UNDERSTANDING THE CONTEMPORARY CARIBBEAN

UNDERSTANDING

Introductions to the States and Regions of the Contemporary World

Donald L. Gordon, series editor

Understanding Contemporary Africa, 3rd edition
edited by April A. Gordon and Donald L. Gordon

Understanding the Contemporary Caribbean
edited by Richard S. Hillman and Thomas J. D'Agostino

Understanding Contemporary China, 2nd edition
edited by Robert E. Gamer

Understanding Contemporary India
edited by Sumit Ganguly and Neil DeVotta

Understanding Contemporary Latin America, 2nd edition
edited by Richard S. Hillman

Understanding the Contemporary Middle East
edited by Deborah J. Gerner

UNDERSTANDING THE CONTEMPORARY CARIBBEAN

edited by
Richard S. Hillman and
Thomas J. D'Agostino

Published in the United States of America in 2003 by
Lynne Rienner Publishers, Inc.
1800 30th Street, Boulder, Colorado 80301
www.rienner.com

and in the United Kingdom by
Lynne Rienner Publishers, Inc.
3 Henrietta Street, Covent Garden, London WC2E 8LU

Published in Jamaica in 2003 by
Ian Randle Publishers
11 Cunningham Avenue
Kingston 6

Library of Congress Cataloging-in-Publication Data
Understanding the contemporary Caribbean / edited by Richard S. Hillman and Thomas J. D'Agostino.
p. cm. — (Understanding)
Includes bibliographical references and index.
Contents: The Caribbean: a geographic preface / Thomas D. Boswell — The historical context / Stephen J. Randall — Caribbean politics / Thomas J. D'Agostino — The economies of the Caribbean / Dennis A. Pantin — International relations / H. Michael Erisman — The environment and ecology / Duncan McGregor — Ethnicity, race, class, and nationality / David Baronov and Kevin A. Yelvington —Women and development / A. Lynn Bolles — Religion in the Caribbean/ Leslie G. Desmangles, Stephen D. Glazier, and Joseph M. Murphy — Literature and popular culture / Kevin Meehan and Paul B. Miller — The Caribbean diaspora / Dennis Conway — Trends and prospects / Richard S. Hillman and Andrés Serbin.
ISBN 1-55587-983-7 (hc: alk. paper)
ISBN 1-55587-959-4 (pbk: alk. paper)
1. Caribbean Area. I. Hillman, Richard S., 1943– II. D'Agostino, Thomas J. III. Understanding (Boulder, Colo.)

F2161. U53 2003
972.9—dc21

2002036826

British Cataloguing in Publication Data
A Cataloguing in Publication record for this book is available from the British Library.

Jamaican Cataloguing in Publication Data
A Cataloguing in Publication record for this book is available from the National Library of Jamaica.
ISBN 976-637-124-5

Printed and bound in the United States of America

The paper used in this publication meets the requirements of the American National Standard for Permanence of Paper for Printed Library Materials Z39.48-1984.

5 4 3 2

Contents

Illustrations

Maps

Tables

Figures

Photographs

Preface

The editors' long-standing collegial relationship and friendship facilitated the productive collaborative process that resulted in this book. We enjoy working together and value the way our complementary operational styles function to our mutual benefit.

We are grateful to the experts representing a variety of disciplines who contributed to *Understanding the Contemporary Caribbean*. Moreover, we believe that this volume will be useful to many readers. The commitment to elucidating the realities of a region that has been misunderstood and neglected but can make an important contribution to global affairs is a tribute to each of the contributors.

We appreciate the participation of John Bogdal, whose eye for detail and sense of the Caribbean region is manifested in his creative maps. Reading this book is undoubtedly enhanced by these excellent graphics.

Richard S. Hillman would like to thank the U.S. Department of State for supporting the Institute for the Study of Democracy and Human Rights (ISDHR), which he directs. One of the ongoing functions of the ISDHR, an outgrowth of a partnership between the Central University of Venezuela and St. John Fisher College, is to foster research on political institutions in regions in the throes of socioeconomic transition. This book, in exploring these issues in the Caribbean, is a case in point.

Professor Hillman also is grateful to the University of Pittsburgh Semester at Sea Program for providing the unique opportunity to visit Cuba and speak with university academics, political leaders (including Fidel Castro), and a variety of Cubans from all walks of life. This experience was particularly illuminating and integral to a more complete comprehension of the Caribbean.

Thomas J. D'Agostino wishes to thank the provost and dean of faculty at Hobart and William Smith Colleges, the vice president for academic affairs at Union College, and the Department of Political Science at Siena College for their support of this project.

The editors remain indebted to Lynne Rienner Publishers for inspiring us to launch this project, encouraging us to complete it, and providing critical editorial assistance throughout the lengthy production process. In this context, we acknowledge the helpful critique and useful suggestions put forth by anonymous reviewers. We, of course, take full responsibility for the book's contents.

Finally, we appreciate the moral support of our families, who at times remained incredulous at the number of hours we logged over the course of this project. Their understanding sustained us throughout. We dedicate *Understanding the Contemporary Caribbean* to our parents, Herman and Edith Hillman and John and Barbara D'Agostino, who instilled in us the value of education and an interest in learning about the world, as well as to our wives, Audrey Hillman and Dawn D'Agostino, and our children, Oliver and Shoshana Hillman and Adriana and Alex D'Agostino, whose love and support enable us to continue these pursuits.

—Richard S. Hillman,
Thomas J. D'Agostino

1

Introduction

Richard S. Hillman

The Caribbean is considerably more important and certainly more complex than its popular image suggests.[1] Widely known as an attractive string of underdeveloped island nations in close proximity to the United States, the region's pleasant climate and natural attributes have attracted large numbers of tourists. Short visits to beautiful beaches and resorts, however, have contributed to a superficial vision of the Caribbean region. It is an interesting, significant, and exciting place for much more profound reasons.

Although there is some truth to the stereotype of the Caribbean as a tropical paradise, the region's historic, cultural, socioeconomic, and political influences far exceed its small size and low status in global affairs. Indeed, political and ideological movements and developments in the Caribbean have provoked international reactions. Moreover, throughout history the people of the Caribbean have been engaged in heroic struggles to liberate themselves from the strictures and exploitation of colonialism, slavery, imperialism, neocolonialism, and dependency.

Historically, the perception of the region has varied from that of an extremely valuable asset to more powerful nations to one of benign neglect. Its role as provider of sun, sand, and surf to Americans and Europeans, for example, has obscured the fact that great power rivalries have been played out in the Caribbean. In fact, the United States has intervened in the Caribbean more than in any other geographical area of the world. The impacts of migration patterns, investment, and commerce, as well as illicit narcotics trafficking, have been significant not only in the Western Hemisphere but also in Europe and throughout the world. Similarly, Caribbean literature, art, and popular culture have had global influences.

Thomas J. D'Agostino

Deep Bay, Antigua

The Caribbean peoples have made outstanding contributions in many fields, both in their home countries and in those countries to which they have migrated. Their presence is apparent in professions such as health care and education, as well as in commerce, construction, music, cuisine, sports, and government. U.S. Secretary of State Colin Powell, who first rose to the position of chairman of the U.S. Joint Chiefs of Staff, is a first-generation U.S. citizen of Jamaican origin. Baseball legend Sammy Sosa was born in the Dominican Republic (in fact, one of every four players in Major League Baseball is from the Caribbean). Many actors like Harry Belafonte and Sidney Poitier, singers like Bob Marley and the Mighty Sparrow, academics like Orlando Patterson, and writers like Derek Wolcott, V. S. Naipaul, John Hearne, Jamaica Kincaid, Aimé Césaire, and Gabriel García Márquez represent the wealth of talent emanating from the Caribbean.

Ironically, as North Americans and Europeans flock to the Caribbean vacationland, the people of the region seek to leave their homelands. Their quest for upward socioeconomic mobility has resulted in large population concentrations abroad. New York City, for example, contains the largest urban concentration of Dominicans outside Santo Domingo. Similarly, New York is the second largest Puerto Rican city next to San Juan. And Miami has become so influenced by Cubans, Jamaicans, and Haitians, among others, that it is commonly referred to as "the capital of the Caribbean."

The Caribbean has always been considered a geopolitical and strategic crossroads (see Maps 1.1, 1.2, and 1.3). From the fifteenth century to the end

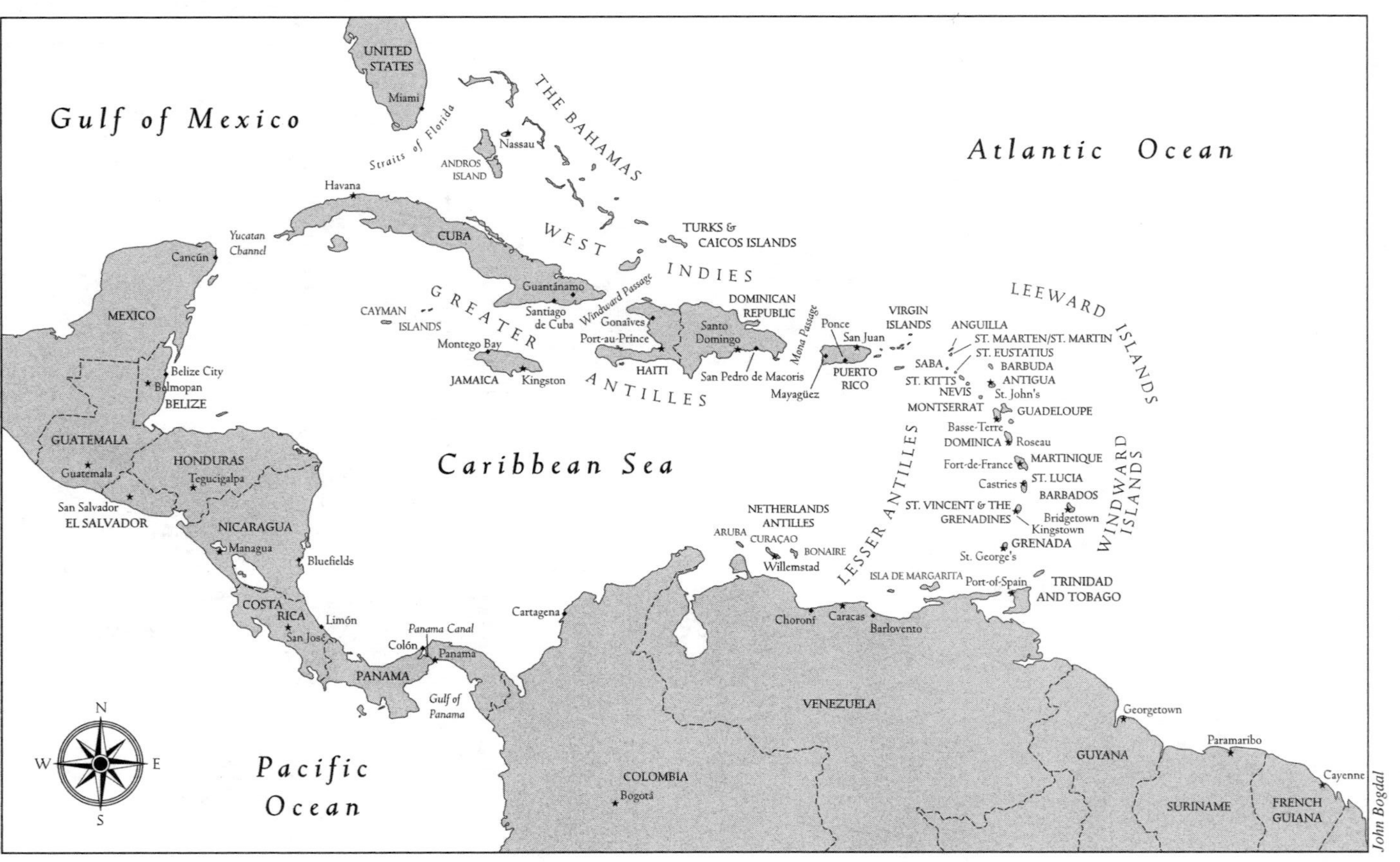

Map 1.1 The Caribbean Region

Map 1.2 The Northern Caribbean

DOMINICAN
REPUBLIC
Santo
Domingo
San Pedro
de Macoris
Mona Passage
Mayagüez
San Juan
Ponce
PUERTO
RICO
BRITISH VIRGIN
ISLANDS
Road Town
Charlotte
Amalie
U.S. VIRGIN
ISLANDS
Anegada Passage
The
Valley
ANGUILLA
ST. MAARTEN / ST. MARTIN
ST. BARTHÉLEMY
ST. EUSTATIUS
SABA
BARBUDA
Basseterre
ST. KITTS
St. John's
ANTIGUA
MONTSERRAT
NEVIS
Plymouth
Guadeloupe Passage
LA DÉSIRADE
GUADELOUPE
Basse-Terre
ILES DES SAINTES
MARIE-GALANTE
Dominica Passage
Portsmouth
DOMINICA
Roseau
Martinique Passage
MARTINIQUE
Fort-de-France
Castries
ST. LUCIA
BARBADOS
ST. VINCENT & THE
GRENADINES
Kingstown
Bridgetown
N
W
E
S
Atlantic
Ocean
Caribbean Sea
NETHERLANDS
ANTILLES
Oranjestad
ARUBA
CURAÇAO
Willemstad
BONAIRE
GRENADA
St. George's
ISLA DE MARGARITA
ISLA LA TORTUGA
Port-of-Spain
TRINIDAD
AND TOBAGO
San Fernando
VENEZUELA
John Bogdal

Map 1.3 The Southern Caribbean

of the twentieth century—from Christopher Columbus to Fidel Castro—the Caribbean has been the focus of external influences (Williams 1979). First, European colonial powers imposed their systems and control. Later the Monroe Doctrine of 1823 conceived of the region as within the sphere of influence of the United States. As a consequence, the Caribbean was thought of as the backyard of the United States—a U.S. lake, so to speak. The Cold War impinged upon emergent pressures within the Caribbean to define itself autonomously by creating confusion as to the origins of national movements. In the post–Cold War era the potential for continued democratization, expanded free trade, and pragmatic regional integration loom large on the horizon. The Caribbean is increasingly perceived as a vital link in the realization of a Free Trade Area of the Americas.

There are, of course, serious challenges confronting the region as a whole, as well as individual countries. The Caribbean comprises ministates endowed with widely dispersed and, in some cases, sparse resources. Thus, economic development has been problematic. Political evolution also has been complicated. In countries that have experienced long periods of colonialism, with the attendant institutions of the plantation and slavery, it is difficult to overcome deeply ingrained authoritarian legacies in order to promote the consolidation of democracy. This does not mean, however, that historical legacies will determine the future. Moreover, disparate developments such as the Cuban revolution, the Haitian transition toward democracy, and the invasion of Grenada further complicate the absence of a singular paradigm or model that would fit the entire region. Thus, generalizations about Caribbean political and economic development must of necessity be multifaceted and intricate if they are to be meaningful. Yet the different countries of the Caribbean have much in common.

Among the most problematic common features are financial weakness and lack of investment capital. Most production in the Caribbean has involved food processing, the making of clothing, and the manufacturing of sugar and rum. Efforts to expand these activities to earn additional income and provide new jobs through programs of import substitution and industrialization by invitation have been relatively unsuccessful.[2] Also, West Indian governments have sought to protect local industries by imposing tariffs on the importation of foreign goods. But this drove up the prices of domestically manufactured goods, which were often inferior in quality to imported goods.

Among the incentives used to attract investment capital are low-cost labor, factories constructed by the island governments, reduction in taxes or complete tax abatements for a number of years (free-trade zones), government-sponsored training programs, political stability, and proximity to the large North American market.

Companies assembling goods for export to the United States benefit from special U.S. tariffs that either reduce or waive import duties for these products. When duties are imposed, they usually are assessed only on the value added to the products by the Caribbean operations. U.S. firms, seeking to escape high-cost unionized labor, have established assembly *maquiladoras* (factories) in the Dominican Republic, Haiti, Jamaica, and Barbados. Predominantly female workers typically earn between U.S.$50 and $100 per week in as many as 1,000 *maquiladoras* throughout the Caribbean employing more than 25,000 workers. A significant portion of the moderately priced clothing sold in the United States is now made in these island factories.

Neoliberal economic philosophy purports that it is more beneficial for island producers to export their products. Accordingly, the World Bank and the International Monetary Fund (IMF) require local governments to devalue their currencies to reduce the costs of their products overseas; lower their import tariffs to increase local competition and efficiency; and reduce domestic spending (so their financial reserves will make the loans more likely to be paid off). The main problem with this philosophy is that it creates austerity in the home country. Currency devaluation raises local prices; competition from imported goods can drive local firms out of business, exacerbating already high levels of unemployment; and decreased government spending reduces the amount of money circulating within the island's economy, causing political pressures.

One of the more successful economic mechanisms used by Caribbean nations to fortify their economies has been offshore banking.[3] Some nations provide advantages such as reduction or elimination of taxes on income, profits, dividends, and capital gains in secret accounts.[4] Moreover, legal fees and licenses are charged by the banks, adding valuable foreign currency to the island's economy. First, the Netherlands Antilles, especially Curaçao, and then the Bahamas, the Cayman Islands, Antigua, the Turks and Caicos Islands, Montserrat, and St. Vincent recently became the leading centers in the Caribbean for offshore banking. In the Bahamas and the Cayman Islands, offshore banking is the second leading industry behind tourism, providing 15–20 percent of each country's gross national product.

In sum, although the Caribbean continues to struggle with political and economic challenges, the global scope of the region's impact is inconsistent with its image and size: the Caribbean contains approximately 36 million people—a small percentage of the Western Hemisphere and only a tiny fraction of the world's population. But their impact has been disproportionate to their numbers, and there are many enclaves of Caribbean peoples living in other areas of the world. London, Toronto, Miami, and New York, for example, have a large West Indian presence.

As the world continues to become more interdependent, a global society is emerging within which the Caribbean must be integrated. Therefore, it is very important to increase our understanding of the contemporary Caribbean. Unfortunately, there has been a theoretical confusion resulting from segregated analyses of the region according to superficial criteria. For purposes of convenience (as opposed to more penetrating factors), one finds reference to linguistic divisions, geographic distributions, and chronological dates of independence, for example. These approaches have reaffirmed obvious differences while obscuring common factors that could contain important information for the production of salutary solutions to pervasive problems.

Our earlier research has shown that the Hispanic countries within the Caribbean have been considered an integral part of Latin America, and the English-speaking countries have been excluded based on the assumption that different cultural heritages require a fundamentally different analytical framework. Thus, scholars of Latin America focus on the Latin Caribbean "often to the almost total exclusion of other areas," whereas scholars of the Commonwealth Caribbean "have usually neglected the Latin Caribbean" (Millet and Will 1979:xxi). We have shown that the Caribbean region provides a microcosm of a fragmented third world in which divisions "tenaciously obscure similarities and impede the evolution of common interests and aspirations" and that the absence of a "single, holistic community" has resulted (Hillman and D'Agostino 1992:1–17).

Some authors have argued that there is a "clear dividing line" separating the English-speaking Caribbean countries from their Hispanic, French, and Dutch neighbors (Serbin 1989:146). Some conclude that conflicts in relations between Caribbean countries are due to "misconceptions, misunderstanding, and lack of communication . . . deriving from historical, cultural, racial, and linguistic differences" (Bryan 1988:41). Others have attributed the absence of a single community to the divisiveness of separate Caribbean societies "often fatally hostile to each other" (Moya Pons 1974:33).

Our approach reveals that beneath obvious differences lie similarities in common historical themes, geopolitical and sociocultural contexts, economic experiences, and accommodation patterns that reflect the pressures of congruent sociopolitical environments. Moreover, we believe that there has been significant convergence of mutual economic and political interests to warrant the promotion of improved relations between the diverse Caribbean states. Nicolás Guillén summarizes this idea succinctly when he characterizes the Caribbean archipelago as one "communal yard" due to its common heritage of slavery, imperial domination, and struggle (Guillén 1976:26). And Pére Labat observed in the eighteenth century that the Caribbean peoples are "all together, in the same boat, sailing the same uncertain sea" (Knight 1990:307). We believe that academic and political navigation in this sea can be enhanced through understanding and appreciating the forces that have shaped the contemporary Caribbean.

Therefore, there is a need for an interdisciplinary introduction to the Caribbean region. Academic, business, and policy interests require understanding this complex and significant area. But the growing numbers of people who wish to learn about the Caribbean are not able to use narrowly focused studies. Comprehending existing theoretical analyses of the region's socioeconomic and political conditions presupposes expertise and experience.

Further, there is much misunderstanding about Caribbean attitudes, values, and beliefs regarding the conduct of politics, business, and life. Sensationalized media coverage of political instability, external debt, immigration, and narcotics trafficking has overshadowed valiant Caribbean efforts to define uniquely Caribbean identities and create autonomous institutions, as well as the consolidation of democracy and the promotion of trade, development, tourism, and regional cooperation.

Moreover, although the strategic geopolitical relevance of the region has been recognized throughout history, the Caribbean has become critically important in the emerging global economy within which the volume of trade will impact significantly on the entire Western Hemisphere. The Caribbean Basin Initiative of the early 1980s is testimony to this idea. Unfortunately, the persistence of flawed policies such as the U.S. embargo against Cuba has impeded, rather than enhanced, regional integration. My visits throughout the region over a number of years have convinced me that there is a great need to promote mutual understanding throughout the hemisphere.[5] The tendency to demonize political leaders with whom there is disagreement has constituted a major obstacle to progress in this area. In an era of opening relations with China and Vietnam, Jimmy Carter's visit to Cuba in May 2002 is testimony

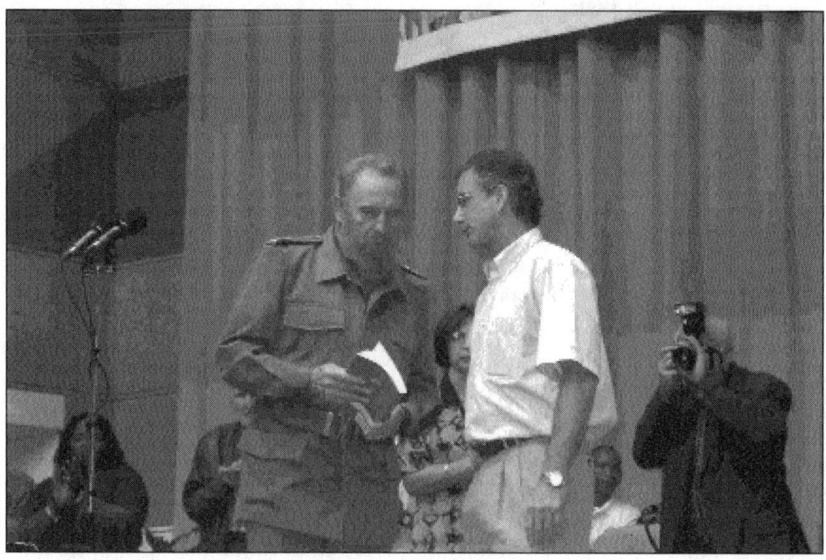

Larry Shuman

Richard Hillman presents Fidel Castro with a copy of his book, *Understanding Contemporary Latin America*, Havana, Cuba, January 25, 2002

to the potential for reevaluation of the U.S. position regarding this Caribbean neighbor.

Attention has been drawn to the region by media accounts of current events, Free Trade Area of the Americas discussions, and tourism, as well as increasing business, commerce, and migration from the Caribbean, which augments the need for basic information. In this context, this book provides a basis for comprehension by introducing fundamental background information, major issues, themes, and trends in countries within the Caribbean region. It is designed as a basic resource that will be useful to those studying the area. The writing style is straightforward, with maps and graphics intended to enhance clarity, comprehension, and appreciation of the traditions, influences, and common themes underlying differences within the Caribbean. *Understanding the Contemporary Caribbean* is intended to contribute to the promotion of interest and basic understanding in college and university classrooms, foreign service seminars, corporate training programs, and the general public.

Because definitions of the Caribbean region vary widely, we provide an integrated text by defining the Caribbean to include the circum-Caribbean, with focus on the insular Caribbean. In other words, each chapter makes primary reference to the Greater and the Lesser Antilles. Secondary reference is made to typically Caribbean enclaves in the Atlantic Ocean and on the South American and Central American coasts.

Specifically, the Greater Antilles consists of Cuba, Jamaica, Hispaniola (Haiti and the Dominican Republic), and Puerto Rico. The Lesser Antilles consists of the Leeward Islands and the Windward Islands. The Leewards include Montserrat, Antigua and Barbuda, St. Kitts and Nevis, Saba, St. Eustatius, St. Martin, and St. Barthélemy. (Notice that the French and Dutch halves of St. Martin are spelled differently, St. Maarten [or Sint Maarten] for the Dutch part, and St. Martin for the French part.) The Windwards include Guadeloupe, Dominica, Martinique, St. Lucia, St. Vincent and the Grenadines, and Grenada. The U.S. and British Virgin Islands, Barbados, Trinidad and Tobago, and the Netherlands Antilles (Aruba, Bonaire, and Curaçao) complete the insular Caribbean. The Bahamas, Bermuda, and the Turks and Caicos Islands, although not within the Caribbean Sea, have much in common with the region. Similarly, Guyana, French Guiana, and Suriname have more in common with the Caribbean than their neighboring South American countries. The same can be said for coastal enclaves in Venezuela and Colombia on the Caribbean coast of South America, as well as the Panamanian, Costa Rican, Nicaraguan, Honduran and Belizean coasts of Central America. Finally, for reasons previously stated, it is not inappropriate to include mention of Miami and South Florida in the context of our expanded definition of the Caribbean.

The theme of unity in diversity, drawn from our previous work, provides an organizing concept (Hillman and D'Agostino 1992). There have been many attempts to describe the Caribbean that reflect our basic thesis. The fused, or blended, cultures are "distant neighbors" (Hillman and D'Agostino 1992), a diverse village, a disparate community characterized by "fragmented nationalism" (Knight 1990). The whole is certainly greater than the sum of its parts in a "continent of islands" (Kurlansky 1992), a tropical paradise that exists "in the shadow of the sun" (Deere 1990). Transcending the obvious differences, we explore similarities in the legacies of the colonial experiences, slave trade, plantation life, the imposition of Eurocentric institutions, the difficulties of transition to independence, obstacles to socioeconomic and political development, and ethnographic patterns.

The Caribbean is a unique and complex concatenation of virtually every ethnic group in the world. There are those of African, European, American, and Asian origins. Africans came to the Caribbean as slaves from tribes of the Ibo, Coromantee, Hausa, Mandingo, Fulani, Minas, Yoruba, Congo, Mohammedan, Calabar, Alampo, Whydahs, and Dahomeans. Europeans—tracing their ancestries to the Spanish, English, Irish, Scots, French, German, and Dutch—came as conquerors. Indigenous to the region by virtue of early migrations from Asia were North American tribes of Taínos, Arawaks, Caribs, Ciboney, and Guanahuatebey. After the abolition of slavery, Indian and Chinese indentured servants were brought to the Caribbean. Later, small waves of immigrants arrived from Spain, Portugal, France, England, Germany, China, the Jewish Diaspora (Ashkenazi and Sephardic Jews), Italy, the Middle East (Syrians and Lebanese), Latin America, and North America (the United States and Canada).

Each group brought particular traits to the Caribbean. The Africans brought popular tales and legends, folklore, music, arts, and religious beliefs, as well as qualities of perseverance and leadership (Herring 1967:109–113). The Europeans brought their religions and culture, military technology, political and social institutions, scientific discovery, as well as diseases unknown in the region. The indigenous contributions are debated due to scant archaeological evidence (Knight 1990:4–22). However, the Arawaks are reputed to have lived in a pacific communal society, whereas the Caribs migrated and were more belligerent. The aesthetic achievements and social structures of the indigenous peoples were almost completely destroyed by conquest, despite the lasting imprint of linguistic adaptations—such as words like *bohío* (shack or hut), *guagua* (bus), *cacique* (Indian chief or political leader), and *guajiro* (peasant).

Far more interesting and significant than the individual contributions of the various groups constituting the contemporary Caribbean is the process whereby their sociopolitical traits have been amalgamated and Eurocentric dominance has been mitigated. The region has truly been a crucible of various cultures. This blending, not only of institutions but also of ethnicity, has produced the uniquely Caribbean Creoles.[6] Thus, racial variation can be understood in the context of a fluid continuum. As Gordon Lewis observed, "Columbus and his followers came to the New World with a baggage of religious intolerance rather than racial phobia" (Lewis 1987:10).

The most popular religious expressions are a result of a syncretizing process that brought together the elaborate African belief systems with those of the European religious traditions. Thus, elitist practice of Catholicism or mainstream Protestantism is nominal compared to the dynamic integration into daily life of Vodou, spiritualism, Obeah, Santería, or other fusions of European and African or Indian religions. Because the Caribbean was "a society founded on the gross exploitation, in the name of Christianity, of both Antillean Indian and African black" people (Lewis 1987:89), these combinations were crucial to a vast majority of non-Europeans attempting to preserve their beliefs and themselves. While many perceived that "Catholic proselytization was a lost cause . . . the Catholic religion saw [its role] as a war against paganism and superstition" (Lewis 1987:195). Thus, evangelical religions have been making inroads in the Caribbean. As one observer asks, "Who with the slightest missionary spirit could resist a region of poor countries whose populations are always looking for new religions?" (Kurlansky 1992:72).

Occasionally, when it had been impossible to integrate their cultures into the dominant society, certain groups rejected that society and alienated themselves. The first of these were the Maroons, slaves who were able to escape into the rugged terrain of the Jamaican hinterland. These *cimarrones* (runaways) have survived as a separate enclave society. Later on the Rastafarians rejected Anglo values, creating an Africanist belief system loosely based on allegiance to Haile Selassie, the former emperor of Ethiopia.

Understanding the forces that tie Caribbean societies together, as well as those that have challenged and transformed their institutions, requires exploration of the impact of the plantation system, slavery, and the processes through which independence (or pseudo-independence) was gained. Moreover, religion, government, society, and current challenges derive in large part from these origins. Simply stated, the relationships between masters and slaves, the rebellions, the heroic struggles, and the tortuous evolution from colonies to independent states reveal inescapable realities that cannot be ignored in our study of the contemporary Caribbean. The resultant attitudes, values, and beliefs inform our understanding of this complex region.

Caribbean attitudes toward the United States are ambivalent, ranging from disdain to infatuation. A version of dependency theory in which problems endemic to the region are attributed to Europe and the United States has become popular in academic circles. Virulent anti-U.S. sentiment developed early in Cuban history, was cultivated by independence leaders, and given ideological expression through *fidelismo* and Castro's revolution. It was given expression in the present day by U.S. as well as Cuban manipulation of the Elián González dispute, in which the question of a father's legal custody over his son became an international incident.

On the one hand, Michael Manley, Maurice Bishop, and other West Indian leaders have flirted with alternative ideologies such as democratic socialism

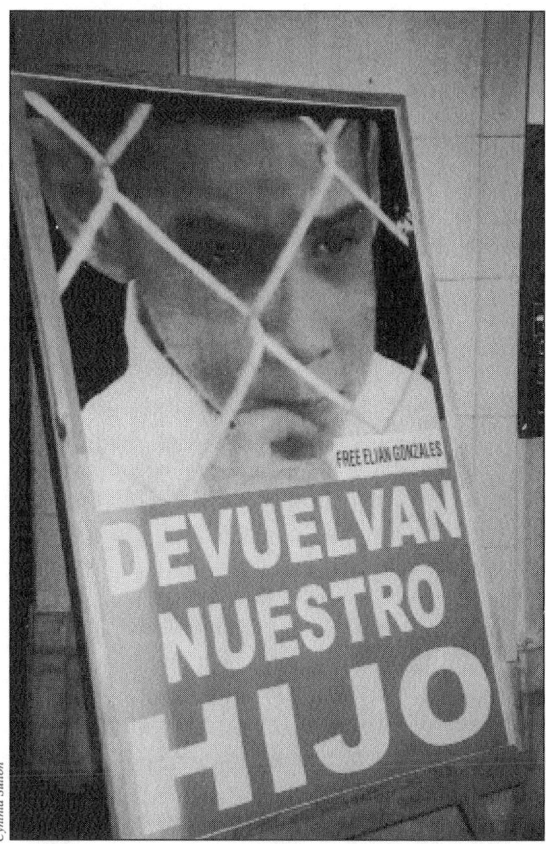

Cynthia Sutton

Poster of Elián González, Havana, Cuba. The poster reads, "Return Our Child."

and Marxism as an antidote to dependence on the United States. On the other hand, some Puerto Rican politicians have championed statehood for the island, whereas others fiercely resist it. Some leaders have consistently supported U.S. international initiatives and have always voted accordingly in world forums such as the United Nations. Also, there has been much envy and idolatry of U.S. culture and economic superiority. This has led to massive immigration—both legal and illegal—into the United States. It has also led to "brain drain," whereby Caribbean professionals and the intelligentsia abandon their own countries for U.S. residency and citizenship. This loss of human resources has been extremely problematic for Caribbean societies.

Also, there has been substantial movement within the Caribbean: Dominicans to Miami and St. Martin; Haitians and Cubans to Puerto Rico, Venezuela, and Miami; Jamaicans to Central America and Miami; Trinidadians to Jamaica and Venezuela; and so on. Movement out of the Caribbean has been a safety valve for overpopulation, political oppression, and especially economic depression. Recently, the European Union began financing border projects on Hispaniola, such that the centuries of animosity between the Dominican Republic and Haiti might be overcome in order to achieve a modicum of economic integration.[7]

Caribbeans nevertheless are proud of their countries, perceiving themselves as holding no candle to the United States or Europe. Michael Manley once remarked to me that "Jamaica is no little dive, it is a sophisticated country" (Hillman 1979:55). Similarly, Edward Seaga told me that "Americans have a dim view" of the third world (Hillman 1979:53). I have known West Indians who have worked their entire lives abroad in order to be able to retire in their homelands. These perspectives ought to be appreciated if we are to develop mutual understanding.

Therefore, *Understanding the Contemporary Caribbean* introduces readers to the region by providing basic definitions, outlining major issues, discussing relevant background, and illustrating the manifestation of these considerations in representative countries. Thus, the text employs both thematic and case-study approaches. Each chapter contains a general discussion, key concepts, ongoing questions, and reference to bibliographic resources (see Table 1.1).

Among the major issues discussed in the text, the most prominent are those related to the Caribbean identity, socioeconomic and political evolution, debt, immigration, narcotics trade, integration, and international relations. These are understood in the context of a background strongly influenced by the legacies of colonialism and the predominant impact of the United States.

The text is part of the series entitled Understanding: Introductions to the States and Regions of the Contemporary World. It is designed to generate knowledge and stimulate interest rather than bring these issues to closure. Each chapter is written as if to teach a class on the subject. In "The Caribbean: A Geographic Preface" (Chapter 2), Thomas Boswell discusses the impact of location, population trends, resource availability, and the environment on economic development and the people in the Caribbean. In "The Historical Context" (Chapter 3), Stephen Randall shows how major themes such as colonialism, plantation life, and slavery have created legacies that persist in influencing contemporary realities. In "Caribbean Politics" (Chapter 4), Thomas D'Agostino analyzes the impact of historical legacies on political development. He shows how different institutions converge in similar patterns of patron-clientelism, elite dominance, and creole fusion.

In "The Economies of the Caribbean" (Chapter 5), Dennis Pantin discusses various attempted solutions to the region's endemic problems and economic programs, the informal economies, the impact of narcotics trafficking, and the emergent trend toward integration. H. Michael Erisman, in "International Relations" (Chapter 6), treats the narcotics trade in more depth due to its bearing on the Caribbean-U.S. relationship. He also discusses regional

Table 1.1 Socioeconomic Indicators for Caribbean States

	Population, 2001	Population Growth, 2002	Urban Population, 2001 (%)	Life Expectancy, 2000 (in years)	Infant Mortality (per 1000), 2000	Literacy, 2000 (%)	GDP per cap PPP U.S.$, 2000[a]
Anguilla	12,446	2.44	N/A	76.5	23.7	95	8,600
Antigua and Barbuda	68,487	0.69	37	73.9	13	86.6	10,541
Aruba	104,000	0.59	51	78.7	6.3	97	28,000
Bahamas	307,153	0.86	89	69.2	15	95.4	17,012
Barbados	268,189	0.46	51	76.8	12	98	15,494
Belize	247,107	2.65	48	74	34	93.2	5,606
British Virgin Islands	21,272	2.16	N/A	75.9	19.6	97.8	16,000
Cayman Islands	36,273	2.03	N/A	79.2	9.9	98	30,000
Colombia	43,035,480	1.6	75	71.2	25	91.7	6,248
Costa Rica	3,886,318	1.61	60	76.4	10	95.6	8,650
Cuba	11,221,723	0.35	75	76	7	96.7	N/A
Dominica	73,199	–0.81	71	72.9	14	96.4	5,880
Dominican Republic	8,505,204	1.61	66	67.1	42	83.6	6,033
French Guiana	182,333	2.57	N/A	76.5	13.2	83	6,000
Grenada	99,000	0.02	38	65.3	21	94.4	7,580
Guadeloupe	435,739	1.04	N/A	77.4	9.3	90	9,000
Guyana	766,256	0.23	37	63	55	98.5	3,963
Haiti	8,114,161	1.42	36	52.6	81	49.8	1,467
Honduras	6,575,264	2.34	54	65.7	32	74.6	2,453
Jamaica	2,668,230	0.56	57	75.3	17	86.9	3,639
Martinique	422,277	0.89	N/A	78.6	7.6	93	11,000
Montserrat	8,437	N/A	N/A	78.2	8	97	N/A
Netherlands Antilles	216,808	0.93	69	75.2	11.1	98	11,400
Nicaragua	5,201,641	2.09	57	68.4	37	66.5	2,366
Panama	2,900,589	1.26	57	74	20.3	91.9	6,000
Puerto Rico	3,950,473	0.51	76	75.9	9.3	89	11,200
St. Kitts and Nevis	41,082	0.01	34	70	21	97.8	12,510
St. Lucia	158,134	1.24	38	73.4	17	90.2	5,703
St. Vincent and the Grenadines	115,881	0.37	56	69.6	21	88.9	5,555
Suriname	419,656	0.55	75	70.6	27.4	94	3,799
Trinidad and Tobago	1,309,608	–0.52	74	74.3	17	93.8	8,964
Turks and Caicos	18,738	3.28	N/A	3.8	17.5	98	7,300
U.S. Virgin Islands	123,498	1.04	N/A	78.4	9.2	N/A	15,000
Venezuela	24,632,376	1.52	87	72.9	23	92.6	5,794

Sources: World Bank, http://www.worldbank.org/data/; United Nations, http://hdr.undp.org/default.cfm; CIA World Factbook, http://www.odci.gov/cia/publications/factbook/index.html.

Note: a. Gross domestic product per capita purchasing power parity in U.S.$.

integration and documents the long history of external intervention in the region. "The Environment and Ecology" (Chapter 7), by Duncan McGregor, contains his treatment of crucial issues such as the ecology of the region—the natural assets and liabilities inherent in essentially tourist economies challenged by hurricanes, depletion of coral reefs, and pollution.

In "Ethnicity, Race, Class, and Nationality" (Chapter 8), David Baronov and Kevin Yelvington elaborate on the significance of large arrays of peoples and groups living in the same small area. They also touch on the impact of Eurocentricity and the contribution of the different ethnic groups, as well as the creolization pattern. The contribution of women is the focus of "Women and Development" (Chapter 9), by A. Lynn Bolles. In "Religion in the Caribbean" (Chapter 10), Leslie Desmangles, Stephen Glazier, and Joseph Murphy show how imposed European religions have been embellished by syncretic belief systems such as Rastafarianism, Obeah, Vodou, and Santería.

"Literature and Popular Culture" (Chapter 11), by Kevin Meehan and Paul Miller, discusses the most notable writers and the politicized nature of their work. It also mentions the widespread impact of folklore and music—like reggae, salsa, merengue, rumba, *son*, *cumbia*, *tambores*, and calypso. In "The Caribbean Diaspora" (Chapter 12), Dennis Conway shows the geographical diversity and impact of the various groups who leave the region and contribute to brain drain, the safety-valve effect, capital flight, and financial remissions. Finally, in "Trends and Prospects" (Chapter 13), Richard Hillman and Andrés Serbin analyze where the region has been as well as the direction in which it appears to be headed.

Notes

1. The terms *Caribbean* and *West Indies* are used interchangeably throughout this book.

2. The phrase *import substitution* refers to a policy of trying to produce goods locally that were formerly imported. *Industrialization by invitation* is a strategy aimed at attracting foreign capital for investment in local industry.

3. Offshore banking includes financial operations conducted by foreign banks that have branches in countries like those in the Caribbean.

4. This has caused speculation that such operations have become money-laundering facilities for illegal activities such as drug trafficking.

5. Among my travels, I visited Cuba as a professor on the faculty of the University of Pittsburgh Semester at Sea Program and presented a copy of my book, Richard S. Hillman, ed., *Understanding Contemporary Latin America* (Boulder: Lynne Rienner Publishers, 2001), to Fidel Castro during his four-and-a-half hour meeting with Semester at Sea students and faculty in Havana, January 25, 2002.

6. *Creole* is a term used in the Caribbean in reference to the unique admixtures of peoples and cultures.

7. Mireya Navarro, "At Last on Hispaniola: Hands Across the Border," *New York Times,* July 11, 1999, sec. 1, p. 3, col. 1.

Bibliography

Bryan, Anthony T. "The Commonwealth Caribbean/Latin American Relationship: New Wine in Old Bottles?" *Caribbean Affairs* 1 (January–March 1988): 29–44.

Deere, Carmen Diana (coordinator). *In the Shadows of the Sun: Caribbean Development Alternatives and U.S. Policy.* Boulder: Westview, 1990.

Guillén, Nicolás. *Jamaica Journal* 9 (1976): 26.

Herring, Hubert. *A History of Latin America.* New York: Alfred A. Knopf, 1967.

Hillman, Richard S. "Interviewing Jamaica's Political Leaders: Michael Manley and Edward Seaga." *Caribbean Review* 8 (Summer 1979): 28–31, 53–55.

Hillman, Richard S., and Thomas J. D'Agostino. *Distant Neighbors in the Caribbean: The Dominican Republic and Jamaica in Comparative Perspective.* New York: Praeger Publishers, 1992.

Knight, Franklin W. *The Caribbean: The Genesis of a Fragmented Nationalism.* 2nd ed. New York: Oxford University Press, 1990.

Kurlansky, Mark. *A Continent of Islands: Searching for the Caribbean Destiny.* New York: Addison-Wesley, 1992.

Lewis, Gordon K. *Main Currents in Caribbean Thought: The Historical Evolution of Caribbean Society in Its Ideological Aspects, 1492–1900.* Baltimore and London: Johns Hopkins University Press, 1987.

Millet, Richard, and W. Marvin Will, eds. *The Restless Caribbean: Changing Patterns of International Relations.* New York: Praeger Publishers, 1979.

Moya Pons, Frank. *Historia colonial de Santo Domingo.* Santiago, Dominican Republic: Universidad Católica Madre y Maestra, 1974.

Serbin, Andrés. "Race and Politics: Relations Between the English-Speaking Caribbean and Latin America." *Caribbean Affairs* 2 (October–December 1989): 146–171.

Williams, Eric. *From Columbus to Castro: The History of the Caribbean, 1492–1969.* New York: Harper and Row, 1979.

2

The Caribbean: A Geographic Preface

Thomas D. Boswell

Defining the Caribbean

Defining regions is not an exact science because not everyone agrees about their borders. In a sense, regions are like beauty—they are in the eyes of the beholder. Thus, there is little general agreement on what area is included within the Caribbean region.[1] To some, it includes only the countries and islands within the Caribbean Sea. To most U.S. geographers it includes those islands in the Caribbean Sea plus the islands of the Bahamas and the Turks and Caicos in the Atlantic Ocean, excluding the Caribbean littoral of Central America and Mexico's Yucatán Peninsula. For many European geographers, as well as residents of the non-Hispanic islands of the Caribbean, it includes all the islands between North America and South America and located east of Central America and Mexico, plus Belize and the northern South American territories of Guyana, Suriname, and French Guiana.

One person has suggested that the best way around the problem is to consider the Caribbean to comprise a set of three concentric zones of Caribbean identity (Elbow 1996:115; see Map 2.1). The innermost zone is the *core* and includes the islands that everyone considers to be part of the Caribbean. The middle zone is the *fringe,* which includes islands farther away from the core such as the Bahamas and the Turks and Caicos, as well as some of the islands located off the Caribbean coast of Central America. In addition, Belize, Guyana, Suriname, and French Guiana are considered part of the fringe. The outermost zone is the *periphery* and covers southern Mexico, including the Yucatán, and all of the Central American countries not included within the fringe. The periphery also includes the northern coasts of Colombia and

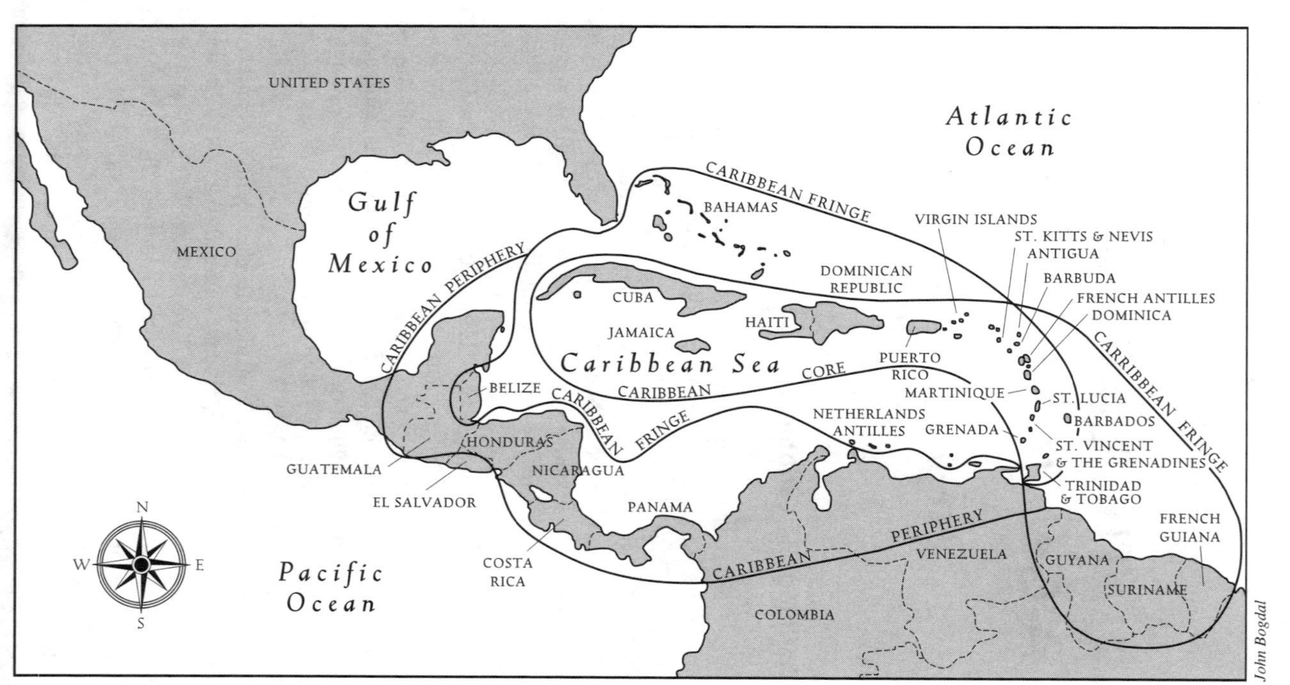

Map 2.1 Subregions of the Caribbean

Venezuela in South America. In this chapter, I concentrate on describing the geographical characteristics of the core of the Caribbean region.

Considering its size, the Caribbean is certainly one of the more diverse areas in the world (Elbow 1996). This diversity manifests in virtually every aspect of the islands in the region, including landforms, climates, vegetation, human history, political systems and degree of independence, levels of economic development, religious preferences, and even the languages spoken by residents. Yet as Richard Hillman proposes in the introduction to this book, there are unifying themes as well.

The thousands of islands, islets, and keys that comprise the archipelago of the Caribbean stretch approximately 2,200 miles from Cape San Antonio on the western tip of Cuba eastward through the islands of Hispaniola, Puerto Rico, and the Virgin Islands, then southward through the small islands of the eastern Caribbean to the northern coast of Venezuela. However, the aggregate land area of the islands in this region is only about 91,000 square miles, less than the area of the state of Oregon and the island of Great Britain.

It is logical to divide the Caribbean islands into five subregions. The largest is the Greater Antilles, encompassing the four islands of Cuba, Hispaniola, Jamaica, and Puerto Rico. Together these islands include 88 percent of the land area in the Caribbean (Table 2.1). The second subregion is the Lesser Antilles, including the smaller islands extending from the Virgin Islands east of Puerto Rico and southward to Trinidad. It contains an additional 4 percent of the area of the Caribbean islands. The Bahamas and the Turks and Caicos Islands are the third subregion and account for almost 6 percent of the land area of the Caribbean. The remaining two subregions collectively contain less than 1 percent of the area of the Caribbean. These are the Cayman Islands, south of Cuba and west of Jamaica, and the Netherlands Antilles (Aruba, Bonaire, and Curaçao) off the coast of Venezuela. Hundreds of other islands are technically located in the Caribbean but are possessions of Central and South American countries; most geographers consider them part of Latin America instead of the Caribbean.

Other terms that require definition are used widely throughout the Caribbean. Perhaps the most important of these is *West Indies,* which is often used interchangeably with *the Caribbean.* When Columbus reached the Caribbean during his first voyage in 1492, he thought he had discovered a shorter western route to the Orient; he called these islands Las Indias, and the natives who lived on them became known as Indians. Later, it was realized that these were not the same islands as those in Southeast Asia; thus they came to be known as the West Indies to distinguish them from the East Indies.

The West Indies were conquered by mainly Spanish, French, Dutch, and British colonialists between the fifteenth and nineteenth centuries and often are subdivided according to their respective colonial histories. Thus, the Netherlands Antilles includes the Dutch possessions of Aruba, Bonaire,

Table 2.1 Land Areas and Population Densities in the Caribbean

Countries and Islands	Area (sq. miles)	Population Density (per sq. mile), 2000
Anguilla	39	319
Antigua and Barbuda	170	394
Aruba	75	1,387
Bahamas	5,382	58
Barbados	166	1,620
Belize	8,867	29
British Virgin Islands	59	361
Cayman Islands	100	363
Colombia	439,737	100
Costa Rica	19,730	200
Cuba	42,804	265
Dominica	290	262
Dominican Republic	18,816	467
French Guiana	34,749	5
Grenada	133	792
Guadeloupe	687	698
Guyana	83,000	9
Haiti	10,714	659
Honduras	43,277	156
Jamaica	4,244	620
Martinique	425	904
Montserrat	39	216
Netherlands Antilles (excluding Aruba)	309	728
Nicaragua	50,193	107
Panama	29,762	101
Puerto Rico	3,435	1,116
St. Kitts and Nevis	101	281
St. Lucia	238	693
St. Vincent and the Grenadines	150	770
Suriname	63,037	7
Trinidad and Tobago	1,981	659
Turks and Caicos Islands	166	113
U.S. Virgin Islands	136	908
Venezuela	352,144	71

Sources: United Nations Population Division, http://esa.un.org/unpp/; National Geographic, http://www.nationalgeographic.com; Population Reference Bureau, http://www.prb.org/pdf/WorldPopulationDS02_Eng.pdf.

Curaçao, St. Eustatius, Saba, and the southern half of St. Maarten.[2] The French West Indies includes the French-owned islands of Martinique, Guadeloupe, the northern half of St. Martin, St. Barthélemy, and Haiti (which became independent in 1804). The British West Indies are the many islands with a British colonial history, including Jamaica, the Cayman Islands, the Bahamas, the Turks and Caicos, the British Virgin Islands, Anguilla, Antigua and Barbuda, St. Kitts and Nevis, Montserrat, Dominica, St. Lucia, St. Vincent and the Grenadines, Barbados, Grenada, and Trinidad and Tobago. Finally, Puerto Rico and the U.S. Virgin Islands are in the U.S. Caribbean, whereas Cuba and the Dominican Republic—former colonial possessions of Spain—are widely considered part of Latin America.

The Lesser Antilles are frequently subdivided by their English- and French-speaking residents into the Leeward Islands and the Windward Islands. The Dominica Passage between Guadeloupe and Dominica is usually regarded as the dividing line, with those to the north called the Leewards and those to the south the Windwards. Interestingly, there is no climate-based logic for such a designation because the islands have similar exposures to the prevailing northeasterly trade winds. One explanation is that Columbus, during his second voyage in 1493, sailed westward between Guadeloupe and Dominica to be on the leeward side of the northern group of Lesser Antilles, thereby gaining some protection from hurricanes that blew in from the east. To complicate matters, the Dutch call their northern islands of St. Maarten, Saba, and St. Eustatius the Windwards, and those to the south the Leewards—the reverse of the British and French uses of these terms. The reason for the Dutch terminology is that Aruba, Bonaire, and Curaçao are much drier than their three northern cousins.

■ Climate and Weather Patterns in the Caribbean

Taxi drivers in the Caribbean are often amused when newly arriving tourists invariably ask, "How has the weather been?" The truth is that the day-to-day weather is almost always the same at any given location, a characteristic of most tropical locations. Of course, there are variations as well as some marked differences, especially in annual rainfall. For example, drier areas include relatively flat islands (like the Netherlands Antilles), valleys shielded by mountains from moderating sea breezes (like the Enriquillo Depression in the Dominican Republic), and the leeward sides of the Greater Antilles (e.g., the southeastern coast of Jamaica). These drier areas typically have a somewhat greater daily range in temperature than other parts of the region (Boswell and Conway 1992:10–15).

With the exception of the northern two-thirds of the Bahamas, all of the Caribbean lies in the tropics. This factor largely controls the uniform temperatures that typify the area. In the tropical latitudes the angle of the sun's rays and the length of the daylight period do not vary like they do in the middle and higher latitudes. The variations in average temperatures for the hottest and coolest months here are almost always less than 10 degrees Fahrenheit, a range that decreases closer to the equator. For example, the annual range of temperatures between the coldest and warmest monthly averages for San Juan, Puerto Rico, is 6 degrees Fahrenheit; for Fort-de-France, Martinique, it is 5 degrees; and for Bridgetown, Barbados, and Port of Spain, Trinidad, it is 4 degrees. Even for Nassau, in the Bahamas just north of the tropic of Cancer, the temperature range is only about 12 degrees. In fact, the major difference between winter and summer seasons in the Caribbean is in the amount of rainfall, not temperature. Summer is the wet season, and winter is the dry season. Daily highs year-round usually range between 82 and 92 degrees Fahrenheit, whereas the lows range between 70 and 80 degrees. Exceptions occur on the rare occasions when a cold north wind (called El Norte in Spanish) blows south into the Caribbean from the interior of North America, but these incursions affect temperatures only in the Greater Antilles and the Bahamas.

The West Indies lie in the belt of the northeasterly trade winds, so called because they blow northeast to southwest and because of the role they played in early European settlement and trading patterns in this region. From a climatological perspective they are significant because their direction determines the leeward and windward sides of the islands, which affects the amount of precipitation and modifies temperature conditions to some extent. Generally, windward coasts are wetter and have somewhat less extreme temperatures. Usually, daily highs on windward coasts range between 2 and 4 degrees Fahrenheit lower than on leeward coasts.

Being surrounded by water has two important climatological consequences for the West Indies. First, the large body of water provides a virtually limitless source of evaporation for the warm tropical northeasterly trade winds that blow over the region, increasing the humidity of Caribbean air masses. Second, because water heats and cools more slowly than land, it helps moderate temperatures on the islands, especially in the coastal locations. Except for a few sheltered locations, like the Cul-de-Sac Depression of Haiti and the Valle Central of Cuba, temperatures as high as 100 degrees and as low as 60 degrees Fahrenheit are rare in the West Indies.

Air masses in the Caribbean are normally warm and moisture-laden. If rainfall is to occur, there must be a mechanism to force this warm, moist air to rise, cooling it enough to create condensation that will result in precipitation. A common geographic feature, island mountain ranges, is one such mechanism. Air is forced to rise on the windward slopes while it subsides on the leeward sides. As a consequence, the windward sides of mountains normally experience heavy rainfall (locally known as relief rainfall), whereas the leeward sides are relatively dry, lying in the rain-shadow of the mountains. These windward and leeward effects are most fully developed in the Greater Antilles, where the mountains are higher and distance traveled by air masses greater. For example, the city of Port Antonio on Jamaica's northeastern coast receives an average of 125 inches of annual precipitation. Higher up in the Blue Mountains, about 15 miles inland, rainfall averages nearly 200 inches per year. In Kingston, on the island's southeastern coast, rainfall averages only about 30 inches annually. On the smaller mountainous islands in the Lesser Antilles, rainfall tends to be more symmetrical without major differences between the windward eastern and leeward western coasts. For example, the coastal lowlands of both the eastern and western sides of St. Vincent average about 70 inches of rainfall, whereas the interior mountains receive more than 125 inches. The flatter island complexes, like the Bahamas and the Caymans, receive much less rainfall than the mountainous ones. Most of the Bahamas receives 40–50 inches of rain, whereas the Netherlands Antilles receives only 20–30 inches per year. In fact, the availability of water for drinking, agriculture, and industry is of major concern in the West Indies. Before the rain that does fall can be used, much of it rapidly runs off to surrounding seas. Some of the islands now strictly ration water. Houses are often built with rain-catching roofs and cisterns, and many of the drier islands, including St. Thomas and St. Martin, have desalination plants. Signs in hotel rooms often urge patrons not to waste water.

A typical summer day on an island in the West Indies will begin with a cool, clear morning with temperatures around 75 to 80 degrees Fahrenheit. By late afternoon the days warm to between 87 and 92 degrees, and a gentle breeze develops as conventional heating creates a slight low-pressure system over the land relative to the somewhat higher pressures over the cooler sea. Late afternoon convectional showers are intense but of short duration (lasting less than an hour). The early evenings are warm and muggy because of the high relative humidity. Later at night (after about 10 P.M.) the earlier daytime onshore breeze reverses itself to a gentle offshore wind because a weak high-pressure cell develops over the land as temperatures drop. Frequently, spectacular lightning flashes can be seen over the warmer sea as rain falls there. During the winter temperatures are only slightly lower, but significantly less rain falls. Although there are variations from place to place, normally about 65–75 percent of the precipitation occurs between May and October.

Tropical cyclonic storms develop most often between the 10th and 25th parallels in the Northern Hemisphere. Although a tropical storm did occur there in 1933, Trinidad is the only island in the Caribbean that is nearly immune to them because it is the southernmost island of the West Indies. Low-pressure systems often develop east of the Lesser Antilles in the middle of the Atlantic Ocean. Current wisdom suggests that some of the more fully developed lows originate as thermal bubbles over the western part of Africa's Sahara Desert. As the thermals travel westward toward the Caribbean they can mature into large and destructive storms, officially becoming hurricanes when sustained winds reach 74 miles per hour.

During a typical hurricane season in the West Indies, which lasts officially from June 1 to November 30, perhaps fifty to sixty tropical depressions will develop, but only between ten and fifteen will evolve into tropical storms, and fewer still (typically between three and seven) will mature into hurricanes. The depressions and storms are notable because of the rain they generate, but hurricanes are the most destructive and dangerous phenomena. A hurricane's sustained winds can reach more than 150 miles per hour, with gusts exceeding 200 miles per hour. Such powerful winds destroy crops, trees, and physical structures, posing danger to human life. But wind is not the only destructive element of a hurricane. The associated heavy rainfall causes massive flooding and pollutes drinking water supplies by overflowing sewage systems. In addition, virtually all hurricanes are accompanied by a storm surge (typically 5–20 feet in height), which causes massive destruction along coastal areas. Small tornados, or vortexes, accompany many hurricanes and add to their destructive effects. Typically, hurricanes follow an east-to-west track through the Caribbean, then curve northward toward the U.S. mainland.

Although the use of satellites and reconnaissance aircraft has improved early detection, hurricane paths remain unpredictable, and each year many deaths and millions of dollars in property damage occur. In 1988 Hurricane Gilbert caused massive destruction in the Caribbean. With sustained winds of 175 miles per hour, Gilbert entered the Caribbean, passing over St. Lucia, and then headed for the Dominican Republic and Haiti. Afterward it continued westward to Jamaica, where it traveled the entire length of the island, leaving 500,000 people homeless and ruining much of the island's coffee and banana crops. Finally it headed for Mexico's Yucatán Peninsula, where it did major damage to the resort areas of Cancún and Cozumel. Damage exceeded U.S.$200 million, hundreds of deaths occurred, and thousands of homes were destroyed or badly damaged. Hurricane Andrew destroyed or badly damaged more than 60,000 homes and caused about $25 billion in damage in August 1992 to South Florida's Miami-Dade County, located on the northern edge of the Caribbean fringe.

■ Landforms in the Caribbean

The diversity of the Caribbean is reflected in its many types of landforms. Some islands are mountainous and others are virtually flat. A few are volcanically active and many experience frequent and devastating earthquakes. Elevations range from a high of 10,417 feet at Pico Duarte in the Dominican Republic to about 150 feet below sea level in the Enriquillo Depression in the same country. But the true range in elevations is much greater than suggested by these figures if the depth of the Puerto Rico Trench, about 35 miles off the northern coast of Puerto Rico, is considered. It plunges more than 30,000 feet below sea level, deeper than Mount Everest is high.

For the most part, the Caribbean is an extraordinarily active geologic region. There are at least seventeen active volcanoes in the Lesser Antilles, and ten of them have erupted since the days of Columbus. On May 8, 1902, the Caribbean's most famous volcanic eruption occurred at Mount Pelée on Martinique. It buried the town of St. Pierre, killing an estimated 30,000 people. One day earlier, on the island of St. Vincent, the La Soufrière volcano erupted, send-

Richard Salter

Mountain view, Dominica

ing a deadly pyroclastic flow of lava and gases down the mountainside, killing 1,500 people.[3] Another volcano named La Soufrière erupted on the island of Guadeloupe in 1976. Most recently, the Soufrière Hills volcano erupted from 1995 to 1997, burying most of Montserrat's capital city of Plymouth.[4]

The volcanic activity and earthquakes that typify this area reflect its location at the zone of contact of six large, colliding tectonic plates (see Map 2.2). At the center of it all is the Caribbean Plate; its northern and eastern edges contain most of the islands of the West Indies. The most violent collision in the West Indies is occurring along the eastern edge of the Caribbean Plate, where the westward-moving Atlantic Plate is plunging under it at a rate of 1–2 inches per year. As the more dense Atlantic Plate dives under the lighter Caribbean Plate, the leading edge of the latter deforms, creating a crumpled mountainous landscape with consequent volcanic activity (Boswell and Conway 1992:6–10).

The geologic details of the Lesser Antilles reflect two roughly parallel arcs of islands. The innermost is volcanic in origin and more mountainous and includes most of the larger islands in the Lesser Antilles (St. Kitts, Nevis, Montserrat, Dominica, Martinique, St. Lucia, St. Vincent, and Grenada). The outer arc is more low-lying, of limestone origin, or deriving from much older volcanic phenomena that is no longer active. Examples include the Virgin Islands, Anguilla, St. Martin, Barbuda, Antigua, and Barbados (West and Augelli 1989:34–35).

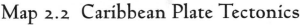

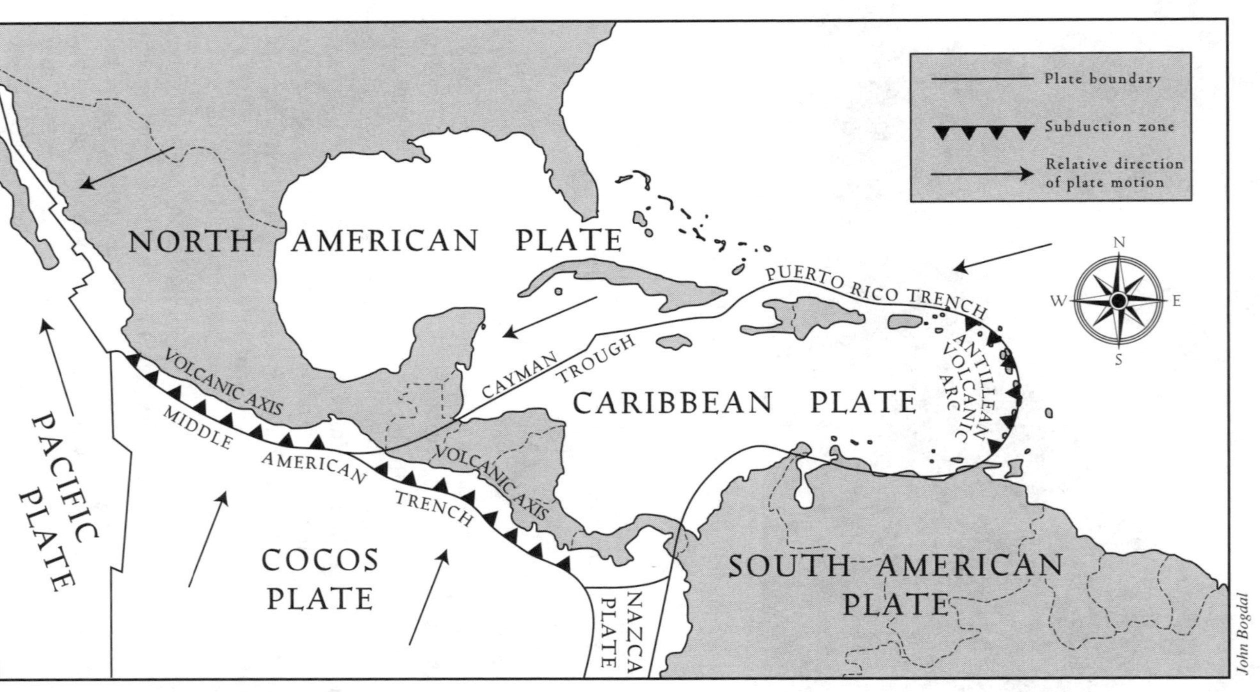

Map 2.2 Caribbean Plate Tectonics

The two halves of the island of Guadeloupe contain examples of both inner- and outer-arc characteristics. The southwestern half, known as Basse-Terre, is a volcanic island whose highest peak (Mount Soufrière) reaches an elevation of 4,812 feet. Conversely, its northeastern half, Grande-Terre, is a low-lying, undulating island of limestone composition. In addition to Guadeloupe's Basse-Terre and Montserrat, evidence of current volcanic activity is found on Martinique and St. Vincent. A number of other islands, such as Nevis, St. Lucia, Redonda, Dominica, and Grenada, contain hot sulfur springs that are also reflections of recent volcanism.

The Greater Antilles are products of much older and probably stronger tectonic forces dating mainly to between 60 million and 90 million years ago. They are not typified by the recent volcanic activity that characterizes the Lesser Antilles, but when they were exposed to uplifting and volcanism they experienced mountain-building that was even greater than that in the eastern Caribbean. As a consequence, the highest mountains on Cuba, Jamaica, and Hispaniola are taller than those on the Lesser Antilles. Even on Puerto Rico, the smallest of the Greater Antilles, the highest elevation of 4,389 feet at Cerro de Punta is comparable to the highest peak in the eastern Caribbean, Guadeloupe's Mount Soufrière. The main difference in the tectonics of the Greater and Lesser Antilles is that volcanism has ceased on the four largest islands, even though they still occasionally experience devastating earthquakes. For example, Port Royal, the old capital of Jamaica, was completely destroyed by an earthquake in 1692. The current capital, Kingston, was destroyed in 1907 and badly damaged again as recently as 1957. Cap Haitien in Haiti was destroyed in 1842; Port-au-Prince, the capital, was devastated twice during the nineteenth century.

The reasons for the occurrence of earthquakes, but not volcanic activity, in the Greater Antilles is also explained by the principles of plate tectonics. Whereas in the eastern islands the Caribbean and Atlantic Plates collide head-on, the movement of the Caribbean and North American Plates is horizontal relative to one another. They slide past each other, rather than one diving under the other. Thus, the force of contact is less intense along the northern coasts of the four larger islands. The friction generated causes pressure to build, and when it is released this causes the infrequent earthquakes that affect all of the northern islands from Cuba to Antigua. In fact, both the Puerto Rican and Cayman trenches were created by this movement, as well as by earlier subduction forces when the Caribbean and North American Plates confronted each other more directly than today.

The ancient volcanism that created the Greater Antilles was followed by a period of submersion beneath the sea. During this period of several million years, coral formations and dying calcareous marine organisms deposited thick layers of limestone. As a result, many of these islands have limestone soils and rocks that cover the lower elevations of their outer edges. The limestone deposits on the higher elevations of these islands were stripped away when another uplift occurred, raising them once again above sea level. The greater steepness of the slopes at higher elevations intensified the erosive effects of the tropical rainfall on the limestone covering, but the inner volcanic cores of the uplands were more resistant to this degradation. The alluvium washed from the mountains was deposited in the valleys and the narrow coastal plains where limestone accumulations are most evident today. The older mountainous cores are composed of igneous rocks, evidence of their volcanic origins. However, the mountains on these islands no longer exhibit the symmetrical shape typical of youthful cinder cones because they have been eroded for millions of years.

Several of the low-lying islands (e.g., those in the Bahamas, the Turks and Caicos Islands, Anegeda in the British Virgin Islands, and the Cayman Islands) are products primarily of coral reefs that grew on top of submerged sea platforms called banks. They were either uplifted above sea level or cov-

Kaieteur Falls, Guyana

Maureen Smith

ered by blowing sand and dying marine organisms that accumulated on top of them. These islands tend to appear to be nearly level, with maximum elevations rarely exceeding 200 feet.

In some places the thick coastal layers of limestone have weathered in geologic formations known as karsts. Here water has dissolved the underlying calcareous materials into caves with spectacular underground features such as stalactites and stalagmites (spines hanging from the ceiling and columns built up from the ground, respectively). In some places, rivers disappear underground, sinkholes abound, and the surface takes on a jumbled appearance of depressions and low rounded hills known as haystacks. These features are particularly prevalent in parts of the Greater Antilles, especially on their wetter northern coasts, and on Grande-Terre in Guadeloupe. Limestone caves, such as those in the Jamaican cockpit country, are present in less spectacular fashion on many of the other smaller islands. There are also formations called blue holes in the British Caribbean caused by deep seawater intrusions.

■ The Caribbean Amerindian Population

Available evidence suggests that the Caribbean islands were occupied by at least three different Amerindian cultural waves prior to the arrival of Christopher Columbus in 1492. The earliest of these was the Ciboney culture, which may have migrated southward from Florida into the Bahamas and then throughout the Greater Antilles as early as 2000 B.C. Because they had almost disappeared by the time the Spanish arrived, very little is known about them. There may have been a few thousand still living on the far western end of Cuba and in the southwestern corner of Haiti. They lived adjacent to the coasts and hunted, gathered, and fished but did not practice agriculture (West and Augelli 1989:61–63).

The arrival of the Arawaks from the northern coast of South America, around 300 B.C., represented the second wave of Amerindians in the Caribbean. Evidence suggests that these people traveled northward through the Lesser Antilles and into the Greater Antilles. By A.D. 1500 they occupied mainly the Greater Antilles. As they swept westward through these larger islands, they either absorbed or annihilated most of the earlier arriving Ciboneys.

The Arawaks had a higher level of technology than the Ciboneys, developing a type of agriculture that is still practiced by many peasant farmers on the mountain slopes of the Lesser Antilles and throughout the Greater Antilles, especially in Haiti and the Dominican Republic. It was a farming strategy known as *conuco*, a variation of the shifting cultivation systems practiced throughout humid tropical areas in other parts of the world. The Arawaks first burned the plot of land to remove weeds and leaves on the trees so more sunlight could reach the ground. Then they piled the topsoil in round mounds that were sometimes knee-high and several feet in diameter. Ashes from the burning of the forest cover enriched these concentrations of more fertile soil. On these relatively fertile mounds—tropical areas are known for their heavily leached poor soils—the Arawaks planted a variety of native crops, including yucca (also known as cassava), yams (sweet potato), arrowroot, peanuts, maize, beans, squash, cacao, various spices, cotton, tobacco, and numerous indigenous fruits such as the mamey and guava. Fish, fowl, and other foods obtained from the nearby water and forests supplemented their diet. When soil fertility declined, the fields were abandoned, new land was cut over, and the process was restarted.

Although the *conucos* looked primitive and unorganized to Europeans because of the way several varieties of crops were intergrown, in fact they represented a logical adjustment to the ecological conditions of the tropical West Indies. Heaping the soil into mounds provided a loose, well-aerated soil; the earthen piles reduced sheet erosion by rainwater; the intercropping of different plants that grew to different heights provided ground cover as further protection against erosion; and the production of a variety of crops offered nutritious variety to the Arawak diet. Additionally, modern research has shown that this kind of companion planting effectively maximizes output of land.

The Caribs, from whom the name Caribbean derived, were the last Indian cultural group to arrive in the region. Like the Arawaks, they also migrated from northern South America. However, they did not begin arriving until about A.D. 1000, and as a consequence they were found mainly in the eastern Lesser Antilles. Evidence suggests that they were just beginning to encroach on Arawak turf in eastern Puerto Rico when the Spanish arrived.

The Caribs were more warlike, fewer in number, and less technologically advanced compared to the Arawaks, but they did practice some agriculture, and like the Arawaks and the Ciboneys, they also hunted, gathered, and fished. They replaced the Arawaks throughout most of the Lesser Antilles except Trinidad, Tobago, and Barbados. The word *Carib* came to mean cannibal because of their fierceness and reputed practice of eating the flesh of captured male enemies, whether for ritual purposes or merely for food.

Estimates of the number of Amerindians that occupied the Caribbean at the time Columbus arrived vary greatly, usually from 750,000 to as many as 10 million. What happened to these people is a tragedy with few precedents in human history. The Ciboneys had all but disappeared before A.D. 1500, and the Arawaks were to virtually vanish from the Caribbean by 1550. The demise of the Arawaks was due to a number of factors, such as the importation of European diseases to which they had no immunity, the wars of European conquest, destruction of their food supplies, and overwork in mines and as laborers on European-owned farms and ranches. In addition, thousands committed suicide, testimony to the cruel treatment they endured.

The Caribs took longer to defeat because of their fiercer nature and because many retreated to the remote forested mountains of the Lesser Antilles. The Spanish did not consider the Lesser Antilles worth the effort it would take to conquer the Caribs; they had become more interested in the riches available on the Latin American mainland. Ultimately, it was the French who defeated the Caribs in Grenada in 1651; the British subdued them on St. Vincent, but not until 1773. Today there are probably no more than 3,000–4,000 people of Amerindian descent living in the Caribbean. The few remaining Caribs are found mainly on St. Vincent and Dominica; people with mixed Arawak ancestry are found on Aruba and very infrequently in the Greater Antilles.

■ Patterns of European Settlement After Conquest

As Stephen Randall details in Chapter 3, Columbus's four voyages throughout the West Indies from 1492 to 1502 paved the way for others to conquer and then settle the new lands in the name of the Spanish crown. With the consolidation of its authority, Spain focused on the exploitation of the region's natural resources. However, Spanish interest in Caribbean possessions quickly diminished except for a few settlements established in the Greater Antilles, especially in Cuba and what is now the Dominican Republic. Still, the Spanish would leave an indelible imprint in the West Indies: the construction of forts and cities, architectural styles, and place-names, even on islands later lost to other European powers. As Thomas D'Agostino points out in Chapter 4, this imprint is also evident within the political systems throughout the region.

Spanish construction of settlements in the Caribbean was determined by the Laws of the Indies, a codified body of laws promulgated by the crown to guide the colonization process. Unless topography demanded otherwise, colonial towns were laid out in a well-defined grid pattern, where streets intersected at right angles. In the center was a town plaza, where activities were focused. The settlement's main church (usually the largest building) was located on or close to the plaza. Also, the most important government offices, such as those of the mayor and town council, were located here. Houses were usually built of stone or brick and covered with white stucco and barrel-tile roofs. Their walls were often made of thick masonry to keep out the tropical heat and to protect against hurricanes. Usually, poor people lived on the periphery of these settlements, whereas the middle class and wealthy lived near the town's center. Later, a few of the colonial towns grew into large modern metropolitan cities and began to acquire some of the characteristics of

North American and European cities; traces of the original structures are still apparent in some cities. The historically reconstructed center of San Juan, known as Old San Juan, and parts of Santo Domingo are outstanding examples of colonial Spanish towns (West and Augelli 1989:63–67).

At least ten different powers would eventually play a role in settling the Caribbean: Spain, the United Kingdom, the Netherlands, France, Denmark, Sweden, the Knights of Malta, the United States, and the two German states of Brandenburg and Courland, in addition to independent privateers—but it was the British, Dutch, and French who competed most notably with the Spanish. The Dutch differed from the British and French in their goals in the West Indies because they were interested primarily in trading rather than settlement. The few small islands they established were primarily for trading purposes, and none played a major role in the sugar industry that emerged during the 1700s. In addition, the Dutch period of influence was shorter, from 1570 until 1678. Spanning little more than a century, their activities nevertheless had a profound and enduring influence on the Spanish. Dutch privateering damaged Spanish prestige and created enough of a diversion that the British and French were able to settle most of the Lesser Antilles. The Dutch introduced the British and French to the plantation system of sugar production, gaining from earlier experiences in Brazil. They also provided, through loans, much of the capital for these early ventures. In addition, the Dutch shipping industry became the main provider of supplies and slaves for the other Caribbean colonies. In fact, they were so successful in trading that the British and French finally passed laws (called exclusives) that required their respective colonies to trade only with the mother country, much like the Spanish had done earlier. However, by 1678 the Dutch were eliminated from a significant role in Caribbean trade. As a consequence, they channeled their energies away from the Americas and into their East Indies empire. The only reminders of Dutch activities in the Caribbean are Suriname and six small island possessions.

Unlike the Dutch, the British and French engaged vigorously in colonization. At first they chose to concentrate their efforts in areas not given much attention by the Spanish, namely, the Lesser Antilles. During the early seventeenth century they occupied most of the Leeward and Windward Islands, with the exception of Dutch settlements and Carib strongholds like St. Vincent and Dominica. The British occupied St. Kitts in 1623, Barbados in 1625, Nevis in 1628, and Antigua in 1632. The French acquired Guadeloupe and Martinique in 1635. During the latter half of the 1600s the British and French competed with the Spanish for possessions in the Greater Antilles and stepped up piracy against Spanish colonies as well as convoys traveling to Spain. In 1655 the British captured Jamaica from the Spanish, and in 1697 the French gained control of what is today Haiti.

The eighteenth century saw frequent wars among the British, French, and Spanish. The greatest concern for each was to maintain the territorial integrity of the home country, so overseas colonies, especially those in the West Indies, often became pawns in diplomacy. The result was a virtual state of sovereignty chaos in the Caribbean during the late 1600s and throughout the 1700s, as individual islands were swapped back and forth many times. For example, St. Lucia changed hands seventeen times, having been held by France nine times, by Great Britain six times, and twice being declared neutral. Similarly, St. Eustatius changed hands nine times, both Guadeloupe and Martinique seven times, Tobago six times, and St. Vincent and Grenada four times each (Richardson 1992:56). Evidence of this confusion is still found in the islands today in their place-names and vernacular speech patterns. For example, although St. Lucia, Dominica, St. Vincent, and Grenada became British possessions during the period 1783–1803 and remained so until their independence during the 1970s, many of their place-names are French, and the local patois spoken informally is a mixture of French and English words.

■ The Rise and Fall of Sugarcane in the West Indies

The first 150 years of settlement in the Caribbean were spent searching for a crop that could be profitably produced and sold in Europe. In addition to food crops grown for subsistence, colonists experimented with cash crops such as indigo, ginger, cotton, and tobacco. But the fact is that they did not grow enough food to feed even themselves, so from the outset they were dependent upon imports of flour, rice, dried meat, and salt fish. Furthermore, by the mid-1600s they began to experience serious competition from the colonies of North America in the production of tobacco and, later, cotton.

Sugarcane is ideally suited to the alternating wet and dry periods characteristic of the tropical climate of the West Indies. It requires a year-round growing season of warm temperatures, and the omnipresence of high-intensity sunlight speeds maturation. Furthermore, sugarcane withstands droughts better than most crops; it benefits from a dry season that makes it easier to harvest; and harvesting can usually be finished before the heart of hurricane season (August and September). The rapidly increasing market for sugar in both Europe and the colonies assured its early success. Because of the strict temperature requirements and the fact that most of the sugar was exported, plantations were usually located on level or gently rolling land along the coasts and in easily accessible valleys.

Around 1640 the Dutch introduced British and French colonialists to the production of sugarcane. Within fifty years the agricultural foundation of the non-Spanish islands had changed radically. Sugar did not catch on as early in the Spanish colonies because of greater interests in exploiting the Latin American mainland. The Hispanic islands were used mainly as way stations for supplying and protecting Spanish fleets and for raising cattle to supply dried meat and leather to both Spain and the mainland. Although Spanish and Portuguese entrepreneurs from the Canary Islands and Madeira, respectively, introduced sugar production in Hispaniola and Cuba by the late 1500s, it did not become of major importance on those islands until 250 years later.

At first, labor was provided by indentured immigrants from the British Isles and France because there was no longer an Amerindian population left to exploit. But soon it was clear that another source of workers was needed, and this led to the black slave trade from western Africa. The infamous triangular trade developed, whereby cloth and manufactured goods were brought from Europe to Africa, Africans were captured and transported against their will to the Caribbean, and sugar, molasses, and rum were shipped back to Europe.

Although estimates vary, some 4–5 million slaves were brought to the Caribbean. This is roughly the same number as were imported to Brazil and approximately ten times as many as were taken to the North American colonies. Most arrived in the eighteenth century during the peak of sugar production in the Caribbean. The massive influx of slaves drastically changed the racial and demographic composition of populations in the British, French, and Dutch colonies. Within a few years blacks were in the majority, a condition that accounts for the prevalence of an African-Caribbean majority today in all but the former Hispanic territories of Cuba, Puerto Rico, and the Dominican Republic. As noted above, the Hispanic islands did not enter the sugar plantation phase until the middle to late 1700s. Thus, they did not import slaves for as long as the other islands, which explains the smaller black populations in Cuba, Puerto Rico, and the Dominican Republic.

The slave trade persisted into the nineteenth century, the British being the first to abolish it in 1807, followed by the Dutch in 1814, the French in 1818, and the Spanish in 1820. The British emancipated slaves in 1834, but this was followed by an apprenticeship of four years, until 1838, when former slaves were required to remain and work on the plantations as wage laborers. The French freed slaves in 1848; Puerto Rico and Cuba released theirs in 1873 and 1886, respectively.

Emancipation created a labor shortage in the Caribbean because many freed slaves left their plantations, mostly to work on their own small farms. As plantations became desperate to find another labor source, indentured workers were enticed to move to the West Indies. Although there were many sources, the largest proportion came from India, the second largest from China. Between 1835 and 1917 almost 700,000 indentured workers were brought in to work in West Indian cane fields (West and Augelli 1989:108). The usual term of indenture was five years, after which most workers left the estates. As a result, indentured workers did not provide a long-term solution to the labor problem. But they did arrive in large enough numbers to significantly affect the populations of Trinidad, Guyana, Jamaica, Guadeloupe, Grenada, and St. Martin. In fact, in Trinidad (as well as in mainland countries such as Guyana) persons of southern Asian descent roughly equal the number of those of African descent. On this island they are still associated with the sugar industry, and many are found in rural areas. The East Indians have had a significant effect on local politics and the landscape, especially through construction of Hindu temples and Muslim mosques. However, on the rest of the islands they represent a much smaller (but still visible) minority and live primarily in cities, where many are merchants.

By the mid–nineteenth century the Caribbean sugar industry was in decline, although the later date of slave emancipation in the Spanish colonies delayed the decline there until the late 1800s. Several factors account for this deterioration. With emancipation, the cost of labor increased. Soils in some areas eroded and lost their fertility. The price supports that the British and French provided to the West Indies were discontinued, and the protected markets with the homelands were opened to outside competition by the mid-1800s. Because their markets used to be protected, there was little incentive for West Indian producers to modernize their operations. When this protection was removed, the inefficiency of the British and French operations made it difficult to compete with new competitors such as Cuba, Mauritius, and Brazil. In addition, sugar beet production in Europe, which was usually heavily protected and subsidized, provided another source of competition. More recent developments, including the use of corn syrup in sugar production and the use of sugar substitutes such as saccharin and aspartame, further eroded the industry.

Today the sugar industry has all but disappeared from most of the Caribbean and is significant only on a few islands such as Cuba, St. Kitts, Barbados, Trinidad, Guadeloupe, the Dominican Republic, and Jamaica. In fact, on all these islands except Cuba there also has been a significant decline in land used for growing sugar. By the mid-1980s Jamaica was producing only about half as much sugar compared to the 1960s. During the early 1970s sugar accounted for almost a third of Barbados's exports by value; by the mid-1980s the figure had declined to about 2 percent. In 1982, for the first time in more than 100 years, Puerto Rico had to import sugar from the U.S. mainland to meet its own needs. To survive at all in the Caribbean, the industry had to renew favorable trade agreements with other countries, especially with the European Union and North America. Similarly, the former Soviet Union and allied East European countries used to buy most of Cuba's sugar production at above-market prices. The dissolution of the Soviet Union in December 1991 put a stop to that practice, but Cuban sugar is still exported to those regions, albeit in smaller amounts.

Population Problems

In the West Indies, island size and population numbers are typically directly related: the larger the island, the larger the population. The Greater Antilles collectively contains more than 90 percent of the region's population, a figure almost identical to its share of total land area. Almost two-thirds (64 percent) live in the former Spanish territories of Cuba, the Dominican Republic, and Puerto Rico. Another 22 percent live in the former French colonies of Guadeloupe, Haiti, and Martinique.

Population growth in the Caribbean over the past five centuries has generated extremely high population densities (Table 2.1 in Chapter 1). In fact, population pressure is nothing new in the West Indies. The population density of the islands has long been much higher than that of the United States, where it is seventy-three people per square mile (73/sq. mile). It has been estimated that the West Indies (not including the Greater Antilles) had population densities that exceeded 100/sq. mile even before the mid-1800s, due largely to the labor demands of sugar production, especially on the British, French, and Dutch islands.

With a population of 36 million and an area of approximately 91,000 square miles, the Caribbean has a population density of 395/sq. mile, almost six times that of the United States. There is tremendous variation within the region, however; the Bahamas has the lowest density with 58/sq. mile, whereas Barbados has a density of 1,620/sq. mile—the highest in the West Indies. However, several of the mainland countries have much lower densities. The Population Reference Bureau, for example, lists Belize at 29/sq. mile, Guyana at 9/sq. mile, Suriname at 7/sq. mile, and French Guiana at 5/sq. mile. Thus, in this context the distinction between the insular and the fringe countries shows significant variation.

Such figures do not truly reflect the implications of population pressures. Due to steep slopes, soil erosion, poor drainage conditions, insufficient rainfall, and competition from urban, residential, and industrial uses, only about one-fourth of the land is used for domestic food production. A better indication: consider only the land being used for agriculture (not including animal grazing), a measure called physiological density. The average for all the West Indies is 1,612/sq. mile of agricultural land, a figure that few regions in the world can match. Coupled with the growing emphasis on cash crop production for export, it is easy to see why Caribbean countries are forced to import food for domestic consumption. Moreover, with nearly 60 percent (and rising) of the region's population living in urban areas, even the concept of physiological density does not fully capture the severity of population pressure. The rapid rate of urbanization has outstripped the ability of national governments to create jobs, build infrastructure, and provide services.

In 1950, the islands in the West Indies had approximately 17 million inhabitants. By the end of the twentieth century, this figure had more than doubled to 36 million, an annual average (geometric) growth rate of about 1.9 percent for 1950–2000. This rate of growth was about twice that of the United States for the same period. Since the 1960s, West Indian birthrates have steadily declined while death rates decreased. As a consequence, by the year 2000 the rate of natural increase (the birthrate minus the death rate) had declined only modestly to about 1.6 percent, a rate at which a population will double in just over forty years. The economic implications of such rapid growth are obvious, although this has been at least partially mitigated in the Caribbean due to opportunities for emigration.

■ Emigration from the Caribbean

From its very beginning, the Caribbean population has been migratory. Even the aboriginal Indians who occupied the area before the arrival of Europeans came from elsewhere, most likely Florida and South America. Despite this long history, I will concentrate this discussion on emigration patterns since World War II.

Emigration from the Caribbean following World War II intensified. Most of the emigrants went to either the European home country—the United Kingdom, France, and the Netherlands—or to the United States and Canada. During the 1950s the movement from the British West Indies to the United Kingdom became so great that in 1962 the British government passed the Commonwealth Immigration Act, which greatly restricted inflow beginning in 1965. Since then, most of those leaving the former British islands have gone to the United States or Canada. By the mid-1980s close to 6 million emigrants from the Caribbean lived either in Europe or in North America, representing about one-fifth of the population still residing in the islands at that time. Approximately three-fourths of the island emigrants lived in the United States, with another 20 percent in Europe and 5 percent in Canada. Of those who migrated to Europe, more than half went to Great Britain, a fourth to France, and a fifth to the Netherlands.

Despite the significant movement to Europe, the United States received by far the greatest number of emigrants. By 1990 some 4.4 million people born in the Caribbean lived on the U.S. mainland.[5] Although this represented only about 2 percent of the total U.S. population, their presence was more noticeable because they tended to concentrate in a few metropolitan areas. For example, Puerto Ricans, Haitians, Jamaicans, Dominicans, and Trinidadians tend to concentrate in the Northeast, especially in New York City. Cuban immigrants congregate mainly in Miami, with a secondary cluster in New Jersey's Union City in the New York metropolitan area. In addition, there was notable migration to the U.S. Virgin Islands from Puerto Rico, the British Virgin Islands, and the nearby less prosperous Leeward Islands between World War II and the late 1970s, but this pattern has diminished considerably.

Because Caribbean immigrants tend to concentrate in a few cities in the United States, the city with the second largest number of an island's natives is often located outside the Caribbean. For example, Miami has more Cubans living there than does Santiago, Cuba's second largest city. Similarly, greater New York City has the second largest number of nationals from Puerto Rico, the Dominican Republic, Haiti, Jamaica, Barbados, and Trinidad. Montreal is the third for Haiti; Paris is the second for both Martinique and Guadeloupe; London is the second for several of the former British Lesser Antilles; and Amsterdam is the second for all of the Netherlands Antilles.

Although emigrants from the Caribbean represent only tiny fractions of the populations of the European and North American countries they moved to, they represent a significant percentage of the islands they moved from. If these people were to return to the West Indies, the result would be catastrophic. In 1990, 44 percent of all Puerto Ricans lived on the U.S. mainland; if they were to return to their island homeland, its population would increase by almost 80 percent. Similarly, Barbadian Americans and Jamaican Americans represent one-fourth and one-fifth of the populations living in Barbados and Jamaica, respectively.

As important as emigration has been to the West Indies in serving as an escape valve for population growth, it should not be viewed as a solution to mounting population pressures. Rather, it should be seen as one factor that temporarily slowed what would otherwise have been ruinous population growth on the islands. Some countries that once received significant numbers of immigrants from the Caribbean are now tightening immigration requirements. In addition to Great Britain's aforementioned Commonwealth Immigration Act of 1962, Canada tightened its immigration policy in 1972, as did the United States in 1986, 1990, and 1996 (Martin and Midgley 1999:17–22).

Even within the Caribbean, serious efforts have been made to reduce interisland movement. For example, Haitian and Jamaican migrations to Cuba have been stopped. The Netherlands Antilles has halted the influx from the British and French islands. Jamaica and Barbados have forbidden the entry of unskilled laborers. Trinidad, much of whose black population initially came from the Windward and Leeward Islands, now has legal barriers against further unrestricted entry. The only islanders not discouraged from immigrating are the skilled and professional groups, and this kind of brain drain is precisely what the islands do not need.

Emigration has served an important function, providing more time for islands to solve the problem of high natural growth rates. Still, it is necessary for Caribbean countries to reduce fertility rates below their current moderately high levels. Fortunately, this appears to be happening, as evidence suggests that fertility is declining generally throughout the region, in part due to the influx of people into urban areas.

■ Urbanization in the Caribbean

People have been migrating from rural to urban areas in the Caribbean since the early 1900s, but this movement has become especially significant since 1945. Today it is one of the most important migration patterns affecting the region, as island populations are rapidly changing from a predominantly rural and agricultural orientation to an urban focus. In 1960 fewer than 40 percent of all the Caribbean population lived in cities. By 1999 the figure had risen to 59 percent, and by 2010 it is expected to be about 65 percent. As Table 1.1 indicates, although there is significant variation, some countries have levels of urbanization comparable to that of the United States (75 percent). The highest level of urbanization is found in the Bahamas, where 89 percent live in the cities of Nassau, Freeport, and Port Lucaya. Martinique, Cuba, Puerto Rico, and Trinidad and Tobago have higher than average percentages of populations living in cities. Conversely, the urban population of Antigua and Barbuda is 37 percent, St. Kitts-Nevis 34 percent, and St. Lucia 38 percent.

Richard Salter

View of Mahaut, Dominica

Two related reasons explain Caribbean urbanization: the decline of economic opportunities in rural areas; and the perceived increase of such opportunities in cities. As a result, rural populations are growing at average rates of less than 1 percent throughout most of the Caribbean, and in some places, such as in Puerto Rico, they are actually declining. Yet the average annual growth rates in the cities generally exceed 3 percent. To put this in perspective, a city whose growth rate remains 3 percent will see its population double in twenty-three years. In the space of about seventy years the population would double three times (actually an eightfold increase because this is a geometric growth rate). Such explosive urban growth creates problems in providing adequate housing, jobs, and social services for new inhabitants, about a quarter of whom are in-migrants either from the countryside or from foreign countries. The remaining three-quarters are the product of natural increase (an excess of births versus deaths).

Much of the growth in the Caribbean is taking place in each island's largest city and its surrounding areas. In 1950 only seven cities in the Caribbean had populations exceeding 100,000, and only Havana had more than 1 million residents. Now there are at least thirty cities with populations of more than 100,000, and five metropolitan areas exceed 1 million: Havana, Santo Domingo, San Juan, Port-au-Prince, and Kingston. Usually, one metropolitan area dominates the urban structure of each island. When the largest city has a population that is more than two or three times as large as its next competitor, it is called a primate city. Primate cities are primary in almost every respect, dominating the island's economy, culture, politics, and social scene. With the exception of Guadeloupe, whose capital is the small city of Basse-Terre, each island's primate city is also its political capital.

The housing problem has become acute in the primate cities of the West Indies. Many residents live in substandard housing in areas called shantytowns. Houses in shantytowns are built from scraps of wood, metal, cardboard, or whatever else the owner can find. They usually have one to three rooms, sometimes with a detached kitchen, and an outhouse or pit latrine. Sometimes standpipes are available as a water source, but many residents still have to buy their water from trucks that travel through the neighborhoods.

If the government does not tear down shantytowns constructed on illegally occupied land, many eventually mature into more substantial housing. As shantytown dwellers find jobs, they begin to make improvements, such as building rooms with cinder blocks and opening a small store in the home. Some suggest that shantytowns help solve the housing problems of the largest Caribbean cities through their self-help nature. Some governments are helping inhabitants provide for themselves by supplying electricity and water pipes to their neighborhoods. They also have built multistory public apartment units in cities like San Juan, Fort-de-France, Pointe-à-Pitre, and Charlotte Amalie (on St. Thomas), but these have rarely provided long-term solutions to the urban housing problem.

The largest Caribbean cities, with populations over 100,000, have evolved considerably in appearance. Originally, even the British, French, and Dutch cities appeared similar to the typical Spanish colonial town. All the primate cities originated as colonial ports with gridiron street patterns focused around a central plaza. Usually, the wealthy lived as near as possible to the plaza, which provided greatest accessibility to public buildings, businesses, and contact with important people. Today automobile use has become widespread, and the largest cities are beginning to resemble cities in North America and Europe. The central business districts of the primate cities now have some high-rise buildings, but the surrounding areas have often deteriorated and become home to the poor instead of the rich. Meanwhile, the wealthy and middle classes have moved to the suburbs, as they have in large U.S. cities, and shopping centers have developed on the periphery of metropolitan areas like San Juan and Kingston.

■ Economic Geography of the Caribbean

Material well-being varies in the Caribbean. There is a wide range of incomes between the more prosperous Bahamas, Barbados, U.S. Virgin

Thomas J. D'Agostino

A barrio in Santo Domingo, Dominican Republic

Islands, Cayman Islands, Netherlands Antilles, and French West Indies; the middle-range Guyana, Jamaica, and Suriname; and the lower-income Haiti and Cuba. These variances are attributable to the availability and use of natural resources.

Caribbean Agriculture Beyond Sugarcane

The decline of the sugar industry has been so far-reaching that it is only a significant agricultural pursuit on several of the islands in the Caribbean. Still, agriculture has not disappeared from most of the islands where sugar is no longer important because other crops have also played a significant role in the agricultural economy of the Caribbean.

Spanish missionaries introduced bananas during the early 1500s, but it did not become a major crop until the 1880s. By the beginning of the twentieth century, bananas had become popular in Europe and the United States, and Jamaica was the world's leading producer. There are two general types of bananas that are important in the Caribbean, the sweet dessert variety (familiar to most Americans and Europeans), and the cooking variety, called plantains. The latter type is used domestically in the West Indies and is not exported in nearly as large quantities as the dessert type. Sweet bananas are most easily grown on fertile alluvial or volcanic soils and on the wetter windward sides of the islands where annual rainfall exceeds 90 inches. Most often they are cultivated on large plantations, where they are grown under carefully supervised conditions. Plantains tolerate less rainfall and are more frequently grown on smaller farms on poorer soils both on coastal lowlands and in the foothills of the mountains. On several of the Windward Islands of the Lesser Antilles, such as St. Lucia, St. Vincent, Grenada, Martinique, the Basse-Terre side of Guadeloupe, and Dominica, sweet bananas have replaced sugarcane as the main agricultural crop (Grossman 1998:208–222). They are also an important secondary product in the Dominican Republic and Jamaica. But the Caribbean is no longer a leading producer of bananas. Far more are grown in Central America, South America, India, and several countries in Southeast Asia.

Tobacco was one of the earliest cash crops grown in the West Indies. In fact, it was used by the pre-Columbian Indians and may have originated in the Caribbean, or possibly in nearby South America. Today, however, it is of greatest significance in Cuba and the Dominican Republic. A little is also grown, mainly for domestic consumption, in Jamaica and Puerto Rico.

Coffee was at one time important as a mountain-grown cash crop on all the Greater Antilles, and its cultivation eventually extended as far south as Trinidad. But production in the Caribbean could not compete with that in some of the Central American countries and particularly Colombia, Brazil, and Venezuela in South America. Some coffee is still grown for export on mountain slopes in the Dominican Republic, Jamaica, and Haiti. A small amount, mainly for domestic use, is also grown in Puerto Rico.

Cacao, used to make chocolate, originated on the adjacent Central American mainland or perhaps in southern Mexico. It is another crop that used to be widely grown throughout the Caribbean but is no longer as widespread (it is particularly vulnerable to high winds from hurricanes). It is still mildly important today only in the Dominican Republic, Trinidad, and several of the Windward Islands. The world's leading region of production has now shifted to western Africa, especially to the Ivory Coast and Ghana.

East Indians introduced marijuana to the Caribbean during the mid-1800s. They brought it with them as a holy plant when they arrived as indentured laborers in the British islands. Marijuana production increased significantly during the 1970s and 1980s, to the point that it is a billion-dollar industry. It is associated with the region's Rastafarians, a cultural sect, and is cultivated in Jamaica as well as in remote mountainous areas throughout the Caribbean despite the fact that it is universally illegal. As H. Michael Erisman shows in Chapter 6, the locations of the islands, some of which are isolated and uninhabited, make them ideal transshipment points for narcotraffickers.

Other significant commercial crops grown both for export and domestic use in the Caribbean today are pineapples, coconuts, and citrus fruits. Pineapples and coconuts are grown almost exclusively on the coastal lowlands, and citrus trees are raised sometimes on the lowlands (as in Cuba) and sometimes in the low mountains (as in Jamaica and Puerto Rico). But these three crops are grown on almost all the islands in small quantities. The Caribbean is not a major producer of any of these on a world scale, although Cuba did provide much of the citrus consumed in Eastern Europe and the former Soviet Union.

Despite the fact that farming is still widely practiced in the Caribbean, it is also true that not nearly enough food is produced to meet domestic needs. At least 50 percent of the food consumed in the region is imported from other countries, usually located outside the region. In some cases, such as Antigua, Puerto Rico, Barbados, Trinidad, and the Bahamas, the amount imported approaches 80 percent of the food locally consumed. At least four factors account for the region's inability to feed itself. First, population densities are so high on many islands that they could feed themselves only by developing an intensive form of farming similar to that practiced in some parts of eastern and southeastern Asia. Second, much of the best agricultural land is used for cash crops. Food crops are usually grown on peasant farms and in residual areas that have steeper slopes, less fertile soils, and generally poorer growing conditions. Third, tastes in the Caribbean have changed, and many people prefer to consume products imported from abroad rather than the locally produced cassava, breadfruit, and rum. Fourth, tourists consume much of the food that might otherwise be eaten by locals. As a consequence of these factors, food prices are 50–100 percent higher in the Caribbean than in the United States, well beyond the means of many local residents.

Mineral Resources

The Caribbean is not blessed with mineral wealth, with three exceptions: Cuba, Jamaica, and Trinidad. Cuba has the greatest variety of metallic minerals, most of which are located in its mountainous eastern end. It exports some manganese, cobalt, nickel, chrome, and iron from this area, and it has small copper reserves west of Havana near Pinar del Río. Proportionately, minerals are not as important in Cuba as they are in Jamaica and Trinidad.

Jamaica has large reserves of bauxite, the ore from which aluminum is made. It is the world's third leading producer of this ore, most of which is found in the valleys among the limestone mountains in the center of the island. No aluminum is manufactured in Jamaica because of the high energy requirements of the final processing stage, and as a result most of the alumina is shipped to either the United States or Canada, where it is refined into aluminum. The exportation of both bauxite and alumina provides for almost 60 percent of Jamaica's exports by value, representing the single most important element in the island's economy.

Trinidad is the only island in the Caribbean to have significant reserves of oil and natural gas. Its oil and gas industry provides for almost 80 percent of the value of its exports and supplies jobs for approximately 20,000 people. The production of oil and gas, and its refinement into various petroleum products, is by far the island's most important industry.

Other islands have refineries, but none produce their own oil, with the partial exception of Barbados, which has small reserves but not nearly enough to satisfy even its own needs. In fact, the Caribbean is badly deficient in traditional energy sources, a dilemma that complicates economic development as petroleum prices continue to rise. Still, the refining of imported oil is big business on some of the islands, including Aruba, Curaçao, and the Bahamas. About one-sixth of the oil consumed in the United States is refined in the Caribbean.

The Caribbean has a number of oil transshipment terminals in addition to refineries. Approximately 50 percent of the oil imported to the United States passes through Caribbean shipping lanes. The reason for this is that the largest oil tankers that transport oil from places like Venezuela, Nigeria, and the Middle East are not allowed access to some ports in the eastern United States because of their size and because of environmental concerns. The supertankers unload their crude oil at Caribbean ports, where it can be transferred to smaller ships to gain access to the lucrative markets on the U.S. eastern seaboard. Most West Indian ports that serve as transshipment terminals take advantage of the unloading of oil to refine some of it, earning some profits from this processing stage.

Tourism in the Caribbean

The natural tropical island environment with some of the world's most beautiful beaches is an idyllic setting for a vacation, and so tourism has become a significant industry in the Caribbean. The varied history has created a diverse cultural setting in which it is easy to visit English-, French-, Dutch-, and Spanish-speaking islands during a single vacation. The proximity of the Caribbean to the affluent North American market has given it an important advantage.

There was a small but significant Caribbean tourist industry prior to World War II, with a primary concentration in Cuba and a much smaller secondary core in Jamaica. But not until the 1950s, when regular and inexpensive air service was available, did the industry become truly significant. The Puerto Rican government developed tourism during the late 1940s and early 1950s, but the demise of tourism in Cuba that resulted from the revolution in 1959 was the major reason for the success of Puerto Rico's tourism during the early 1960s. This success spurred similar government promotion and development in the U.S. Virgin Islands and the Bahamas during the 1960s and 1970s. Their success, in turn, motivated other islands to promote tourism. Today, tourism accounts for at least 10 percent of the gross national product (GNP) of the Caribbean. This sector of the economy also generates about 20 percent of the region's export earnings, making tourism the number-one earner of foreign currency.

Of course, the importance of tourism differs throughout the West Indies. For example, tourism generates 70–80 percent of the legal GNP of the Bahamas and the Cayman Islands.[6] It accounts for 35–50 percent of GNP in the U.S. Virgin Islands, Antigua, and Barbados. But it provides less than 10 percent of GNP in some of the Lesser Antilles like Dominica, St. Vincent, St. Lucia, Martinique, Guadeloupe, and Trinidad and Tobago and in the Greater Antilles countries of Haiti and the Dominican Republic.

Although tourism is the leading earner of foreign currency for the West Indies, the industry here is not big by world standards. The region receives only about 3 percent of the world's tourists (an estimated 16.8 million in 1998) and about 5 percent of its earnings. The number of tourists and the dollars they generate are much smaller than in Europe and North America, yet compared to other developing areas tourism is well established in the Caribbean.

Almost two-thirds of tourists who visit the Caribbean live in the United States, 8 percent live in Canada, and 10 percent come from Europe. Although the number of interisland tourists traveling within the Caribbean has increased, as a proportion of the total they have decreased since 1970. With the rise of a substantial middle class in the region, more local people are traveling to areas outside the region for vacations rather than traveling within it from one island to another.

Some people argue that there is a downside to tourism, questioning the logic of depending on this sector as a development strategy. They assert that because tourism is a seasonal venture it does not provide the type of year-round income and employment that the West Indies need. Also, they note that much of the profits earned by tourism are leaked outside the islands and back to the countries that send most of the tourists. For example, many of the tourist facilities are foreign-owned, and much of the revenue they generate is repatriated rather than reinvested in local economies. In addition, overdependence on tourism promotes a monocultural economy that is vulnerable to outside influence beyond the control of local governments and entrepreneurs. Tourism is vulnerable to economic fluctuations, and when recessions occur the number of people taking vacations decreases. They also point out that Caribbean government budgets are a zero-sum game in the sense that money invested in tourism results in less money that can be spent elsewhere in other sectors to promote economic growth. Thus, even though tourism generates some revenue and creates some jobs, its contribution to the region's long-term development is problematic. Finally, it is argued that the local culture is degraded by the large influx of pleasure-seeking tourists.

■ Conclusion

Although the Caribbean's geographic diversity is apparent, there are at least five unifying characteristics that enable us to view it as a single region.[7] First, except for the northern Bahamas, all of the Caribbean is located within the tropics. This affects the climates, soils, vegetation patterns, the clothing worn, the food eaten, and many other characteristics. Second, the roles of the Caribbean Sea and the Atlantic Ocean serve as a homogenizing factor. Both bodies of water are routes for interisland trade as well as for trade with countries outside the region. Many islanders derive sustenance from the oceanic surroundings that have also functioned as a source for food and a place of adventure and recreation. Third, this is a region containing developing countries, all of which are disadvantaged in their trading relations with the prosperous first world nations in North America and Europe. What the islands do have to export (primarily food products, minerals, tourism) usually costs less than what they need to import (including technology, managerial and advertising skills, and manufactured products) from the more industrialized countries of the world. Fourth, each island had a long history of colonial domination, and many only recently became independent. After independence, a new type of economic dependency upon North American and European countries replaced the old-style political colonialism. Despite proximity to one another, the island countries still trade primarily with North America and Europe, more so than with each other. Fifth, the Caribbean's geographical location (sandwiched between the United States to the north, South America to the south, and Mexico and Central America to the west) has been of great importance. It has affected the trading patterns that all the West Indian islands have with both one another as well as with the nearby United States, Canada, and Latin America. Furthermore, the fact that all these islands are located close to each other (with much interisland migration and interaction) has created a sense of kinship and neighborhood despite their diversity.

■ Notes

1. Two years ago I was asked to provide expert testimony in a legal case involving a yacht that had run aground on the Colorado Archipelago, a string of small islands located off the northwestern coast of Cuba. The boat was maneuvered off the reef it had hit and began to limp northward toward Miami. However, the boat never made it. It sunk in the Straits of Florida, about a third of the way between Havana and Key West. The yacht had been insured and the policy covered the boat while it was in the Caribbean (not the Caribbean Sea, just the Caribbean). The insurance company involved argued that it was not liable because the boat had not sunk in the Caribbean Sea and, therefore, it had not sunk in the Caribbean. The question I was asked was whether where the boat had sunk was in the Caribbean region. I explained that although there was no unanimity regarding the exact boundaries of this region, it was generally accepted by most scholars that it extended beyond the limits of the Caribbean Sea to include the Straits of Florida, outside the limit of the territorial waters of the United States. The court accepted my explanation, and the insurance company agreed to settle with the yacht's owner.

2. Aruba withdrew from the Netherlands Antilles in 1986 and has since become an autonomous member of the kingdom of the Netherlands, the same status as the whole of the Netherlands Antilles. Notice that the French and Dutch halves of St. Martin are spelled differently, St. Maarten for the southern Dutch part, and St. Martin for the northern French part.

3. A pyroclastic flow occurs when magma, rocks, mud, and gases mix together and roll down the side of a volcano at speeds up to 60–70 miles per hour. This utterly destructive and often deadly avalanche resembles a mass of boiling boulders.

4. In French the word *soufrière* means "sulfur," a chemical that is always present during volcanic eruptions and produces an egglike smell. This word appears repeatedly throughout the mountainous islands of the eastern Caribbean.

5. This figure includes all foreign-born persons plus all Puerto Ricans living in the United States in 1990. Since Puerto Ricans are U.S. citizens, they are not classified as being foreign-born by the U.S. Bureau of the Census (U.S. Bureau of the Census 1995:51–52).

6. The illegal drug industry has become very well developed in the Bahamas. Because it is a clandestine industry, nobody knows what its precise contribution to the

Bahamian economy is, but there is no doubting that it does add very significantly to this country's economy. The 70–80 percent figure just stated for tourism's contribution does not take into consideration profits from the drug industry.

7. For an alternative list of unifying factors, see Elbow 1996:16–18.

Bibliography

Ashdown, Peter. *Caribbean History in Maps.* London: Longman Caribbean, 1979.

Boswell, Thomas D., and Dennis Conway. *The Caribbean Islands: Endless Geographical Diversity.* New Brunswick, NJ: Rutgers University Press, 1992.

Cameron, Sarah, and Ben Box, eds. *2000 Caribbean Islands Handbook.* New York: Prentice Hall, 1999.

Elbow, Gary S. "Regional Cooperation in the Caribbean: The Association of Caribbean States." *Journal of Geography* 96, no. 11 (1996): 13–22.

Espenshade, Edward B. Jr., ed. *Goode's World Atlas.* Rand McNally, 1995.

Fukuda-Parr, Sakiko, and Richard Jolly, eds. *Human Development Report 1999.* New York: Oxford University Press, United Nations Development Programme, 1999.

Grossman, Lawrence S. *The Political Ecology of Bananas: Contract Farming, Peasants, and Agrarian Change in the Eastern Caribbean.* Chapel Hill: University of North Carolina Press, 1998.

Klack, Thomas D., ed. *Globalization and Neoliberalism: The Caribbean Context.* New York: Rowman and Littlefield, 1998.

Martin, Philip, and Elizabeth Midgley. "Immigration to the United States." *Population Bulletin* 54, no. 2 (June 1999).

Michener, James A. *Caribbean.* New York: Random House, 1989.

Population Reference Bureau. *2002 World Population Data Sheet,* available at http://www.prb.org/pdf/WorldPopulationDS02_Eng.pdf.

Richardson, Bonham C. *The Caribbean in the Wider World, 1492–1992.* Cambridge, UK: Cambridge University Press, 1992.

U.S. Bureau of the Census. *Statistical Abstract of the United States, 1995.* Washington DC: U.S. Government Printing Office, 1995.

———. *International Data Base, 1999.* International Programs Center, available at http://www.census.gov/ipc/www/idbnew.html.

West, Robert C., and John P. Augelli, eds. *Middle America: Its Lands and Peoples.* Englewood Cliffs, NJ: Prentice Hall, 1989.

3

The Historical Context

Stephen J. Randall

The Caribbean has a complicated historical legacy. Christopher Columbus, searching for a passage to China, first landed in the area at the end of the fifteenth century. From then on the region has played an important role in international relations, as detailed by H. Michael Erisman in Chapter 6. The Caribbean was often at the center of European colonial rivalries. Even when the region was of peripheral concern to competing European and North American imperialism, the competition invariably impacted domestic politics, society, and economics.

As Richard S. Hillman indicates in the introduction to this book, both unity and diversity characterize the Caribbean. There is a striking cultural and linguistic diversity within the region, as well as significant differences in terms of socioeconomic development and political traditions. For example, some of the islands of the West Indies have traditions of British parliamentary government, whereas Cuba and the Dominican Republic, former Spanish colonies, experienced authoritarianism and strong presidential regimes. There are contrasts between larger nations such as the Dominican Republic, Haiti, and Cuba, which have played a major role in hemispheric politics in the past century, and the smaller islands of the eastern Antilles. There are also critical differences between the island nations of the Caribbean that remained within the imperial system into the twentieth century and the larger, more powerful mainland nations. African slavery had a substantially lesser impact on Colombia, Venezuela, and Mexico, each of which attained independence from Europe in the early nineteenth century.

Notwithstanding such diverse currents, the countries of the Caribbean have endured common experiences. Settled primarily by English, Spanish, French, and Dutch colonists with imperial interests and who rapidly destroyed all but a small remnant of the indigenous populations, the Caribbean took on a different appearance with the massive forced migration of African slaves from the seventeenth century through the middle of the nineteenth century. Africans' forced migration, combined with the institution of slavery and the postemancipation importation of indentured workers from India and China, essentially created the human contours of the region.

Moreover, slavery, economic exploitation, and political domination have profoundly impacted the evolution of converging cultural, socioeconomic, and political patterns within the region. Thus, as Thomas J. D'Agostino discusses in Chapter 4, contemporary Caribbean governments and their leaders face similar socioeconomic and political challenges. These governments, despite their disparate structures and traditions, have developed common ways of addressing these challenges.

This chapter introduces the major historical developments in the Caribbean region since the end of the fifteenth century and provides background and context for the more specialized chapters that follow. The approach is necessarily synthetic and interpretative, touching on the main historical currents and highlights of the region with focus on the insular Caribbean.

■ Conquest and Colonization, 1492–1800

Although debate continues in regard to Christopher Columbus's arrival being the "discovery" of the Americas, there can be little disagreement about the historical importance of the colonization of the Caribbean by European imperial powers after 1492. As Thomas Boswell details in Chapter 2, that first voyage ultimately led to the large-scale movement of European, African, and Asian peoples to the Americas, completely altering the demographic composition of the region. It also led to the formation of European colonies throughout the Western Hemisphere, many of which would become independent states during the course of the nineteenth and twentieth centuries.

Columbus conducted four voyages to the Caribbean between 1492 and 1502. The primary interest of Queen Isabella of Spain was not in the settlement of a new world but rather in mineral wealth—particularly gold—believed under the economic theories of the age to be the source of all national wealth. It was only on Columbus's third voyage in 1498 that gold was discovered in Santo Domingo and not until 1508 that Juan Ponce de Léon would locate deposits in Puerto Rico. Columbus's initial forays into the area, therefore, were of less economic significance than the major developments that followed in Mexico, Peru, and Bolivia, which became the main sources of gold and silver.

Between Columbus's first voyage in 1492 and 1519, when Hernán Cortes invaded Mexico, the Spanish held unchallenged supremacy in the Caribbean.

By the time of Cortes's onslaught on the Aztec and Mayan peoples of Mexico, the Spanish had established varying degrees of authority and settlement in Cuba, Santo Domingo (the island of Hispaniola, which became Haiti and the Dominican Republic), Puerto Rico, Jamaica, Trinidad, and Martinique. What was especially important about this period was the rapidity with which the Spanish sought to turn the region into one that could be successfully exploited in the interest of the metropolis, and that interest soon went beyond the quest for gold. Juan de Esquivel, for example, shortly after establishing a colony in Santo Domingo in 1509, set up sugarcane cultivation and processing, within a few years sending the first shipments of sugar back to Spain.

The Spanish quickly sought to institutionalize the relationship between the metropolis and the new colonies and their peoples (including the indigenous population) and to regulate trade. The indigenous population, prior to the advent of the African slave trade, was the most pressing social concern. At the time of the Spanish arrival in the Caribbean, the indigenous population is estimated to have been 750,000, composed primarily of the Ciboney, the Arawak, and the Carib, with the main concentration of the population on the island of Hispaniola (Knight 1978:6) There, the population of perhaps 200,000 was reduced to only a few thousand in less than two decades as the result of warfare, enslavement, and disease. Although there was some outrage in Spanish circles about this devastation, by the time any effort was made to address the problem the population was already hovering on the brink of extinction. In the Laws of Burgos (1512), the first of the European colonial charters, King Ferdinand sought to address the persistent problems over the treatment of indigenous peoples, recognizing the need for some degree of regulation. The Laws of Burgos, which permitted colonial officials to free native people from the *encomienda* system (in which they were enslaved) when they were Christianized and capable of self-government, in practice simply continued the policy of *repartimiento* (distribution of lands and forced labor) granted to the conquistadors by the Spanish crown. More significant, although perhaps equally ineffectual, was the appointment of friar Bartolomé de las Casas as protector of the Indians. De las Casas, who arrived in Hispaniola in 1502, himself utilized forced Indian labor on his allotted lands until 1515, when he renounced his *repartimiento* of Indians and returned to Spain in an effort to alter Spanish policy. In his efforts to improve the condition of indigenous peoples throughout the region, de las Casas underlined the deficiencies and tragedy of Spanish policies. His historical legacy was to become one of the major inspirations of modern liberal attitudes toward indigenous peoples and to produce an account of Spanish atrocities toward the first inhabitants of the Americas.

Spanish mistreatment of native peoples, the unwillingness of Spanish colonists to engage in agricultural labor, and the singularly exploitative nature of Spanish colonial policy had other, farther-reaching consequences. The rapid decimation of the potential labor force left Spain with few options except to seek alternative sources of manual labor. In 1518 the Spanish crown authorized the importation of African slaves. That initiative would ultimately bring several million African slaves across the Atlantic Ocean to the Americas and create new societies that were an amalgam of European, African, and Asian cultures and peoples.

By the early sixteenth century Spain began to face increasing challenges to its exclusive presence in the Caribbean, although it was almost another century before it was forced by other European powers to relinquish its monopoly. For much of the sixteenth century the other major European countries were distracted by other ventures or were too weak to confront Spain. Spain controlled the Netherlands until 1568, and though France was in the financial position to challenge Spain in the Americas, its exploration of North America inspired little initial interest. For much of the century, French raiders were little more than an irritant to Spanish authority in the Caribbean, resulting in intensified security, improved fortifications, and the use of convoys to move shipments of gold to Spain. France made a brief foray into present-day Florida in the 1560s and an equally unsuccessful attempt to colonize in the area of Port Royal in what is now South Carolina. The more serious challenge came from England during the reign of Queen Elizabeth I (1558–1603). English merchants initially sought to legitimately challenge the closed Spanish trading system in the Caribbean. However, the officially sanctioned voyages in the 1560s of John Hawkins, which met a favorable response from Spanish colonists anxious to obtain goods Spain could not provide, provoked a hostile military response from Spain. In 1569 the majority of Hawkins's ships were captured at Veracruz by a Spanish fleet.

Spain's refusal to allow trade with its West Indian colonies gave the other European nations little option but privateering and warfare if they wished to crack the Spanish monopoly. English privateers were the most successful during the balance of the sixteenth century, with Francis Drake the most notable. Having narrowly escaped capture at Veracruz with his cousin John Hawkins, Drake became a major threat to Spanish interests. Operating from a base in Central America and employing native allies and escaped slaves, Drake captured Nombre de Diós on the isthmus in 1572 as well as Spanish ships carrying South American silver to Europe. The following year he captured Panama City, in the process looting its shipments of silver as well. Drake returned from subsequent privateering ventures on the Pacific coast of South America to raid major Spanish ports in the Caribbean region, including Cartagena and Santo Domingo, as well as St. Augustine in Florida.

England and Spain moved to open warfare in 1588, although the Caribbean colonies were almost irrelevant to the conflict. The startling defeat of the Spanish armada by seemingly inferior English naval forces in the English Channel was a minor setback to Spanish power, yet it heralded a more aggressive European challenge to Spanish authority. In 1604 in the Treaty of London and five years later in the Truce of Antwerp, Spain conceded that it could not maintain a monopoly in the Americas. The seventeenth century thus became a period of dramatic change in the Caribbean and of radically increased colonization and mercantile efforts by other European nations, led by the English, the Dutch, and, to a lesser extent, the French.

As much as these nations challenged Spain for hegemony in the Caribbean, they did not seriously threaten the major Spanish colonies or Spain's economic status. The focus of England was on British North America and, like the Dutch, on the smaller islands in the eastern Antilles and on the northern coast of South America in the area that would eventually become the countries of Guyana, Suriname, and French Guiana. Their colonial strategy also differed radically from that of the Spanish, with a stronger emphasis on colonization, the development of agriculture and imperial trade, and less emphasis on the quest for mineral wealth. The Dutch moved expeditiously to establish a salt industry on the Caribbean coast of Venezuela. By 1616 they had a foothold in the area that would become Dutch Guiana and later Suriname, and in 1621, as a reflection of trading opportunities in the region, established the Dutch West India Company. A few years later they joined the English in settling St. Croix, and the English in turn gained control in the 1620s over Barbados and St. Kitts. During the seventeenth century the Dutch moved into Tobago, Curaçao, St. Maarten (the French portion is St. Martin), St. Eustatius, and Saba, all of which, with the exception of Tobago, became part of the Netherlands Antilles. The English gained control of Antigua, Montserrat, and St. Lucia; took Jamaica by force from the Spanish in 1655; and established a firm foothold on the Central American coast in British Honduras (present-day Belize), which proved to be a useful military base and source of tropical timbers and dyes. All of this came at the expense of the Spanish monopoly, although with the exception of Jamaica, given its strategic importance, such gains were made only on the periphery of Spain's Caribbean empire. French acquisitions were even more modest, taking control in the 1630s of Martinique and Guadeloupe and establishing a claim to a portion of Guiana. Its major inroad against Spain was the acquisition of the western portion of Santo Domingo in 1697 through the Treaty of Ryswyck, ending the Nine Years' War in Europe. Under French control, St. Domingue (as the colony that would ultimately become Haiti was called) became the wealthiest non-Spanish possession during the eighteenth century.

These inroads by the other European powers may not have threatened Spanish hegemony, but they proved profitable to the other nations and became the source of imperial wars in the seventeenth and eighteenth centuries. Once the other nations had established a presence in the Caribbean, conflict ensued among the other European powers as well as between them and Spain. Between 1652 and 1678 the English and the Dutch fought three wars; in 1669 the Dutch monarch William of Orange ascended to the throne with his English wife, Queen Mary, cementing a military-economic alliance that resolved half a century of conflict. The English, Dutch, and French were also more successful in establishing the economic basis for longer-term prosperity in their colonies, moving quickly to nurture a profitable sugar industry that Spain brought to Cuba only in the nineteenth century. England exported its first shipments of sugar from Barbados in the late 1640s. In St. Domingue, French settlers mixed agriculture and stock-raising with their share of piracy, and their very occupation of the western half of the island was made possible by the Spanish decision to move Spanish settlers out of that area to reduce support for pirates and smugglers. The Dutch from early in the seventeenth century held a virtual monopoly over salt production and trade. Yet none of these gains did more than nibble at the edges of Spanish authority and hegemony in the area. Spain lost only one major possession—Jamaica—and even what would become Saint Domingue had a long road toward economic prosperity after 1697.

For much of the seventeenth century, officially condoned buccaneering by English, Dutch, and French privateers sought to undermine Spain's power in the region. The privateers, often provisioned by colonial officials and given safe haven in colonial ports, cut a swath of terror through the Spanish Caribbean until the end of the seventeenth century, attacking and looting Spanish treasure ships. Such activities also provided a means to attain social, political, and economic mobility for a privileged few. For example, the Englishman Henry Morgan, perhaps the most notorious of the buccaneers, was later appointed governor of Jamaica. By that time, the other major powers found piracy as disturbing to their own interests in the Caribbean as they had hoped it would be to Spanish authority, with the result that the English and Dutch began to turn their own military might against the buccaneers, bringing to an end a colorful—if violent—period in Caribbean history.

European imperial rivalries, a series of major wars, and continued expansion of and debate over slavery dominated developments in the eighteenth century. The century began with the demise of the Spanish Hapsburg dynasty and the ascendancy of the more reformist Spanish Bourbons, triggering war with Great Britain, which feared a French-Spanish alliance. The War of the Spanish Succession (1701–1714) involved naval actions in the Caribbean as well as land conflicts in North America and Europe. However, the treaties at the end of the war had only limited significance for Spain and other imperial powers in the Caribbean. England's main gain for the Caribbean area was the Spanish concession of the *asiento* (license) to enable England to trade in slaves and other goods in the Spanish colonies. French gains from these conflicts were far more peripheral to Spain's main Caribbean possessions, focusing on the coastal areas of Florida and Texas.

Between 1739 and the mid-1780s war was constant. One source of conflict between England and Spain was disagreement over the application of the *asiento* at the conclusion of the War of the Spanish Succession. Rather than liberalizing its colonial trade, Spain sought to tighten controls at a time when Spanish demand for European goods continued to increase. With Spain lagging behind both France and England in industrial production, it was unable to meet that demand, and its effort to curtail imports from England only served to exacerbate tensions. War between Spain and England erupted in 1739 over claims by English Captain Robert Jenkins that Spanish authorities mandated to curtail English trade severed his ear. The English fleets failed to take the heavily fortified Cartagena and were equally unsuccessful in their attack on Santiago de Cuba, but they seized control over Portobello in Panama, which had considerable strategic value. The War of Jenkins's Ear involved only England and Spain, but it was evident that in subsequent conflicts England could expect to be confronted by a Bourbon alliance between Spain and France.

By 1740 hostilities had widened into the War of the Austrian Succession, an eight-year conflict. Although the war ended inconclusively, the Spanish decision to remove the British *asiento* meant the inevitability of future conflicts over trade access to the Caribbean. Furthermore, the increased competition between England and Spain's ally, France, suggested that an Anglo-French war loomed on the horizon. When this conflict (the Seven Years' War) erupted in 1756, the focus of the combat was on French and British North America, but inevitably the conflict spilled into the West Indies. With France as an ally of Spain, Spanish possessions in the region were fair targets for

Maureen Smith

The High Court, Georgetown, Guyana

England's men-of-war, and England—in a crushing blow to Spain's strategic interests as well as its pride—captured the major port of Havana.

Unlike the conclusion of the War of the Spanish Succession, the War of the Austrian Succession, and the War of Jenkins's Ear, the Seven Years' War led to dramatic transfers of power in the Caribbean and the North American mainland. England returned Havana to a humbled Spain, which retained control over the Floridas. Developments on the North American continent also had far-reaching consequences for future rivalries in the region. France transferred to Spain possession of the lands west of the Mississippi River and its Louisiana Territory at the same time that military losses to the English ended French control over New France as well as disputed territories east of the Mississippi River and south of the Great Lakes. England had emerged as the undisputed hegemon in North America; ironically, when that hegemony was challenged, the challenge came not only from its European rivals but also from North American colonists attempting to sever imperial ties. In diverting its naval and military power to confront the rebellious American colonies after 1775, Britain's capacity to fend off imperial challenges elsewhere in the region was weakened, as evidenced by Spain's regaining control over much of the Floridas as well as temporary possession of British Honduras and the Bahamas.

The French Revolution, hastened not only by an incompetent and arrogant French government but also by the financial disaster occasioned by the unsuccessful Seven Years' War, further changed the face of Europe as well as the Caribbean. The most significant impact in the Caribbean was France's loss of St. Domingue (Haiti), its most profitable colony with a massive investment in sugar cultivation, processing, and export. When France erupted into revolution in 1789, St. Domingue had an overwhelming majority population of enslaved and free Africans. There were only slightly more than 40,000 whites on the French part of the island, in contrast to more than 440,000 black slaves and some 26,000 free blacks and mulattos (Knight 1978:149–152). In liberating one of the largest slave populations in the Western Hemisphere, the revolt in what would become Haiti also had significance throughout the slaveholding areas of the Americas, including the southern United States.

Slave revolts were not a new phenomenon in the colonial Caribbean in the eighteenth century. In most of the colonies the existence of communities of escaped slaves, or *maroons,* were vivid reminders to colonial authorities of the resistance to slavery that was always just below the surface even in times of relative stability. There were large and well-established colonies of escaped slaves in the interior mountainous regions of Jamaica, as there were in the less accessible interiors of St. Domingue and eastern Cuba. Such *maroon* communities were a constant threat not only to the white slaveholding populations of the Caribbean but also to the institution of slavery itself, although the *maroons* were not in themselves above trading and holding slaves. Although most of the slave opposition to forced labor came in the form of day-to-day resistance, there were also large-scale revolts. White slaveholders, especially on the larger, more isolated plantations, where the ratio of black slaves to white slaveholders overwhelmingly favored the former, lived in constant fear of slave rebellion. There was a serious *maroon* war in 1734 in Jamaica and another in 1795.

The slave revolt with the longest-term impact, however, began in St. Domingue in 1791, two years after the outbreak of the French Revolution. The French government not only increasingly lacked the capacity to control its colonies; the ideology of the French revolutionary governments in the early 1790s, with their emphasis on liberty, fraternity, and equality, tended to favor the end of slavery. In 1791 the French assembly granted full political rights to the free colored population in St. Domingue, and when the white elite refused to accept this act of political enfranchisement, the free colored leaders, perhaps unwittingly, unleashed the mass of black slaves. The French also ended the legal slave trade in 1793 and slavery the following year, but by then the revolt could not be contained. By the end of the decade, the Haitian revolution was led by free blacks and former slaves, the most important of whom were the educated, propertied freedman Toussaint L'Ouverture and his main military commander, Jean-Jacques Dessalines, an African-born former slave. L'Ouverture was imprisoned in France, where he died. By 1804, with France shifting back to empire under Napoleon and departing from its revolutionary ideology, Dessalines had firm control not only of Haiti but also briefly of the

Carolyn Watson

Monument commemorating the slave revolt, with the National Palace in the background, Port-au-Prince, Haiti

rest of the island. Although slavery remained a viable institution elsewhere in the Caribbean for another eight decades, the Haitian revolution was a vivid reminder of the potential for change.

The diversion of French attention from its colonies in the 1790s and its alliance with Spain also provided an opportunity for other imperial powers in the region. England captured Trinidad in 1797 and seized the Dutch islands when France defeated the Netherlands as well as Spain. England also gained temporary control over Martinique, St. Lucia, and Guadeloupe. The Treaty of Amiens in 1802 confirmed English control over the harbors of Trinidad, which occupied a key strategic location near the South American coast.

The Napoleonic Wars and political instability in Spain had a more significant impact on the mainland areas than on the insular Caribbean. Napoleon's conquest of Spain in 1808 disrupted Spain's already tottering capacity to control its American colonies. Spanish energies initially were devoted to resistance to the French occupation. In the colonies, loyalties were divided between those who favored a restoration of the Spanish monarchy and liberals who sought political reforms, which they achieved to some degree in the 1812 constitution. By the time Ferdinand II restored the Spanish monarchy in 1814, the level of resistance to Spanish colonialism in the Americas was intense. This resistance served to thwart recolonization efforts over the next decade, as did opposition from other European powers, especially the English, whose efforts to promote trade would be undermined by the reassertion of Spanish authority. By the early 1820s, Mexico and the rest of Central America, Venezuela, and Colombia had achieved independence from Spain, although Great Britain retained control over British Hondorus and Nicaragua's Mosquito Coast. On the northern coast of South America, Britain, the Netherlands, and France still had firm possession of the Guianas. Spain's loss on the mainland was only marginally compensated by its retention of Puerto Rico and Cuba, which remained a powerful foothold in the region for another century.

■ Nation Building and Socioeconomic Transition in the Nineteenth Century

Nothing was of such profound importance in the nineteenth-century Caribbean as the debate over slavery. In the eighteenth century, the Caribbean was the destination for approximately 60 percent of the African slaves forcibly removed to the Americas, with some 5 million total brought to the Caribbean during the course of the slave trade. Eighteenth-century Enlightenment ideas on the equality of man provided an intellectual context for the debate, although more practical considerations led to the termination of the trade and then slavery itself during the nineteenth century. The socioeconomic and demographic impacts of slavery in the Caribbean were profound, as was the impact of emancipation, which opened the door for tens of thousands of immigrant laborers from various parts of the world.

The English and French Caribbean colonies dominated the trade in the eighteenth century, with Dutch vessels providing most of the shipping. In that period the Spanish Caribbean absorbed only some 10 percent of the traffic, in contrast to the nineteenth century, when the Cuban sugar industry took flight, creating a huge demand for labor (Randall and Mount 1998:20). Despite any opposition to slavery and the trade that existed in the Caribbean colonies in the nineteenth century, the critical decisions affecting the institution were made in the metropolitan capitals, which were more insulated from local considerations of racial balance.

Great Britain and the United States declared the international slave trade illegal in 1807–1808, and it was the effort of the British Admiralty to enforce its own decree that significantly curtailed traffic from Africa. Parliamentary action to end the slave trade followed more than a decade of rising opposition within Britain. Antislavery forces established the Society for the Abolition of the Slave Trade in 1787, under the leadership of William Wilberforce, Thomas Clarkson, and others. Wilberforce was clearly the most powerful voice for reform, and his close association with William Pitt added credibility to his cause. Antislavery forces secured passage of the Foreign Slave Bill in 1806, prohibiting the importation of slaves into Britain's territories that had been acquired as a result of the Napoleonic Wars. The following year the British Parliament went farther by banning the slave trade in all British territory.

The Dutch agreed in 1814, at the end of the Napoleonic Wars, to comply with British policy. Britain concluded a treaty with Sweden shortly after ending a rather marginal Swedish involvement in the traffic. France followed the Dutch example, agreeing by treaty with Britain to end its involvement in the African slave trade by 1818. Responding to critics who found the British expenditure on the initiative excessive, Wilberforce asked: "How can money be so well employed as in thus effecting the deliverance of so great a portion of our fellow creatures from the most cruel scourge that ever afflicted the human race?" (Wilberforce 1840). However, like officials in the other major slaveholding imperial powers, French authorities turned their backs as another 80,000 slaves entered Guadeloupe and Martinique before the 1830s. Spain paid at least lip service to the policy by 1820, although there was widespread violation by Spanish colonial officials, with the result that in the decade after official Spanish adherence to that policy approximately 500,000 African slaves were forcibly removed to Cuba alone, and another 50,000 to Puerto Rico, to toil in the sugarcane fields and processing factories.

Reformers were increasingly disillusioned by the difficulties of enforcement, as even Britain was not vigilant in its enforcement efforts until after it declared slavery illegal in its colonies after 1833. Reformers realized that the institution was unlikely to crumble solely through the restriction of international slave traffic. Thus, Wilberforce and his compatriots turned their attention to the abolition of slavery itself in the British Empire, and the legislation finally succeeded in 1833, the year after his death. This was more complicated economically and sociologically than simply ending the traffic, for the end of slavery would result in the loss of a massive investment in forced labor and create an unpredictable racial situation in a number of the colonies. The British government was also sensitive to the fact that its ill-conceived imperial policies had contributed only a few decades earlier to the successful rebellion of the thirteen American colonies. The British approach to emancipation was consequently cautious, but it was still well in advance of thinking in Spain, France, and the southern United States. In 1815 the Parliament passed legislation requiring the registration of all slaves in its colonies. This measure was partially designed to control trafficking, but it was seen as necessary preparation for emancipation. Britain followed its registration policies with legislation in the 1820s to improve the conditions in which slaves lived and worked, although local slaveholders largely ignored and resented such interference. Nonetheless, Britain persisted and appointed an abolitionist, Sir James Stephen, as the administrator of Caribbean affairs within the Colonial Office.

Colonial officials continued to impede application of such legislation, however. In Jamaica, it was not until 1831, two years before actual emancipation, that the colonial legislature passed legislation adhering to the spirit and letter of the Amelioration Acts of the 1820s; even then it did so largely as a response to the massive rebellion that swept through the northwestern section of the island. There, some 40,000 slaves, in part inspired by Baptist lay preacher Sam Sharpe, destroyed several hundred plantations, although the loss of life among white planters was minimal. The rebellion struck fear into planters throughout the Caribbean, but it also inspired the optimism of British abolitionists.

In the aftermath of Sharpe's rebellion the British Parliament passed the Abolition Act in 1833 ending slavery in British territory. The act provided £25 (25 pounds) sterling per capita for compensation to slaveholders as well as a period of indenture for newly emancipated slaves to ensure the continuity of the labor force. That indenture requirement did not apply to all of the colonies. Antigua and Barbados, for example, were exempted. In areas where the policy applied, the indenture was six years for field hands and four years for domestic slaves. There seemed no recognition of the irony of compensating slaveholders for their loss of property but not the slaves for their years of free labor and lost freedom.

Although in Cuba and Puerto Rico both the slave trade and slavery itself continued into the late nineteenth century, the passing of the Abolition Act raised serious labor questions in the British colonies. At the time of emancipation, the overwhelming majority of the slaves—some 300,000—were in Jamaica, with 80,000 in Barbados, 22,000 in Trinidad, 15,000 in British

Guiana, and a scattered population in British Honduras. Although there is some evidence that the majority of emancipated slaves remained on the plantations, largely for want of real economic alternatives, there was a near universal belief that slaves would not work the plantations with any enthusiasm after gaining their freedom. Many former slaves in the British colonies also seized the opportunity to become freeholders themselves, even if the landholdings they were able to acquire were often too small to be economically viable. In Jamaica it is estimated that the number of black freeholders in the twenty years after 1838 increased from 2,000 to more than 20,000. In Antigua, freedmen and freedwomen brought thousands of new acres into cultivation after emancipation. In British Guiana, freed slaves between the 1830s and 1848 purchased more than 400 estates with an estimated value of U.S.$100,000 (Randall and Mount 1998:23).

Consequently, there was great interest in attracting immigrant labor in the British Caribbean, particularly in those colonies where the shortage of unskilled labor was most acute. Despite the pressing need for labor, European immigration to the Caribbean in the nineteenth century never approached levels found in North America, Argentina, and Brazil. This may be attributed to several factors, including the climate, the lack of economic diversification in the largely monocultural economies, and the racial composition of the islands. Interestingly, Cuba, despite the continuation of slavery, was, along with Costa Rica, the most attractive to European (almost exclusively Spanish) immigrants, primarily because of the economic boom that accompanied the expansion of the sugar industry.

In the non-Spanish Caribbean, the main immigration was of indentured East Indian workers into Trinidad and British Guiana along with some Chinese to various colonies. More than 140,000 East Indians arrived in Trinidad between the end of slavery there and World War I. British Guiana was even more active in recruiting East Indian labor, with approximately 238,000 arriving prior to World War I. More than 30,000 East Indians and Chinese came to Jamaica in the nineteenth century, and smaller numbers were brought to St. Kitts, St. Vincent, and Grenada. The indenture system in Trinidad remained in place until 1917, when the British government ended the practice. By that time East Indians and their descendants constituted one-third of the island's population, and the existence of that substantial population was further incentive for continued movement from South Asia (Laurence 1971; Lai 1993). The East Asian and South Asian migration into the Caribbean created one of the other enduring features of modern Caribbean history: tension between the Indo-Caribbean and Afro-Caribbean populations. This tension has been especially pronounced in British Guiana and Trinidad.

The pattern of development in Cuba throughout the nineteenth century stood in marked contrast to that of the British Caribbean. With the thriving Cuban economy generating great demand for slave labor, the slave trade (and slavery itself) persisted long after Spain had agreed to end its involvement in 1820. The proportion of Cuban slaves relative to the population increased markedly between the late eighteenth and the mid–nineteenth centuries with the expansion of the sugar industry. Between 1774 and 1827, while the Cuban population increased from approximately 170,000 to more than 700,000, slaves increased from 25 percent to more than 40 percent of the total population (Knight 1978:96–97, 101). That dramatic increase had significant implications for the independence movement as well as for the social and political history of modern Cuba. By 1860, the free colored population in Cuba was only 16 percent of the total population, compared to more than 40 percent in Puerto Rico. Not surprisingly, there was less racial tension in Puerto Rico than in Cuba and less resistance to emancipation (Knight 1978:105). Although the distribution of Cuba's free colored population tended to parallel the urban concentration in the other colonies, Cuba was distinct in the high percentage of the free black population in the largely rural areas of eastern Cuba that a century later provided Fidel Castro with his strongest base of support.

The wealth of the Cuban sugar plantations and slaveholders in the nineteenth century paralleled that of the plantation aristocracy in the United States. They also held a similar degree of political power, although in Cuba this was not muted by the tensions of sectionalism. The white population in Cuba and Puerto Rico also bore greater similarity to that of the southern United States in terms of its size relative to the black and slave populations than to the rest of the Caribbean, where slave societies were characterized by the dominance of the small white elite over a massive black majority. As late as 1870, approximately 60 percent of the Cuban population and some 50 percent of the Puerto Rican population were classified as white (Knight 1997: 130; Engerman and Genovese 1975).

Between the late 1840s and 1868, small groups of U.S. privateers known as "filibusters"—mainly Southerners anxious to extend the area of slavery by annexing Cuba—attempted invasions in Cuba. Unsuccessful as their efforts were, the filibusters were one important manifestation of a long-standing U.S. interest in Cuba, underlined as well by several equally unsuccessful efforts to purchase Cuba from Spain. With the end of the U.S. Civil War in 1865 and the emancipation of U.S. slaves, combined with the extensive trade ties that had emerged between Cuba and the United States, Cuba's colonial status as well as the institution of slavery became increasingly anachronistic. In 1868 Cuban creole nationalists, frustrated by Spain's refusal to permit a greater degree of political autonomy or to implement meaningful economic reforms, launched their first struggle for independence in what came to be known as the Ten Years' War.

The revolt had little support from the large slaveholding planters in wealthier western Cuba, who had too much at stake to support such an initiative. Neither was there a slave revolt to bolster the ranks of nationalists, led by Carlos Manuel Céspedes, in large part because the rebels had no clear policy on the abolition of slavery. Although the rebels failed to gain the independence they sought from Spain, the lengthy rebellion had major consequences. The most important was the emancipation of Cuba's slaves over the next few years, providing an additional base of support for later rebellions and reducing some of the power of the slaveholding planter class.

Another important consequence was that the conflict clearly demonstrated that Spain lacked the military power, and perhaps the political will, to suppress a large-scale war for independence. Yet it was also apparent that the rebels did not possess the means to defeat Spain militarily. Without external assistance, Cuban nationalists would likely be condemned in the future to another drawn-out stalemate.

Another significant consequence was the massive destruction of property and the high level of indebtedness that sugar planters and producers suffered. U.S. investors moved in quickly to acquire sugar properties, helping to establish a strong U.S. presence by the time another war for independence broke out in Cuba in the 1890s. By that time U.S. private direct investment in Cuba exceeded $50 million; bilateral trade, primarily in sugar, industrial goods, and consumer goods, was worth $100 million. Spain had already lost the economic war for its wealthy colony.

Finally, the war spawned nationalist heroes as well as the poet laureate of Cuban nationalism—José Martí. After exile in Spain and Mexico and a brief return to Cuba, Martí settled in New York, where he and other Cuban nationalists established a government-in-exile. Martí wrote extensively on the United States as well as Cuba during his lengthy exile, and his writings on the United States reflected a complex mixture of admiration for U.S. political and economic successes with a fear of the threat the Colossus of the North posed for the Americas' future. Martí by the late 1880s had become a passionate, idealistic, revolutionary nationalist prepared to lay down his life for his *patria* (country). He had also by that time moved away from his earlier disinterest in labor and the peasants to adopt a broader stance of egalitarian, democratic, and racial equality that gave him legendary status with Fidel Castro's revolutionary movement more than half a century later (Ruiz 1968: 62–71).

Support for the nationalist cause from Cubans was strong in the United States, where Martí and other exiles raised funds and recruited forces for the independence struggle. Powerful Cuban exiled nationalists also worked from bases in other countries, including Antonio Maceo in Costa Rica and Máximo Gómez in the Dominican Republic. Ultimately, Cuban discontent with continued Spanish imperial control and unfulfilled promises of political and economic reforms spilled over into open revolt in February 1895.

Although insurgent forces were stronger and domestic Cuban public opinion more supportive of the independence movement than during the Ten

Years' War, this conflict rapidly moved toward a bloody stalemate. Pro-independence sentiments were inflamed by the Spanish antiguerrilla warfare tactic of reconcentration of the civilian population in the countryside, designed to cut off insurgent forces from food and other supplies. Although the tactic of moving civilians into what were little more than concentration camps was brutal indeed, Spanish forces had little choice if they were to regain control of the insurgent-dominated countryside. For their part, insurgents burned sugarcane fields and destroyed processing plants, plantations, and infrastructure, a good deal of which was U.S.-owned by that time. The widespread violence directed against property and the brutality of Spanish policy under Governor General Valeriano Weyler—which included the destruction of crops and livestock in an effort to starve out the insurgents—served further to provide a cause célèbre for the yellow press in the United States, primarily Joseph Pulitzer's *New York World* and William Randolph Hearst's *New York Journal*, which vied for circulation with lurid stories of Spanish atrocities.

By 1898 war still raged. Although under U.S. pressure the Spanish government promised to end the policy of reconcentration and move toward political reform, neither the U.S. public, Congress, nor William McKinley's administration were confident that anything short of Cuban independence would end the persistent conflicts on the island. Not only were Cuban-U.S. trade and U.S. investment constantly disrupted by Spain's inability to control its colony; the instability in such a strategic area of the Caribbean threatened U.S. security. President McKinley called Cuba's instability a "constant menace" and reluctantly moved toward war (D. Smith 1965:284–286). A combination of domestic politics, genuine humanitarian concerns, pressure from U.S. commercial interests, and U.S. security concerns, especially following the February 1898 sinking in Havana Harbor of the battleship USS *Maine,* thus led to the U.S. declaration of war against Spain in April of that year.

The rapid destruction of the Spanish fleet in the Philippines and Cuban waters ended Spain's claim to great power status and marked a significant movement of the United States into world affairs. More than 200,000 Cubans and Spaniards had already perished prior to the U.S. declaration of war, and more than 3,000 U.S. personnel died in the conflict, all but a few hundred from yellow fever and malaria. The war also brought the United States into a new role as colonial administrator in the Caribbean, setting the stage for the next century of U.S. hegemony in the region. The United States established protectorate status over Cuba, formally occupied the island from 1898 through 1902, and returned troops again to restore domestic order in 1906. Under the terms of the Platt Amendment, the United States exercised a high degree of control over Cuba until the amendment was abrogated in 1934. Whereas Cuba was only a protectorate, Puerto Rico, the Philippines, and Guam became U.S. possessions. As such, the United States wielded considerable influence over the evolution of the Puerto Rican political system. Initially, the U.S. president appointed the governor, cabinet, and all judges sitting on Puerto Rico's supreme court. In contrast to the later occupations of Haiti and the Dominican Republic, where officials appointed to such positions were not nationals of the respective countries, the situation in Puerto Rico was such that at least these appointees were Puerto Rican. In addition, Puerto Ricans were able to elect an assembly on the basis of a franchise that was much wider than in the English and French Caribbean. In 1910, Puerto Ricans elected their first resident commissioner to the U.S. Congress, Luis Muñoz Rivera; seven years later, with the passage of the Jones-Shafroth Act, Puerto Ricans gained U.S. citizenship.

The Non-Spanish Caribbean in the Early Twentieth Century

The British Caribbean in the late nineteenth century enjoyed a greater degree of stability than the Spanish colonies even before the final collapse in the Spanish-American War. The earlier end of slavery in the British colonies and the arrival of East Indian immigrants in many of the colonies set them on a path toward political maturity and economic development more rapidly than in the Spanish Caribbean, although none of them approximated the wealth of Cuba. However, while Cuba was plagued by turmoil and suffered widespread destruction during the war, the British were able to maintain order and stimulate development in their colonies.

Politically, Jamaica and Trinidad and Tobago (united in 1888) remained rigidly under the control of small, mostly white elites. Even the gradual introduction of British parliamentary institutions did not obscure the fact that these societies were neither democratic nor free of imperial dominance at the turn of the century. Jamaica's black population did not gain a legislative majority until the 1920s, although women gained the right to vote just before that, paralleling that development in the United Kingdom and preceding it in the United States. Property and literacy requirements for the franchise remained in effect until 1938, and full racial and gender equality before the law did not come to Jamaica until the adoption of a new constitution in 1944.

In both Jamaica and Trinidad and Tobago, the effort to improve agriculture and trade involved crop diversification, pest control, and low-interest loans to facilitate the improvement of infrastructure, including the expansion of rail and road links to ease the movement of goods. The attempt to diversify the Jamaican economy met with some success. Although large sugar estates retained their importance, the number of plantation workers declined from 30,000 in 1860 to 20,000 in 1910; the relative importance of sugar to the Jamaican economy also declined, by 1896 representing only 18 percent of the value of Jamaican exports (Randall and Mount 1998:47). Conversely, the number of smaller freeholders operating banana plantations increased, and the country began to export bananas. There was a significant level of Canadian and U.S. investment in the bauxite industry in Jamaica over the next few decades, providing a higher degree of economic diversification on the island. Yet the demand for labor and the opportunities for economic advancement in Jamaica remained limited, and the lure of either seasonal migratory work or permanent migration from the island became constant. Thousands of Jamaican workers and their families migrated to Panama in the mid–nineteenth century to assist in the construction of the Panama Railroad linking the Caribbean and the Pacific. After the United States gained control of Panama from Colombia in 1903, thousands more sought employment in the construction of the Panama Canal.

Like Jamaica, Trinidad experienced some degree of economic diversification in the first half of the twentieth century, in particular with the development of an oil industry after World War I. However, such economic development had little impact on political democratization. Given the high percentage of East Indian immigrants, many of them indentured workers, Trinidad enjoyed less self-government than most of the other British colonies until the end of the indenture system in 1917. Most of the residents were people of color, and most of the Europeans were Roman Catholics. What minimal representative government there was disappeared in 1898 as part of the so-called reforms organized by Colonial Secretary Joseph Chamberlain. Chamberlain, who assumed office in 1895 as part of Lord Robert Arthur Salisbury's Conservative cabinet, envisioned a centralized British Empire—a Greater Britain—which would be competitive with the United States, Russia, and Germany. Before 1898, Trinidad's Legislative Council, which advised the governor, was hardly representative, dominated by wealthy planters, businessmen, and professionals. Even that was too much for Chamberlain. As of 1898, appointees of the Colonial Office would outnumber Trinidadians. Chamberlain also abolished the elective local council in Port of Spain, which had existed since 1853. Despite a high property franchise, blacks as well as mulattos had served as councilors, with the result that the abolition of the local council eliminated one of the few avenues for the colored population to participate actively in colonial politics. As late as 1934 only 25,000 Trinidadians out of a total population of more than 400,000 had the right to vote, and in Barbados the franchise was even more restricted, with only 2.5 percent of the population entitled to cast a ballot as late as 1937 (Knight 1978:161).

In terms of its degree of democratization, British Honduras fared little better than Trinidad in the nineteenth and early twentieth centuries. One factor accounting for the limited local self-government in British Honduras was the ongoing threat posed by Guatemala, which had maintained a long-standing claim to the territory. From 1814 until 1851, authority rested with the superintendent, a British military officer, and the Public Meeting. At first all free citizens could attend the Public Meeting, but as the society grew, property qualifications—higher for people of color than for whites—became mandatory. A civilian superintendent was appointed in 1851, and in 1854 British Honduras abandoned the Public Meeting, establishing a legislative assembly of eighteen elected members plus three members appointed by the superintendent. Voters had to meet the property requirements; assembly members had to meet even higher ones. In 1862, while the United States was embroiled in the Civil War, Great Britain constituted British Honduras as a formal colony. In 1871 the legislative assembly voted itself out of existence and transferred authority to the governor and his appointees. The threat from Guatemala was not the only factor; the tiny European minority did not want to be governed by the large nonwhite majority. A legislative assembly did not return until 1954, when all literate adults gained the right to vote. In 1964, British Honduras gained full internal self-government, a significant advance but a far cry from the independence enjoyed by Jamaica and Trinidad.

There were similar pressures for more representative government in British Guiana in the late nineteenth century. The emerging Afro-Guyanese middle class was pressing for constitutional reforms, in particular the conversion of the governor-appointed Court of Policy into an elected assembly, as well as easing qualifications for the franchise. Yet as in most of the colonies, wealthy planters, who had little difficulty exercising their political influence in London with the West India committee, vigorously resisted such reforms. Nevertheless, by the early 1890s the pressures began to work; voter qualifications were gradually relaxed, the College of Electors was abolished, and eight elected members were added to the Court of Policy to balance the eight appointed members. Still, the governor and planters retained the real power, as the executive duties of the Court of Policy were transferred to an Executive Council that the court controlled. It was not until 1909 that electoral reform made Afro-Guyanese the majority of the voting population. Those reforms were sparked in part by the massive 1905 Ruimveldt riots, which began with a strike by Georgetown stevedores and turned into the country's first general strike uniting urban and rural workers. The strikes and the rioting were quelled by British troops, but the uprising underlined the depth of the discontent that the masses felt with their economic and political condition.

French colonial policies underwent considerable evolution from the early nineteenth through the early twentieth centuries. St. Domingue, prior to its successful revolt against France, had representation in the French National Assembly, as did Martinique and Guadeloupe by 1815. This status went far beyond what England and the United States accorded their possessions by the early twentieth century. The surviving colonies lost that status until after the 1848 revolution in France, although in the intervening years there were some advances in the development of elected councils in both Guadeloupe and Martinique, restricted as the franchise was to men of property. After the failure of the Paris Commune in 1871 and the establishment of the French Republic, French colonial representation in the National Assembly was restored, paving the way for recognition as actual overseas departments of France after World War II (Knight 1978:161).

The legal end of slavery in 1863 in the Dutch West Indies (Aruba, Bonaire, Curaçao, St. Eustatius, St. Maarten, Saba, and Suriname) brought, as elsewhere in the region, economic decline and the search for alternative sources of labor and alternative economic activities. In Bonaire, abolition was followed by a serious and prolonged decline in the production of salt, long the mainstay of the economy. In Aruba, gold mining remained an important economic factor until World War I. Later, as the Venezuelan oil industry experienced rapid growth during the 1920s, Aruba became an important locale for oil refining, by 1929 boasting the largest refinery in the world. Curaçao followed a similar pattern. There the major investments by Dutch-Shell in oil refining in the 1920s revived a stagnant economy, and World War II stimulated the development of an offshore oil industry as well. Shell's refinery remained operational until the 1980s, and in the interim the island had also developed, along with Bonaire and Aruba, a vibrant tourist industry.

The experience of Suriname deviated somewhat from that of the other Dutch colonies in this period. As in the others, the abolition of slavery in 1863 was followed by a ten-year transitional period of indentured labor for former slaves, but indentured workers from South Asia significantly supplemented the labor force. Between 1873 and 1916, when the indenture system ended, some 34,000 East Indian contract workers reached Suriname, most of them Hindus but also many Muslims. As with most immigrant labor experiences in the West, the return rate of the Indian indentured workers was high, with an estimated one-third returning to India before the system was discontinued. They left an indelible imprint on the politics, language, culture, and economics in Suriname, and in 1927 their importance was recognized by the grant of eligibility for Dutch citizenship (Hoefte 1998). The Surinamese economy in the twentieth century came to be dominated by foreign-owned bauxite production and export, most of which was destined for the United States. Rice remained the main agricultural product, supplemented by citrus fruits, bananas, and other tropical crops. In Suriname, as in Curaçao, a complex racial and ethnic mixture of Dutch Europeans, Afro-Caribbeans, Spanish, and Indians has engendered societal divisions and at times spilled over into conflict.

■ The Emergence of U.S. Hegemony, 1898–1930s

After 1898 the United States emerged as the unchallenged power in the Caribbean region. French interest in the construction of a canal across the isthmus of Panama collapsed late in the nineteenth century. With the 1903 separation of Panama from Colombia and the conclusion of the Panama Canal Treaties with Panama, the United States moved rapidly ahead with its plans for a canal linking the Atlantic and Pacific Oceans to facilitate commercial and military naval operations. Distracted with its own colonial problems, mainly in South Africa during the Boer War, and confronted by an increasingly powerful Germany, Great Britain ceded dominance in the Caribbean to the United States. Prime Minister Arthur Balfour renounced any intention of acquiring additional territory in the Americas and explicitly accepted the principles set forth in the 1823 Monroe Doctrine.

No other European power had either the capacity or the political will to challenge the United States in what became a special sphere of influence. Germany, however, briefly presented a challenge early in the century when its warships were active in the Caribbean, protecting and expanding commercial and strategic interests. Without formal colonies in the Caribbean, Germany nonetheless had extensive commercial interests in Venezuela at the time. Confronted with the failure of Venezuelan officials to meet their international financial obligations, Germany blockaded Venezuelan harbors in 1901. During the next few years German, Italian, and French naval vessels all made shows of force in Caribbean waters. This spurred President Theodore Roosevelt to take a stronger stand against European encroachment as well as what he considered to be the irresponsible economic practices of Caribbean countries that led them into increased indebtedness abroad.

In the Roosevelt Corollary to the Monroe Doctrine, the president declared that the United States had a responsibility to exercise police power in the Caribbean.[1] His successor, William Howard Taft, pursued a policy called dollar diplomacy that substituted financial controls to promote greater political stability and reduce the threat of further European involvement in the region, a concern made more acute with the outbreak of World War I. In fact, the greater willingness of Woodrow Wilson's administration to dispatch U.S. troops, as occurred in Mexico in 1914 and 1917 and in Haiti in 1915, may be attributed as much to the war in Europe as to instability in the Americas.

Much like the specter of communist expansion in the 1920s and the rise of fascism and Nazism in Italy and Germany in the 1930s, the possibility of European encroachment in the Caribbean was perceived as threatening to U.S. security. In response, the United States assumed substantial responsibility for security in the region, as evidenced by the protectorate status of Cuba, the level of control exerted in Puerto Rico, and the establishment of military occupations and/or customs house controls in Nicaragua, Haiti, and the Dominican Republic. This degree of involvement was basically limited to the Caribbean region; with the exception of Mexico during World War I, the more powerful and independent mainland countries remained relatively untouched by direct U.S. action.

Harper's Weekly, November 21, 1903

"Held Up the Wrong Man"
President Theodore Roosevelt strong-arms Colombia to secure control of territory for the construction of the Panama Canal.

Haiti was especially vulnerable and of strategic importance because of its deep-water harbor at Môle St. Nicolas. Although the United States had no pressing need for another naval base beyond those it possessed at Guantánamo in Cuba, in Puerto Rico, and in Panama, U.S. officials did not want the port to fall under German control. Seeking stability following the collapse of the government of Guillaume Sam in 1915, President Wilson ordered U.S. forces to occupy Haiti, where they remained until 1934 as the effective power behind a series of governments. Brenda Plummer (1992:110) concludes:

> The Haitian protectorate was unprecedented in its duration, the racism that characterized U.S. behavior in the black republic, and the brutality associated with pacification efforts. . . . The devaluation of Haitian culture by

> Protestant, positivist and dogmatic North Americans recalled an age of imperialism that was rapidly becoming obsolete in other parts of the world.

The governance structure imposed by the United States provided for financial oversight of Haitian affairs by U.S. officials, Marine officers to command a national police force, and the power to deal unilaterally with Haiti's creditors. There were improvements in health, education, and infrastructure development, as occurred in Cuba and elsewhere in the Caribbean where the United States exercised direct or indirect controls. But U.S. policy measures were universally unpopular in Haiti, and the attitudes as well as the practices of U.S. officials during the lengthy occupation provoked violent resistance.

The political impact of the U.S. occupations was, on the whole, even less positive. In contrast to the British, Dutch, and French colonies, where a variety of civic organizations and political institutions were emerging, the lessons in democracy meted out by U.S. officials seemed to breed more authoritarian than democratic impulses. In the Dominican Republic, for example, where the United States began an eight-year military occupation in 1916, the congress was dissolved and all senior Dominican officials were replaced with U.S. military officers, many of whom did not even speak Spanish. Here, as elsewhere, there were improvements in education, sanitation, and infrastructure. But for all the rhetorical commitments U.S. officials made to equality and democracy, there was little if any change in the distribution of wealth and power. Culturally, the U.S. occupation produced a Dominican passion for baseball, which over the coming decades provided a small window of opportunity for economic mobility. But even in that game the racism that characterized the U.S. presence tended to prevail.

Decades of interventionism and intimidation under the guise of the Roosevelt Corollary, dollar diplomacy, and Wilson's "democratic crusade" engendered considerable ill-will within the region (P. Smith 1996:64). In recognition of the implications of mounting anti-U.S. sentiment, the United States changed its policy approach toward Latin America and the Caribbean. In his inaugural address on March 4, 1933, Franklin Delano Roosevelt made reference to this new approach: "I would dedicate this nation to the policy of the good neighbor—the neighbor who resolutely respects himself and, because he does so, respects the rights of others." Roosevelt's Good Neighbor Policy sought to enhance the image of the United States and to develop a spirit of cooperation within the hemisphere. Following Herbert Hoover's withdrawal of U.S. forces from Nicaragua in 1933, Roosevelt brought home the remaining troops from Haiti and the Dominican Republic and abrogated the infamous Platt Amendment in 1934. Such measures aside, the United States clearly did not abandon the Monroe Doctrine as the basis of its hemispheric policy. Rather, it was able to pursue its objectives through less confrontational means, including economic leverage and diplomatic pressure (G. Smith

1994). Although the Good Neighbor Policy appeared to portend improved U.S.-Caribbean relations, the previous era of intervention and occupation left an inauspicious legacy. This legacy set the stage for the eventual rise of brutal dictators such as Rafael Trujillo in the Dominican Republic, Anastasio Somoza in Nicaragua, Fulgencio Batista in Cuba, and François Duvalier in Haiti.

■ The Emergence of Labor Organizations

The Caribbean colonies and independent states in the first few decades of the twentieth century continued to experience political and economic change. As foreign (especially U.S.) investment increased, economic growth, continued imperial control over many colonies, and the growing strength of foreign-owned enterprises stimulated an emergent nationalism. In those nations still under U.S. or European control, this meant an increasingly strong desire for independence. Despite periods of economic growth, high levels of poverty among the majority of previously indentured and enslaved peoples persisted while political systems throughout the region remained dominated by small, typically white, elite groups. However, the growth of the working class and the slow emergence of a middle class contributed to the formation of labor movements and political parties as much of the Caribbean achieved a greater degree of political institutionalization.

A major development that occurred throughout the Caribbean during the interwar period was the emergence and growing political power of labor organizations. World War I, with the rising cost of living and frequent shortages of basic commodities, including foodstuffs and housing, provoked popular discontent. There were strikes of oil and asphalt workers in Trinidad in 1917, and from 1918 to 1924 strikes and labor violence became more common throughout the region. There were labor disturbances and strikes in Jamaica in 1918 and 1924; in Trinidad in 1919 and 1920; in St. Lucia in 1920; in the Bahamas in 1922; and in British Honduras in 1919 and 1920.

On the mainland, banana workers in the Santa Marta area of Colombia began to organize in the 1920s, with the assistance of European socialist and anarchist groups, which targeted the subsidiaries of the United Fruit Company (UFCO), the main foreign interest in the banana industry throughout the region. Workers tended to have the sympathy as well of local Colombian planters who were seeking with limited success to break UFCO's monopoly over crop transportation and export. Tensions between labor and UFCO climaxed in 1928 in a bloody strike that ended with Colombian troops firing on unarmed civilians, a scene that inspired Gabriel Gárcia Márquez in his brilliant novel *One Hundred Years of Solitude* and that also brought to prominence the young socialist politician Jorge Eliécer Gaitán.

Trade union activity gained momentum in British Guiana, Jamaica, and Trinidad. Led by the popular cricketer Herbert Critchlow, the British Guiana Labour Union, beginning with black dockworkers and then expanding to encompass East Indian agricultural workers, claimed a membership of 10,000 by the early 1920s. Restricted as trade unions were in Jamaica, the labor movement met with limited success in the 1920s, with only the longshoremen organized briefly by the mid-1920s. Workers realized more success in Trinidad in the interwar years, where Arthur Andrew Cipriani played a crucial role as a labor organizer, encouraging returned veterans and workers to join the Trinidad Workingmen's Association (TWA) in a major dockworkers strike in 1919. Their success emboldened workers who later struck across the island, reflecting a broadened base of participation by sugar workers and tradesmen. Alarmed by the rising level of militancy and violence on the part of labor, British authorities made strike action illegal while simultaneously paying lip service to the need to investigate workers' concerns about wages. Cipriani then shifted his focus to political action, converting the TWA into the Trinidad Labour Party in 1934. In addition to Cipriani, a number of other trade union leaders emerged in Trinidad during the 1930s, including Uriah Butler, who formed the British Empire Workers and Citizens Home Rule Party in 1938. Butler and Adrian Rienzi, a young East Indian lawyer and Leninist activist, contributed to the general strike among oil workers in 1937, the most important labor action in the country to that date.

Jamaica also experienced major labor actions in the late 1930s as workers, whose standard of living continued to decline as economic conditions deteriorated, voiced their growing discontent. The 1938 disturbances began with a major strike on a sugar estate, where striking workers clashed with police. Conflict quickly reached the docks of Kingston and then spread to include public works employees, former soldiers, and cane and banana workers in the rural areas. Suppressed though they were, these strikes led to the establishment of the West India Royal Commission (the Moyne Commission) to study the problems of labor unrest and then to the formation of the Bustamante Industrial Trade Union, which by the end of World War II was the largest labor organization in the Caribbean. (Randall and Mount 1998:66–69).

War and Cold War, 1939–1959

The period from the end of the Great Depression to the Cuban revolution was turbulent in the Caribbean, although the attention of the great powers was diverted largely to European and Asian affairs. World War II brought tensions to the region, especially with the German defeat of the Netherlands and France, which threatened the future of their Caribbean colonies. Britain's weakness, the defeat of the Dutch and French, and the threat that German submarine activity posed to shipping all contributed to a strengthening of U.S. power in the Caribbean. The war also created unprecedented demand for Caribbean products, from petroleum and bauxite to sugar and other foodstuffs. The unsettled nature of the imperial connections during the war also served as further stimulus to sentiments favoring a greater degree of self-government and liberalization of laws governing political participation.

Events in Europe during World War II sparked concern over the transfer of colonial territories in the Caribbean. When Germany defeated the Netherlands and France by June 1940, U.S. and British officials feared that those countries' Caribbean possessions would fall into German hands. There was also concern that Great Britain, given the threat of German invasion, would be unable to defend its West Indian colonies. In response, the United States and other states signed the Act of Havana on July 30, 1940, committing to the principle that no territory in the Americas could be transferred from one power to another. They agreed that in the event of an imminent German takeover of colonial territory, one or more of the American states could establish a trusteeship for the duration of the war. In addition, with British consent, Canadian troops moved into Jamaica, the Bahamas, Bermuda, and British Guiana to replace British forces needed in Europe from 1940 to 1946 (Randall and Mount 1998:71). In return for transferring U.S. destroyers to Britain in 1941, the United States also acquired control of a number of British air bases in the region. In the end, although Vichy control over the French colonies posed some problems, there was no transfer of any Caribbean colonies to a hostile power, and no serious security threat emerged during the war.

With European powers debilitated by war, increased political mobilization in their colonies stimulated a growing sense of nationalism and demands for reform. In British Guiana, for example, the Moyne Commission's inquiry underlined the rift between the Afro-Guyanese and the larger Indo-Guyanese population, the latter of which had played little role to that date in the colony's politics. The commission recommended increased democratization of government as well as socioeconomic reforms, including extending the franchise to women and those who did not own land. In contrast to prewar British policy, the commission also encouraged the emerging labor movement. Among the reforms introduced by governor Sir Gordon Lethem were reduced property qualifications for holding office and voting, and elected members were made a majority of the Legislative Council in 1943. By 1952 there was universal adult suffrage, prefacing the movement toward independence.

This political liberalization, albeit limited and with little impact on the distribution of wealth and power, occurred elsewhere, particularly in the British Caribbean. In 1944 suffrage was extended to women in British Guiana, Barbados, and Bermuda. In that same year Jamaica and Trinidad achieved universal adult suffrage, and Jamaica also gained limited self-government. Martinique and Guadeloupe were made overseas departments of

France in 1946. Universal adult suffrage came to Barbados in 1950 and to the Leeward and Windward Islands in 1951. After years of debate over its political status, Puerto Rico obtained its first taste of local self-government since the U.S. occupation in 1898, ultimately gaining commonwealth status in 1952. In 1954 the Netherlands Antilles and Suriname were granted the right of internal self-government and universal suffrage and became autonomous parts of the kingdom of the Netherlands.

Along with decolonization, economic development and Cold War tensions dominated the regional agenda in the postwar decades. Puerto Rico experimented with aggressive economic change under the program Operation Bootstrap. Intended to promote industrialization and to diversify the economy, Operation Bootstrap sought to attract large corporations from the mainland with tax incentives and comparatively inexpensive labor. In the short term, at least, the island boomed with manufacturers anxious to take advantage of their ability to export into the U.S. market duty-free. Throughout the region, state planning became increasingly popular in the postwar era, led to a large extent by the United Nations Economic Commission for Latin America and the influential ideas of the Argentine economist Raul Prebisch. The model of industrial development behind protectionist tariff walls was widely adopted in the area during these years, contributing to increased rural-urban migration and the decline of the rural labor force. Economic changes notwithstanding, the traditional polarity between an impoverished rural peasantry and urban proletariat, and a small, largely white urban and landed elite, remained the norm. With inflation rampant by the 1960s there were few signs that poverty and disparities of wealth were on the wane.

Politically, the non-British Caribbean had slipped decidedly into an authoritarian mold beginning in the 1930s, with the Somozas in Nicaragua, Trujillo in the Dominican Republic, and later with Batista in Cuba and Duvalier in Haiti. Even Colombia slipped briefly under the control of the military under Gustavo Rojas Pinilla until 1958. Throughout the 1950s democracy reeled under the onslaught of right-wing dictators considered by the United States to be safe bets in the Cold War struggle. That trend was particularly evident in Guatemala, which emerged with more progressive elements under the leadership of Juan José Arévalo and Jacobo Arbenz. Their efforts to bring sorely needed reforms to landholding, agriculture, and the rights of labor ran up against U.S. Cold War paranoia as well as the vested economic interests of private capital, in particular UFCO. Confronted with what U.S. officials considered to be a wedge for communism, Dwight Eisenhower's administration in 1954 gave support (through the Central Intelligence Agency) to the reactionary forces of the Guatemalan military, led by U.S.-trained Colonel Carlos Castillo Armas, in overthrowing the democratically elected government of Arbenz. In addition to rolling back a decade of socioeconomic and political reform, this coup ushered in three decades of repressive military rule.

The British Caribbean in the postwar years experimented less with revolution than with political evolution, including a failed attempt at federation between 1958 and 1962 (the West Indies Federation) involving Jamaica, Barbados, Trinidad, and the Windward and Leeward Islands. The federation was less a colonial initiative than one inspired by British officials anxious to curtail the costs of empire for a weakened postwar Britain while seeking to minimize the impact of decolonization on the smaller island economies unable to survive on their own. The federation was doomed to fail as an artificial creation that represented accurately neither the political will of the majority nor the historical reality of the ties among the British West Indies. Ultimately, Jamaica's physical separation from and weak economic links to the other islands led to its withdrawal. When Trinidad followed suit, the British House of Commons was left with little choice but to end the short-lived federation in 1962. The failure of the West Indies Federation presented an early indication of the obstacles to political changes that might address historical inequities in the Caribbean.

The onset of severe East-West tensions heightened concerns in the United States and other imperial powers over the threat of communism specifically and political radicalism generally. However, it was Fidel Castro's seizure of power in 1959 and the Cuban revolution's turn to socialism that brought home the realities of the Cold War in the Western Hemisphere.

■ The Cuban Revolution

No event in the postwar years had a more significant impact on the Caribbean than the 1959 Cuban revolution. In toppling the regime of dictator Fulgencio Batista, Fidel Castro initiated a true revolution that resulted in the massive redistribution of political, social, and economic power in the insular Caribbean's largest and most powerful nation. This revolt, and Castro's subsequent embrace of Soviet-style socialism, dramatically impacted the East-West balance of power and made Castro and Cuba a symbol of defiance against the United States, one that has endured for more than forty years.

Cuba's alliance with the Soviet Union appeared to provide communism a beachhead in the Western Hemisphere. It conditioned the U.S. response to political change in the area that seemed to portend radical socioeconomic transformation or provide more leverage for Soviet- and Cuban-supported insurgencies. The first and only direct U.S. effort to overthrow Castro, with the use of a surrogate force of Cuban exiles, ended in disaster at the Bay of Pigs in April 1961. The Cuban missile crisis in October 1962 resulted in a more cautious, if still determined, effort to undermine the Castro regime. The rupture of diplomatic relations and the U.S.-imposed economic embargo by the Organization of American States in 1962 heightened Cuba's isolation within the region, ultimately leading to a greater level of dependence on Soviet aid and trade with Eastern bloc countries. Although the embargo did take a toll on the average Cuban, for whom basic necessities would become scarce, as well as on the infrastructure of the island, it failed to bring about Castro's demise. In fact, he and the revolution have endured, and Cuba has wielded considerable influence both within the Caribbean as well as on the world stage.

Among other things, the Cuban revolution served to increase the paranoia and sensitivity of Western powers and Cuba's neighbors to political change in the region. Thus, after civil war broke out in the Dominican Republic in 1965 when supporters of ousted president Juan Bosch tried to return him to power, Lyndon Johnson's administration sent 23,000 troops to forestall what was perceived as a threat of revolutionary change. Ultimately, U.S. forces helped to defeat the pro-Bosch movement, preventing the restoration of the democratically elected government and facilitating the establishment of an authoritarian regime headed by longtime Trujillo associate Joaquín Balaguer.

The Cuban revolution and the Cold War also brought tension to the British Caribbean, in particular to British Guiana (independent Guyana after 1966) and Jamaica. In the former, U.S. and British authorities were concerned with the political dominance in the early 1960s of the left-leaning Cheddi Jagan and his People's Progressive Party (PPP). Canada also had extensive economic investments in the country, primarily in the financial sector, and generally shared the U.S. desire to avoid a political crisis. Under U.S. pressure, the British government in 1964 introduced a new electoral system employing proportional representation, a significant departure from traditional British electoral politics, in order to provide an opportunity for the People's National Congress (PNC) under Forbes Burnham and other opposition parties to break the stranglehold of the PPP. The tactic worked, with the PNC winning the election and establishing a minority government in alliance with the United Force Party in 1964. Ironically, Burnham himself drifted to the left and adopted a more radical stance in the early 1970s, nationalizing a number of foreign-owned enterprises, including the extremely important bauxite holdings of the Canadian-owned Alcan, and establishing closer links with Cuba, Libya, North Korea, and East Germany.

Further evidence of the Cuban influence can be found throughout the 1970s. With the nationalization of bauxite production in Guyana, greater attention was focused on production in Jamaica, where Alcan's holdings had more potential and where there were also extensive investments by Anaconda, Kaiser, Revere, and Reynolds. The political situation in Jamaica in the early 1970s was viewed with alarm in the United States, as the electoral victory by the People's National Party (PNP) in 1972 led to the formation of a government committed to a program of democratic socialism under the leadership of Michael Manley. Manley and the PNP won reelection in 1976 and proceeded to establish diplomatic relations with the Soviet Union and to host an official visit by Fidel Castro in late 1977, provoking an ever-more hostile response from the United States.

By the end of the decade the worst fears of the United States—the potential expansion of Cuban and Soviet influence—seemed to have been confirmed. Cuba's military activism in Africa, particularly its remarkable success intervening in conflicts in Angola (beginning in 1975) and Ethiopia (1977), did much to enhance the country's global stature as did Havana's hosting of the Sixth Nonaligned Summit in 1979. The success of the Sandinista National Liberation Front in overthrowing the regime of Anastasio Somoza in Nicaragua in 1979 provoked a crisis within the region and raised U.S. fears of a second Cuba in what had become known as the Caribbean Basin. That same year, Maurice Bishop's New Jewel Movement came to power in Grenada after overthrowing the regime of Eric Gairy and made immediate overtures to Castro. With Cuba attempting to expand its economic and political ties throughout the region, this period marks the high point of Cuban power and prestige in the Caribbean. However, as H. Michael Erisman examines more fully in Chapter 6, such revolutionary change precipitated ongoing hostilities with the United States and varying degrees of military intervention that contributed to a diminishing of Cuban influence as time went on.

Conclusion

Some historical patterns have emerged from this discussion. Today the West Indies contains a variety of political entities, ranging from independent countries to various types of overseas possessions. These varying forms of political status, and the distinctive political system types found in the region, reflect divergent colonial experiences and traditions. Significant disparities in the nature and timing of the decolonization process are also apparent, ranging from the bloody slave revolt in Haiti to the evolutionary tutelary method employed by the British.[2] Overall, the presence of different colonial powers, imparting different traditions, values, and institutions, has contributed to the popular perception of the Caribbean as an area divided by linguistic, cultural, and political barriers.

Such superficial differences, however, must not obscure the fact that the countries of the Caribbean have endured a common historical experience of slavery, economic exploitation, and political domination. This common experience has engendered similar cultural, socioeconomic, and political patterns, resulting in a sort of convergence within the region.

At the onset of the twenty-first century, the politically independent Caribbean remains economically dependent. There is a continuing high level of out-migration, diminishing the region's human resources. As Dennis Pantin demonstrates in Chapter 5, the economic dependency of the region may have lessened somewhat with greater diversification of national economies, but dependency rather than self-sustaining economic growth is more the norm than the exception. In Chapter 4, Thomas J. D'Agostino explores the political implications of this condition.

Notes

1. On December 6, 1904, in a message to Congress, Roosevelt stated:

> Any country whose people conduct themselves well can count upon our hearty friendship. If a nation shows that it knows how to act with reasonable efficiency and decency in social and political matters, if it keeps order and pays its obligations, it need fear no interference from the United States. Chronic wrong-doing, or an impotence which results in a general loosening of the ties of society, may in America, as elsewhere, ultimately require intervention by some civilized nation, and in the western hemisphere the adherence of the United States to the Monroe Doctrine may force the United States, however reluctantly, in flagrant cases of such wrong-doing or impotence, to the exercise of an international police power. (P. Smith 1996:38)

2. The current and former British West Indies had the most complicated road to independence of the Caribbean territories. Some, like Anguilla, the British Virgin Islands, the Cayman Islands, Montserrat, and the Turks and Caicos Islands, remain possessions of the United Kingdom with internal self-governments. Others, like most of the former British Lesser Antilles and the Bahamas, have become independent. The first to become independent were Jamaica and Trinidad and Tobago in 1962. Barbados became independent in 1966, and the rest achieved independence during the 1970s and early 1980s, with St. Kitts and Nevis being the most recent to become independent in 1983.

Bibliography

Andie, F. M., and T. G. Mathews, eds. *The Caribbean in Transition: Papers on Social, Political and Economic Development*. San Juan: University of Puerto Rico Press, 1965.

Bryan, Anthony. *Trading Places: The Caribbean Faces Europe and the Americas in the Twenty-first Century*. Occasional Paper 27. Miami, FL: University of Miami North-South Center, 1997.

Buhle, Paul. *C.L.R. James: The Artist as Revolutionary*. New York: Verso, 1988.

Curtin, Philip D. *The Atlantic Slave Trade: A Census*. Madison: University of Wisconsin Press, 1969.

Domínguez, Jorge. *International Security and Democracy: Latin America and the Caribbean in the Post–Cold War Era*. Pittsburgh: University of Pittsburgh Press, 1998.

Domínguez, Jorge, Robert A. Pastor, and R. DeLisle Worrell, eds. *Democracy in the Caribbean: Political, Economic, and Social Perspectives*. Baltimore: Johns Hopkins University Press, 1993.

Engerman, Stanley, and Eugene Genovese, eds. *Race and Slavery in the Western Hemisphere*. Princeton, NJ: Princeton University Press, 1975.
Gordinga, Cornelius. *A Short History of the Netherlands Antilles and Suriname*. The Hague: M. Nijhoff, 1979.
Green, W. *British Slave Emancipation: The Sugar Colonies and the Great Experiment, 1830–1865*. Oxford, UK: Clarendon Press, 1965.
Hartog, Johannes. *Curaçao: From Colonial Dependence to Autonomy*. Aruba: De Wit, 1968.
Henry, Paget, and Paul Buhle, eds. *C.L.R. James's Caribbean*. Durham, NC: Duke University Press, 1991.
Hoefte, Rosemarijn. *In Place of Slavery: A Social History of British Indian and Javanese Laborers in Suriname*. Gainesville: University of Florida Press, 1998.
Ince, B., ed. *Contemporary International Relations of the Caribbean*. Trinidad: University of the West Indies Press, 1978.
James, C.L.R. *The Black Jacobins: Toussaint L'Ouverture and the San Domingue Revolution*. 2nd ed. New York: Vintage, 1963.
Knight, Franklin W. *The Caribbean: The Genesis of a Fragmented Nationalism*. New York: Oxford University Press, 1978.
———, ed. *General History of the Caribbean, Volume 3: Slave Societies of the Caribbean*. London: UNESCO and Macmillan, 1997.
Lai, Walton Look. *Chinese and Indian Migrants to the British West Indies, 1838–1918*. Baltimore: Johns Hopkins University Press, 1993.
Langley, Lester D. *Struggle for the American Mediterranean: United States–European Rivalry in the Gulf-Caribbean, 1776–1914*. Athens: University of Georgia Press, 1976.
———. *The United States and the Caribbean, 1900–1970*. Athens: University of Georgia Press, 1980
Laurence, K. O. *Immigration into the West Indies in the Nineteenth Century*. Barbados: Caribbean Universities Press, 1971.
Lewis, Rupert, and Patrick Bryan, eds. *Garvey: His Work and Impact*. Jamaica: Institute of Social and Economic Research, 1988.
de Onís, Juan. *The America of José Martí*. New York: Funk and Wagnalls, 1953.
Parry, J. H., and P. M. Sherlock. *A Short History of the West Indies*. London: Macmillan, 1965.
Pastor, Robert A. *Whirlpool: U.S. Foreign Policy Toward Latin America and the Caribbean*. Princeton, NJ: Princeton University Press, 1992.
Plummer, Brenda Gayle. *Haiti and the United States: The Psychological Moment*. Athens: University of Georgia Press, 1992.
Randall, Stephen J., and Graeme S. Mount. *The Caribbean Basin: An International History*. London: Routledge, 1998.
Raup, Henry. *The Life and Writings of Bartolomé de las Casas*. Albuquerque: University of New Mexico Press, 1967.
Ruiz, Ramón Eduardo. *Cuba: The Making of a Revolution*. New York: Norton, 1968.
Smith, Daniel, ed. *Major Problems in American Diplomatic History*. Boston: D. C. Heath, 1965.
Smith, Gaddis. *The Last Years of the Monroe Doctrine, 1945–1993*. New York: Hill and Wang, 1994.
Smith, Peter H. *Talons of the Eagle: Dynamics of U.S.–Latin American Relations*. New York: Oxford University Press, 1996.
Solnick, B. B. *The West Indies and Central America to 1898*. New York: Knopf, 1970.

Thomas, Hugh, *The Slave Trade: The Story of the Atlantic Slave Trade, 1440–1870*. New York: Simon and Schuster, 1997.

Turton, Peter. *José Martí: Architect of Cuba's Freedom*. London: Zed Books, 1986.

Wilberforce, Robert Isaac, and Samuel Wilberforce, eds. *The Correspondence of William Wilberforce*. London: John Murray, 1840.

Wilgus, A. C., ed. *The Caribbean: Its Hemispheric Role*. Gainesville: University of Florida Press, 1967.

4

Caribbean Politics

Thomas J. D'Agostino

■ The Past as Prelude

The protracted and disparate colonial experiences that Stephen Randall discusses in Chapter 3 have profoundly influenced contemporary Caribbean political systems. The Caribbean contains remarkably diverse institutional structures and constitutional traditions, ranging from Cuba's revolutionary communist system to Westminster-style parliamentary democracies in the Commonwealth Caribbean to emerging democracies elsewhere; from independent states to colonial dependencies to states with varying relationships with metropolitan powers (see Basic Political Data, pp. 371–376). Thus, on the surface at least, generalizing about Caribbean politics is a challenging task.

The perception that Caribbean political systems are too different from one another to merit serious comparison has led to the tendency to segregate analyses by subregions, defined primarily by linguistic and cultural criteria. The result has been a dearth of pan-Caribbean political studies that are truly comparative.

Superficial differences between Caribbean societies, however, have tended to obscure underlying commonalities in their political systems. Some scholars observe that Caribbean societies, despite their unique features, have all been shaped by a host of common experiences (Lewis 1985; Knight 1990). The legacies of conquest, European colonialism, the plantation system, African slavery, and the persistent influence of external powers have produced similar patterns of political change and are evident in the values, practices, and institutions prevailing throughout the region. Contemporary Caribbean political systems reflect the blending of traditional and modern patterns, yielding hybrid systems that exhibit significant structural variations and divergent constitutional traditions yet ultimately appear to function in similar ways (Wiarda and Kryzanek 1992). In other words, though they may diverge in theory, the political systems across the Caribbean converge in practice.

This becomes apparent when evaluating the performance of Caribbean governments over time. Conventional wisdom has maintained that by virtue of their British colonial heritage the states of the Commonwealth Caribbean are more likely to sustain stable democratic governance than other countries in the region. To be sure, many of the difficulties experienced by Haiti and some of the Spanish-speaking countries of the circum-Caribbean may be attributed to highly centralized authoritarian rule derived from the colonial and postcolonial era and the concomitant paucity of viable political institutions. In contrast, the democratic structures and values Britain imparted to its Caribbean possessions, coupled with its policy of gradual decolonization in the region, facilitated the transition to independence and contributed to the relative success of democratic governments among the Commonwealth states. However, British rule also included long periods of semiauthoritarian "crown colony" administration and the imposition of a plantation economic system sustained by African slavery and indentured labor. The legacies of this colonial experience are reflected in contemporary political systems that manifest, like many throughout the region, the trappings of formal democracy yet remain elite-dominated and exclusionary, operating on the basis of personalism and patron-clientelism. Political crises in Grenada, Guyana, Jamaica, and Trinidad and Tobago since the early 1980s have tarnished the popular image of Anglo-Caribbean democracy, revealing these countries to be vulnerable to similar socioeconomic and political pressures as elsewhere in the region.

Though many scholars point to the record of democratic stability as the feature that has most distinguished the Caribbean from other developing areas, recent trends are unsettling (Griffin 1993; Ryan 1994; Huber 1993; Domínguez et al. 1993; Edie 1994). Since the onset of a devastating economic crisis in the 1970s and 1980s, governments across the Caribbean have struggled to meet the basic needs of their populations. As frustration and cynicism mount, the exodus of West Indian peoples accelerates, and many of those who remain increasingly question the efficacy of political systems that they believe have failed to sufficiently provide for or represent them. At present, then, the challenges confronting regional governments and leaders—regardless of cultural, linguistic, and political traditions—as well as the constraints—both internal and external—under which they operate are daunting.

What are the primary factors that have contributed to the development and maintenance of democratic political systems in the Caribbean? What has hindered the ability of governments to meet popular demands? What, if anything, can be done to make governments more responsive and to enhance their capacity to provide for citizens? Is the future of democracy in the Caribbean imperiled—and, if so, what might this lead to? This chapter explores the political repercussions of historical processes and current trends in order to address these questions and assess the future of Caribbean politics.

■ External Influences, Internal Dynamics, and New Forms

For more than five centuries the Caribbean has been impacted by events and processes originating outside the region. The islands of the West Indies and the mainland areas bordering the Caribbean Sea were irrevocably transformed as a result of European conquest and colonization. Following the consolidation of Spanish control, other European powers sought to challenge Spain and intensified efforts to make inroads in the region. By the early 1600s Spanish hegemony was beginning to erode, precipitating major changes throughout the Caribbean.

Nearly constant warfare among the British, Dutch, French, and Spanish resulted in many colonies changing hands throughout the sixteenth and seventeenth centuries (e.g., Jamaica was ceded to Britain from Spain in 1655). Of even greater importance was the introduction of the plantation system by Dutch colonizers expelled from Brazil around 1640.

This innovation sparked the "sugar revolution" that transformed the agricultural, demographic, and socioeconomic character of the Caribbean and greatly enhanced its economic and strategic value. For example, land tenure patterns were altered dramatically as vast tracts were concentrated in the hands of the wealthy planter class, with production geared for export to metropoles. More significantly, the demand for labor far exceeded the available pool, stimulating the growth of the African slave trade. As David Baronov and Kevin Yelvington discuss in Chapter 8, the importation of millions of African slaves as laborers forever changed the demographic composition of the region and led to the formation of a rigid three-tier social hierarchy (white minority elite on top, black slaves on the bottom, and a mixed colored population in the middle), the legacies of which remain evident today (Knight and Palmer 1989:7). Although the nonwhite population dwarfed the white European population throughout virtually the entire region, whites retained their economic and political dominance, reflecting the pervasive elitism within Caribbean societies.

The French colony of St. Domingue (later to become Haiti) provides another example of how external events have impacted the Caribbean. After France gained control over the western third of Hispaniola in 1697, the introduction of a slave-based sugar plantation economy enabled St. Domingue to become one of the most lucrative colonies in the world. However, the onset of the French Revolution in 1789, with its ideals of liberty, equality, and fraternity, contributed to the outbreak of a slave revolt in 1791 and the first challenge to colonial rule in the region. Even the abolition of the slave trade in

1793 and of slavery itself in 1794 in St. Domingue could not stop the revolt that culminated in the formation of the first independent black republic in the Americas: Haiti.

Stephen Randall notes in Chapter 3 that efforts to abolish slavery in the Caribbean were subject to fits and starts. Once again, external forces proved to have a major impact, as the debate over slavery in Britain during the early 1800s set into motion events that slowly curtailed the practice of slavery in the region. The actual implementation of policies to end the slave trade and then slavery itself occurred at different intervals by the respective colonial powers (Williams 1970). Regardless of when abolition occurred, the implications for Caribbean political systems and societies were extraordinary.

One of the most significant implications in the Anglo-Caribbean, where emancipation occurred earliest, was the need for an alternative source of labor. Attention turned to Asia, resulting in the influx of tens of thousands of indentured laborers primarily from India but also from China and elsewhere. The two countries impacted the most are Guyana and Trinidad, where sizable segments of the populations (around 41 percent in Trinidad and more than 50 percent in Guyana) are of East Indian descent. Ethnic and racial divisions are evident in both societies, manifested in tensions between Afro-Caribbean and Indo-Caribbean segments of the populations and in the political organizations created to represent them.

Although abolition technically gave freedom to millions of slaves, it did not alter the inequitable distribution of economic resources or political power.[1] The rigid stratification of Caribbean societies by race and class persisted, with the white minority planter class still in control. Nevertheless, it began a long process of enfranchisement that ultimately challenged the political dominance of elites, who opposed any measures that would open political systems to the nonwhite majority. Literacy and property requirements were imposed to delay the extension of the franchise and thereby preserve elite control over local representative institutions (i.e., legislative assemblies). As pressure to open systems escalated, several assemblies, including those in British Honduras and Jamaica, voted themselves out of existence rather than allow the nonwhite majority to gain control. This paved the way (along with the 1865 Morant Bay Rebellion in Jamaica) for the end of the "old representative system" that had been established in 1661 and the implementation of "crown colony" administration throughout the British Caribbean. Designed to perpetuate British control over increasingly vocal colonial societies, this inhibited political development and bestowed a legacy of semiauthoritarian centralized executive power that contrasts with the democratic structures inherent in Anglo-Caribbean systems.

Whereas Britain retained tight control over its colonies well into the twentieth century, Spain's power in the Americas deteriorated dramatically by the early 1800s following the loss of its mainland possessions and the

Dominican Republic, leaving only Cuba and Puerto Rico under its control by 1825. This decline was paralleled by the gradual emergence of the United States as a significant presence in the region. As H. Michael Erisman shows in Chapter 6, the 1823 Monroe Doctrine underscored U.S. interest in Latin America and the Caribbean, particularly the countries in closest geographic proximity to its borders. Initially, this did little to curtail European interventionism, as the United States had no means to enforce the doctrine. However, following the end of the Civil War the United States began to assert itself, and the flow of U.S. investment into the region greatly increased. Thus, concerns about regional stability precipitated a more aggressive approach that enabled the United States to exert enormous influence across the region.

A variety of actions underscored the centrality of the circum-Caribbean to U.S. economic and national security interests, as well as U.S. determination to consolidate its hegemony within the region. U.S. involvement in the 1895 border dispute between Venezuela and British Guiana reflected a heightened assertiveness and European recognition of the growing stature of the United States. The construction of the Panama Canal facilitated U.S. commercial and strategic dominance. But it was the defeat of Spain in the Spanish-American War that brought the Caribbean within the U.S. sphere of influence and marked the advent of U.S. preeminence in the region.

U.S. intervention in Cuba's struggle for independence had major regional implications. Spain's defeat and its loss of colonial possessions (Cuba, Puerto Rico, Guam, and the Philippines) effectively ended its reign as a colonial power. Although Britain, France, and the Netherlands each retained a number of Caribbean possessions, the mantle of power had been passed to the United States (Richardson 1992). This marked the beginning of the "American Century" in the Caribbean, during which U.S. preeminence would be established, challenged, and later confirmed with the end of the Cold War.

By intervening in the military conflict between Spain and those forces seeking Cuban independence, the United States denied Cuba its opportunity to gain independence on its own. Instead, after defeating Spain the United States established a protectorate over Cuba, motivated in part by the magnitude of U.S. investments there. The insertion of the infamous Platt Amendment as part of Cuba's 1902 constitution—which forbade Cuba from incurring foreign debt, provided for the establishment of a U.S. naval coaling station at Guantánamo Bay (still in operation), and gave the United States the right to intervene in Cuban affairs—provoked strong anti-U.S. sentiment that later fueled the fight for Cuban "independence" in the 1950s.

Elsewhere in the Caribbean, the early part of the twentieth century witnessed varying forms of U.S. intervention and heightened anti-U.S. sentiment. The U.S. preoccupation with regional stability was exemplified by President Theodore Roosevelt's 1904 Roosevelt Corollary to the Monroe Doctrine. In asserting the right of the United States to exercise an "international police power" in the hemisphere, Roosevelt was "extending the Monroe Doctrine to justify U.S. intervention to prevent European intervention" (Molineau 1990: 41). Over the next three decades U.S. policymakers acted to protect commercial and strategic geopolitical interests from the threat of European encroachment. For example, fears that mounting Caribbean debts might provoke a response from European creditors led to the establishment of customs receiverships in the Dominican Republic, Haiti, and Nicaragua. At the same time, concerns that instability would threaten U.S. interests and invite European incursions in the region (particularly given the escalation of tensions prior to World War I and during the interwar period) led to direct military interventions and occupations in a number of countries.

Notwithstanding the fiscal benefits derived from the receiverships, as well as the infrastructure improvements carried out by U.S. occupation forces, the political repercussions of U.S. interventionism were more problematic. Despite efforts to tout the U.S. democratic mission in the circum-Caribbean, these interventions not only stultified the development of democratic institutions and values; they actually paved the way for the emergence of a number of repressive authoritarian regimes. Ironically, even though President Franklin Delano Roosevelt's Good Neighbor Policy was intended to improve relations with Latin American and Caribbean countries by putting an end to direct U.S. intervention, the withdrawal of U.S. forces in favor of local institutions ("national guards") designed to maintain stability actually facilitated the rise of notorious dictators such as Rafael Trujillo, Fulgencio Batista, Anastasio Somoza, and François Duvalier. In each case, domestic political development was sacrificed in the interest of preserving the status quo and safeguarding U.S. national security, sowing the seeds of future conflict that would involve further U.S. intervention, albeit in different forms.

Table 4.1 U.S. Military Involvement in the Caribbean During the Era of Intervention, 1898–1934

Country	Years
Cuba	1898–1902, 1906–1909, 1912, 1917–1922
Dominican Republic	1912, 1916–1924
Haiti	1915–1934
Mexico	1914, 1916–1917
Nicaragua	1909–1910, 1912–1925, 1926–1933
Panama	1903
Puerto Rico	1898–1900

Source: Harold Molineau, *U.S. Policy Toward Latin America* (Boulder: Westview, 1990), p. 51.

The Case of Puerto Rico

Puerto Rico represents something of an anomaly in the study of U.S. involvement in the Caribbean. Acquired by the United States from Spain concurrently with Cuba, Puerto Rico was subject to military intervention and occupation like the cases discussed above. By contrast, however, the U.S. occupation of Puerto Rico was comparatively brief and gave way not to brutal dictatorship but to stable civilian rule closely tied to the United States. Puerto Rico is further distinguished from the other cases in that it never gained independence, remaining a U.S. possession to this day.

Puerto Rico's central location in the Caribbean, its special relationship with the United States, and the relatively advanced level of development on the island have brought attention to it as a unique case. Yet despite its distinctiveness, Puerto Rico has much in common with its Caribbean neighbors, especially in terms of social problems, economic challenges, and external domination.

A brief overview of past developments helps to clarify the similarities and differences between Puerto Rico and the rest of the Caribbean. After Spain ceded Puerto Rico to the United States in 1898, the U.S. military occupied the island until President William McKinley signed the Foraker Act in 1900, providing for a civilian government. Under that act—whereby Puerto Rico became an unincorporated territory of the United States—the U.S. president appointed the Puerto Rican governor, the members of an executive council, and the justices of the Supreme Court. And though the House of Delegates and resident commissioner were popularly elected, the United States continued to exercise substantial governmental control.

The Foraker Act also facilitated U.S. control over the Puerto Rican economy. In providing "the legal framework for economic dependency," the act extended the U.S. tariff structure, currency, and commercial regulations to the island (Silvestrini 1989:148). Among other things, this prevented Puerto Rico from entering into commercial treaties with other nations and required that U.S. vessels transport all products shipped between the island and the mainland. Coupled with its administration of the education, health care, and criminal justice systems, deemed "pivotal in the Americanization process," it is evident that U.S. control was pervasive (Silvestrini 1989:153).

In response to demands from Puerto Rican political leaders for increased autonomy and self-rule for the island, the 1917 Jones-Shafroth Act provided for the popular election of the nineteen-member Senate as well as U.S. citizenship for the island's residents. Although this did enhance local authority to a degree, continued U.S. control was ensured by virtue of the U.S. president's appointment power.

The Puerto Rican economy underwent significant change during the early part of the twentieth century, growing more closely integrated with the U.S.

economy in the process. This sparked changes in the social structure as well as land tenure and employment patterns. The pace of rural-urban migration increased and, after the onset of economic problems in the 1930s, so did the exodus to the United States. Debate continued on the political status question, however, with political parties emerging to represent the three options: autonomy, independence, and statehood.

More far-reaching changes occurred in the 1940s. Following its creation in 1938, the Popular Democratic Party (Partido Popular Democrático) swept the 1940 legislative elections under the leadership of Luis Muñoz Marín. Its decision to shift from agriculture to industrialization as the development focus led to the implementation of Operation Bootstrap in 1947. This program of "industrialization by invitation"—designed to attract foreign investment with tax breaks and other incentives—triggered substantial economic growth, with profound implications for Puerto Rican society and politics in the coming decades.

After World War II, the United States was under increasing pressure from the United Nations to modify its colonial relationship with Puerto Rico. President Harry Truman signed the Elective Governor Act in 1947, paving the way for the election of Muñoz as the island's first elected governor the following year. In 1950 the U.S. Congress approved Public Law 600, which set into motion the process of establishing a constitution for Puerto Rico. Following its approval by referendum in Puerto Rico, where it was opposed by the independence movement, the process culminated on July 25, 1952, with the creation of the Estado Libre Asociado de Puerto Rico—the Free Associated State (or Commonwealth).

The new constitution modified the structure of government in Puerto Rico, allocating more power to the elected government and legislature. Even still, the United States retained considerable powers that had been provided in the Foraker and Jones Acts. It has been suggested that the 1952 constitution bestowed "a new veneer of respectability to the home rule provided for Puerto Rico," an important international consideration for the United States at the time, but "did not in fact bring any fundamental change in the powers of government" (Gautier-Mayoral 1994:167). This situation is characterized as one of "limited democracy," whereby the elected government has control of local matters while a host of key areas and issues (including, aside from defense and foreign relations, customs, citizenship, immigration, the post office, and minimum wages) that impact the daily lives of people on the island remain under U.S. control. As a result, the debate over the status question did not end with the promulgation of the Commonwealth constitution. On the contrary, it has continued over the past half-century with no definitive resolution in sight.

Despite impressive rates of economic growth achieved during the 1950s and 1960s, producing a level of prosperity exceeding that of most regional neighbors, it became apparent that the Puerto Rican developmental model was beset by problems (Silvestrini 1989; Gautier-Mayoral 1994). First, in promoting the development of capital-intensive industry, the number of new jobs that were created was far less than that needed to reduce already high levels of unemployment. This was exacerbated by the collapse of the rural agricultural economy and displacement of peasant farmers, a trend that sparked large-scale urban and out-migration (mainly to the United States) and necessitated costly food imports as production declined.

Second, the influx of U.S. companies and investment capital, though stimulating growth, also had a downside. The government undertook a massive infrastructure development program in order to accommodate the emerging industrial economy, causing public debt to skyrocket. At the same time, much of the profit generated by the companies, most of which received substantial tax breaks to locate on the island, was repatriated rather than reinvested locally. Thus, aside from the jobs that were created, the presence of these companies in Puerto Rico was not nearly as beneficial to the local population as statistical growth rates would seem to suggest.

Finally, over time Puerto Rico grew increasingly dependent on the United States as a source of capital, markets, technology, and expertise as the island economy became more closely integrated with the U.S. economy. In addition, the level of U.S. federal assistance increased dramatically as more and more island residents came to rely on public services and social welfare programs. Puerto Rico receives more than U.S.$3 billion annually in federal grants. This heightened dependence has had significant political ramifications, for it represents "a formidable obstacle in the quest for self-determination" (Gamaliel Ramos and Rivera 2001:7). This point is echoed by another scholar, who concludes that the massive transfer of federal funds has produced "a bipartisan political system with alternation and cogovernance of the two major parties and fewer opportunities for a political status change" (Gautier-Mayoral 1994:168). Efforts to promote greater local autonomy or pursue statehood were thus "largely neutralized."

For all of its idiosyncrasies, Puerto Rico faces challenges similar to those in other small, dependent, resource-scarce Caribbean states seeking to adapt to a global economy dominated by the world's major industrial powers. It has much in common with other "welfare colonies" in the region, including the Dutch and French possessions, whose decolonization has been "deferred" and who enjoy "prosperous dependence" through heavy subsidies from metropolitan powers (Gautier-Mayoral 1994). This extreme dependence breeds a "politics of immobility" with regard to the status issue. In the case of Puerto Rico, this has been evident in recent elections and referenda where support has been more or less evenly divided between those favoring statehood and those favoring the existing commonwealth status. The lack of consensus among island voters, mirrored in the U.S. Congress, suggests that it is unlikely that a change in status will occur anytime soon. Nevertheless, Puerto Rico's political status continues to be an important question, which determines the kind of relationship the island can have with its Caribbean neighbors as well as with other countries of the world.

■ Socioeconomic Conditions and Political Consciousness

Outside Central America and the non–English speaking Greater Antilles, where U.S. interventionism was most pervasive, the late nineteenth and early twentieth centuries saw substantial socioeconomic changes. The political repercussions were particularly profound in the Anglo-Caribbean, where export-driven development contributed to the expansion of the nascent urban working and middle classes, primarily non-Europeans. As the level of popular political consciousness rose, however, political systems throughout the region remained under the firm control of a small, predominantly white elite. Largely excluded from the political process, the working and middle classes recognized that despite divergent objectives they had a mutual interest in reforming the anachronistic colonial political order (Knight and Palmer 1989:12).

And whereas the middle classes sought more gradual constitutional reform, the working classes demanded immediate change. Despite the proliferation of organizations promoting popular interests, their limited access to legitimate political channels compelled them to employ extralegal methods to express their demands. The depth of popular discontent throughout the Anglo-Caribbean was manifested by a plethora of violent disturbances, including the water riots in Trinidad in 1903 and the 1905 Ruimveldt riots in British Guiana. These events, calling attention to deteriorating socioeconomic conditions and exclusionary political systems, served as a precursor to the turmoil that engulfed the region in the 1930s.

With the onset of the Great Depression, tensions within the working classes were exacerbated by massive return migration on top of already heightened levels of unemployment (Knight and Palmer 1989). Amid intensifying nationalist fervor and demands for self-rule, violent labor disturbances culminated in the 1938 riots in Jamaica and British Guiana. In the aftermath, the Moyne Commission's inquiry into the causes of the unrest focused on the dire poverty afflicting the masses and led to a call for sweeping reform within the British territories.

The impact of external events on Caribbean affairs was again evident with the outbreak of hostilities in Europe in the late 1930s. As noted by Stephen Randall in Chapter 3, this conflict led the United States to assume greater responsibility for security in the Caribbean and also bolstered nationalist sentiments within the region. Coupled with the repercussions of the labor disturbances, this brought pressure on the European powers to reassess their colonial policies and set the stage for significant change in the postwar era.

France and the Netherlands pursued a policy of decolonization very different from that of the British. Confronted with escalating tensions in other colonies following World War II, France and the Netherlands took measures to more fully integrate their respective Caribbean possessions with the metropolitan center. Following a plebiscite in which each approved political union with France, French Guiana, Guadeloupe, and Martinique became *départements d'outre mer* (French overseas departments) in 1946. Among other things, this arrangement entitles the departments to elected representation in the French legislature as well as government subsidies. The Dutch granted internal self-government and universal suffrage to the Netherlands Antilles (Aruba, Bonaire, Curaçao, Saba, St. Eustatius, and St. Maarten), which in 1954 was granted autonomy in international affairs and attained constitutional equality with the Netherlands and Suriname joining with them to form the kingdom of the Netherlands. Suriname went on to acquire full independence in 1975. In 1986 Aruba became a separate self-governing unit in anticipation of a ten-year transition to independence. In 1990, however, Aruba rescinded its petition in order to remain within the kingdom.

■ Postwar Transitions

In contrast to the French and Dutch approach to colonial reform, Britain responded to demands for reform by initiating a gradual process that differed markedly from its policy in Africa and Asia. A lengthy period of "tutelary democracy" ensued whereby the structural apparatus of Britain's Westminster parliamentary system was introduced to facilitate the transition to local self-government and, ultimately, independent statehood. Such an institutional inheritance, in and of itself, has not necessarily guaranteed democratic stability, for "form seldom defines function" (Knight 1993:32). In the case of the Anglo-Caribbean, ostensibly democratic institutional structures were grafted onto societies that had experienced a protracted period of highly centralized, semiauthoritarian governance under crown colony administration. Through a process of "institutional adaptation" (Stone 1985:15), the Westminster parliamentary system was "Caribbeanized" (Payne 1993:72), or adapted, to the socioeconomic, political, and cultural realities of the Caribbean. This process has yielded hybrid or blended political systems that combine first world theory and institutions with third world conditions (Hillman and D'Agostino 1992; Payne 1993). Such systems boast formal democratic institutions and processes, yet in practice they tend to operate on the basis of personalism, patron-clientelism, and the exclusion of the popular classes.

As compared to other developing areas, the Anglo-Caribbean historically has maintained an impressive record of stable democratic rule. Many scholars attribute this, at least in part, to the institutional and attitudinal legacies imparted by Britain to its Caribbean colonies.[2] The colonial inheritance received by these states (though perhaps not as democratic as is widely perceived) was a great deal more beneficial to that received by Haiti and the former Spanish colonies of the circum-Caribbean. After centuries of colonial rule these states, with deep-rooted authoritarian political cultures, were ill-prepared for nation-building, much less democratization. With the removal of colonial authority, the newly independent states were confronted by a vacuum of power in societies devoid of any viable political institutions and democratic traditions.

Into this vacuum stepped rival military leaders, such as Henry Christophe and Alexandre Pétion (following the death of Jean-Jacques Dessalines) in Haiti and Pedro Santana and Buenaventura Báez in the Dominican Republic, competing to assert control over the state and its resources. The dominance of powerful *caudillos* (strong leaders, often military figures who dominate politics through the use of force) had profound repercussions throughout Central America and the Greater Antilles, perpetuating the dearth of institutions by impeding the development of those central to democratic societies. What followed, in the wake of the Great Depression, the Good Neighbor Policy, and the withdrawal of U.S. forces from the region, was the emergence of brutal regimes such as those led by Trujillo, Somoza, Batista, and Duvalier.

The repressive rule and instability experienced in these countries following World War II stood in stark contrast to the gradual process of decolonization that characterized the territories controlled by the British, as well as the processes of reform employed by the Dutch and the French. These divergent experiences may be attributed to a variety of factors. Some scholars point to the disparity in the level of institutionalization in explaining the relative stability of the non-Hispanic Caribbean (excluding Haiti) as compared to other areas (Grugel 1995; Stone 1985). The emergence of a vibrant civil society, particularly labor unions and political parties, served to channel heightened levels of social mobilization engendered through modernization in the Anglo-Caribbean while enhanced linkages with the metropolitan centers helped to preserve stability in the Dutch and French territories as well as in Puerto Rico. The paucity of viable institutions in Haiti and many of the former Spanish colonies, however, left opposition groups little choice but to pursue extraconstitutional means to challenge authoritarian regimes and effect change.

Scholars also focus on the response of elite groups to demands for reform in explaining divergent experiences since World War II (Grugel 1995:10; Stone 1985:47–48). In the Anglo-Caribbean, the rapidly growing and increasingly well organized popular classes posed a significant threat to the political dominance of elites. Following the disturbances of the late 1930s, elites took measures to provide working classes with improved benefits and limited opportunities to participate in the political process under their tutelage within the existing power structure (Hillman and D'Agostino 1992).

The situations in the Hispanic Caribbean (excluding Puerto Rico) and in Haiti were very different. In these cases the growth of the urban working class was more gradual, and the labor movements were much smaller, less dynamic, and not nearly as well organized. Consequently, those in power (and their elite supporters) did not feel compelled to accommodate pressures for reform and, instead, utilized coercion and repression to marginalize and depoliticize the popular classes.

It is important to consider the impact of the United States in these areas during the early post–World War II era. U.S. activism and interventionism was primarily confined to the non–English speaking Greater Antilles and Central America in what some consider to be the true U.S. sphere of influence (see, e.g., Molineau 1990). The onset of the Cold War heightened U.S. sensitivity to the potential for instability and communist insurgency within the region. Seeking to forestall revolutionary change that might threaten its interests, the United States supported self-professed anticommunist dictatorships (such as those identified above), effectively "putting the Good Neighbor Policy in mothballs and giving the Monroe Doctrine new life" (Maingot 1994:87). Through the Central Intelligence Agency, the United States also supported forces that ousted the democratically elected government of Jacobo Arbenz in Guatemala in 1954.[3] Arbenz was perceived by conservatives in the U.S. government as being too far to the left because his reformist agenda threatened U.S. business interests, especially the United Fruit Company. With the removal of Arbenz, the Caribbean again took center stage in the struggle between the world's great powers.

The Case of Cuba

The 1959 Cuban revolution, by effecting a complete social transformation in the largest insular Caribbean state, was a regional and global watershed. The revolution produced a unique alternative political and socioeconomic model within the Caribbean.

The 1898 U.S. intervention and subsequent occupation compromised Cuban independence. A pattern of strongman rule and military intervention in politics ensued. The overthrow of Gerardo Machado, elected in 1924 but who maintained power illegally until 1933, led to a brief revolutionary period under Ramón Grau San Martín. Then Fulgencio Batista led a military revolt, leading to his domination of Cuban politics over the next decade, initially behind the scenes and later through direct rule from 1940 to 1944. During this period the United States strengthened its economic and political ties to Cuba. Any democratic alternative, severely undermined by widespread corruption and endemic political violence, was eliminated in March 1952 when Batista again seized power.

UN Photo 152636, Maggie Steber

People gather in Bayamo, Cuba, July 1982, to hear President Fidel Castro's address at a celebration commemorating the Cuban revolution

Batista cultivated ties with the United States, which maintained close scrutiny over Cuban affairs given its proximity and the extensive U.S. business interests on the island. Cuba, compared to other Caribbean nations, was relatively prosperous, yet there were considerable disparities in the distribution of wealth as well as between urban areas and impoverished rural areas. Thus, broad opposition to Batista's increasingly repressive regime emerged. Among the various groups seeking to oust the dictator was the 26th of July Movement, named after the date in 1953 on which its leader, Fidel Castro, launched an ill-fated attack on the Moncada military barracks. After his release from prison, Castro went to Mexico, where he plotted the overthrow of Batista. The struggle began in 1956, when Castro and his forces (numbering less than 100) returned to Cuba and waged a remarkably effective guerrilla campaign against Batista's well-equipped (by the United States) army of some 40,000. With his forces unable to quell the rebellion, Batista increased repression against students and other groups who led urban-based opposition to the regime, as well as those suspected of sympathizing with the rebels. Lacking any substantial popular support and having lost U.S. backing, Batista fled into exile on January 1, 1959, and Castro marched triumphantly into Havana.

As the broad revolutionary coalition began to splinter, Castro's faction, including his brother Raúl and the Argentine revolutionary Ernesto "Che"

Guevara, became the dominant force. The ultimate direction that the revolution would take was unclear at this time, largely due to uncertainty as to Fidel's ideological orientation. Although Guevara, an avowed Marxist, maintained that Fidel was not a Marxist prior to the revolution, Fidel Castro himself has given conflicting accounts. He was not a member of the prerevolutionary Communist Party, instead focusing his appeal on the middle sectors as a nationalist reformer. However, initial uncertainty as to his intentions gave way to the realization that Castro was committed to a radical program intended to transform Cuban society and to assert Cuban sovereignty and independence from U.S. influence.

The Castro regime immediately set about dismantling the country's dependent capitalist economy, nationalizing property of both domestic and foreign owners. This action, coupled with the movement toward an authoritarian single-party state, led to the exodus of thousands of upper- and middle-class

Cynthia Sutton

Mural depicting Ernesto "Che" Guevara, Havana, Cuba

Cubans. This exodus (and subsequent ones like the 1980 Mariél boatlift) served as a kind of safety valve for Castro, helping to defuse internal opposition.

His charismatic presence did much to fill the institutional void left in the wake of Batista's collapse, and Committees for the Defense of the Revolution and other organizations were formed to mobilize support for the regime. Support was also generated by an ambitious program to address the glaring inequalities that characterized pre-1959 Cuba. Land redistribution, educational reform, a literacy campaign, and improvements in health care and other services were introduced to raise the standard of living of Cuba's masses and to ensure that their basic daily needs would be met.

Emboldened by Cuba's deepening ties with the Soviet Union, which provided a market for Cuban sugar and a new source of technology (and, later, military assistance), Castro's anti-U.S. rhetoric intensified. The revolution's increasingly radical tone, coupled with the seizure of U.S. holdings, prompted John Kennedy's administration in 1961 to launch a Guatemala-style invasion by U.S.-backed Cuban exiles at the Bay of Pigs. Instead of fomenting a counterrevolution within Cuba, the poorly organized operation failed miserably. A monumental victory for Castro and for Cuban nationalism, the Bay of Pigs substantiated Castro's contention that the United States was the mortal enemy of revolutionary Cuba; many contend that the failed invasion pushed Cuba further into the embrace of the Soviet bloc.

Castro then formally declared himself, and the revolution, Marxist-Leninist. Within months, Soviet leader Nikita Khrushchev ordered the installation of missile bases on the island, transforming Cuba into a stage for a confrontation that brought the world's superpowers to the brink of nuclear war. The Cuban missile crisis of October 1962 was resolved when Khrushchev, under pressure from the Kennedy administration, agreed to withdraw Cuba-based Soviet missiles in exchange for a U.S. pledge not to invade the island.

Over the next three decades Cuba became a key Soviet ally in the third world. The relationship provided the Soviets with access to a strategic location in the Western Hemisphere, and Soviet efforts to assist communist movements in Africa were bolstered by Castro's desire to export revolution and his willingness to contribute troops and other personnel to missions in Angola and Ethiopia. In return, the Soviet Union provided the military support and economic and technical assistance that facilitated institutionalization of the revolution and enabled Cuba to survive the embargo imposed by the United States in 1960.

Critics of the revolution argue that Castro, despite his rhetoric about asserting Cuba's independence from foreign powers, merely exchanged U.S. dependence for Soviet dependence. Although supporters counter that since 1959 Cuba has belonged to Cubans rather than to foreign investors, Soviet influence was pervasive. Castro maintained a greater degree of autonomy than the leaders of most Soviet satellites, but his longevity in power has been due, in part, to Soviet backing. To be sure, Castro depended heavily on Soviet aid to provide the benefits that endeared him to the Cuban masses. But Castro's popularity has also derived from his willingness to confront the United States, which has greatly enhanced Cubans' sense of national pride and dignity. His longevity may also be attributed to a centralized authoritarian state in which legitimate opposition is not tolerated and dissent is severely repressed.

The Cuban revolution has been influenced profoundly by the prevailing international context. The bipolar structure institutionalized during the Cold War enabled Castro to parlay Cuba's strategic geopolitical location into leverage in dealing with the Soviet Union. However, the situation changed dramatically with the emergence of Soviet leader Mikhail Gorbachev in 1985 and the introduction of reforms such as *glasnost* and *perestroika*. Soviet rapprochement with the West meant that Cuba soon became a costly burden, both economically and politically. As the Cold War wound down and the Soviet domestic crisis deepened, the Soviet Union's diminished ability, and willingness, to subsidize Cuba led to a reduction in assistance. Further, as Cuba's trade partners began to demand hard currency payments, Cuba was forced to borrow from abroad, accruing a substantial foreign debt.

The collapse of regimes throughout Eastern Europe and the dissolution of the Soviet Union deprived Cuba of its primary trading partners and its source of economic and technical assistance. Coupled with the long-standing embargo imposed by the United States in 1960, the loss of Soviet-bloc assistance has caused serious economic hardship in Cuba. Ironically, with Castro left to fend for himself, Cuba may be considered truly independent for the first time since formally gaining independence a century ago.

Despite rhetorical slogans like "Socialism or Death!" Castro has adopted a more pragmatic approach to maintaining the revolution in the long term. For example, in an effort to attract much-needed hard currency, Castro allowed for the dollarization of the Cuban economy in 1993, enabling people to trade in U.S. dollars. He has also sought foreign investment, establishing joint ventures with foreign firms to stimulate the economy. In particular Cuba is banking on a revitalization of the once-vibrant tourist industry to keep the economy, and possibly the regime itself, afloat. However, the influx of tourists has exacerbated the sense of deprivation felt by many Cubans. This could prove especially troubling among Cuba's youth, who face bleak prospects with few opportunities and who lack the strong emotional attachment to Castro and the revolution felt by the previous generation. Nevertheless, as the Elián González case illustrates, Cuban nationalism is tied inextricably to anti-U.S. sentiment and the desire for Cuba to chart an independent course.

For countries in the Western Hemisphere, the repercussions of the Cuban revolution were far-reaching. Castro's consolidation of power and Cuba's alliance with the Soviet Union aroused U.S. fears of the potential for socioeconomic and political change throughout the Americas. After 1959 U.S. policy in the region focused on preventing a "second Cuba." In 1961, the Alliance for Progress was introduced by the Kennedy administration to stimulate development and ameliorate the conditions that were believed to foster communism. The determination to confront regimes deemed leftist was evident in Guyana, where pressure on Britain to alter electoral laws brought down the government of Marxist Cheddi Jagan in 1964 and, on a grander scale, in the Dominican Republic following its 1962 elections.

■ The Case of the Dominican Republic

After coming to power in 1930, Rafael Trujillo established a highly centralized authoritarian state whereby he would rule until his assassination in 1961. During this time the Dominican Republic evolved into a police state in which Trujillo came to exercise absolute control and the regime relied upon intimidation, repression, and terror to maintain power. Although the country was transformed from a traditional rural society to a more urban modern one under Trujillo, his unwillingness to accommodate the demands of an increasingly mobilized populace, particularly the emerging urban working and middle classes, contributed to his demise. Political development had been so constrained under his rule that "the country was only slightly more advanced in 1961, when Trujillo was assassinated, than in 1844, when independent life began" (Wiarda 1989:434).

Rapid modernization in the post-Trujillo era continued to alter the composition and structure of Dominican society, as well as the expectations and values of the populace. The Dominican Revolutionary Party (Partido Revolucionario Dominicano; PRD), led by Juan Bosch, mobilized the newly emergent groups and won the nation's first competitive democratic election in 1962. However, the PRD's democratic experiment faced serious obstacles, including opposition from domestic elites who, along with the United States, feared Bosch's progressive policies and viewed events in the Dominican Republic as a prelude to Cuban-style revolution.

Whereas the PRD's victory appeared to promise an opening of the political system, Bosch's ouster by a coalition of powerful elites and the military after only seven months in office underscored the lack of national consensus as to the future direction of Dominican politics. The suppression of the PRD and its supporters following the coup did not bode well for the maintenance of stability. Mass discontent and violence ultimately erupted in April 1965, when Bosch supporters attempted to restore him to the presidency.

Lyndon Johnson's administration sent some 23,000 troops to assist loyalist forces in quelling the revolt, seen as a threat to stability and U.S. hegemony in the region. After the defeat of the pro-Bosch constitutionalist forces,

Thomas J. D'Agostino

Dominican presidential candidate Juan Bosch during his 1990 campaign

Dominicans returned to the polls in 1966 to elect Joaquín Balaguer, a former Trujillo associate. Balaguer's conservative agenda endeared him to the Dominican elites, the international business community, and particularly the U.S. government, whose overt support of Balaguer over Bosch was one of several factors that compromised the electoral process. Over the next twelve years Balaguer ruled in a manner reminiscent of the Trujillo era, employing electoral fraud and repression in a process of authoritarian restructuring that stultified democratic development in the Dominican Republic.

The Anglo-Caribbean

While Cuba embarked on a period of revolutionary change and the Dominican Republic reverted to its authoritarian past, the Anglo-Caribbean was on the verge of a new era as well. As Stephen Randall describes in Chapter 3, the West Indies Federation (WIF) was created in 1958 to facilitate the transition to independence for a number of British colonies. However, the WIF faced substantial obstacles from its inception and was "doomed from the start by lukewarm popular support" (Knight and Palmer 1989:15). Many of the obstacles derive from Britain's own colonial policies. For example, Britain fostered a sense of division among its colonies as a way to enhance its control. There was little direct communication and trade among the colonies, as each dealt primarily with London. Significant disparities in the level of economic and political development among the British colonies also undermined efforts to promote a sense of cohesiveness and unity of purpose.

Thus, there was little sense of regional identity or regionwide nationalism within the British Caribbean (Grugel 1995:115–116). On the contrary, one of the commonalities that emerged among the British colonies was a fierce sense of nationalism in the early twentieth century. This nationalism was island-specific and fostered a strong desire for independence rather than a desire to belong to an artificial supranational creation. That regional interests would be subordinated to those of individual states became evident early on: the federation "quickly foundered on the uncompromising insular interests, especially of its principal participants, Trinidad and Jamaica" (Knight and Palmer 1989:15).

The eventual demise of the federation came as a result of Jamaica's decision to withdraw following a referendum held on September 19, 1961. The legacies of fragmentation and uneven development played a significant role as Jamaica's ties to the other members were limited and there was a widespread perception among Jamaicans that their country, as the federation's largest economy, would be subsidizing its less developed partners. With Trinidad subsequently announcing its decision to withdraw, the WIF was officially dissolved on May 31, 1962. Later that year, on August 6, Jamaica became the first British colony in the region to gain its independence.

■ The Case of Jamaica

Jamaica provides an interesting case in exploring the transition to independence as well as the challenges confronting newly independent states. Such analysis demonstrates the extent to which the legacies of British colonial rule shaped the postindependence political systems in the Anglo-Caribbean (Payne 1993).

Jamaica's independence marked an end to more than 300 years of British colonial rule. During this time political institutions and values inherent in the British parliamentary tradition were transplanted in Jamaica, along with the crown's other West Indian possessions. These institutions and values have been adapted over time to the country's socioeconomic realities, producing a uniquely Jamaican political system—yet one that has been influenced deeply by the country's colonial heritage.

Following its seizure from Spain in 1655, Jamaica experienced a brief period of military rule. The "old representative system" was in place from 1661 to 1865, dominated by a governor and a council forming an upper house appointed by the king. The lower house consisted of a representative assembly chosen by an electorate limited by a variety of restrictions. This assembly represented the interests of the landowning plantocracy and, in the nineteenth century, some professional and mercantile interests as well. The system was exclusionary, leaving the vast majority without representation.

In the wake of emancipation in 1838 (slavery itself was abolished in 1834) and the subsequent arrival of indentured workers from Asia, disturbances erupted periodically between landowners and laborers frustrated with the lack of responsiveness to their demands. This turmoil culminated in the 1865 Morant Bay Rebellion, which resulted in the dismantling of the old representative system and its constitution and the imposition of a crown colony government in which the governor enjoyed nearly autocratic power and in which political activity was discouraged. It wasn't until 1944, after a series of disturbances in 1937–1938, that crown colony rule was rescinded. A new constitution was proclaimed, restoring representative government and facilitating the transition to self-rule.

The labor unrest and incipient nationalism that emerged in the 1930s gave rise to charismatic leaders and organizations that would lead Jamaica into independence. Frustrated by the dearth of institutions through which their demands could be effectively channeled, workers began to organize. Movement toward the unionization of labor provided a vehicle for the organization of political expression. One of the leaders of this movement was Alexander Bustamante, who formed the Bustamante Industrial Trade Union in 1938 and captured the imagination of the Jamaican masses. At the same time, as sentiment for self-government mounted, Norman Manley established the People's National Party (PNP) as a nation-building organization. Bustamante subsequently founded the Jamaica Labour Party (JLP) while the PNP was initially linked to the Trade Union Council and later established its trade union affiliate, the National Workers' Union. This nexus between political parties and labor unions played a critical role in Jamaica's transition to independence and democratic rule, facilitating the institutionalization of a dominant two-party system in which both major parties relied upon labor organizations for electoral support.

This support was secured through an elaborate system of patron-client relations through which political parties and their leaders are linked to the masses in a system that distributes employment and other material benefits in exchange for loyalty and support. In this manner, "the Jamaican ruling groups have been able to anesthetize popular discontent by a politics of clientelism, keeping the masses quiet by a politics of 'jobs for the boys' at every social level" (Lewis 1985:227). Party loyalty was also derived from the dominance of "big personalities" such as Bustamante and Manley, a pattern in Caribbean politics where "loyalties have traditionally been given to leaders on a highly deferential, almost messianic, basis" (Payne 1993:72).

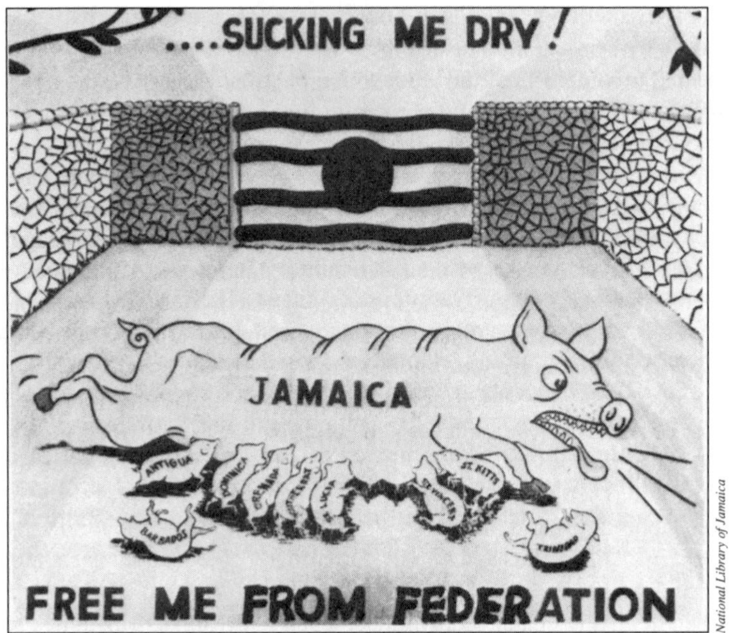

National Library of Jamaica

"Free Me from Federation"
Opponents of the West Indies Federation in Jamaica argued that their country would suffer as smaller member states would drain resources from the federation's largest economy.

Beginning with the 1944 election, Jamaica's first with universal adult suffrage, the JLP and PNP went on to alternate as majority and opposition, with Bustamante and the JLP winning in 1944 and 1949, and Norman Manley and the PNP prevailing in 1955 and 1959. These parties were representative of the two main ideological tendencies in the post–World War II Caribbean. However, both the "working-class and peasant-based populism" of Bustamante's JLP and the Fabian-inspired "social democracy" of Manley's PNP had much in common and "represented dual types of centrist ideological tendencies that supported economic and social reform on behalf of the majority classes but rejected either right-wing conservatism or left-wing Marxism/Leninism" (Stone 1985:41). The moderate platforms supported by each party attracted broad support, minimizing ideological conflicts and contributing to an orderly transition to independence.

Jamaica's transition to becoming an independent democratic state was facilitated by several factors deriving from its colonial experience. However, it is important to note that the country's gradual evolution toward self-rule differed markedly not only from the experiences of its non–English speaking neighbors but also from those of Britain's possessions in other areas. As one scholar has noted:

> Unlike their counterparts in Britain's African and Asian colonies, the nationalist movements that emerged in the Commonwealth Caribbean during this time eschewed armed struggle and stuck to legal methods of bringing about change. Ruled directly by Britain under the Crown Colony system from the mid-Victorian period until decolonization, the Caribbean possessions never knew sustained and crude repression of the sort that Spain visited upon Cuba and Puerto Rico. As a result, violent anti-British sentiment never reached significant proportions in these countries. (Griffin 1993:88)

In addition, the duration and intensity of the colonial experience in the Commonwealth Caribbean set the region apart from other areas controlled by Britain. For example, "unlike in Africa and Asia, British rule in the Caribbean had been uninterrupted for centuries" (Domínguez et al. 1993:16). Consequently, the institutions and values imparted by Britain could become more firmly embedded in Jamaican society.

Most observers agree that Anglophone Caribbean states have benefited from the Westminster parliamentary system, firmly rooted by the time of independence. In contrast to the presidential system found in former Spanish colonies, the parliamentary system, coupled with a stable party system, enables governments to function more efficiently by virtue of their control over both the executive and legislative branches (Huber 1993).

A vibrant civil society developed during the colonial era also contributed to the solid institutional base upon which Jamaican democracy was established. In particular, the emergence of labor organizations, political parties, and other civic associations provided opportunities for political expression and some degree (albeit limited) of political participation. The ties between the major parties and their union affiliates were critical to both the transition to independent statehood and the consolidation of Jamaican democracy. At the time of independence in the Commonwealth Caribbean, the "party-union complex was firmly established in terms of electoral effectiveness and as one pillar of the democratic order" (Domínguez 1993:16–17).

A dynamic democratic political culture also took root in Jamaican society during the colonial era. According to one scholar,

> The record suggests that Anglophone Caribbean societies are *structurally* and *culturally* hospitable to democratic attitudes, institutions, and processes. These countries hold traditional values that reflect a distaste for excessive and arbitrary authority and a belief in individual autonomy. (Griffin 1993:89)

The broad acceptance of democratic values has bolstered democratic governments in Jamaica and throughout the Anglophone Caribbean. The movement toward self-rule, for example, was aided by the fact that with few exceptions "the leading political figures who contested power in the Commonwealth Caribbean at the time of independence possessed values that were more deeply rooted in liberal democratic politics than in any other ideology" (Payne 1993:60). At the same time, democracy was widely embraced by the masses, who demonstrated their support through their active participation in the electoral process.

Yet it is also true that certain aspects of the British colonial legacy inhibited Jamaica's pursuit of independence and democratic stability. Some contend that the decolonization process deprived Jamaicans of a true "revolutionary" experience and that independence amounted to "separation but not transformation." Formal independence created no abrupt alterations in a political culture defined by great continuity with the past, and the basic socioeconomic and political structures and traditions remained intact, with indigenous Jamaican elites replacing British colonial elites.

The legacy of elitism inherent in British colonial rule endured in the postindependence era, and "as a result, Jamaican politics acquired a markedly elitist character" (Grugel 1995:118). This was apparent within the political parties created by elites in order to integrate the masses into the existing framework of power (Edie 1991). In the absence of real ideological differences between them, support for the rival parties derived from emotional images of charismatic leaders (Bustamante and Norman Manley) who consolidated power through personalistic appeal and promises to provide material benefits in the form of jobs, housing, access to education and health care, and other kinds of social welfare. Thus, with power highly concentrated within a narrow leadership, the parties served (and continue to serve) as vehicles of elite dominance rather than as aggregators of mass interests.[4] In coopting the masses into a corporatist framework through such patron-client linkages, the party system channeled popular participation and served as a stabilizing agent during Jamaica's transitional period. However, even though this method of mobilizing mass support ensured maintenance of the status quo in the short term, its tenability has been challenged.

Jamaica's parliamentary system enjoyed a high degree of legitimacy from a broad cross-section of society in the immediate postindependence era. To a large extent this was due to a period of substantial economic growth spurred by favorable market conditions for Jamaican exports. Rising export revenues, coupled with increased investment and aid flows, helped to sustain the "statist bargain," enabling the government to provide material benefits and foster the perception that it was "delivering" (Domínguez et al. 1993; Huber 1993). As Trevor Munroe observed:

> The period of decolonization saw the consolidation of the system based on a version of party clientelism and state welfarism that improved the standard of living of the people and facilitated upward social mobility of the underclass. On this foundation, the postcolonial state, democracy, and constitutional government retained sufficient legitimacy among the people and performed effectively until the beginning of the 1970s. (Munroe 1996:104)

In fact, the system began to show signs of strain during the late 1960s. A series of disturbances broke out, including the 1968 Rodney riots (sparked by the deportation of a popular university professor). These outbursts reflected rising frustration and discontent among the Jamaican masses and served as the latest in a long tradition of violent uprisings against the deep-seated inequities inherent in Jamaican society. As was the case following the 1865 Morant Bay Rebellion and the 1938 labor disturbances, the unrest of the late 1960s ushered in a period of substantial change.

It is ironic that while the postwar economic boom in Jamaica provided the resources to mollify a broad range of society through the provision of patronage, it also created conditions that ultimately provoked instability. This economic expansion has been characterized as "growth without development," meaning that expansion was generated externally through foreign investment in tourism, bauxite and other mineral extraction, and light manufacturing (Payne and Sutton 1993:11). Most of the wealth produced was repatriated, with little reinvested in Jamaica, and the number of jobs created was far below that needed to reduce unemployment. Working-class Jamaicans, relatively speaking, benefited little from their country's economic success.

With the economic boom came rapid social changes: increased urbanization, greater access to media outlets and other forms of communication, heightened levels of social mobilization, and improvements in education and literacy. Over time the public demonstrated a greater degree of political awareness, and popular expectations and demands upon government increased. Unfortunately, this trend coincided with a period of economic decline in the late 1960s and early 1970s that undermined the government's ability to maintain the statist bargain and the extensive clientelistic linkages it relied upon for support. As the quality of life for Jamaica's masses deteriorated, they blamed the JLP government that had been in power since independence.

In 1972 the Jamaican electorate turned to the PNP and its new leader, Michael Manley (Norman's son), whose campaign featured slogans like "Power to the People" and "Better Must Come." Over the next eight years Manley pursued an agenda that asserted Jamaica's economic and political independence, sparking a sharp ideological division within Jamaican society and rancor in relations with the United States. The rift between the PNP, which aligned with the anti-imperialist rhetoric prevailing throughout the third world, and the more conservative JLP was indicative of the ideological polarization that typified the region over the next two decades.[5]

* * *

Franklin Knight asserts that the 1960s was "a major turning point" marking "the beginning of some fundamental restructuring of the politics and society of the Caribbean region. . . . Politically the Caribbean entered a period of intensified restlessness" (Knight 1993:29–30). This restlessness and restructuring were evident in Jamaica in the late 1960s and the 1970s. The disturbances fueled by the black power movement and deep socioeconomic inequalities were a portent of rioting that erupted elsewhere, including in Curaçao in 1969 and Trinidad in 1970. As discontent swelled, Manley and other Caribbean leaders explored common interests and forged links with other developing countries. This effort to diversify relations, coupled with the influx of alternative ideological currents, was viewed by the United States as a threat to regional stability and provoked a strong response.

■ Decades of Challenge and Change: The 1970s and 1980s

Reflecting the restlessness of the 1960s, the 1970s and early 1980s saw numerous instances of political restructuring and a host of regime changes. In the context of these regime changes, some states experienced a transition from colonial status to become independent liberal-democratic states (Antigua [1982], Belize [1981], Dominica [1978], St. Lucia [1979], and St. Vincent [1979]); in others liberal-democratic systems gave way to "leftist-socialist one-party states" (Grenada, Guyana, and Suriname); and one (the Dominican Republic) evolved from a conservative authoritarian system to establish an embryonic liberal democracy (Stone 1985).[6]

In other cases significant restructuring occurred. In Haiti, François "Papa Doc" Duvalier died in 1971, having ruled the country since 1957. He was succeeded by his then nineteen-year-old son, Jean-Claude "Baby Doc" Duvalier. Although the Duvalier dynasty endured under Jean-Claude's direction until 1986, his style of leadership and the nature of his regime differed from that of his father. His ties to the mulatto business community centered in Port-au-Prince contributed to the erosion of the regime's traditional base of support among the rural black peasantry. Its collapse in 1986 ushered in a period of violence and instability that underscored the dearth of viable political institutions in Haiti.

In Jamaica, Michael Manley's pursuit of "democratic socialism"—an alternative model of development independent of Western capitalism and Soviet communism—was a significant departure from his predecessors' policies. The decided shift to the left during the 1970s, in Jamaica and much of the region, reflected the influx of new ideological currents as well as Cuba's increasing influence. Analysis of these patterns reveals many challenges confronting governments across the Caribbean and provides insight into conditions under which democracies flourished—or foundered.

In contrast to other cases to be examined, Jamaica's shift to the left occurred within the framework of the country's parliamentary system, the result of a peaceful transfer of power. Manley and the PNP were not seeking to fundamentally restructure Jamaican society or its political system but rather to experiment with an alternative developmental model.

Jamaica's experience from 1972 to 1980 is illustrative of the considerable external constraints under which many Caribbean governments have had to operate. For example, the oil crises and the economic decline that beset the developed world severely hindered the ability of Manley and other leaders to sustain patron-client linkages. In addition, Manley's program of democratic socialism aroused U.S. concerns in light of his aggressive stance toward multinational corporations operating in Jamaica. In particular, a new tax (or levy) imposed on foreign-owned bauxite companies was viewed as a potentially dangerous precedent for other exporters of raw materials.

Manley's cordial relations with Cuba and his close ties to Fidel Castro also earned him the enmity of the United States. The concern was that this relationship served to further legitimize Castro at a time when Cuba's global stature was peaking. Some observers, as well as Manley himself (Hillman and D'Agostino 1992), maintain that U.S. opposition to Jamaica's socioeconomic and political agenda at this time led to a campaign aimed at isolating the PNP government and destabilizing the Jamaican economy. The bauxite levy engendered strong opposition from the companies as well as the U.S. government, including production cutbacks and transfers, lawsuits, and a media campaign designed to undermine the tourist industry (Edie 1991:95). Plagued by significant international and domestic constraints, the Jamaican economy deteriorated in the late 1970s, hindering Manley's ability to deliver for his constituents. In an election marred by unprecedented political violence (some 800 people were killed during the campaign), Edward Seaga and the JLP soundly defeated Manley and the PNP in 1980. This marked the end of democratic socialism in Jamaica and was part of a wave of electoral victories between 1979 to 1982 by conservative candidates in Barbados, Dominica, and St. Lucia.

The situations in British Guiana/Guyana, Grenada, and Suriname differed sharply from that in Jamaica, where the shift to the left occurred within the existing liberal-democratic political framework. In these cases, the emergence of leftist-socialist regimes with close ties to Cuba resulted from the collapse of liberal-democratic systems inherited from the colonial era.

In Suriname, allegations of corruption, unfulfilled promises of political and socioeconomic reform, and widespread discontent within the military undermined support for the government of Henck Arron that had come into power at the time of independence in 1975. Arron was ousted in a coup d'état on February 25, 1980, and by early 1981 Suriname had embarked on a revolutionary socialist course under the leadership of Desi Bouterse.

The erosion of democratic institutions and values in Guyana and Grenada illustrated the fragile nature of liberal democracy in the face of endemic corruption, severe repression, and elite-dominated exclusionary political systems. It also underscored the fact that Westminster-type parliamentary democracy—a remnant of British rule adapted to the realities of the Caribbean—has not always functioned as envisioned in the region. The electoral victories by Cheddi Jagan, an avowed Marxist, in British Guiana in 1953, 1957, and 1961 sparked concern in both London and Washington of the potential for expanded Soviet influence in the region. In 1953, with Jagan in office only five months, the constitution was suspended, and Jagan and the People's Progressive Party (PPP) were removed from power. Britain's decision in the aftermath of the 1961 contest to introduce a new type of electoral system (proportional representation, replacing the traditional first-past-the-post system used throughout the Anglo-Caribbean) enabled Jagan's former associate, Forbes Burnham, to win the 1964 election and to lead British Guiana into independence.

Burnham unleashed a campaign of repression against Jagan's PPP in advance of the 1968 election, which his People's National Congress (PNC) won amid allegations of massive fraud. Initially viewed as a social-democratic alternative to Jagan, Burnham himself disavowed the capitalist economic model and declared Guyana to be a socialist cooperative republic in 1970. By the mid-1970s more than three-quarters of the national economy was under state control as Guyana evolved into a militarized single-party state. Racial and ethnic conflicts escalated as the Afro-Guyanese-based PNC, which retained power through blatantly fraudulent elections, dominated at the expense of the PPP, whose strength was centered in the majority East Indian community. Burnham's power was further augmented with a new presidential-style constitution introduced in 1980, although the onset of a severe economic crisis and mounting tensions with Ronald Reagan's administration plagued his regime until Burnham's death in 1985.

As in Guyana, Grenada's Westminster-type system was undermined by rampant corruption, extensive state-sponsored repression, economic decline, as well as the extreme centralization of power and concomitant exclusion of the masses from the political process. However, Grenada merits special attention given the extraordinary international context in which its revolution occurred. In July 1979 in Nicaragua, just months after the ouster of Grenada's longtime leader Sir Eric Gairy, the Sandinista National Liberation Front (FSLN) toppled the regime of Anastasio Somoza Debayle. Later that year in December, the Soviet Union invaded Afghanistan. Coupled with the 1980 election of U.S. President Ronald Reagan, these events sparked a resurgence of Cold War tensions with major implications for the nations of the Caribbean. Indeed, the perceived threat posed by the revolutionary turmoil resulted in a new era of U.S. interventionism.

■ The Case of Grenada

The March 1979 coup that toppled Gairy marked the first time that a leader in the Anglo-Caribbean had been removed from power by force. Gairy first emerged in 1951, establishing a labor union (the Grenada Manual and Mental Workers Union) and, later, a political party (the Grenada United Labour Party) that enabled him to take power with the support of the newly enfranchised masses. With the exception of 1962–1967, Gairy ruled Grenada for nearly three decades, during which time the political system deviated from the traditional British parliamentary model and increasingly centered on his individual leadership. Often known simply as Gairyism, this was a system of authoritarian rule in which political power was highly personalized, extensive patron-client linkages assured the regime of mass support, and coercion and intimidation were regularly employed to quell opposition. According to one scholar:

> The trajectory of a matter-of-fact, routine liberal parliamentary democracy which brings in the masses as voters, producers of wealth, and consumers of colonial hegemony while leaving real political, social, and cultural power in the hands, pockets, and institutions of a minority elite—the Gairy Revolution and administration derailed that. Gairyism was its replacement—that synthetic, contradictory mix of part popular empowerment and part open dictatorship, with the personal and political figure of Gairy—not English rule—as the icon of ideology and politics. (Williams 1970:100)

By the early 1970s, amid a deepening economic crisis in which unemployment reached a staggering 44.6 percent and underemployment was estimated at nearly 75 percent, opposition to Gairy escalated. Popular disillusionment over the regime's assaults on civil liberties and democratic institutions, rendered all but meaningless, also undermined Gairy's support. After opponents of the regime, including the New Jewel Movement (NJM; formed in 1973), carried out a series of strikes and demonstrations aimed at forcing Gairy from office, they faced even greater levels of repression carried out by the notorious Green Beasts (a paramilitary group) and Mongoose Gang (Gairy's secret police). With the NJM asserting itself as the leading opposition, the regime fell in March 1979, paving the way for the emergence of the People's Revolutionary Government (PRG)—the second successful socialist revolution in the hemisphere.

The PRG inherited leadership of a country beset by a host of socioeconomic and political problems. Long-standing democratic institutions had been seriously debilitated, subordinated to the highly centralized personal power wielded by Gairy. The inequitable distribution of wealth, pervasive unemployment and underemployment, inadequate infrastructure, and foreign domination of key sectors of the economy posed daunting challenges to the new government (Smith 1993). The PRG attributed these conditions to the legacies of Gairyism and British colonial domination, as well as to neocolonialism. In rejecting the Westminster model and Grenada's links to Western capitalism, the PRG pursued an alternative form of political organization and socioeconomic development that sparked tensions with neighbors as well as with the United States.

If Gairy contributed to the degradation of the Westminster-type representative democracy in place in Grenada, the PRG and its leader, Prime Minister Maurice Bishop, were determined to eliminate it altogether. They viewed this system, considered by many to be central to the maintenance of relative stability throughout the Anglo-Caribbean, as elite-dominated and nonrepresentative. Their objective was to replace the system they derisively referred to as "two-second democracy" (for the amount of time they claimed a citizen would actually participate in the system every five years, i.e., by voting) with a system of community-based "participatory democracy." This new structure was intended to foster grass-roots organization and the integration of the masses into the political process.

Seeking to facilitate the transition to socialism and to address mounting economic problems, the PRG adopted the Soviet Union's model of noncapitalist development. A program of socioeconomic restructuring was initiated in which the state was to play a dominant role in a mixed economy. Seeking to boost productivity and enhance the quality of life among Grenada's masses, a variety of agrarian reform initiatives and physical and social infrastructure projects were undertaken. To reduce the country's external dependence, the government sought to diversify its international relations to include other developing and socialist states. Tourism was the key to the PRG's program of economic restructuring, appearing to offer the best opportunity for short-term growth that would generate the revenue needed to invest in both the agricultural and manufacturing sectors. Ironically, the focal point of the PRG's policy to bolster the tourist sector—the construction of the international airport at Point Salines—was to be cited by the United States as one of the primary factors leading to the U.S. invasion of October 1983.

The economic performance of the PRG was decidedly mixed (Smith 1993). Overall growth rates from 1979 to 1982 were positive, enabling the government to deliver substantial improvements in the so-called *social wage*—a PRG term referring to benefits in areas like education, health care, housing, and transportation. However, this image was misleading, for it did not reflect the serious sectoral imbalance in the economy. Most of this growth was the result of government-funded construction aimed at infrastructure development, whereas state and cooperative sectors lagged. Expectations for growth in tourism were dashed as arrivals and receipts declined precipitously, particularly from the United States, given the PRG's pro-Soviet rhetoric. Dwindling private-sector investment weakened the manufacturing sector as well. These trends, exacerbated by the dearth of external funding, hindered the PRG's ability to reduce unemployment and deliver benefits. Thus, even though some socioeconomic gains occurred, they were tempered by the regime's inability to sustain growth. Ultimately, to forestall the deepening economic crisis, the PRG entered into an agreement with the International Monetary Fund (IMF) in August 1983. Such a step was inherently at odds with the PRG's agenda and did much to erode regime support.

Although the deteriorating economic conditions were problematic, the PRG's efforts at political restructuring were even more damaging. Its attempt to establish a more participatory system did stimulate the development of a number of mass-based organizations, albeit under the direction of NJM officials. The extent to which this integrated the masses into the political process in a meaningful way was limited, as "there was little real popular involvement in policy making and implementation" (Thorndike 1993:163). This failure to open the system and broaden participation, coupled with frustration with the lack of elections and limitations on basic civil liberties, further undermined popular perceptions of the PRG. Bitter infighting within the PRG, pitting Bishop against the more militant Bernard Coard, did little to enhance its public image.

Although a variety of factors contributed to the revolution's demise, the principal cause of its collapse was the imposition of Marxism-Leninism in a context ill-suited for it. "The Grenadian revolutionary experiment, in both theoretical and practical terms, was far removed from the values that informed the traditional Eastern Caribbean model" (Thorndike 1993:158). The 1979 coup and formation of a one-party militarized state were an aberration in the eastern Caribbean, an area in which democracy is deeply rooted and a culture of constitutionalism pervades. Given the centrality of competitive elections and peaceful transfers of power, the events of October 1983 proved particularly unsettling for regional observers. More ominously, the coup in which Bishop was arrested and executed—with power shifting to a Revolutionary Military Council led by General Hudson Austin—provided a pretext for the U.S.-led invasion (Operation Urgent Fury) that toppled the regime and marked a renewed era of U.S. intervention.

■ The Resurgence of U.S. Interventionism

U.S. policy in the Caribbean Basin during the 1980s differed markedly from the approach employed by President Jimmy Carter (1977–1981). The

Carter administration's role in pressuring the military in the Dominican Republic to respect the results of the country's 1978 election, along with its agreement to transfer control of the Panama Canal to the government of Panama, engendered positive relations with Latin American and Caribbean countries. However, the Soviet invasion of Afghanistan, the revolutions in Grenada and Nicaragua (and turmoil elsewhere in Central America), and the election of Ronald Reagan in 1980 sparked a resurgence in Cold War hostilities that exacerbated tensions within increasingly polarized societies. Coupled with the devastating economic crisis that engulfed the region, this trend ensured that the 1980s would be volatile. Events during this period illustrated the extent to which politics in the Caribbean continues to be shaped by the power of external actors and by changes in international geopolitics.

This was clearly illustrated by the 1983 invasion of Grenada as well as the Reagan administration's actions in Central America, included within its definition of the Caribbean Basin. In Nicaragua, the 1979 revolt brought an end to a U.S.-backed dynasty that dated back to the mid-1930s. Although the United States initially sought amicable ties with the revolutionary coalition led by the Sandinista National Liberation Front, relations deteriorated, and by 1981 the Reagan administration had initiated a campaign to destabilize what it saw as a Marxist-Leninist ally of Cuba and the Soviet Union. The U.S. policy of economic sanctions and support for anti-Sandinista counterrevolutionary forces (the contras) exacted a considerable toll on the regime. The physical and economic devastation caused by the sanctions and the contra war, which threatened to engulf Honduras and Costa Rica (the longest-standing democracy in Central America), prevented the Sandinista government from delivering on its pledge to improve the standard of living, undermining its popular support. Thus, even though U.S. policy never brought about military victory over the Sandinistas, it contributed to their electoral defeat in 1990 and the demise of their revolution.

In El Salvador, the Reagan administration continued its quest to confront communist aggression. Massive economic and military assistance, totaling nearly U.S.$2 billion from 1981 to 1986, was provided to a succession of military-backed governments threatened by an insurgency led by the Farabundo Martí Front for National Liberation. U.S. involvement dramatically escalated the conflict and prolonged a civil war that dragged on for more than a decade, with neither side able to gain a decisive victory. Aside from the billions of dollars in damage and lost productivity caused by the conflict, some 75,000 lives were lost, mainly civilians. Among them was Oscar Romero, the popular archbishop of San Salvador who was assassinated while saying mass in March 1980.

In the insular Caribbean, Reagan's first term (1981–1985) coincided with an ideological shift to the right. Electoral victories by conservative parties brought to power Edward Seaga in Jamaica, Tom Adams in Barbados, Eugenia Charles in Dominica, and John Compton in St. Lucia. In addition, the first postinvasion election in Grenada was won by the New National Party, a coalition of parties led by Herbert Blaize. These leaders cultivated close ties with the United States, campaigning on the basis that their ideological affinity with the Reagan administration would bring a foreign aid and investment windfall. This struck a chord of resonance among electorates weary of economic stagnation and seeking amelioration of endemic socioeconomic problems.

Great optimism accompanied the emergence of these leaders and the regional economic development program proposed by the United States, yet the 1980s proved to be a trying period for the Caribbean. The Reagan administration's eagerly awaited Caribbean Basin Initiative (CBI), originally conceived by Adams and Seaga as a mini–Marshall Plan, could not stem the economic crisis that gripped the region. This "lost decade," as the 1980s became known, was characterized by skyrocketing inflation, rising unemployment and external debt, and deteriorating living conditions. With limited resources and heightened demands, the challenges confronting governments across the Caribbean were daunting, and many fell victim to their inability to fulfill expectations. This is perhaps best illustrated by events in Jamaica and the Dominican Republic during the mid-1980s.

It is ironic that Jamaica, which under Seaga was considered by the Reagan administration as the centerpiece of the CBI, would experience the level of economic strife that it did. As a proponent of the neoliberal free-market economic policies favored by international lending agencies, Seaga quickly endeared himself to Reagan. However, despite a substantial infusion of assistance from the United States, the economic performance of the Seaga government was disappointing at best. What went wrong?

An analysis of this case reveals the structural constraints under which Caribbean leaders must operate. Seaga worked closely with the IMF, implementing the prescribed structural adjustment measures in return for a series of loan packages. Jamaica's economic recovery, however, was derailed by a confluence of factors. The global economic slowdown of the 1980s proved especially problematic, limiting foreign investment and shrinking markets for traditional exports such as bauxite. Domestic political reaction to the imposition of austerity measures, including currency devaluations, tax increases, and public-sector layoffs, was oftentimes swift and furious, as illustrated by rioting that broke out in January 1985. Seaga, therefore, had to contend with the conflicting demands of dual constituencies, one external and one internal, neither of which he was able to satisfy. His government repeatedly failed to meet benchmarks set forth in its agreements with the IMF, and the leverage he enjoyed through his once cordial ties with the United States diminished over time. So, too, did his and his party's stature with the Jamaican electorate, culminating in the JLP's defeat in 1989 and the return to power of Michael Manley.

The experience in the Dominican Republic during this period closely parallels that of Jamaica. In the historic 1978 election, the opposition PRD and

Richard S. Hillman

Political street rally for Joaquín Balaguer during his reelection campaign in 1990, Santo Domingo, Dominican Republic

its candidate, Antonio Guzmán, defeated three-term incumbent Joaquín Balaguer. Guzmán's death shortly before the end of his term led the party to nominate Salvador Jorge Blanco to be its candidate in 1982. Widely viewed as a reformist, Jorge Blanco's pledge to raise the standard of living and respect human rights and civil liberties helped him to defeat Balaguer. Soon after taking office, however, Jorge Blanco negotiated with the IMF for an emergency loan that was conditioned on the imposition of an austerity program. The announcement of a currency devaluation in April 1984 dramatically increased the cost of many basic items and sparked rioting that was brutally suppressed. By 1986 the PRD was deeply divided and badly discredited in the eyes of its traditional popular constituency, which had expected reform but was rewarded with austerity.

Both of the cases reveal the lack of real autonomy for Caribbean political leaders who, despite domestic political considerations, are compelled to follow strict policy guidelines in order to qualify for desperately needed funds. With little choice but to accept the loan conditions, Seaga and Jorge Blanco carried out austerity programs and suffered the political consequences. This also points to the extent to which the leaders of Caribbean countries located within the U.S. sphere of influence are subjected to external pressures. With respect to Jamaica,

> this gives substantial power over the Jamaican political directorate to a range of external forces, from U.S. political leadership in the White House and various U.S. departments of state, to the officials of the IMF, the World Bank, and other U.S.-dominated international financial agencies, to the managers of major multinational corporations with investments and interests in Jamaica. (Payne 1993:51)

The fact that Seaga's JLP and Jorge Blanco's PRD were defeated at the polls following IMF-related riots reveals the depth of popular outrage with these programs as well as with governments that impose them. However, in both cases power was transferred peacefully to the opposition through competitive elections (Manley and the PNP in Jamaica, and Balaguer and his Social Christian Reformist Party in the Dominican Republic), a testament to the level of democratic institutionalization attained in each society. The stability that characterized these transitions, however, stands in stark contrast to the experience of Haiti during the late 1980s and 1990s. A dearth of viable institutions, extreme inequalities, a deeply entrenched elite, and a praetorian military have frustrated efforts to introduce democratic reforms following the collapse of the Duvalier regime in 1986.

■ The Case of Haiti

Under French rule Haiti became one of the most valuable colonial possessions in the world. Nearly two centuries after acquiring independence, it is now widely regarded as the most impoverished country in the Western Hemisphere.

The massive importation of slave labor required for Haiti's sugar plantation economy engendered profound social and racial divisions that persist to the present day. The slave uprising that began in 1789 culminating in independence in 1804 left the country in economic ruin. In addition, the removal of colonial authority left the country without viable political institutions, a void filled by a succession of personalistic authoritarian military leaders.

As a result of postindependence economic decline, Haiti fell deeply into debt. Coupled with escalating political strife, this prompted the U.S. intervention and occupation from 1915 to 1934. The U.S. failure to foster the development of democratic institutions paved the way for the election of François Duvalier in 1957. Papa Doc employed Vodou, *noirisme* (a political ideology aimed at empowering the black majority), and the repressive Tonton Macoutes (a private security force) to consolidate power, appealing primarily to the rural masses. He declared himself president for life in 1964, transferring power prior to his death in 1971 to his son, Jean-Claude.

Baby Doc's policies, particularly his close ties with the mulatto elite in Port-au-Prince, alienated many traditional supporters of Duvalierism. Economic decline in the rural areas and the mobilization of church opposition, particularly following the 1983 visit of Pope John Paul II, further undermined the regime. The withdrawal of long-standing U.S. support hastened the collapse of the dictatorship, and Baby Doc Duvalier fled into exile after pilfering the national treasury in February 1986.

Several aborted attempts at democratic transitions preceded the 1990 election of Jean-Bertrand Aristide. Enormously popular among Haiti's poor majority and perceived as threatening by elites and the military, Aristide was overthrown less than a year into his term. Following the coup, security forces and paramilitary groups killed an estimated 3,000 supporters of Aristide's Lavalas movement, and thousands more fled to the United States. Protracted negotiations, an international embargo against the Haitian military government led by Raoul Cedras, and the threat of U.S. military action succeeded in returning Aristide to power in October 1994. This marked the first time that the United States had intervened in order to restore a democratically elected Caribbean leader (Stotzky 1997).

Aristide's return and the subsequent peaceful transfer of power to his ally and successor, Rene Preval—the first such transfer between democratically elected leaders in Haiti's history—were positive steps in the promotion of democracy. However, significant obstacles remained. Although Preval's victory in the 1995 election (he officially took office in 1996), coupled with Lavalas's sweep of legislative contests, seemed to bode well, a dispute erupted within the movement that led Aristide and his supporters to break and establish a rival organization, Fanmi Lavalas (FL). Senate and local elections

Sean Newell

Thomas J. D'Agostino and Haitian President Jean-Bertrand Aristide held in 1997, marred by allegations of fraud and extremely low voter turnout, were followed by a period of gridlock; the split had fueled partisan rancor and brought the legislative and executive branches into conflict and the government to a standstill.

This gridlock prevented the organization of local and legislative elections scheduled for late 1998. With members' terms having technically expired in the absence of these elections, virtually the entire legislature—all members of the Chamber of Deputies and two-thirds of the Senate—were dismissed, enabling the president and prime minister to rule by degree. After further delays, elections were finally held on May 21, 2000. Despite a strong turnout (more than 60 percent) and a broad range of candidates, the electoral process was seriously compromised by the manipulation of results to benefit the governing coalition and the poor performance of the Provisional Electoral Council charged with overseeing the contest. Opposition groups coalesced to protest and to pressure the government to call for new elections. International efforts to resolve the crisis, led by the Organization of American States and the Caribbean Common Market and Community (or CARICOM—a Caribbean economic community), were unsuccessful, prompting all major opposition groups to boycott the subsequent presidential and Senate elections held on November 26, 2000. Aristide returned to power, winning nearly 92 percent of the vote, and his FL party swept the Senate contests. Since that time tensions between the government and opposition have remained high, and sporadic political violence has flared despite ongoing international mediation efforts.

Haiti's turbulent past, lack of experience with participatory institutions, debilitated economy, and polarized citizenry have combined to produce a political culture that provides very little foundation for democracy. Although many aspects of these problems are specific to Haiti, the country also faces a host of challenges typical of other countries within the region.

■ An Era of Uncertainty: The 1990s and 2000s

Given its past, Haiti's struggles with its first real experience with democratic governance might have been anticipated. However, the problems afflicting some of the region's well-established democracies in the late 1980s and 1990s came as a surprise to many and served as a portent of the adversities that have come to confront governments across the region. In Trinidad and Tobago, a coup attempt was launched by a Muslim extremist group, the Jamaat al Muslimeen, in July 1990. Although the group surrendered after holding the prime minister and most of the cabinet hostage for almost a week, their demand that the government address the economic burden stemming from IMF austerity measures reflected popular frustration with inequities and deteriorating living standards.

In Venezuela—one of the most advanced democracies in the Americas—the imposition of an IMF austerity program sparked massive riots in 1989. Despite the country's relative prosperity, the lower classes were largely excluded from the rapid economic growth of the 1970s. Deepening inequalities, an elite-dominated exclusionary political system, and allegations of massive corruption heightened opposition to the government of Carlos Andres Pérez and prompted two coup attempts in 1992. These attempts dealt a serious blow to Venezuela's democratic system, as did the eventual removal and impeachment of Pérez. Ironically, the leader of the first coup attempt, Hugo Chávez, a former military officer who was imprisoned after the attempt, went on to win the presidency in 1998. His success and the subsequent dismantling of the institutional structures that had been in place since 1958 underscored the depth of the discontent with a system that was viewed as serving only the interests of the privileged (Hillman 1994). However, Chávez's attempts to promote a "social revolution" alienated the middle and upper classes, who recently have supported protests and work-stoppages designed to leverage an early election. Consequently, Venezuela has been paralyzed since December 2002 and the crisis continues as of late January 2003. César Gaviria, secretary general of the Organization of American States, and former U.S. President Jimmy Carter have been unsuccessful in their attempts to mediate. A nonbinding referendum on Chávez's presidency is scheduled for February 2, 2003.

The health of democratic political systems across the Caribbean increasingly has been called into question. The defeat of numerous incumbent governments points to the seemingly insurmountable challenges confronting Caribbean leaders. In a region where voter participation rates traditionally have been extremely high (particularly in the Anglo-Caribbean), sharp declines since the early 1990s reflect mounting alienation and frustration, especially among Caribbean youths (Munroe 1996). Potentially more devastating are declining rates of political party identification and loyalty. The demise of some of the region's most noteworthy political parties, especially in Venezuela, raises serious questions given the critical role that parties play in the consolidation of democratic regimes (Huber 1993; Mainwaring and Scully 1995).[7]

The Caribbean, especially the Anglo-Caribbean, has been widely recognized as the most democratic and stable of all the developing areas. Given that Caribbean political systems are subjected to many of the same adversities confronting these other areas, what accounts for the region's distinctive record in promoting democracy? Most important, what do the trends outlined above mean for the democratic systems prevailing throughout the Caribbean today?

With respect to the former British colonies, many observers point to the nature and duration of colonial rule as key to the region's success. The introduction of the Westminster-type parliamentary system provided the necessary framework within which Caribbean democracies could flourish, and the liberal political culture that would sustain this system became deeply rooted in West Indian societies. The long, gradual process of decolonization in the

Anglo-Caribbean differed markedly from the experiences of British colonies in Africa and Asia, providing the opportunity for institutional development, nation-building, and "tutelage" in the ways of democratic governance.

Among the other pillars upon which Caribbean democracy has rested is the institutional infrastructure that has been established. The emergence of strong political party systems, regular competitive elections, and vibrant civil societies including labor unions, professional associations, and the like has done much to bolster the cause of democracy in the Caribbean. Although the level of institutionalization in the Anglo-Caribbean has been greater than that in some other parts of the region, particularly the former Spanish colonies in Central America (excluding Costa Rica) and Hispaniola, significant progress has been achieved in a number of countries.

To a large extent, the legitimacy of democratic institutions and governments in the Caribbean has derived from their ability to deliver material benefits to the people. Thus, perhaps the most important pillar on which Caribbean democracy has been based has been the statist bargain:

> Caribbean states invested the income derived from favorable international circumstances (high prices for commodities, new investments in tourism and other sectors, and foreign aid) to improve the standard of living for many Caribbean citizens. The Caribbean state was the midwife; economic growth gave birth to social welfare. Because this practice continued in the 1960s even after independence in the larger countries of the Anglophone Caribbean and in the 1970s in the Dominican Republic . . . as it democratized gradually, the allegiance of citizens to democratic states was enhanced: Democracies delivered material gain. (Domínguez 1993:12)

State-sponsored patron-clientelism, then, contributed significantly to the legitimization of emerging democracies across the region. As Caribbean citizens gained access to an array of social services, including improved education and health care, they increasingly viewed political parties (as the primary dispensers of patronage) and democratic governments as worthy of their loyalty and electoral support.

More recently, however, economic decline has undermined the statist bargain. As the fiscal resources needed to sustain patron-client linkages have diminished, the foundation of Caribbean democracy has eroded.

Ironically, the Caribbean has suffered from a *lack* of U.S. interest in recent years. With the end of the Cold War, U.S. security and economic interests have been focused on other areas, including the former Soviet Union and Eastern Europe, China, and the Middle East. The terrorist attacks of September 11, 2001, on New York and the Pentagon also caused the United States to direct huge amounts of political and financial resources toward the war on terrorism. As a result, there has been a significant reduction in U.S. aid and investment to the Caribbean. At the same time, commodity prices for many traditional Caribbean exports have stagnated or, in some cases, declined.

While the tourist sector has remained strong, foreign exchange revenues have struggled to keep pace with spending in many countries.

The adoption of neoliberal economic policies has limited the ability of Caribbean governments to fund social welfare programs and thereby maintain the statist bargain. This has had a deleterious impact on the quality of life for millions across the region, a problematic trend given the heightened expectations held by increasingly mobilized populations. The failure to fulfill such expectations has undermined the public's faith in political parties, popularly elected leaders, and democratic politics in general.

This loss of confidence has been exacerbated by popular perceptions that the institutions of democracy have failed to represent the interests of the masses, as evidenced by the tendency for the burden of structural adjustment to fall squarely on their shoulders. The traditional pattern of elite domination of parties, with mass participation effectively limited to providing electoral support, is no longer tenable. The prospects for long-term stability within the Caribbean will remain tenuous at best until democracy is deepened and the masses are integrated into the democratic process in meaningful ways.

Despite their divergent origins and structures, political systems throughout the Caribbean have much in common. All have been influenced by the legacies of colonialism—slavery, economic exploitation and dependence, external domination, and elite-dominated exclusionary rule. The evolution of these systems has been conditioned by external forces, in many cases the United States being the most obvious. Caribbean leaders are confronted by a host of common problems, including deteriorating living standards; pervasive frustration and alienation; corruption and violence stemming, in large part, from the illicit narcotics traffic; and the inherent constraints imposed upon small, resource-scarce states in the global economy. These political systems function in similar ways in seeking to address these issues. Unfortunately, they have demonstrated a common inability to find long-term solutions to the endemic problems within the region.

■ Notes

1. "It is almost a truism that emancipation did not transform the nature of Caribbean societies, nor the fundamental pattern of race relations, nor the way power was held and exercised, nor even the values and attitudes that had most prestige" (Brereton 1989:85).

2. "Similar institutional inheritances collapsed quickly enough in other ex-British colonies, notably in Africa" (Payne 1993:59); this underscores the point that a variety of other factors also contributed to the region's record of democratic success.

3. For the best account of this event, see Stephen Schlesinger and Stephen Kinzer, *Bitter Fruit: The Untold Story of the American Coup in Guatemala* (Garden City, NY: Doubleday, 1982).

4. According to one scholar:

> There is a deep gulf which separates the political elite, composed of important members of both parties and their allies in the trade unions, business and the administration, and the mass of Jamaican citizens. Politics 'at the top' has very little relevance to the needs and concerns of the ordinary Jamaican citizen, with the parties functioning to ensure votes and to promote party identification but without creating channels for the incorporation into the political agenda of demands from the party bases. The parties operate from the top downwards. (Grugel 1995:118)

And here a comment on the role of political parties throughout the Commonwealth Caribbean: They "have generally been conceived . . . as tools for mobilizing the vote and winning elections. They have not been built up as mass organizations in the sense of constituting vehicles by which ordinary members can enter the policymaking process" (Payne 1993:71).

5. According to one scholar:

> Between the Black Power revolt in Trinidad in 1970 and the implosion of the Grenada revolution in 1983, significant social sectors in the region turned toward radical Left alternatives within and outside the framework of liberal democracy and market-driven economies. The successive administrations headed by Michael Manley in Jamaica (1972–80), the People's Revolutionary government in Grenada (1979–83), and the Forbes Burnham government in Guyana represented the highest development (and also the deformation) of these tendencies in the Commonwealth Caribbean. This turn to the Left was influenced by the reality as well as the perception that the democratic governance and state interventionist market economies of the 1960s in the region had deepened, rather than reduced, economic and social inequalities. (Munroe 1996:104)

6. According to the broad definition of *circum-Caribbean* employed in this book, Nicaragua should be recognized as having experienced a regime change. In 1979 the FSLN ousted the dictator Anastasio Somoza Debayle, marking a shift from a conservative authoritarian regime to a leftist-socialist one-party state.

7. In his introduction to *Democracy in the Caribbean: Political, Economic, and Social Perspectives*, Jorge Domínguez (1993) writes: "Can democratic regimes survive if the partisan institutions that have been at the heart of politics can no longer provide organized political support and opposition?"

■ Bibliography

Brereton, Bridget. "Society and Culture in the Caribbean: The British and French West Indies, 1870–1980." In *The Modern Caribbean*, edited by Franklin Knight and Colin Palmer, pp. 85–110. Chapel Hill: University of North Carolina Press, 1989.

Domínguez, Jorge I. "The Caribbean Question: Why Has Liberal Democracy (Surprisingly) Flourished?" In *Democracy in the Caribbean: Political, Economic, and Social Perspectives*, edited by Jorge I. Dominguez, Robert A. Pastor, and R. DeLisle Worrell, pp. 1–25. Baltimore: Johns Hopkins University Press, 1993.

Domínguez, Jorge I., and Abraham Lowenthal. *Constructing Democratic Governance: Latin America and the Caribbean in the 1990s—Themes and Issues*. Baltimore: Johns Hopkins University Press, 1996.

Domínguez, Jorge I., Robert A. Pastor, and R. DeLisle Worrell. *Democracy in the Caribbean: Political, Economic, and Social Perspectives*. Baltimore: Johns Hopkins University Press, 1993.

Edie, Carlene. *Democracy by Default: Dependency and Clientelism in Jamaica*. Boulder: Lynne Rienner Publishers, 1991.

———. *Democracy in the Caribbean: Myths and Realities*. Westport, CT: Praeger Publishers, 1994.

Gamaliel Ramos, Aarón, and Angel Israel Rivera. *Islands at the Crossroads: Politics in the Non-Independent Caribbean*. Boulder: Lynne Rienner Publishers, 2001.

Gautier-Mayoral, Carmen. "Puerto Rico: Problems of Democracy and Decolonization in the Late Twentieth Century." In *Democracy in the Caribbean: Myths and Realities*, edited by Carlene Edie, pp. 163–179. Westport, CT: Praeger Publishers, 1994.

Griffin, Clifford E. "Democracy in the Commonwealth Caribbean." *Journal of Democracy* 4, no. 2 (April 1993): 84–94.

Grugel, Jean. *Politics and Development in the Caribbean Basin*. Bloomington: Indiana University Press, 1995.

Hartlyn, Jonathan. *The Struggle for Democratic Politics in the Dominican Republic*. Chapel Hill: University of North Carolina Press, 1998.

Hillman, Richard S. *Democracy for the Privileged: Crisis and Transition in Venezuela*. Boulder: Lynne Rienner Publishers, 1994.

Hillman, Richard, and Thomas J. D'Agostino. *Distant Neighbors in the Caribbean: The Dominican Republic and Jamaica in Comparative Perspective*. New York: Praeger Publishers, 1992.

Huber, Evelyne. "The Future of Democracy in the Caribbean." In *Democracy in the Caribbean: Political, Economic, and Social Perspectives*, edited by Jorge I. Domínguez, Robert A. Pastor, and R. DeLisle Worrell, pp. 74–95. Baltimore: Johns Hopkins University Press, 1993.

Knight, Franklin. *The Caribbean: The Genesis of a Fragmented Nationalism*. 2nd ed. New York: Oxford University Press, 1990.

———. "The Societies of the Caribbean Since Independence." In *Democracy in the Caribbean: Political, Economic, and Social Perspectives*, edited by Jorge I. Domínguez, Robert A. Pastor, and R. DeLisle Worrell, pp. 29–41. Baltimore: Johns Hopkins University Press, 1993.

Knight, Franklin, and Colin Palmer. *The Modern Caribbean*. Chapel Hill: University of North Carolina Press, 1989.

Lewis, Gordon. "The Contemporary Caribbean: A General Overview." In *Caribbean Contours*, edited by Sidney W. Mintz and Sally Price, pp. 219–250. Baltimore: Johns Hopkins University Press, 1985.

Maingot, Anthony. *The United States and the Caribbean*. Boulder: Westview, 1994.

Mainwaring, Scott, and Timothy R. Scully. *Building Democratic Institutions: Party Systems in Latin America*. Stanford: Stanford University Press, 1995.

Mintz, Sidney W., and Sally Price. *Caribbean Contours*. Baltimore: Johns Hopkins University Press, 1985.

Molineau, Harold. *U.S. Policy Toward Latin America*. Boulder: Westview, 1990.

Munroe, Trevor. "Caribbean Democracy: Decay or Renewel?" In *Constructing Democratic Governance: Latin America and the Caribbean in the 1990s—Themes and Issues*, edited by Jorge I. Domínguez and Abraham Lowenthal, pp. 104–117. Baltimore: Johns Hopkins University Press, 1996.

Payne, Anthony. "Westminster Adapted: The Political Order of the Commonwealth Caribbean." In *Democracy in the Caribbean: Political, Economic, and Social Perspectives*, edited by Jorge I. Domínguez, Robert A. Pastor, and R. DeLisle Worrell, pp. 57–73. Baltimore: Johns Hopkins University Press, 1993.

Payne, Anthony, and Paul Sutton. *Modern Caribbean Politics*. Baltimore: Johns Hopkins University Press, 1993.

Peeler, John. *Building Democracy in Latin America*. Boulder: Lynne Rienner Publishers, 1998.

Richardson, Bonham C. *The Caribbean in the Wider World, 1492–1992: A Regional Geography*. Cambridge, UK: Cambridge University Press, 1992.

Ryan, Selwyn. "Problems and Prospects for the Survival of Liberal Democracy in the Anglophone Caribbean." In *Democracy in the Caribbean: Myths and Realities*, edited by Carlene Edie, pp. 233–250. Westport, CT: Praeger Publishers, 1994.

Silvestrini, Blanca G. "Contemporary Puerto Rico: A Society of Contrasts." In *The Modern Caribbean*, edited by Franklin Knight and Colin Palmer, pp. 147–167. Chapel Hill: University of North Carolina Press, 1989.

Smith, Courtney. "The Grenadian Revolution in Retrospect." In *Modern Caribbean Politics*, edited by Anthony Payne and Paul Sutton, pp. 176–197. Baltimore: Johns Hopkins University Press, 1993.

Stone, Carl. "A Political Profile of the Caribbean." In *Caribbean Contours*, edited by Sidney W. Mintz and Sally Price, pp. 13–54. Baltimore: Johns Hopkins University Press, 1985.

Stotzky, Irwin. *Silencing the Guns in Haiti: The Promise of Deliberative Democracy*. Chicago: University of Chicago Press, 1997.

Thorndike, Tony. "Revolution, Democracy, and Regional Integration in the Eastern Caribbean." In *Modern Caribbean Politics*, edited by Anthony Payne and Paul Sutton, pp. 176–197. Baltimore: Johns Hopkins University Press, 1993.

Von Mettenheim, Kurt, and James Malloy. *Deepening Democracy in Latin America*. Pittsburgh: University of Pittsburgh Press, 1998.

Wiarda, Howard. "The Dominican Republic: Mirror Legacies of Democracy and Authoritarianism." In *Democracy in Developing Countries*, vol. 4, edited by Larry Diamond, Juan J. Linz, and Seymour Martin Lipset, pp. 423–458. Boulder: Lynne Rienner Publishers, 1989.

Wiarda, Howard, and Michael J. Kryzanek. *The Dominican Republic: A Caribbean Crucible*. Rev. ed. Boulder: Westview, 1992.

Will, W. Marvin. "A Nation Divided: The Quest for Caribbean Integration." *Latin American Research Review* 26, no. 2 (1991): 3–37.

Williams, Eric. *From Columbus to Castro: The History of the Caribbean*. London: Andre Deutsch, 1970.

5

The Economies of the Caribbean

Dennis A. Pantin

The current and projected economic problems and challenges of the Caribbean cannot be fully comprehended without an appreciation of the historical evolution of these economies. There are, in fact, twenty-eight distinct political entities, most of which are islands, within what is called the insular Caribbean, among which twelve are dependent territories in a region with a total population of 36 million people. There are many areas of commonality among these individual economies as a result of their post-Columbian history of colonization by one or other European power for the primary purpose of growing sugarcane for export. This chapter, therefore, begins with a historical overview of the Caribbean and then turns to a review of current economic structure and performance and future challenges.

The idea of a singular Caribbean is a recent development.[1] In keeping with the theme set forth by Richard S. Hillman in the introduction, I will focus on the insular Caribbean and refer to the island economies within the Caribbean Sea together with the bordering mainland countries of Belize, Guyana, French Guiana, and Suriname; some mention also will be made of other countries on the northern coast of South America and eastern coast of Central America.

■ Common Economic History

The region shares a prehistory, that is, the period prior to the European colonization initiated by Christopher Columbus's voyage in 1492. Today, little remains—other than historic artifacts and a few isolated communities throughout the Caribbean—of the indigenous peoples who inhabited the region. It is in this sense that the term *prehistory* is used relative to the indigenous peoples, who still make up a significant share of the population in some South American countries. All Caribbean economies are also linked by a common economic history and, in particular, two specific economic characteristics.

The first common point of economic history is that of plantation slavery together with the indentureship that followed the end of the slave trade and the subsequent abolition of slavery itself. This occurred by 1838 in the English-speaking Caribbean, following which indentured laborers were introduced from India and elsewhere, particularly in Trinidad, Guyana, and Suriname. The result has been the creation of multiracial and plural religious societies, the legacies of which are evident today in the social, political, and economic systems in these countries.

There is a particular school of Caribbean economics—the plantation economy school—that has sought to explain the functioning of the Caribbean economy on the basis of this historic origin.[2] The plantation economy literature was influenced by the notion of "plantation America," which encompassed the southern U.S. states, northeastern Brazil, and other pockets of slavery throughout North, South, and Central America, in addition to the Caribbean (Wagley 1960).[3] What is specific and special about the Caribbean, according to the plantation economy school, is that plantation economic systems have continued to persist. But some of the other countries of plantation America, by contrast, have become integrated into more complex economic systems, including settler agriculture, manufacturing, and scientific and technological development. The United States is the best example of this.

UN Photo 154202, Nicole Toutounji

An outdoor market in Port-au-Prince, Haiti

The plantation economy school hypothesizes that the original (slave) plantation economies of the Caribbean have been bequeathed with a legacy of nondynamic responses to changes in the external world economic environment (see Best and Levitt 1968:32). The plantation economy theorists suggest that this legacy is not only persistent in the traditional agricultural sectors that still exist (especially sugarcane production) but also evident in other sectors, notably minerals, manufacturing, and services.

A second common legacy among Caribbean economies is dependence on natural resources for the generation of export earnings. These small, open, export-led economies began as totally dependent for their internal production, employment, income, and consumption on the generation of sugarcane exports. Therefore, soil fertility determined fortunes as cane producers shifted to newer territories and hence virgin soils. Following the emancipation of slaves and the collapse of the sugar industry in the nineteenth century, diversification was marked by a shift to other agricultural exports such as cocoa, coffee, citrus, and, later, bananas.[4] In the twentieth century, there was also the growth of mineral export dependence, whether bauxite (Jamaica, Guyana, Suriname), oil or, more recently, natural gas (Trinidad and Tobago); and tourism (all Caribbean economies). Regional economies therefore remain largely dependent on natural resources for their economic survival.

■ Some Differences

There are several points of difference among Caribbean economies. First, the dominant language in the insular Caribbean, in terms of the sheer number of speakers, is Spanish. The primary language in Cuba, the Dominican Republic, and Puerto Rico, Spanish is spoken by 60 percent of the region's population. The second most common language is French—but particularly the creole variant, as spoken in Haiti, Martinique, and Guadeloupe (combined, roughly 22 percent of the regional population) but also alongside English in St. Lucia and Dominica. English is the third language (17 percent), Dutch the fourth (1 percent).

These language differences are, of course, the result of the source country of the most dominant or long-lasting metropolitan colonization.[5] Most language groups have tended to retain a closer linkage—in both economic and informational senses—with the country of original metropolitan colonization than with each other, although the United States became a more significant and, in some senses, unifying metropolitan country of influence throughout the twentieth century. Language differences have contributed to limited economic relations within the Caribbean, as well as in terms of cooperation among these economies in interacting with the rest of the world. Intraregional trading and investment opportunities are therefore sometimes constrained by these language barriers.

A second point of difference is in political systems and their status. All Caribbean countries have effectively embraced the legal, juridical, and political systems of the original colonial power, although as Thomas J. D'Agostino notes in Chapter 4, some local adaptation has been added. Cuba is, of course, a significant exception to this generality. Such differences also can serve as an impediment to trade and investment within the Caribbean given the lack of familiarity within language- and political-system subgroupings about other subsystems, a tendency exacerbated by language differences.

The third significant difference derives from Caribbean states' political status. Most are, at least formally, politically independent, but a minority still retains a formal political linkage with a metropolitan power. Puerto Rico, Martinique and Guadeloupe, Montserrat, and the Netherlands Antilles are in this category.[6] On the one hand, those that have acquired their political independence enjoy a degree of self-determination unknown among those that have maintained metropolitan ties. On the other hand, Caribbean economies in which formal quasicolonial relations have been retained benefit in several ways, including free movement of labor and access to metropolitan institutions for education, health care, and sometimes other social services.

A fourth distinction among Caribbean economies involves the ideological underpinnings of the various economic system types found throughout the region. One may contrast, for example, Cuba's socialist economic system with variants of the market economy that prevail throughout the remainder of the region.

A fifth point of difference flows from size as defined in population and area terms. In terms of population, Caribbean economies range from Cuba with some 11 million people and the Dominican Republic with 8.5 million to, at the other extreme, Montserrat with less than 10,000.

The most populous and largest (in terms of area) Caribbean economies exist in the northern Caribbean—Cuba, Hispaniola (Dominica Republic and Haiti), Puerto Rico, and Jamaica—and the southern Caribbean (Guyana, with roughly 83,000 square miles, though a population of 766,000) and the 1.3 million population of Trinidad and Tobago. The size of Caribbean economies (in population and area size) decreases as one moves south of Hispaniola or north of Guyana and Trinidad and Tobago. As will be discussed below, there appears to be no particular advantage of size in terms of economic performance in the Caribbean.

The sixth area of difference is in terms of linkages among Caribbean economies. As H. Michael Erisman details in Chapter 6, the English-speaking countries of the Caribbean share a relatively higher degree of intercountry linkages. In 1967, the English-speaking Caribbean economies formed the

Caribbean Free Trade Agreement, which was transformed in 1973 into the Caribbean Common Market and Community (CARICOM, a Caribbean economic community). Within this grouping there are even closer linkages between the subgroup of the Organization of Eastern Caribbean States that share a common currency and central bank (the Eastern Caribbean Central Bank [ECCB]).

More recently, there have been several efforts to broaden the base of intraregional cooperation. These initiatives include the Caribbean Forum (known as CARIFORUM), which links CARICOM with Haiti (now a member of CARICOM) and the Dominican Republic. Another development has been the formation of the Association of Caribbean States (ACS) linking Caribbean and Central American countries with Mexico, Columbia, and Venezuela. The ACS has identified trade, transportation, and tourism as its three areas of policy focus (see, e.g., Byron 1998; Girvan 2001).

A seventh and final area of difference among Caribbean economies is the extent of diversification away from the original dependence on sugarcane or a substitute traditional agricultural export. In the twentieth century, there was an increasing divergence away from traditional agricultural exports. The main form of diversification was seen in the growth of tourism.[7] However, there also was a shift to mineral exports (bauxite in the case of Jamaica, Guyana, and Suriname and petroleum in the case of Trinidad and Tobago) and, more recently, a smaller shift to information processing (Barbados, the Dominican Republic, and Jamaica), offshore financial services (Antigua and Barbuda, the Bahamas, Barbados, the Cayman Islands, the Netherlands Antilles, St. Vincent, and the Grenadines), and some specialty agroindustrial and medical/pharmaceutical exports (particularly Cuba).

■ Current Economic Structure

Caribbean economies continue to be dominated by their export sectors, which in turn tend to be concentrated on one to three products based on the region's natural resource endowment. Caribbean economies vary in the significance of nonexport-producing sectors. Domestic food production is the most common area of nonexport production. However, in some islands (particularly the more arid or limestone islands such as Aruba, Curaçao, and Barbados) there is little domestic agricultural production. Manufacturing also exists in some Caribbean economies, although there tends to be a dependence on imported products.

Tourism has been the most dynamic sector throughout the Caribbean. For some Caribbean economies tourism is the dominant sector. In all other regional economies (including Cuba and Trinidad and Tobago) the tourist sector has been targeted for substantial growth. Table 5.1 shows that visitor expenditures are estimated to have grown by 48 percent between 1991 and 1996 while employment in the sector grew by 28 percent over the same period and actual visitors by 23 percent. Table 5.2 details hotel room capacity in selected Caribbean economies in support of the tourist industry along with the number of individuals employed in related areas. Table 5.3 highlights the national economic significance of foreign exchange receipts from tourism relative to overall gross domestic product (GDP).

There are also three other sectors of significant growth, although all from a low initial base, in some Caribbean economies. The first is offshore financial services, which are of particular importance in Antigua and Barbuda, the Bahamas, Barbados, the Cayman Islands, the Netherlands Antilles, and St. Vincent and the Grenadines. A second growth area has been export-processing zones.[8] These have become important in the Dominican Republic and, to some extent, Jamaica.[9] A third sector of dynamic growth has been information

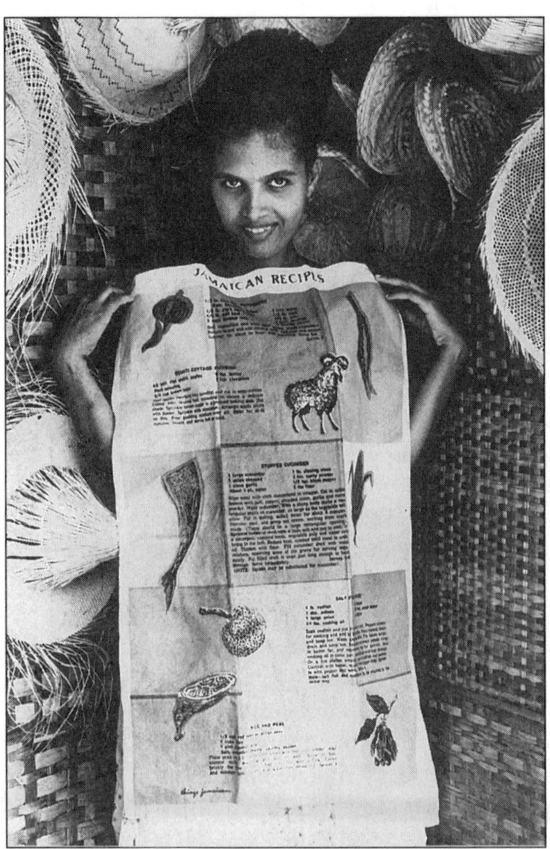

A Jamaican recipe cloth from the Things Jamaican shop, Kingston, Jamaica

UN/ILO/JMcG

Table 5.1 Selected Indicators of Tourism in the Caribbean

Indicator	1991	1995	% Change, 1991–1995	1996	% Change, 1995–1996	% Change, 1991–1996
Estimates of visitor expenditure in the Caribbean (U.S.$ in millions)	9,018	12,631	40	13,340	6	48
International visitor arrivals (millions)	12	14.5	21	14.8	2	23
Employment in accommodation establishments	108,367	122,237	13	138,734	13	28

Source: Caribbean Tourism Organization, *Caribbean Tourism Statistical Report 1996* (St. Michael, Barbados: Caribbean Tourism Organization, 1997), pp. 21, 67, 69.

Table 5.2 Hotel Room Capacity and Related Employment, 1996

Country	Number of Rooms	Persons Employed	Employee/Room Ratio
Anguilla	978	1,064	1.09
Antigua and Barbuda	3,317	3,649	1.10
Aruba	6,150	7,995	1.30
Bahamas	13,398	16,078	1.20
Barbados	5,685	5,685	1.00
Belize	3,708	2,107	0.57
Bermuda	4,152	4,029	0.97
British Virgin Islands	1,446	2,110	1.46
Cayman Islands	4,432	1,630	0.37
Curaçao	2,200	1,980	0.90
Dominica	764	415	0.54
Dominican Republic	28,967	34,760	1.20
Grenada	1,085	1,200	1.11
Jamaica	20,422	27,937	1.37
Martinique	5,730	2,307	0.40
Puerto Rico	10,299	11,900	1.16
St. Eustatius	77	41	0.53
St. Lucia	4,203	5,200	1.24
St. Kitts and Nevis	1,593	1,599	1.00
Trinidad and Tobago	3,198	4,160	1.30
U.S. Virgin Islands	4,070	2,890	0.71
Total	125,874	138,736	1.10

Source: Caribbean Tourism Organization, *Caribbean Tourism Statistical Report, 1996* (St. Michael, Barbados: Caribbean Tourism Organization, 1997).

Table 5.3 Estimates of Visitor Expenditure, Selected Years (U.S.$ in millions)

					as % of GDP			
Country	1987	1990	1993	1996	1987	1990	1993	1996
Anguilla	20	35	43	48	73	68	84	87
Antigua and Barbuda	191	298	277	257	80	89	71	55
Aruba	24	353	464	606	38	39	N/A	N/A
Bahamas	1,146	1,333	1,304	1,450	50	43	43	42
Barbados	379	494	528	685	30	33	38	41
Belize	47	91	70	84	20	27	16	N/A
Bermuda	468	490	505	472	40	37	32	26
British Virgin Islands	111	132	196	268	N/A	N/A	N/A	N/A
Cayman Islands	146	236	271	368	36	33	32	N/A
Curaçao	94	238	194	186	11	23	13	N/A
Dominica	13	25	29	37	12	18	19	N/A
Dominican Republic	571	900	1,070	1,755	16	18	13	17
Grenada	42	38	48	60	35	24	26	24
Jamaica	595	740	942	1,100	20	19	31	N/A
Martinique	210	240	332	411	8	7	N/A	N/A
Puerto Rico	955	1,367	1,628	1,930	4	4	4	4
St. Lucia	126	154	221	N/A	52	46	59	66
St. Kitts and Nevis	47	58	70	N/A	53	43	42	32
Trinidad and Tobago	79	95	82	105	2	2	2	2
U.S. Virgin Islands	639	705	902	687	51	N/A	N/A	N/A
Total	5,904	8,020	9,175	10,508				

Source: Caribbean Tourism Organization, *Caribbean Tourism Statistical Report, 1996* (St. Michael, Barbados: Caribbean Tourism Organization, 1997).

Note: N/A indicates that data is not available.

processing. In 1993, the level of employment in this sector in the region was estimated at some 5,000 persons. By the mid-1990s there were some seventy-four export-oriented information processing firms in the Caribbean, employing 7,500 persons, an increase of 50 percent within two to three years.

A fourth sector is exported labor, as indicated by remittances by the Caribbean population living abroad. The significant economic role of this Caribbean diaspora, examined in greater detail by Dennis Conway in Chapter 12, is reflected in the impact of remittances on home country economies. The percentage of native-born Jamaicans living abroad in the late 1980s relative to the resident population on the island was 40 percent, similar to Guyana. The remittances provided by diasporic Jamaicans were equal to 29 percent of their country's export earnings in the early 1990s, and the roughly 1 million Haitians living abroad (15 percent of the resident population) provided remittances valued in excess of 30 percent of Haiti's exports. Incredibly, during this same period émigrés from the Dominican Republic remitted an amount equal to 71 percent of export earnings (Girvan 2001).

■ Current Economic Performance

In terms of economic performance, the Caribbean can be grouped into four categories: independent larger island states (Cuba, Dominican Republic, Haiti, and Jamaica); smaller island states (Antigua and Barbuda, the Bahamas, Barbados, Dominica, Grenada, St. Lucia, St. Kitts and Nevis, St. Vincent, and Trinidad and Tobago); mainland states (Belize, Guyana, Suriname); and the twelve dependent territories (Girvan 2001). Table 5.4 provides a summary comparison of these groupings in terms of size (population and territory) and GDP; further details on the individual countries within each group are shown in Table 5.5. Seventy-six percent of the Caribbean population inhabits the four larger island states that together occupy nearly 28 percent of the region's land area. The nine smaller island states account for 6.4 percent of the region's population and 3 percent of its land. The mainland countries occupy 55 percent of the land area of the Caribbean but contain only 4 percent of its population. The twelve dependent territories reflect roughly similar shares of the region's population (13.9 percent) and land area (14.4 percent). Table 5.4 also reveals that dependent territories have the highest average per capita GDP of some U.S.$11,000, followed by the smaller island states with a per capita GDP of $5,215, then the mainland states with $1,174, and finally the larger island independent states with per capita GDP of $1,101.

The level of labor force absorption tends to be reflective of the GDP trends, and as a result countries with higher economic growth rates (as

Table 5.4 The Caribbean: Gross Domestic Product, Population, and Land Area

	Per Capita GDP, 1995[a]	Percent Total		
		GDP	Population	Land Area
Larger island states	1,101	30.3	75.9	27.6
Smaller island states	5,215	12.0	6.4	3.0
Mainland	1,174	1.6	3.8	55.0
Dependent territories	11,099	56.1	13.9	14.4
Total	2,759	100.0	100.0	100.0
CARICOM states	2,923	18.0	17.0	59.6
Non-CARICOM states	1,036	25.0	69.1	26.0

Source: Norman Girvan, "Reinterpreting the Caribbean," in *New Caribbean Thought,* edited by Folke Lindahl and Brian Meeks (Kingston, Jamaica: University of the West Indies Press, 2001).

Note: a. Weighted averages.

reported in Table 5.5) have been able to record higher levels of employment creation.

Table 5.5 also illuminates the performance of the four groups of Caribbean countries between 1991 and 1998 based on the Human Development Reports of the United Nations Development Programme (UNDP). The UNDP produced its first world Human Development Report in 1990, introducing a new Human Development Index (HDI) based on combined indicators of life expectancy, educational attainment, and income. The HDI offers an alternative to GDP in comparing development trends across countries.

Table 5.5 The Caribbean: Human Development, Growth, and Poverty

	GDP Per Capita, 1995 (U.S.$)		Human Development Category	HDI Change, 1991–1998[c]	Growth[a]		
	Current	Real PPP$[b]			1965–1980	1980–1995	Poverty[d]
Larger island states							
Cuba	1,113	3,100	Medium	–23	0.6	—	15[e]
Dominican Republic	1,663	3,923	Medium	–8	3.8	1.1	21
Haiti	285	917	Low	–34	0.9	–4	65[f]
Jamaica	1,762	3,801	Medium	–25	–0.1	1.4	32
Smaller island states							
Antigua and Barbuda	6,640	9,131	High	17	–1.4	5.2[g]	12
Bahamas	12,258	15,738	High	–4	1	–0.1	5[f]
Barbados	7,120	11,306	High	–2	3.5	1.2	8[f]
Dominica	2,574	6,424	High	12	–0.8	4.3	33
Grenada	2,344	5,425	High	13	0.1	3	20
St. Kitts and Nevis	3,083	10,150	High	15	4	4.9	15
St. Lucia	4,642	6,503	High	10	2.7	4.4[g]	25
St. Vincent	2,032	5,969	High	22	0.2	4.5	17
Trinidad and Tobago	4,101	9,437	High	–1	3.1	–1.5	21
Mainland							
Belize	2,696	5,623	High	4	3.4	1.7	35
Guyana	809	3,205	Medium	–11	0.7	–1.7	43
Suriname	1,066	4,862	Medium	–10	5.5	3.4	47[f]

Source: Caribbean Tourism Organization, *Caribbean Tourism Statistical Report, 1996* (St. Michael, Barbados: Caribbean Tourism Organization, 1997).

Notes: a. Average annual real per capita GDP growth for period, from UN Development Programme, *Human Development Report* (New York: United Nations, 1998), available online at http://hdr.undp.org/reports/global/1998/en/.

b. Adjusts GDP for differences in purchasing power between countries, from UN Development Programme, *Human Development Report* (New York: United Nations, 1998), available online at http://hdr.undp.org/reports/global/1998/en/.

c. Change in global HDI rank, 1991–1998.

d. Proportion of population below national poverty line estimate, 1989–1994, except where otherwise indicated, from UN Development Programme, *Human Development Report* (New York: United Nations, 1998), available online at http://hdr.undp.org/reports/global/1998/en/.

e. Urban population at risk of not accessing supply of essential goods and services.

f. Head Count Poverty Index, mid-1990s, as reported by the World Bank, see www.worldbank.org, accessed January 2003.

g. 1980–1993, from UN Development Programme, *Human Development Report* (New York: United Nations, 1997), available online at http://hdr.undp.org/reports/global/1997/en/.

It is noticeable, in Table 5.5, that by 1998 the most significant declines in HDI in the Caribbean over the 1991–1998 period were recorded in Haiti, Jamaica, and Cuba. Two of the three mainland countries also experienced negative HDI trends (Guyana and Suriname). Most of the smaller island states recorded positive trends in the HDI over the period, excluding small declines for Barbados, the Bahamas, and Trinidad and Tobago.

Tables 5.4 and 5.5 suggest that the dependent territories and smaller island states have been faring better than the larger independent Caribbean states—whether larger island states or mainland states. A number of factors may be advanced to explain this divergence in economic performance. The first, of course, is size of economy. The smaller the economy, the easier it is for any positive microtrends to express themselves in macroeconomic significance. A second and related factor has been the role of tourism. The Caribbean economies with more positive macroeconomic trends have been largely those with growing, or already dominant, tourism sectors.

A third factor to explain the variation in economic performance would appear to be macroeconomic management, particularly exchange-rate management. The former refers to the use, by governments, of fiscal, monetary, and other economic policies to influence the level of overall economic activity. One component of this is exchange-rate policy between a national currency and foreign currencies.

The exchange rate is extremely important to small Caribbean economies that are highly dependent on imports for both consumption and production. Significant volatility in the exchange rate can have deleterious impacts on the standard of living and, by inference, on social stability.

There are four exchange-rate options open to small economies. The first is to have no national currency, as occurs in Panama, which relies on the U.S. dollar. A second option is to fix, or peg, the exchange rate to a hard currency such as the U.S. dollar. A third strategy would be to permit one's national currency to float and hence be determined by the forces of demand and supply. A final option is to link the supply of national currency to reserves in hard currency, or foreign exchange. This final option is termed a currency board. It was long practiced in the British colonies. Under the currency board arrangements the national currency is backed—completely or partially—by reserves of hard currencies. The currency board is similar to a fixed exchange-rate system. However, the difference is that the units of national currency created are backed, in whole or part, by hard currencies. In this sense, a currency board is analogous to a casino where, upon entry, players convert their hard currency to chips and then, if they are so lucky, reconvert their net winnings back to hard currency upon leaving the casino.[10]

Most Caribbean economies currently operate pegged or floating single-currency systems. One exception is the members of the Eastern Caribbean Central Bank, who share a common currency as well as one based on a modified currency board system. ECCB member countries have recorded a more stable economic performance relative to their larger cousins in the English-speaking CARICOM. The latter set of countries (Jamaica, Guyana, Trinidad and Tobago, and Barbados) have operated with fixed exchange rates, subject to devaluation, and more recently (with the exception of Barbados) with floating exchange rates, subject to depreciation. Puerto Rico, of course, uses the common U.S. currency, and the French departments draw on the French franc. The Netherlands Antilles share a common guilder currency.

Current and Projected Economic Challenges

There are perhaps five main economic problems that Caribbean economies will face, in common, in the near term. These are the collapse of preferential arrangements for traditional exports; overnight liberalization in the context of globalization (the World Trade Organization [WTO] and the Free Trade Area of the Americas [FTAA]); stubborn unemployment, particularly among youths, and concomitant growing social deviance, including violence, crime, and drugs; foreign debt burdens; and market risks faced by more dynamic sectors of recent years—tourism, offshore finance, and information processing. Vulnerability to natural disasters, exacerbated by climate change, is a sixth and longer-term concern.

Collapse of Preferential Arrangements

Although there has been substantial economic diversification in the Caribbean, traditional agricultural exports still loom large. Cuba, Jamaica, St. Kitts, Trinidad and Tobago, and Guyana continue to operate significant sugarcane industries, particularly in terms of employment.[11] Some other Caribbean economies, like those in the Windward Islands, share a similar dependence on banana exports.

These exports continue to be dependent on long-established preferential agreements with the European Union (EU) under the Lomé convention, which is a cooperation agreement between the European Union and the seventy-plus countries in the African, Caribbean, and Pacific (ACP) group of states. Under the Lomé convention, some ACP products enter EU markets duty-free.

This preferential agreement is now under threat. The most serious threat is to the banana industry. As a result of several recent WTO rulings, the preferential banana regime of the European Union with the grouping of ACP countries has been ruled to be in breach of the preferential banana regime under the Lomé convention.[12] Already, the Caribbean banana industry has declined. This is evident among the four banana-producing Windward countries in the English-speaking Caribbean. Over the 1992–1998 period, for example, the Dominican Republic experienced a 46 percent decline in the number of active farmers. The comparable decline in St. Lucia was 36 percent, in St. Vincent and the Grenadines 12 percent, and in Grenada 80 percent. This dramatic decline in active farmers poses several risks to these micro–island states. First, it has led to growing unemployment and increasing social tension. Second, it may lead to the kind of negative social behavior that would have a domino effect on other competitive sectors, such as incipient tourism industries. Finally, it has created the need for Caribbean governments to import foodstuffs to feed growing populations, diverting scarce financial resources from other key sectors.

The second most vulnerable sector is the sugarcane industry. With the exception of Cuba, Caribbean sugarcane producers benefit from the sugar protocol with the European Union. This protocol is considered to be independent of the Lomé convention between the European Union and the ACP countries. In addition, the Lomé convention has been effectively extended. (Caribbean countries entered Lomé I [1975] and Lomé III [1984]. Negotiations continued in 1998 and concluded in 2000. The EU-ACP agreements were signed June 23, 2000, for post-Lomé cooperation over a period of twenty years, with a clause for revision every five years.) However, it is difficult to assume that the Lomé convention and the related sugar and rum protocols will not come under the same pressure as the European Union's banana regime before 2010. There is a likely repetition of the banana-industry experience, with a falloff in the number of active farmers and their related jobs creation.

Adjusting to Liberalization and Globalization

The near-term collapse of preferential arrangements for small Caribbean economies is complicated by globalization and its institutional expression in economic liberalization. Globalization may be defined, generally, as the increasing integration of the world economy. Liberalization involves negotiation of binding contracts by nations to remove barriers to the opening of their economies. The WTO is the forum for such negotiations, which are reinforced in many instances by loan agreements signed by countries with the World Bank or International Monetary Fund.

One of the key issues in negotiations is the time period that individual countries will be allowed to adjust to the demands of liberalization. In the case of the WTO, for example, countries such as the United States have been able to negotiate a decade-long transitional period to liberalize markets for textiles and garments. The Caribbean, to date, has not had the negotiating clout to achieve similar results for some traditional export industries such as bananas.

In the case of the Americas there also are discussions under way for the Free Trade Area of the Americas. In the FTAA discussions, the notion that small economies require special and differential treatment—including longer transitional terms—does not appear to have found favor, particularly with the dominant player, the United States.[13]

The implications of globalization and liberalization include differential treatment for nationally owned firms in the tourism, financial, agricultural, and manufacturing sectors. According to some interpretations of WTO rules, for example, Caribbean economies may no longer be able to require significant or total local ownership of small hotels, tour operators, and the like. If this proves to be the case, then the share of national ownership in many Caribbean industries may come under threat from transnational corporations. Although some increased competition is not without benefits, a sudden and large-scale denationalization of industry is likely to have negative impacts. These are likely to include resentment toward foreign ownership of major industries, particularly those that were previously nationally owned. The commitment of foreign firms to national developmental objectives also is likely to be weaker. It is perhaps for not dissimilar reasons that the United States places constraints, for example, on foreign ownership of its mass media and financial institutions.

Unemployment, Underemployment, Poverty, Crime, and Drugs

Another constraint is the existence of unemployment, underemployment, and poverty throughout the region, particularly in the more populous Caribbean economies. The data reveal a concentration of unemployment among the youth of the region. Therefore, it is not difficult to suggest a link between the frustration of unemployed youths and growing levels of crime, particularly drug-related offenses. In Chapter 4, Thomas J. D'Agostino also notes that mounting frustration and cynicism among Caribbean youths has undermined support for political parties and elections, critical components of the democratic systems within the region. Trade and investment patterns are sensitive to national stability that can be disrupted, in small economies, by factors such as youth crime and general deviance.

The Foreign Debt Burden

One of the constraints that some Caribbean economies face, particularly those with significant socioeconomic problems, stems from substantial foreign debt burdens that consume a large share of fiscal revenue. This is true of Jamaica and Guyana and, to a lesser extent, the Dominican Republic and Trinidad and Tobago. Facing the challenges noted above is likely to require substantial fiscal expenditures to fund programs, including retraining of displaced workers in the process of globalization and liberalization and upgrading infrastructures for new investments (e.g., telecommunications). However, countries with significant debt burdens are constrained to service such prior liabilities before addressing future needs.

Risks Facing Nonpreferential Export Sectors

Even the nonpreferential and globally competitive export industries of the Caribbean will not remain unaffected by global trends. Tourism, for example, is the most dynamic sector in the Caribbean. However, the prospects are not always bright. The larger question is the sustainability of the regional tourism industry. The Caribbean faces the danger, for example, of killing the goose that lays the golden egg by expansion of tourism beyond its ecocultural carrying capacity. The challenge is to develop sustainable tourism, which is simultaneously within carrying capacity limits (whether sociocultural, economic, or ecological) while maximizing the retention of the majority of the economic rents accruing from the sector.[14]

The prospects are not as bright for other sectors with the partial exception of the natural-gas sector in Trinidad and Tobago. However, the distribution of rents from that sector is still problematic, given substantial tax holidays and dominant foreign ownership.

The offshore financial sector faces decline in light of changing metropolitan tax laws targeting centers of money laundering and tax evasion. A 2002 report by the Organization for Economic Cooperation and Development (OECD) on harmful tax competition listed forty-seven countries, including fifteen from the Caribbean with offshore financial services and nominal corporation taxes, claimed to be causing injury to tax regimes in OECD countries (OECD 2002). Offshore investment trusts, foreign sales corporations, and offshore insurance companies have been identified as instruments of OECD tax losses. The Caribbean has been attempting to seek support from individual OECD countries, particularly in the European Union, to stave off punitive changes in the relevant tax laws.[15]

The information processing sector, as noted earlier, is dominated by low-end data-entry activities subject to competitive erosion by the increasing automation of such functions, which, among other things, is facilitating use of non–English speaking data entry services in lower-labor-cost regions of the world, particularly Asia.

Vulnerability to Natural Disasters and Climate Change

The frequency and intensity of hurricanes have increased in recent years. Anguilla, to take one example, has been hit by three hurricanes and one tropical storm since 1995. Some southern coast resorts were still closed in January 2000 as a result of Hurricane Lenny in November 1999. Anguilla's Cap Juluca Hotel was not expected to reopen until seven months later in July 2000. Hurricane Lenny also swept away the beach at the Young Island resort of St. Vincent and caused damage elsewhere in the region, including the Coco Reef Hotel in Tobago. In November 2001 Hurricane Michele was the strongest to hit Cuba since 1952; Cuba was hit again in August 2002. The latest summary data also indicate that in 2000 Antigua/Barbuda, Dominica, Grenada, and St. Lucia were hit by hurricanes at an estimated damage cost of U.S.$268 million. In 2001, the estimated damage cost for Cuba alone was U.S.$87 million.

Although this recent intensified pattern may be the result of a cyclical active and less active periods, there is virtual consensus that climate change is likely to exacerbate the frequency and intensity of hurricanes in particular. For example, it has been projected that the sea-surface temperature in the region of the Caribbean Sea will increase 1.5 degrees Celsius and that this could lead to about 40 percent more hurricane activity in the area.

It also is anticipated that global warming will result in a greater heating of water via thermal expansion. This thermal expansion, coupled with melting glaciers and ice sheets, could cause sea levels to rise, although it should be noted that the rise will not be uniform but will be influenced by other factors such as currents, winds, and tides. One projection suggests that sea levels could increase by an average of 0.2 inches yearly (Intergovernmental Panel on Climate Change 1998:341).

Conclusion

The challenge facing Caribbean economies is to find mechanisms for regional collaboration and cooperation in addressing seven key issue areas: loss of preferences; liberalization and globalization; unemployment, poverty, crime, and violence; foreign debt; risks to dynamic sectors of tourism and offshore finance; information processing; and vulnerability to natural disasters. In all of these instances, the advantages of cooperation should be obvious.

Three of these challenges—the collapse of preferential agreements, liberalization and globalization, and foreign debt burdens—require individual Caribbean economies to enter into negotiations with the same global players, whether multilateral or national. Cooperation among them can therefore facilitate their leverage in such negotiations. The same holds true for the threats facing the offshore financial sector. The commonality of concerns as to the other challenges—such as unemployment, drugs, and crime and vulnerability to natural disasters—also suggests benefits from the sharing of experiences. In terms of tourism, the Caribbean Tourism Organization already joins regional governments with the mission of promoting the regional industry. The quest for sustainable tourism reinforces this need for cooperation and collaboration, including the sharing of experiences.[16]

Already some forms of cooperation and collaboration exist. The conclusion drawn in this chapter is that these need to be both deepened and expanded to new areas.

Notes

1. See Girvan (2001) for a helpful review of differing definitions of the Caribbean and of the view of Gaztambide-Geigel (1996), as cited in Girvan, that the very concept of the Caribbean originated only toward the end of the nineteenth century.

2. See Best (1967), Beckford (1972), and Best and Levitt (1968) for elaboration on the plantation economy school. For a review of critiques and update on this school, see Pantin (1980) and Pantin and Mahabir (1999).

3. For more general reviews of Caribbean economic thought, see Brown and Brewster (1974), St. Cyr (1984), and Lalta and Freckleton (1992). See Lewis (1950) for a pioneering effort to analyze Caribbean economic reality from the perspective of the majority peoples of the region.

4. See Eric Williams's seminal articulation (1944) of the linkage between the economic fortunes of the sugar industry and slavery and then emancipation.

5. Some Caribbean countries have run the gamut of European colonizers—French, Spanish, English, or Dutch.

6. The relationship between Caribbean countries and more urban countries cannot be simply described as colonial because the majority of the population of the former continues to support these links.

7. For a discussion of the cultural, economic, environmental, and social repercussions of the growth of tourism in the Caribbean, see Polly Pattullo (1996).

8. The export-processing zone (EPZ) is a demarcated physical area within a country in which a range of host-country domestic laws—particularly trade-related laws—do not apply and in which the entire output of resident firms is normally exported.

9. The first EPZ in the Dominican Republic was established in 1969. By 1980 some 16,440 jobs had been created, and by 1992 an estimated 101,300 people were employed in nearly twenty EPZs. The vast majority—an estimated 70 percent—are involved in the production of apparel and textiles. Companies have been attracted to the Dominican EPZs because of low wages, relative political stability, and access to the North American market. For further analysis of EPZs in the Dominican Republic, see Jonathan Hartlyn (1998) and Emelio Betances (1995).

10. Similar proposals for currency-board arrangements have been discussed in the former Soviet bloc (see Schwartz 1992); Argentina introduced such a system in the 1990s.

11. In these instances there are linked rum industries that also face preferential-type markets.

12. For details on this WTO ruling on the European Union's banana regime and the implications for the Caribbean, see Pantin, Sandiford, and Henry (1999).

13. A working group on the smaller economies has been established in the negotiations for the Free Trade Area of the Americas, but this appears to be more of a cosmetic than a substantive concession.

14. For a review of the literature on sustainable tourism and its application to the Caribbean, see Pantin (1999). Also see Pattullo (1996) for a critical review of the contribution of the tourist industry to Caribbean development.

15. A report in the *Trinidad Guardian* of March 11, 2000, on a meeting between French President Jacques Chirac and sixteen CARIFORUM countries in Guadeloupe, is captioned "Region Wants French to Halt [OECD] Offshore [Financial Sector] Assault."

16. The Association of Caribbean States has set a target of 2020 for the achievement of a sustainable tourism zone in the Caribbean.

■ Bibliography

Beckford, George. *Persistent Poverty: Underdevelopment in the Plantation Economies of the Third World.* New York: Oxford University Press, 1972.

Best, Lloyd. "A Model of Pure Plantation Economy." *Social and Economies Studies* 17, no. 3 (September 1967).

Best, L., and Kari Levitt. "Externally Propelled Industrialisation and Growth in the Caribbean." 4 vols. Montreal: McGill Centre for Developing Area Studies (mimeo), 1968.

Betances, Emelio. *State and Society in the Dominican Republic.* Boulder: Westview Press, 1995.

Brown, Adlith, and H. Brewster. "A Review of the Study of Economics in the English-Speaking Caribbean." *Social and Economies Studies* 23, no. 1 (March 1974).

Byron, Jessica. "The Association of Caribbean States: Growing Pains of a New Regionalism?" *Pensamiento Propio* 3, no. 7 (May–August 1998): 33–57.

Gaztambide-Geigel, Antonio. "La invención del Caribe en el Siglo XX. Las definiciones del Caribe como problema histórico e metodológico" (The invention of the Caribbean in the twentieth century: Definitions of the Caribbean as a historical and methodological problem). *Revista Mexicana del Caribe* 1, no. 1 (1996): 75–96.

Girvan, Norman. "Reinterpreting the Caribbean." In *New Caribbean Thought*, edited by Folke Lindahl and Brian Meeks. Kingston, Jamaica: University of the West Indies Press, 2001.

Hartlyn, Jonathan. *The Struggle for Democratic Politics in the Dominican Republic.* Chapel Hill: University of North Carolina Press, 1998.

Intergovernmental Panel on Climate Change. *Contribution of Working Group 1 to Second Assessment Report of the Intergovernmental Panel on Climate Change.* Cambridge, UK: Cambridge University Press, 1998.

Lalta, Stanley, and Marie Freckleton. *Caribbean Economic Development: The Second Generation.* Kingston, Jamaica: Ian Randle Publishers, 1992.

Lewis, W. Arthur. "The Industrialisation of the British West Indies." *Caribbean Economic Review* 12 (May 1950).

OECD (Organization for Economic Cooperation and Development). "Harmful Tax Practices." *Annual Report 2002*. Paris: OECD Public Affairs Division, 2002, p. 41.

Pantin, Dennis A. "The Plantation Economy Model and the Caribbean." *IDS Bulletin* 12, no. 1 (December 1980): 17–23

———. "The Challenge of Sustainable Development in Small Island Developing States: Case Study on Tourism in the Caribbean." *Natural Resources Forum* 23, no. 3 (August 1999): 221–234.

Pantin, Dennis A., and Dhanyshar Mahabir, eds. "The Plantation Economy Revisited." *Maroonage* 1, no. 1 (March 1999).

Pantin, Dennis A., W. Sandiford, and M. Henry. *Cake, Mama Coka or ? Alternatives Facing the Caribbean Banana Industry Following the April 1999 WTO Ruling.* Study for the West Indian Farmer's Association, the Caribbean Development Policy Center, and OXFAM (September 1999).

Pattullo, Polly. *Last Resorts: The Cost of Tourism in the Caribbean.* New York: Monthly Review Press, 1996.

St. Cyr, Eric. *Caribbean Economic Thought.* Occasional Paper. St. Augustine, Trinidad: Institute of International Relations, University of the West Indies, 1984.

Schwartz, Anna J. *Do Currency Boards Have a Future?* Twenty-second Wincott Memorial Lecture. Occasional Paper 88. Mona, Kingston, Jamaica: Institute of Economic Affairs, University of the West Indies, 1992.

Wagley, Charles. "Plantation America: A Culture Sphere." In *Caribbean Studies: A Symposium,* edited by Vera Rubin. Seattle: University of Washington Press, 1960.

Williams, Eric. *Capitalism and Slavery.* Chapel Hill: University of North Carolina Press, 1944.

6

International Relations

H. Michael Erisman

As Richard S. Hillman illustrates in the introduction to this book, the popular stereotype does not portray the Caribbean states as *active* participants in international affairs. Instead, the conventional image of the West Indies, especially in the minds of people from the more developed countries who are seeking relief from the rigors of northern winters, is usually that of a vacation playground. In short, this perspective tends to define the region's essential role in the larger global community as that of providing foreign tourists with ready access to its three abundant *s*'s: sun, sand, and surf.

As is almost inevitably the case when relying on such cursory glances, this view presents a rather distorted picture of reality. Thus the casual observer can easily overlook important and interesting aspects of the Caribbean's long tradition of involvement in world politics, such as:

- The area's colorful history as a cockpit of great power conflict. Indeed, because of its strategic location astride the crossroads of the Americas, foreign nations have fought and schemed to control the Caribbean from almost the very moment that Columbus first came ashore on San Salvador Island (also known as Watling Island) in the present-day Bahamas. Certainly the most melodramatic of these combatants were the pirates, whom many people mistakenly assume operated as completely free agents while pursuing their violent profession. But in fact privateers were often acting as agents of European governments, which "licensed" their expeditions. The Welshman Henry Morgan, who sailed under English authorization, is probably the most famous and successful of these officially sanctioned swashbucklers. There are numerous foreign powers that established a presence in the Caribbean at one time or

United Nations

A beach along undeveloped shoreline near Runaway Bay, Jamaica

another: England, France, Spain, the Netherlands, Denmark, Sweden, the United States, and the Soviet Union.

• The advances that the English-speaking Caribbean countries have made in the field of small-state regional integration. The main institutional vehicle that has been used to facilitate this process is the Caribbean Common Market and Community (CARICOM), which was established in 1973 as the successor to the Caribbean Free Trade Association. CARICOM has not only been active in the Caribbean region; it has also played a leading role in organizing a large number of former European colonies into the African, Caribbean, and Pacific (ACP) group of states and then collectively bargaining the Lomé convention for preferential trade ties with the European Union.

• The Cuban revolution's unique and often highly controversial ventures on the world stage. Among the Fidelistas' most noteworthy exploits have been their promotion of guerrilla-based armed struggles in Latin America and elsewhere; their Cold War alignment with the Soviet bloc; their deployment of combat units to help win two African wars (in Angola and Ethiopia); and their numerous successes in playing the Caribbean David to Washington's Yankee Goliath.

In this chapter we will explore these and other dimensions of the Caribbean's complex personality, highlighting in the process the historical and contemporary developments that have been most important in shaping the region's evolving international role, as well as examining some of the most serious foreign policy challenges confronting it as it moves into the twenty-first century.

Caribbean International Relations: A Historical Overview

The Caribbean that Christopher Columbus stumbled upon in his quest to find a western route to Asia soon found itself, like many other parts of the world, embroiled in Europe's wild scramble for colonies. Some indication of the pandemonium involved can be seen from the fact that the small island of Tobago (now part of the independent state of Trinidad and Tobago) changed hands twenty times over the years. Initially, Spain dominated the region, but during the 1600s its position was increasingly overshadowed by England and, to a somewhat lesser extent, France. Ultimately, the only Spanish holdings of any significance were Cuba and Puerto Rico, both of which it lost to the United States in the Spanish-American War of 1898. The two main motivations behind this imperialistic rivalry were strategic considerations and the lure of enormous wealth.

The key players in this initial drive to dominate the West Indies—Spain, England, and France—were all great seafaring powers. Consequently, it was almost inevitable that they would seek to acquire island colonies, for to do so would in effect provide them with staging bases from which they could fan out to impose their control over the key ocean routes between the Western Hemisphere and Europe that crisscrossed the Caribbean Sea and the Gulf of Mexico. Especially important were those territories adjacent to several narrow choke points that the maritime traffic had to traverse, the most prominent being the Yucatán Channel, the Straits of Florida, and the Windward, Mona, and Anegeda Passages (see Maps 1.1, 1.2, and 1.3 in Chapter 1). Probably more compelling than these naval concerns, however, was the lure of the Caribbean as a treasure trove.

Prior to the Industrial Revolution the West Indies was, despite its relatively small size, truly remarkable in its ability to generate vast fortunes. During its heyday (roughly the mid-1600s to the mid-1800s) it represented a regional source of natural resource wealth comparable to that of the oil-rich

Middle East in the twentieth century. As Stephen Randall shows in Chapter 3, the two central pillars upon which this prosperity rested were sugarcane cultivation and the large pool of cheap agricultural labor provided by the African slave trade. Europe's demand for sugar (and its by-products such as rum) was insatiable, and the Caribbean's ability to produce it cheaply in vast quantities quickly transformed the West Indies into highly prized pieces of real estate. The following two examples illustrate how coveted these sugar-producing territories were:

- London was at one point so interested in acquiring the French-controlled sugar islands of Guadeloupe and Martinique that it seriously considered offering to trade *all of Canada* for them.
- In 1673 the Dutch, who had lost and then regained control of New York from the English within the context of a larger colonial conflict between the two countries, concluded a peace treaty with London wherein they exchanged most of present-day New York State for British recognition of Dutch authority over the area that comprises present-day Suriname, a sector of northeastern South America near Venezuela that was suitable for growing sugarcane. In short, the Dutch used New York as a bargaining chip to consolidate their position in what they considered the more desirable territory—Suriname.

Much like the U.S. gold prospectors of 1849 who stampeded west in the hope of striking it rich, the Europeans were mesmerized by the Caribbean's economic potential and therefore moved quickly to extend the boundaries of their empires into the region.

A critical by-product of this era was the emergence throughout the West Indies of what have been called plantation societies (or plantation cultures). Although the nature of these European-spawned entities was multifaceted and complex, their essential characteristic in terms of international relations was extensive, if not total, imperial mastery of the colony's political affairs and its economy (especially foreign trade). The fact that such was the case is hardly surprising, for the primary economic function of plantation societies was to generate wealth that would then be transferred to the home country through a variety of mechanisms. To assure that this process functioned smoothly, the central authorities in Europe had to maintain tight control over political as well as economic decisionmaking powers in their Caribbean domains.

As was the case in many other areas where European imperialism sank its exploitive roots, its impact on the West Indies was far-reaching, for the flaws that the plantation societies nurtured did not disappear entirely with imperialism's demise. Instead, as Thomas J. D'Agostino shows in Chapter 4, the legacy of the plantation society would long plague the Caribbean's developmental aspirations and distort the dynamics of Caribbean relations with the outside world. Stephen Randall documents the flaws of the plantation system (monocultural economies, authoritarian political systems, and others) in Chapter 3.

The decolonization process in the Caribbean began in Haiti. In 1697 Spain had formally ceded the western third of the island of Hispaniola to the French, who called the area St. Domingue and had already established a flourishing slave plantation system there. This acquisition proved to be fortuitous, for by the late 1700s St. Domingue (the French form of Santo Domingo, early name of Haiti) was considered by many to be among the most profitable colonies in the entire world. But then the French Revolution burst on the scene, inspiring a slave uprising in 1791 led by Toussaint L'Ouverture and Jean-Jacques Dessalines. By 1801 the rebel forces were for the most part in control of the situation, although they suffered a major setback in 1802 when Toussaint was captured by the French and later died in prison. The struggle, however, continued under Dessalines's leadership, with Haiti finally achieving full independence in 1804 and thereby becoming the Western world's first black republic.

Events in the remaining two-thirds of Hispaniola, initially controlled by the Spanish and known as Santo Domingo, were equally chaotic. The French, who had previously established themselves in its western environs, finally gained control of the entire island in 1795. Shortly thereafter, of course, the French position was undermined by the slave rebellion that created an independent Haiti. Santo Domingo, however, remained a French colony for another five years until it reverted to nominal Spanish control in 1809. But Madrid's tyrannical proclivities generated increasing discontent, and in 1821 the Dominicans rose in revolt, drove out the Spanish, and declared their independence. Their victory celebrations proved, however, to be premature, for in 1822 Haitian President Jean Pierre Boyer invaded and annexed the new country, thus bringing all of old Hispaniola under his authority. Boyer ruled until overthrown in 1844, when Santo Domingo once again broke free, forming the modern-day Dominican Republic.

The next chapter in the Caribbean's anticolonial saga was written in Cuba, where revolutionaries under the leadership of Carlos Manuel de Céspedes proclaimed independence from Spain in 1868. The ensuing Ten Years' War (1868–1878) ended inconclusively in a truce that, while granting some concessions to the rebels, still left the island under Madrid's control. Lingering discontent in the ensuing years led to a resumption of the fighting in February 1895 under the leadership of José Martí (who, although killed just three months later in a minor skirmish, is widely revered today as the godfather of Cuban independence) and General Máximo Gómez. The U.S. government intervened on behalf of the insurgents in April 1898, precipitating the Spanish-American War. Many nationalistic Cubans were not particularly enthused by this development, for there was considerable suspicion that Washington's involvement was motivated primarily by its own long-standing hegemonic designs (e.g., the United States had for years expressed an interest in buying and/or annexing the island) rather than by an idealistic commitment to Cuban emancipation. These fears would in many respects prove to be valid once the war was over.

The conflict ended on December 10, 1898, with Spain withdrawing and transferring power to a U.S. military government that ruled the island until an independent republic was formally established on May 20, 1902. However, the new nation's sovereignty was from the very beginning severely undermined by the Platt Amendment. Grafted into the Cuban constitution of 1902 in return for the withdrawal of U.S. troops, it basically guaranteed Washington the unilateral right to intercede in the island's affairs (by armed force or other means) anytime it wished to do so. Over the next thirty-two years the United States repeatedly exercised this option; it militarily occupied the country on several occasions and routinely conspired to ensure that governments acceptable to Washington were installed or maintained in power. This interventionist legacy would later be a major factor contributing to tensions between the United States and Fidel Castro's revolutionary government.

The final wave of Caribbean decolonization came rather late, at least in comparison to the rest the hemisphere. Almost all the countries involved were English colonies (Dutch-controlled Suriname being the main exception), and all would subsequently become members of CARICOM, the area's foremost organization for promoting regional cooperation. The various dates for independence are: Jamaica, Trinidad and Tobago (1962); Barbados, Guyana (1966); the Bahamas (1973); Grenada (1974); Suriname (1975); Dominica (1978); St. Lucia, St. Vincent and the Grenadines (1979); Antigua and Barbuda, Belize (1981); and St. Kitts and Nevis (1983).

There are, of course, still some non–self-governing territories in the Caribbean, the main example being Puerto Rico, which the United States acquired as a result of the 1898 Spanish-American War.[1] The island's complex and often controversial relationship with Washington allows its inhabitants a considerable degree of jurisdiction over local affairs, but ultimate power still resides with the U.S. Congress. In recent years elections and other measures of public opinion have indicated an almost equal split between those favoring a continuation of the current commonwealth arrangement and those desiring statehood, with support for the independence option lagging significantly behind.

In any case, many countries soon discovered that breaking free from the shackles of classical colonialism does not necessarily produce freedom in its most pristine form. Instead, the harsh reality—especially for relatively small states such as those in the West Indies—is that they remain highly vulnerable to various kinds of control and exploitation by outside powers. William Demas, who at the time was serving as president of the Caribbean Development Bank, nicely summarized the problem with this observation:

> Many people in the region . . . hold pessimistic and deterministic positions regarding our prospects for any degree of *effective* independence vis-à-vis the outside world. They believe that we are doomed to abject subordination because of our small and in some cases minuscule size, and because of our long colonial history as mere political, economic, military, and cultural appendages of the metropolitan countries. They consider that we can only be "specks of dust" [that are] impotent, unable to control our destiny, . . . and inevitably subject to the decisions, and indeed the whims, of outside countries. (Demas 1986:12)

Demas's key point involves the need to recognize the crucial difference between *formal* and *effective* sovereignty. The former is more symbolic than substantive, for its main focus centers on acquiring such ceremonious badges of independence as diplomatic recognition by other states, admission to the United Nations, and other similar manifestations of acceptance into the international community. Effective sovereignty, in contrast, refers to circumstances where a country and its people *truly control* their own destinies; they are, in other words, exercising their right of national self-determination in the fullest sense of the term. Establishing and especially sustaining these conditions is no simple matter, for constant vigilance must be maintained against any attempts by outside elements to usurp a nation's power to make and implement its own decisions concerning its political, economic, and/or social affairs.

The picture becomes somewhat complicated when formal sovereignty exists (as it can) without its effective counterpart, a situation often considered by observers to represent a modern manifestation of classical colonialism. Although various concepts such as neocolonialism, neoimperialism, and dependency have been developed to describe and explain this quandary, all are in the final analysis referring to a hegemonic relationship in which one state dominates another's affairs through a complex system of indirect controls, often using its superior position for exploitive purposes. Such inequities were eloquently characterized by William Appleman Williams as constituting an informal empire wherein

> the weaker country is not ruled on a day-to-day basis by resident administrators, or increasingly populated by emigrants from the advanced country, but it is nevertheless an empire. The poorer and weaker nation makes its choices within limits set, either directly or indirectly, by the powerful society, and often does so by choosing between alternatives actually formulated by the outsider. (Williams 1962:47–48)

Given Caribbean countries' long history as targets of European subjugation and the fact that the Colossus of the North (i.e., the United States) has continued to cast a long shadow over the region even after many of its peoples became independent, it should not be surprising that Caribbean countries still

"Next!"
In the early twentieth century, the United States perceived itself as responsible for the states of the circum-Caribbean.

are apprehensive about any possible threat of hegemonic intervention into their affairs. Indeed, such nationalistic sentiments have often emerged as a crucial element in the West Indian perspective on international relations today, to which we now turn our attention.

■ The Dynamics of Caribbean International Relations in the Modern Era

The international agendas of the West Indian states during the second half of the twentieth century were for the most part dominated by two themes; first, the Cold War competition for global supremacy waged by the world's two superpowers; and second, various initiatives launched by Caribbean countries (especially Anglophone nations) in the realm of economic coalition-building. The latter category includes efforts to create or to gain admission to organizations dedicated to expanding the scope of their members' economic and commercial relations, often via such mechanisms as free-trade agreements and similar arrangements.

These two key dimensions did not, of course, play out independently. Instead, there were, at least until the early 1990s, when the U.S.-Soviet Cold War rivalry faded from the scene, complex links between them, with developments in one area often having a significant impact on what happened in the other. For simplicity's sake, however, they will be discussed separately here, with primary emphasis on economic coalition-building, for it remains a major concern of West Indian governments. Finally, two other urgent foreign affairs challenges that will continue to confront the Caribbean as it moves into the new millennium—migration issues and drug trafficking—will be explored.

The Cold War in the Caribbean

The international stage underwent a radical transformation after World War II. European countries such as England and France, which had monopolized the limelight for centuries, were no longer the central actors. Instead, attention focused on the United States, the Soviet Union, and the global power struggle that exploded between their two camps after Nazi Germany and imperial Japan had been defeated. The Caribbean countries, as was the case with many other small developing nations, were not able to avoid the turmoil that had been unleashed. And so in light of the political tentacles cast over the region by their northern neighbor, they increasingly found their international agendas being heavily influenced by Washington and its Cold War concerns. Basically, then, what transpired was that the United States incorporated the West Indies into its overall strategy of trying to prevent the expansion of Soviet influence in particular and the spread of communist ideology in general.

Washington's interest in establishing itself as the Caribbean's dominant outside power was not, of course, simply a by-product of the Cold War. Rather, almost from the very moment that it gained its independence, the United States considered the region (along with Mexico, Central America, and the northern coast of South America) as falling within its sphere of influence. This hegemonic mentality derived from Manifest Destiny. The central notion of the Monroe Doctrine of 1823, Manifest Destiny became popular in the mid-1800s as a rationale for the annexation of Texas and related frontier areas and was based on the belief that God had assigned the United States the mission of spreading its democratic and Protestant ideals westward across the continent. In other words, much like the Spaniards before them, these proselytizing Yankees (Spanish: Yanquis) viewed their territorial expansion as the logical outgrowth of a divine natural law whose operation resulted in "higher civilizations" (i.e., the United States) taking charge of lands inhabited by "backward peoples" (i.e., Native Americans and Mexicans). By the end of the nineteenth century Manifest Destiny's geographic scope had been enlarged to include the Caribbean and Central America. As this drama unfolded, outright annexation was abandoned in favor of more sophisticated policies of indirect control that some critics would later characterize as neocolonial. Perhaps the most infamous initiative along these lines occurred in 1904 when President Theodore Roosevelt issued the Roosevelt Corollary to the Monroe Doctrine. Like the Platt Amendment with regard to Cuba, the Roosevelt Corollary claimed Washington's unlimited unilateral right to intervene forcefully into the affairs of Latin American and Caribbean states.[2] Although the Roosevelt Corollary was repudiated by the U.S. government in 1928 with the Clark memorandum, its key contention that the United States should function as the hemispheric policeman remained firmly embedded in Washington's policy psyche.

These attitudes were compatible with the basic Cold War approach that the United States adopted for dealing with the Soviet Union. The three fundamental operating principles involved were: (1) *bipolarity* (the United States and the Soviet Union represented the world's only significant power centers); (2) *macrolinkage* (practically all international political and security issues were considered integral to the bipolar struggle for power and had to be handled accordingly); and (3) vigilant *containment* of communism (any expansion of which was seen as a victory for Moscow that served to enhance its position within the all-important global balance of power and thereby increase the security threat confronting the Western camp in general and the United States in particular). Given the strategic significance that Washington has historically accorded the Caribbean region, it quickly became a prime locale for the application of the containment doctrine. Any challenges to the status quo, especially those employing violence to seize power, that were considered communist in nature or simply leftist-inspired (a term that was defined very broadly) were equated with threats to the policy of global containment. As such, Washington felt compelled and justified in bringing its power to bear to restore stability and pro-Western political orthodoxy, often undermining or even completely destroying the principle of effective West Indian sovereignty in the process. The 1954 overthrow of the Jacobo Árbenz regime in Guatemala is generally considered to have been the first major example of such U.S. Cold War interventionism in the Western Hemisphere, but revolutionary Cuba ultimately emerged as Washington's most enduring and most frustrating target.

The specific moves undertaken to implement containment in the Caribbean and elsewhere fell for the most part into two broad categories of action that could be employed individually or in some combined fashion. The first involved economic options, the most common tactics being:

• the institution of aid programs for particular countries or even entire regions, which usually entailed direct financial support (e.g., outright grants or loans on highly favorable terms), technical advice and training, and/or trade preferences. Such assistance was predicated on the assumption that societies that are economically stable and are becoming, at least according to U.S. standards, increasingly modernized will be immune to communist subversion. The Marshall Plan in Western Europe was Washington's first major Cold War attempt to put this theory into practice, its counterparts in the Western Hemisphere being John Kennedy's Alliance For Progress and Ronald Reagan's Caribbean Basin Initiative (CBI).

• the destruction of governments unacceptable to Washington by wielding U.S. economic power to destabilize them. By employing such techniques as trade embargoes and manipulation of private investment, it was hoped that the ensuing economic chaos would either cause the targeted regime to self-destruct or would erode its popular support to the point where it would eventually be overthrown. Among the CARICOM countries, efforts were made to undermine Michael Manley's first administration in Jamaica (1972–1980) and Maurice Bishop's New Jewel movement in Grenada (1979–1983). However, Fidel's Cuba has borne the brunt of Washington's economic warfare in the Caribbean. Indeed, policies maintaining and even intensifying the U.S. economic blockade of the island continued despite the Cold War's demise, two graphic examples of this ongoing anti-Castro sentiment being the 1992 Torricelli Amendment and especially the 1996 Helms-Burton Act.

The second set of options were military or paramilitary, taking such various forms as:

• aid programs designed to bolster the ability of recipient governments and their armed forces to counter threats to their security. Often the greater danger was posed by homegrown rebels rather than foreign invaders, with Washington in these instances responding by providing counterinsurgency trainers and advisers.

• covert operations, sometimes characterized as "dirty tricks," which were usually carried out by the U.S. Central Intelligence Agency (CIA). Among these escapades, the general public is probably most familiar with the ill-fated 1961 invasion of Cuba at the Bay of Pigs. This fiasco was a major embarrassment for the Kennedy administration, as were subsequent revelations about CIA plots to assassinate Castro. A less well known, but in this case successful, Caribbean undertaking was the 1964 joint U.S.-British campaign to nullify the preindependence elections in British Guiana (later known as Guyana) won by Cheddi Jagan, an avowed Marxist.

• calling upon regular U.S. armed forces to enforce containment. This is, of course, the most drastic (and often highly controversial) measure available to Washington, and therefore one might expect that it would very seldom, if ever, be used in such a relatively small area as the West Indies. In reality, however, there were *three* major combat deployments in the Caribbean during the Cold War: to the Dominican Republic in 1965; to Grenada in 1983; and during the 1962 Cuban missile crisis, an extremely dangerous confrontation considered by many experts to be the closest that the United States and the Soviet Union ever came to nuclear war.

Although it is true that the Caribbean's strategic importance was diminished in Washington's eyes once the Cold War ended, the United States certainly did not abandon its traditional affinity for trying to manipulate developments there. Generally gone, however, was the image of U.S. ruthlessness often exhibited during containment's heyday. Politically, for example, Washington stopped openly embracing governments, no matter how brutal or corrupt, simply because they had impeccable anticommunist credentials. No longer on public display were the attitudes exemplified by Franklin Roosevelt's famous observation about the Dominican Republic's dictator, Rafael Trujillo: "He is an SOB, but at least he's *our* SOB." Instead, Washington began to use its influence to promote democracy and human rights. Its biggest success in this respect was Haiti. In October 1991 a coup occurred there when Jean-Bertrand Aristide, a radical priest who had won the country's December 1990 presidential elections and had subsequently implemented reforms benefiting the country's long-suffering lower classes, was driven from power by a military junta. In 1994, however, the generals finally capitulated and stepped aside under heavy international pressure led by Bill Clinton's administration, which included tough economic sanctions and the threat of a U.S. invasion. Subsequently, Washington, along with other members of the United Nations, dispatched peacekeeping forces to Haiti, which helped to maintain stability as Aristide reassumed office and then peacefully transferred power to his democratically elected successor in 1996. The last U.S. troops were withdrawn from the country shortly thereafter.

This enthusiasm for democracy has, however, had some limits in the case of Fidelista Cuba. For example, in a provision generally ignored by most U.S. observers relating to Washington's demand for a democratic presidential campaign as a precondition for lifting the U.S. economic blockade of the island, the 1996 Helms-Burton Act stated unequivocally that the United States will refuse to accept as legitimate *any* Cuban election (including, presumably, one that is totally open and fair) won by Fidel Castro or his brother Raúl. Havana understandably reacted with disdain, portraying U.S. policymakers as brazen

UN Photo 177252

Supporters of Jean-Bertrand Aristide celebrate his presidential election victory, Haiti

hypocrites with absolutely no respect for the principle of effective sovereignty who embrace the electoral process only when it produces results that advance their hegemonic pretensions.

The Caribbean Countries and Economic Coalition-Building

As Dennis Pantin discusses in Chapter 5, no country in the modern interdependent world can afford, if it expects to exist at anything beyond a bare subsistence level, to ignore the exigencies of international finance and commerce. This maxim applies particularly to small states like those in the Caribbean because their prospects for significant progress in socioeconomic development almost always depend on their ability to operate in the larger global economy. Such nations do not normally have, for example, the large reserves of natural resources (e.g., minerals and fuels) necessary to support industrialization and related aspects of modernization. Thus, international trade in commodities, manufactured goods, and even services becomes a crucial element in their developmental processes.

A profile of some recent economic trends for the West Indies as a whole, which admittedly can vary considerably from one country to another, suggests that the region's developmental momentum has lagged behind its Latin American counterparts. For example, if per capita gross domestic product (GDP) performance is used as a basis for comparison, Table 6.1 indicates that Caribbean growth rates were (except for the Dominican Republic) well below the hemispheric norm during the 1990s. This pattern seems to be a new phenomenon, for Figure 6.1 shows the West Indies faring markedly better in per capita GDP figures than Latin America in the late 1970s and early 1980s. But clearly adjusting to the economic environment that emerged in the 1990s has been more difficult in the Caribbean than on the mainland.

Table 6.1 Latin America and the Caribbean: Per Capita Gross Domestic Product (percentages based on values at 1990 prices)

	Average Growth Rates							Average Annual Rate	
	1991	1992	1993	1994	1995	1996	1997[a]	1981–1990	1991–1997
Latin America	1.7	1.2	2.1	3.7	–1.5	1.9	3.5	–1.0	1.8
CARICOM	1.0	–0.3	–0.5	1.1	1.4	1.1	1.2	–0.9	0.5
Cuba	–11.6	–11.8	–15.2	0.0	1.8	7.3	2.9	2.8	–4.2
Dominican Republic	–1.2	4.6	0.3	2.3	2.9	5.2	6.4	0.2	2.8
Haiti	2.8	–14.9	–4.4	–10.2	2.3	0.7	1.3	–2.4	–3.7

Source: ECLAC (Economic Commission on Latin America and the Caribbean), on the basis of official figures converted into U.S. dollars at constant 1990 prices. Downloaded from ECLAC's Internet homepage at www.eclac.cl.

Note: a. Based on official figures converted at constant 1995 prices.

Figure 6.1 Caribbean Gross Domestic Product (1990 U.S.$)

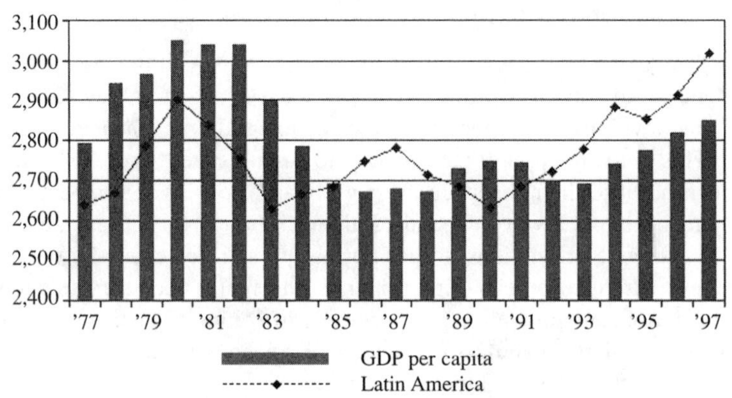

Source: Compiled by author from CARICOM data, available online at http://www.caricom.org/statistics, accessed 2001.

Numerous considerations have helped to produce this situation. For example, in the post–Cold War period it obviously is no longer possible for third parties to benefit by being courted by the Western and Eastern camps. One important casualty of this development has been the superpower foreign aid programs (such as the CBI) that had the potential to contribute to the economic health of developing states; they have been drastically reduced and, in some cases, have totally disappeared. Undoubtedly, Cuba is the Caribbean country that has suffered the most in this respect, its economy having shrunk approximately 40–45 percent when its preferential ties to the socialist bloc disappeared in the early 1990s. Indeed, Caribbean nations, like many elsewhere in the world, have found that they are now on their own in international economic relations.

Lending added importance and even urgency to these new rules of the economic game is the fact that export-oriented growth, operating within the context of a neoliberal system of global free-market competition, has become widely accepted as the most effective strategy for enhancing a country's economic strength. In other words, foreign trade and its related activities are increasingly seen as the keys to prosperity.

Unfortunately, most Caribbean states have not been faring too well in this area, as is illustrated by Figure 6.2, which summarizes the CARICOM members' aggregate trade balance from 1977 through 1997. Note in particular that their performance, which was never particularly strong in terms of producing surpluses, has nose-dived in the post–Cold War period. This decline is to a great extent rooted in the configuration of CARICOM's trading partners and

Figure 6.2 Caribbean Trade Balance, 1977–1997 (U.S.$ in millions)

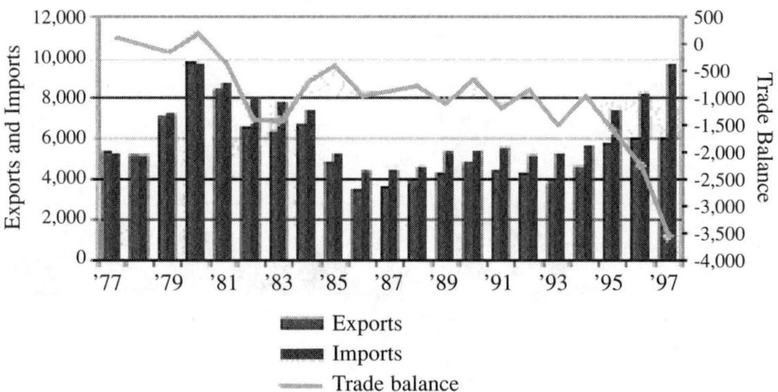

Source: Compiled by author from CARICOM data, available online at http://www.caricom.org/statistics, accessed 2001.

shows the United States as the overwhelmingly dominant outside commercial force in the region (Figures 6.3 and 6.4). Approximately 40 percent of all CARICOM trade takes place with the United States, the European Union ranking a rather distant second with a percentage in the upper teens. The crux of the problem, of course, is that during the 1990s the CARICOM nations were selling less and buying more from their northern neighbor, the result being a seriously deteriorating trade balance, which is very much reflected in the overall data presented in Figure 6.5. These statistics (along with the Cuban case) illustrate the danger of becoming overly reliant upon any single business

Figure 6.3 Destination of CARICOM Exports, Selected Years (percentage)

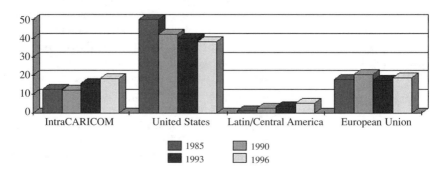

Source: Compiled by author from CARICOM data, available online at http://www.caricom.org/statistics, accessed 2001.

Figure 6.4 Sources of CARICOM Imports, Selected Years (percentage)

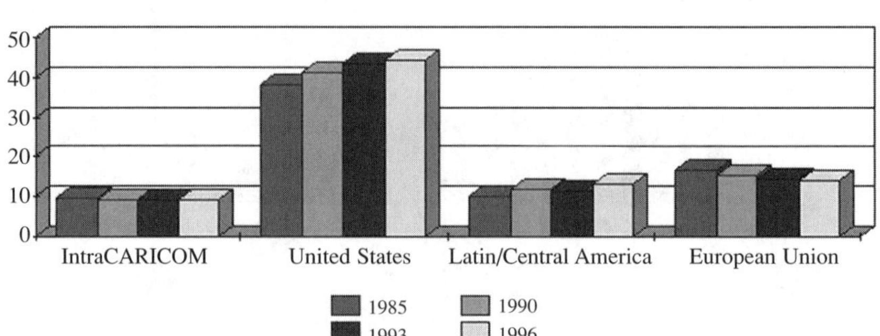

Source: Compiled by author from CARICOM data, available online at http://www.caricom.org/statistics, accessed 2001.

Figure 6.5 CARICOM's Trade Balance with the United States, 1980–1996 (Eastern Caribbean $)

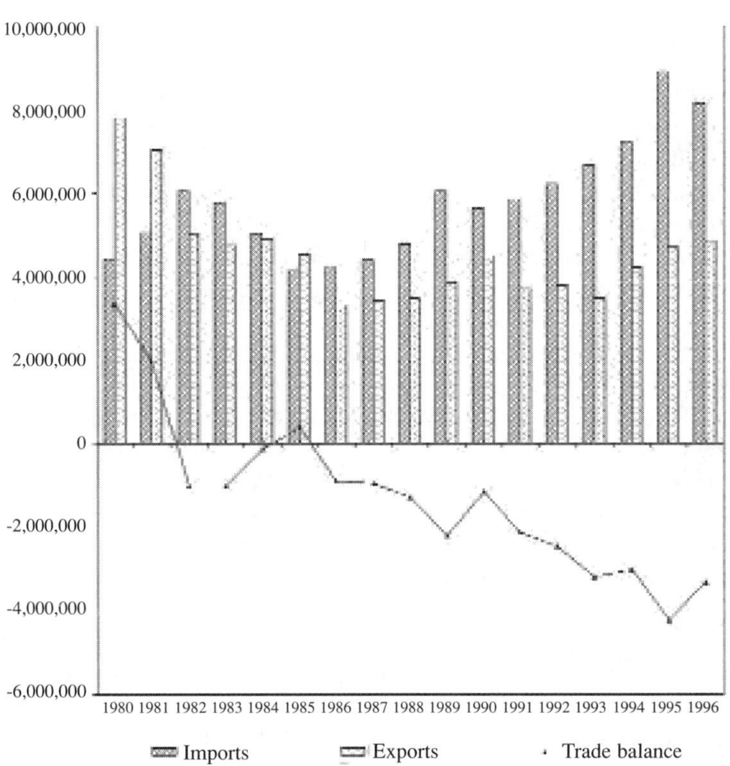

Source: Compiled by author from CARICOM data, available online at http://www.caricom.org/statistics/graphs/figure, accessed 2002.

relationship, which can raise the specter of dependency and the loss of effective economic sovereignty. One strategy to avoid this fate and, hopefully, to enhance their ability to compete more effectively in the global free market system with which Caribbean states (both CARICOM members and others) have experimented is economic and developmental coalition-building.

The concept of such coalition-building is, at least in this context, fairly straightforward. Basically, it involves the establishment of economic arrangements whereby the participating countries garner various advantages, trade preferences being the most common. Normally these special relations will be fully institutionalized by being incorporated into an official longer-term agreement (i.e., a treaty) and operating under the aegis of an administrative structure (e.g., a commission or a secretariat) that is fully empowered to oversee and coordinate implementation. In short, coalition-building entails some movement by a country toward economic integration with a clearly defined, and limited, set of partners. Typically, the first step taken is membership in a free-trade association.[3]

Beyond the obvious economic benefits that may be involved, the prospect of enhanced collective bargaining power can be a major incentive for cooperation among small developing countries like those in the Caribbean. The key idea here is to use coalition-building as a mechanism for members to coalesce around a grand strategy for dealing with the main centers of global economic strength (i.e., either individual countries such as the United States, or groups like the European Union), thereby putting them in a better position to negotiate more advantageous deals with the world's great economic powers.

Intra-Caribbean initiatives. The flagship vehicle for coalition-building within the confines of the Caribbean has been and remains today CARICOM. Created in 1973, its twelve charter members (four of which were independent at the time) were all nations that were or had been part of the British Empire.[4] The Bahamas joined the fold in 1983, and in 1995 Suriname became the first country to be admitted that did not have an English heritage (it had been a Dutch colony). The organization's most recent addition as a full member state is Haiti, which was granted provisional membership in 1997 and then became a full participant in July 1999.

Certainly the most audacious and controversial move that CARICOM made was its overtures toward Castro's Cuba. This process began to gain momentum in the 1990s, when the CARICOM heads of state decided at their eleventh summit conference (Jamaica, August 1990) to launch serious discussions with Havana regarding possibilities for increased economic cooperation. A series of meetings followed in which significant progress was made toward an agreement covering a range of topics. The culmination of this essentially exploratory phase occurred at the thirteenth CARICOM summit conference (Trinidad, June 1992). Although Havana's request for official observer status was not approved (reportedly due to intense counterlobbying by the United States), CARICOM did agree to establish a joint commission to explore prospects for greater CARICOM-Cuban cooperation in the areas of trade, developmental programs, and cultural exchanges. A formal accord setting up this body was concluded at the fourteenth CARICOM summit (the Bahamas, July 1993).

This budding relationship further expanded when CARICOM used its influence to promote Cuban involvement in economic negotiations with the European Union. Such an initiative was important to the Castro regime because Havana was in the unenviable position of being the *only* government in the entire Caribbean–Latin American community that did not have an official trade agreement with the European Union. The Caribbean Forum

(CARIFORUM), the body used by CARICOM to formulate and represent its interests in negotiations with the European Union to update the Lomé convention (see below for details on the Lomé process), provided the arena for this evolving cooperation. In late March 1998 Cuba formally applied for admission to CARIFORUM as an observer, a designation that would allow it to join the group's preparatory activities in a nonvoting capacity and to closely monitor any subsequent formal talks with the European Union. This petition was approved by CARICOM in May 1998, and the European Union endorsed the acceptance in June 1998, thereby for the first time giving Havana some degree of official standing within the Lomé framework. Shortly thereafter, at an August 1998 CARIFORUM summit meeting in the Dominican Republic that Castro attended, Cuba was upgraded to full membership. But despite such positive developments, CARICOM has remained reluctant to approve Havana's long-standing request for similar observer status (which is often seen as a precursor to regular admission) in the main organization.[5]

This opening to Cuba proved to be quite lucrative, for CARICOM's trade with Cuba exploded from a meager U.S.$17.7 million in 1992 to $444 million over a twelve-month period during 1996–1997 (an increase of 2,048 percent). The latter figure must, however, be approached with some caution, for it is inflated by the fact that it includes a large amount of petroleum produced outside the Caribbean that the Fidelistas purchased through West Indian brokers. Such transactions, although obviously benefiting both parties, did not represent "trade" in the purest sense of the term because the product that Havana was buying was not produced in the Caribbean country that was selling it. Although good longitudinal information that excludes brokered oil is not readily available, it is probably safe to say that such entries would account for at least half of the 1996–1997 total. However, even assuming this to be the case, the upward trend (especially percentage-wise) in Cuba-CARICOM trade during the 1990s would be impressive. But most important to CARICOM was the fact that by 1996–1997 it was registering a healthy surplus in these exchanges; its exports constituted U.S.$405 million of the $444 million total, which translated into a $366 million profit.

CARICOM's thriving Cuban connection represented just one aspect of a larger process of trade diversification (especially with regard to export destinations) that was attributable in part to the organization's coalition-building efforts both within and beyond the West Indies. This phenomenon is illustrated by Table 6.2, which indicates that in 1985 the United States and the European Union far overshadowed the other major centers of CARICOM export activity; their market share was almost five times greater than that of their less-developed competitors. But by 1996 this differential had been cut almost in half. In other words, though still trading heavily with these traditional partners, the CARICOM group as a whole was succeeding in becoming *less* export dependent upon them. This pattern can be seen as contributing to

Table 6.2 Market Share of CARICOM Members' Exports (percentage)

Percentage of Exports Going to	1985	1996
United States and the European Union	68.0	56.9
Other CARICOM members and Latin/Central America	13.8	23.8

Source: Compiled using data downloaded from CARICOM's Internet homepage at www.caricom.org/statistics, accessed 2001.

the CARICOM countries' quest for economic sovereignty, for they are moving away from a situation where their economic health can become so closely tied to their relationship with certain countries that they may become vulnerable to trade sanctions and other kinds of commercial blackmail. In extreme cases this could escalate into economic warfare that would seriously threaten their basic security.[6]

Extra-Caribbean initiatives. CARICOM's greatest achievement with regard to extending its economic coalition-building operations beyond the Caribbean's horizons has involved its leadership in the Lomé process, which basically entails periodic renegotiation of economic and trade preferences that the European Union has agreed to extend to a large group of former European colonies. The genesis of Lomé can be traced to England's decision in the late 1960s to join the European Community. London's pending entry sent shockwaves through the third-world members of the British Commonwealth, who feared that their privileged access to English markets was now in jeopardy. Consequently, when the opportunity arose in 1972 to establish an institutionalized association with the *entire* European Community, the developing Commonwealth nations formed the ACP Group to serve as their agent.

ACP membership was quickly expanded to include the former colonies of other European powers (especially France), and the forty-six participating governments then proceeded to enter discussions for a comprehensive new relationship with the European Community. The result was the 1975 Lomé convention, which has subsequently been renegotiated every five years: 1980, 1985, and 1990.[7]

CARICOM states have played a vanguard role in the Lomé process from the very beginning. They were, for example, the driving force behind the move to increase the ACP Group's ranks, the idea being to translate larger numbers into a stronger negotiating position. Subsequently they have tried, often with a considerable degree of success, to serve as a catalyst for greater strategic consensus within the ACP Group and thereby enhance its ability to present a more united front in discussions with the Europeans, who during their colonial years had become highly skilled in the use of divide-and-conquer tactics.

Although the Lomé experience has not always lived up to CARICOM's (and others') expectations, it nevertheless represents a major accomplishment in furthering sovereignty with regard to international commercial and financial affairs. Specifically, it represents the use of coalition-building to acquire and regularly exercise collective bargaining power to establish the exact terms of at least some important aspects of CARICOM's trading and related relationships with one of the world's great centers of economic power.

The most recent foray by West Indian countries, led by CARICOM, into economic coalition-building on a broad international scale led to the emergence of the Association of Caribbean States (ACS). The first step toward creating the ACS was taken by CARICOM when it endorsed the idea during its fourteenth summit meeting (the Bahamas, July 1993). Three months later (in October 1993) CARICOM officials met with representatives of Mexico, Venezuela, and Colombia in Trinidad, where they issued a declaration calling for the formation of the ACS. Subsequently, a treaty formally launching the organization was signed on July 24, 1994, in Cartagena, Colombia.

The ACS's list of full-fledged participants numbered, as of November 2002, twenty-five West Indian and mainland Caribbean Basin nations, with three other countries affiliated as associates.[8] One entry on this roster that attracted particular attention was Cuba, for much to Washington's chagrin the ACS had flouted the U.S. policy of trying to isolate Castro's government by accepting Havana as a charter member.

As the 1990s drew to a close the ACS, unlike CARICOM, had yet to establish a track record substantial enough to allow its worthiness as a developmental coalition to be evaluated. This situation was hardly surprising to many observers, for opinion has been widespread that the ACS is unlikely ever to become a truly viable organization. Such skeptics would point, for example, to the fact that Central America's landscape is littered with failed attempts at economic coalition-building, the troubled history of the Central American Common Market (CACM) being a case in point.[9] Also, the two main regional groups within the ACS—the CARICOM nations and the mainland Hispanic states—have never displayed much capacity for sustained cooperation, instead often regarding one another with considerable suspicion.

Another problem confronting the ACS involves the possibly lackluster commitment that some members might have to the organization, with Mexico posing the largest question mark, for that country already participates in both the ACS and the North American Free Trade Agreement (NAFTA). Theoretically, such dual membership could allow Mexico to serve as a convenient bridge between the two groups and to represent the interests of its ACS partners within NAFTA. Realistically, however, Mexico is likely to find itself severely cross-pressured in many situations, and if Mexico were ever forced to choose where its primary interests lie, the NAFTA connection will almost certainly prevail. This quandary will, of course, intensify if other ACS members who have displayed strong NAFTA aspirations (e.g., Jamaica and Trinidad and Tobago) are admitted, for then the specter of fragmentation will arise.

International Challenges Confronting the Caribbean

Economic coalition-building, which as noted above has been and remains a high-priority item on the international agenda of Caribbean countries, involves two vital challenges: *broadening* the process and *deepening* the process. Broadening means expanding the scope of one's activities, which in practice means expanding existing networks of collaboration by bringing in new participants or by forging alliances that create new groupings. The Caribbean countries were, by and large, successful in this regard during the 1990s. CARICOM, for example, went beyond its traditional Anglophone base by bringing Suriname and Haiti into the fold and by markedly improving its relations with Castro's Cuba. Moreover, via the ACS, the larger West Indies community helped to create a mechanism that its supporters hope will serve as a vehicle for unprecedented cooperation across the entire Caribbean Basin.

It has, however, been a different story in the context of deepening the process, which concentrates on achieving greater degrees of teamwork and integration (e.g., moving from a free-trade to a common-market arrangement). Progress in this area has not been terribly significant. It was noted previously that the considerable skepticism that exists as to the ACS's prospects to develop into an effective, influential body has yet to be refuted. Likewise, there are observers who feel that CARICOM's depth has been lacking, citing as evidence several points:

- CARICOM's vulnerability to fragmentation, which was demonstrated in 1981 when several of its smaller participants, without withdrawing from CARICOM, formed a parallel group called the Organization of Eastern Caribbean States (OECS) to service their special developmental needs.[10] The goals of the OECS are quite similar to CARICOM's, and it often functions as a lobbying group for its constituents within its CARICOM parent.
- CARICOM's failure, despite describing itself as such, to implement various policies and to create various institutions that characterize an authentic functioning common market. For example, although preliminary agreements have been reached and action plans have been formulated, CARICOM has not yet fully acquired such attributes of a common market as uniform external tariffs, a regional stock market, and unimpeded movement of labor among its members.

Although both the broadening and the deepening dimensions of economic coalition-building are intrinsically desirable and useful, they have become imperative in the face of another major challenge confronting the Caribbean countries: the advent of NAFTA and its possible expansion into other hemispheric markets. The harsh reality is that no *single* country in the region can match NAFTA's power and resources; individually, each is relegated to play the role of David to the NAFTA Goliath.

The basic problem confronting Caribbean governments as they try to deal with this emerging megacenter of international financial and commercial power has been nicely summarized by Denis Benn, who notes that NAFTA

> presents the Caribbean with a major dilemma. Whereas, on the one hand, the region's economic viability, or even survival may depend on favorable access to NAFTA, some of the conditions for accession impose significant constraints on the development options available to those countries. For example, it is clear that the Caribbean countries would have to subscribe to market-oriented policies sanctioned by the IMF [International Monetary Fund] and the World Bank, and demonstrate commitment to a liberalized international trading system. Despite governmental statements of commitment to liberalization, it will be difficult for Caribbean countries to succeed in putting their economies on a firmer footing that would enable them to compete [effectively]. (Benn 1997:18)

In other words, Caribbean nations may be confronting a situation where they will be damned if they do and likewise damned if they don't join or somehow affiliate with NAFTA. To forgo participation entails the risk of losing trade, foreign investment, and other developmental benefits to member countries who receive preferential treatment. But to become involved may be equally dangerous, for there is serious doubt that such small countries would be able to handle the competitive pressures when pitted against much larger states in the cutthroat arena of free trade. Indeed, the most pessimistic scenarios see the Caribbean islands losing so often and so thoroughly that their effective economic sovereignty may be threatened.

An obvious response to this quandary is to try to employ regional economic coalitions as collective bargaining units, the goal being to negotiate a special NAFTA connection (e.g., akin to the various Lomé agreements) that will ensure some protective preferences for Caribbean countries. CARICOM has experienced some success in launching initiatives along these lines aimed at preserving its members' CBI benefits in any future NAFTA association. But it is the larger ACS, whose member populations total approximately 217 million and whose combined GDPs in 1995 (the first full year of the ACS's existence) were roughly U.S.$549 billion, that appears at least on paper to have the stronger negotiating position. However, this potential has not yet been realized in any significant way.

Although economic concerns are extremely important to Caribbean governments, a major issue for the general public (especially in the United States), and perhaps the region's greatest problem, is the international drug trade. The Caribbean is not the major production center for illegal narcotics, but it is a conduit in the industry's transportation network. It has, for example, been estimated that 40 percent of all cocaine produced in South America for the U.S. and European markets moves through the area. Initially, the Bahamas, Belize, and Jamaica were the main countries used as transshipment centers. More recently, however, such activity has expanded to include Barbados, the Dominican Republic, Guyana, Haiti, Trinidad and Tobago, and many of the smaller eastern Caribbean islands. Also, drug cartels have often turned to the region to launder their huge profits, using friendly banks, paper corporations, and other ruses to hide their narcodollars in legitimate business activities. The focal point for such financial alchemy has been the Cayman Islands, whose strict laws guaranteeing bank secrecy are extremely attractive to customers seeking to avoid scrutiny by regulators or law enforcement officials.

In the Caribbean, as elsewhere, narcotics trafficking has brought with it a depressing litany of social ills. Drug-related crime rates are up, and corruption of government officials has increased. Combating such problems can, of course, require a reallocation of personnel and resources that might otherwise be dedicated to developmental projects, the result perhaps being a serious deterioration of the overall quality of life. In certain respects, however, some islands may, due to their extremely small size, the openness of their democratic societies, and their physical isolation, be susceptible to a very unique and extreme threat: subversion and indirect control of their governments by drug barons.[11] In short, the fear is that their effective sovereignty might be jeopardized by the narcotics trade.

Recognizing, as have other countries like Colombia and Mexico, that drug trafficking is a truly international problem that cannot be addressed effectively in a unilateral fashion, the Caribbean's counteroffensive has relied on various international agreements and joint programs, particularly with the United States. In most cases these endeavors, which have involved fairly conventional undertakings such as sharing intelligence, providing aid funds for equipment and training, and combined interdiction operations, have proceeded smoothly. Controversy has erupted, however, over Washington's heavy-handed efforts to persuade Caribbean governments to enter into so-called shiprider agreements. These accords are designed to permit U.S. antidrug agencies to conduct land, sea, and air patrols, maritime searches and seizures, and arrest and detention operations *within* the national boundaries of the Caribbean signatories. Some critics complained that these understandings, which more than a dozen countries in the region had embraced in one form or another by 2000, were grossly one-sided, giving Washington prerogatives that in many cases infringed on Caribbean sovereignty without providing anything significant (e.g., increased developmental aid) in return. In such instances, they have complained, the narcotrafficking cure might be as bad as the ailment.

Although not a source of serious international contention for most West Indian nations, the migration issue is one final challenge always looming on the Caribbean horizon. Indeed, the region holds the dubious distinction of having a greater percentage of its people relocate to other lands than any other part of the world. Dennis Conway discusses the Caribbean diaspora in Chapter 12. Usually motivated at the individual level by economic self-interest (e.g., the desire for employment or a better job), emigration has functioned in a larger social sense as a two-edged sword. It has, for example, been beneficial in serving as an outlet for surplus labor, whose frustration might otherwise lead to serious internal dissension, and as a source of valuable foreign currency, because migrants often send back large remittances to relatives still living in the region. Cuba's economy, to cite just one example, profits enormously from the approximately U.S.$800 million that flows in annually from the U.S. exile community. But because the people who leave are often the brightest and most ambitious, they may represent a serious brain drain that undermines the developmental progress of the countries they leave behind.

Because the most popular destination is the United States, the potential exists for migration quarrels to erupt between Washington and Caribbean governments. By and large, however, this has not occurred. The United States did make often restrictive changes in its immigration laws in the 1980s and 1990s, but generally West Indians were not adversely affected. Indeed, legislation passed in 1990 actually increased the Caribbean's total number of permissible immigrants, although admittedly limitations were placed on some categories within the overall pool that reduced their prospects. The two main exceptions to this tranquil scenario have been Haiti and Cuba. Most Haitians who illegally left the island in the pre-Aristide period claiming that they were refugees fleeing oppression were turned back by U.S. authorities, the rationale being that their motivation was actually economic and therefore they were not eligible for political asylum. This policy was denounced as racist by many in both Haiti and the United States, the anger inflamed by the fact that any Cuban in similar circumstances was *automatically accepted* and given assistance in establishing U.S. residency. No other nationality in the entire world was extended the carte blanche given to those abandoning Castro's revolution, and Havana, as might be expected, did not react well to such generosity.

The Fidelistas' basic complaint was that Washington was encouraging illegal emigration and thereby creating a no-win situation for Havana. When people were leaving, the United States tried to use that fact as evidence to bolster its claim that Castro's government lacked popular support. Yet if Havana tried to prevent such departures, it was then accused of police-state terrorism. Castro's most famous retaliatory move was known as the Mariél boatlift. In April 1980 he announced that any exiles in the United States who wanted to take their relatives out of the country could come to the port of Mariél near Havana to retrieve them. Thus began a frenzied boatlift that deposited about 125,000 refugees on U.S. shores before it was shut down in October 1980. This chaotic influx often had a disruptive impact, especially because it included some hardened criminals and other undesirables that Cuba was, in effect, covertly deporting to an unsuspecting United States. Subsequently, Havana and Washington would negotiate various migration agreements designed to assure a more orderly process. In August 1994, as economic problems drove increasing numbers of Cubans to sea on flimsy homemade rafts that they hoped would get them to Florida, the White House finally abandoned its unconditional open-door policy by announcing that it would no longer provide automatic asylum to illegal Cuban refugees. Thus, most of the tensions between the two countries over migration were relieved.

* * *

The task of meeting these challenges makes it quite likely that the Caribbean nations will endure as vibrant actors on the international stage. Admittedly, the chances are slim that their situation will be as melodramatic as when pirates prowled the region or when the twentieth century's two superpowers brought their Cold War to the West Indies. In any case, the area's proximity to the United States practically guarantees that it will continue to attract Washington's attention. Thus, regardless of whether they like it or not, the futures of the Caribbean as well as that of the colossus to the north appear destined to remain closely intertwined as the two parties move forward.

■ Notes

1. The list of external powers and the main Caribbean territories still involved in some sort of nonindependent relationship with them includes: the United States—Puerto Rico and the U.S. Virgin Islands (along with the special case of the Pentagon's naval base at Guantánamo Bay in Cuba); Great Britain—Anguilla, the British Virgin Islands, the Cayman Islands, Montserrat, and the Turks and Caicos Islands; the Netherlands—Aruba, Bonaire, Curaçao, St. Eustatius, St. Maarten, and Saba; and France—Guadeloupe, Martinique, and French Guiana, which are considered overseas departments of France and thus have a formal legal status similar to states in the United States.

2. As Stephen Randall notes in Chapter 3, the key section of the Roosevelt Corollary (for the original text, see Roosevelt (1906: 857) proclaimed that:

> If a nation shows that it knows how to act with reasonable efficiency and decency in social and political matters; if it keeps order and pays its obligations, it need fear no interference from the United States. Chronic wrongdoing, or an impotence which results in a general loosening of the ties of civi-

lized society, may in America, as elsewhere, ultimately require intervention by some *civilized nation*, and in the Western Hemisphere the adherence of the United States to the Monroe Doctrine may force the United States, however reluctantly, in flagrant cases of such wrongdoing or impotence, to the *exercise of an international police power*. (italics added)

3. The four most common forms of economic coalition-building are as follows (ranked from the least to the most complex):

- Free-trade agreements: the main goal is to radically lower or ideally remove all major impediments to trade, such as tariffs and related barriers, among members.
- Customs unions: similar to free-trade agreements, but these add common external tariffs with regard to commercial relations among participants and nonmembers.
- Common markets: these add various provisions to a customs union structure, the most important being assurances that there will be an unimpeded flow of labor and capital among participating countries.
- Complete economic unions: these incorporate all of the traits mentioned in the previous three categories and then factor in provisions that function to centralize control over the monetary and fiscal policies of all participants.

4. The independent charter members were Barbados, Guyana, Jamaica, and Trinidad and Tobago. The eight others, all of which except Montserrat would subsequently become independent, were Antigua, Belize (known at the time as British Honduras), Dominica, Grenada, St. Lucia, St. Vincent and the Grenadines, St. Kitts and St. Nevis, and Montserrat.

5. As of late 2002, those holding observer status in CARICOM were Colombia, the Dominican Republic, Mexico, Venezuela, Aruba, Bermuda, the Cayman Islands, the Netherlands Antilles, and Puerto Rico; associate members included Anguilla, the Brtitish Virgin Islands, and the Turks and Caicos Islands.

6. Cuba underwent such a wrenching experience in the early 1960s when the United States, which bought most of the sugar that was the mainstay of the island's economy, stopped all purchases as part of a larger plan to destabilize and ultimately destroy Castro's infant revolution.

7. The 1990 version differed from its predecessors in that it was agreed that it would run for ten years. The Lomé convention became obsolete, one key reason being the relative deprioritizing of North-South relations by the European Union as it devoted increasing attention to its ties with countries in the former Soviet bloc. However, the EU and the ACP signed an agreement on trade, aid, and sustainable development on June 23, 2000, in Cotonu, Benin.

8. The twenty-five full members of the ACS are Colombia, Costa Rica, Cuba, the Dominican Republic, El Salvador, Guatemala, Honduras, Nicaragua, Panama, Mexico, and Venezuela plus fourteen of the fifteen CARICOM countries (Montserrat, a member of CARICOM, is not included because it is not independent). The associate members are Aruba, the Netherlands Antilles, and France (on behalf of French Guiana, Guadeloupe, and Martinique).

9. The CACM was established in 1960 with the ultimate goal of creating a Central American free-trade zone. The 1969 fighting between Honduras and El Salvador

(the so-called Soccer War) effectively paralyzed the whole process, with the CACM henceforth existing only as a paper organization. Efforts to reinvigorate it were made in the early 1990s, but little was accomplished as area governments focused most of their attention on dealing with the fallout of the severe political instability that plagued the region in the 1980s.

10. The seven members of the OECS are Antigua and Barbuda, Dominica, Grenada, Montserrat, St. Kitts and Nevis, St. Vincent and the Grenadines, and St. Lucia.

11. Among the independent CARICOM countries, for example, four have populations under 100,000, and five fall into the 100,000–300,000 range. As such, they are no larger and often significantly smaller than such U.S. cities as Tampa, Florida, and Akron, Ohio.

■ Bibliography

Benn, Denis. "Global and Regional Trends: Impact on Caribbean Development." In *Caribbean Public Policy: Regional, Cultural, and Socioeconomic Issues for the 21st Century*, edited by Jacqueline Braveboy-Wagner and Dennis Gayle. Boulder: Westview, 1997.

Bryan, Anthony T., J. Edward Greene, and Timothy M. Shaw. *Peace, Development, and Security in the Caribbean*. New York: St. Martin's, 1990.

Demas, William. *Consolidating Our Independence: The Major Challenge for the West Indies*. Distinguished Lecture Series, Institute of International Relations, University of the West Indies. St. Augustine, Republic of Trinidad and Tobago, 1986.

Domínguez, Jorge I., ed. *International Security and Democracy: Latin America and the Caribbean in the Post–Cold War Era*. Pittsburgh: University of Pittsburgh Press, 1998.

Domínguez, Jorge I., and Abraham F. Lowenthal, eds. *Constructing Democratic Governance: Latin America and the Caribbean in the 1990s—Themes and Issues*. Baltimore and London: Johns Hopkins University Press, 1996.

Ebel, Roland H., Raymond Taras, and James D. Cochrane. *Political Culture and Foreign Policy in Latin America: Case Studies from the Circum-Caribbean*. Albany: State University of New York Press, 1991.

Erisman, H. Michael. *The Caribbean Challenge: U.S. Policy in a Volatile Region*. Boulder: Westview, 1984.

Fauriol, Georges A. *Foreign Policy Behavior of Caribbean States: Guyana, Haiti, and Jamaica*. Lanham, MD: University Press of America, 1984.

Heine, Jorge, and Leslie Manigat, eds. *The Caribbean and World Politics: Cross Currents and Cleavages*. New York: Holmes and Meier, 1988.

Klak, Thomas, ed. *Globalization and Neoliberalism: The Caribbean Context*. Lanham, MD: Rowman and Littlefield, 1998.

Langley, Lester D. *The United States and the Caribbean in the Twentieth Century*. Athens: University of Georgia Press, 1982.

Maingot, Anthony P. *The United States and the Caribbean*. Boulder: Westview, 1994.

Mullerleile, Christoph. *CARICOM Integration Progress and Hurdles: A European View*. Kingston, Jamaica: Kingston Publishers, 1996.

Pastor, Robert. *Exiting the Whirlpool: U.S. Foreign Policy Toward Latin America and the Caribbean*. Boulder: Westview, 2001.

Roosevelt, Theodore. "The Roosevelt Corollary." In *Compilation of the Messages and Speeches of Theodore Roosevelt,* vol. 2, edited by A. H. Lewis. Washington, DC: Bureau of National Literature and Art, 1906.
Tulchin, Joseph S., and Ralph H. Espach. *Security in the Caribbean Basin: The Challenge of Regional Cooperation.* Boulder: Lynne Rienner Publishers, 2000.
Williams, William Appleman. *The Tragedy of American Diplomacy.* New York: Dell, 1962.

7

The Environment and Ecology

Duncan McGregor

Many have argued that the Caribbean environment has been, and is being, altered at a pace that is resulting in significant environmental degradation (Watts 1987; Paskett and Philocette 1990; McElroy et al. 1990; Richardson 1992; McGregor 1995; Eyre 1998). There are three major foci of this degradation. Widespread *ecological degradation* has occurred through the depletion of both flora and fauna. *Soil degradation* is exemplified by the removal of topsoil by erosion as well as pollution of the land by agrochemicals and a range of human and industrial wastes. *Marine degradation* is most clearly seen in reef degradation, though a general depletion of marine life through overfishing and pollution has been a fact of Caribbean life for decades.

As Dennis Pantin shows in Chapter 5, economic development in most, if not all, of the Caribbean has been achieved in three ways: agriculture, extractive industry, and tourism (with industry and tourism leading to ever-increasing urbanization, particularly in the coastal zone). Each of these has had, and continues to have, a significant effect on the environment. The longest acting of these is agriculture, and in this respect environmental degradation has been a fact of Caribbean life for centuries. Regionwide increases in soil erosion associated with the conversion of natural forest to plantation agriculture have been documented (Watts 1987; Richardson 1992). It has also been argued that historically entrenched land use patterns virtually ensured that soil erosion and land degradation would continue to be a problem after emancipation, once rural population pressures built up in agriculturally marginal hillside farming regions (Barker 1989).

Today, environmental degradation and loss of topsoil is ubiquitous throughout the Caribbean and is at critical levels in Haiti in particular (Watts 1995). It has continued apace despite numerous attempts at watershed rehabilitation (see, e.g., Paskett and Philocette 1990; McGregor and Barker 1991; McGregor 1995; Edwards 1998). Watershed deforestation leads to increased levels of soil erosion as well as to deteriorating water supplies; negative impacts on stream, estuarine, and marine plant and animal life; and the reduction of reservoir capacity. Again, the interdependence of natural and human systems is apparent, and a holistic perspective is critical to inform the discussion of environmental degradation.

The roots of environmental degradation can be found in the history of the plantation economies and the colonial legacy (Watts 1987; Richardson 1992; Potter 2000). However, the colonial legacy is more than environmental degradation and economic dependency on the exploitation of natural resources; it is also about the greater ability of national governments to control interactions between humans and their environment (Bryant and Bailey 1997). A common manifestation is exploitation at the expense of the environment (e.g., Jamaica's bauxite industry and the effects of tourism; France and Wheeller 1995; Pattullo 1996). This is most often driven by global economic forces, which are largely controlled by national governments or by individuals and groups who have the opportunity to influence government thinking. The outcome for local people and their environment is frequently disadvantageous. The agriculture industry will serve as an example.

Much of Caribbean agriculture suffers from entrenched *structural dualism*, defined in this context as a situation whereby a large-scale commercial sector uses the best land for produce destined for the export market, and whereby a small-scale traditional sector produces mainly for the local market, often relying on marginal land such as steeply sloping hillsides (Barker 1993).

A second major constraint on agriculture is the periodic disruption caused by natural hazards, such as hurricanes, floods, storm surges, and landslides, as well as hazards exacerbated by human activity, such as accelerated soil erosion. Additionally, the economic vulnerability characteristic of small states is linked to this hazardous nature and arises from a number of underlying causes, principally the limited supply of quality agricultural land, high population densities of many Caribbean islands, limited aquifer (groundwater) storage of water, and small catchments with rapid transfer of the effects of environmental damage (Potter 2000; Brookfield 1990; McElroy et al. 1990; Barker 1993). A good example: soil eroded from cultivated upland slopes in small islands such as Dominica and St. Lucia is rapidly incorporated into the hillside streams, with their relatively steep gradients and rapid flows, and is rapidly transported by these streams through the catchments and out into the near-shore sea zone.

■ The Physical Setting

Although Thomas Boswell discusses the geographic setting in Chapter 2, I begin with a brief explanation of the nature of the environment and of recent environmental change in order to understand fully the pressures that shape human behavior in the contemporary Caribbean.

Geologically, the islands of the Caribbean may be divided into four main groups. The Bahamas consists of more than 700 islands, most of which are composed of limestone and many of which are uninhabited. The four largest islands in the Caribbean—Cuba, Hispaniola, Puerto Rico, and Jamaica—form the Greater Antilles and owe their origins to tectonic activity at the interface between the North American Plate and the northward- and eastward-moving Caribbean Plate, most notably during the late Miocene and Pliocene geological periods, between about 10 million and 4 million years ago (Draper et al. 1994).

The Lesser Antilles comprise two parallel chains of islands: an inner arc built around volcanic cones or cone groups (such as Montserrat, Dominica, St. Lucia, and St. Vincent), and a discontinuous outer arc of islands of coral limestone (Anguilla, Barbuda, Antigua, Grande Terre, and Barbados). These islands have been constructed from mid-Eocene times (about 45 million years ago) along the arc-shaped eastern edge of the Caribbean Plate. A number of the volcanic cones are still intermittently active, as witnessed most dramatically by the recent eruptions of Soufrière in Montserrat; many islands experience intermittent earthquake activity.

A fourth group of islands close to the South American mainland, including Trinidad and Tobago, although geologically varied, owe their current form and position to Andean folding and faulting, predominantly of Miocene age.

The region is characterized by northeasterly trade winds and relatively high temperature regimes with little seasonal variation. Rainfall is generally highest in the summer months, and a drier period is commonly present between December and April. Orographic rainfall is important, where rain-bearing clouds are forced to rise upon encountering mountain ranges, causing the air to cool and precipitate its moisture as rain on the northeasterly-facing mountain slopes. "Rain-shadow" effects are common on the larger islands or those such as Dominica, which are dominated by mountain terrain, where relatively little rain remains to fall in the southwest-facing side of the mountains. For example, the eastern slopes of the Jamaican Blue Mountains have up to 197 inches of rainfall in the average year, but this drops to 31.52 inches in Kingston, only a short distance to the leeward side of the Blue Mountains peaks.

Tropical storms and hurricanes are regular features of Caribbean life, with most heavy storms being experienced during August and September. They are born in the warm waters of the western Atlantic or the Caribbean Sea, in areas where sea temperatures exceed the critical threshold of 26 degrees Celsius required to provide the heat energy for their development. Although varied and unpredictable, most hurricanes track from east to west across the Caribbean before frequently moving to a more northerly track as they approach the Lesser Antilles or the North American or Central American mainlands.

In this area of relatively abundant rainfall and equable tropical temperatures, natural vegetation consists mainly of tropical and seasonal rainforest, except in rain-shadow areas, where drier forms of seasonal rainforest are found (Table 7.1). Cactus-thorn forest-scrub communities are found on the dry coastal fringes of many islands, more extensively in the Bahamas and other well-drained limestone areas. Significant vegetation community types include lowland savanna grasslands, freshwater and saltwater swamp vegetation, mountain forest formations, and coastal fringe formations including mangrove communities. Mangrove communities were formerly much more widespread, formed an important buffer to coastal erosion by waves and storm surges, and acted as a trap of material eroded from cleared land and natural erosion.

Another result of the combination of high temperatures and rainfall: high natural rates of chemical weathering. The soils that are produced are deeply weathered, heavily leached, and highly susceptible to erosion. On steeper slopes in particular, attempts at permanent forms of agriculture inevitably lead to accelerated soil erosion and thin soils of relatively low chemical fertility (see, e.g., Paskett and Philocette 1990; McGregor 1988, 1995). Younger volcanic soils and soils developed on low-lying coral limestone may, in contrast, be very fertile, and these soils have formed a long-term basis of successful agriculture where carefully husbanded (Watts 1987). Examples of fertile vol-

Table 7.1 Lowland Vegetation Formations in the Caribbean

Vegetation Type	Tropical Rainforest	Seasonal Rainforest	Seasonal Rainforest (dry)	Cactus-thorn Forest-scrub
Annual precipitation (inches)	78.74	49.21–78.74	29.53–49.21	19.69–29.53
Number of dry months	0–2	3–5	6–7	8–10
Predominant soils	Ferralitic[a] latosols and podsols	Relatively rich organic; some concretions near surface	Relatively rich organic; some concretions near surface	Young, often closely related to bedrock
Nutrient cycling	Rapid; storage in vegetation	Slower; litter accumulation, some storage in soil as well as vegetation	Slower; litter accumulation, some storage in soil as well as vegetation	Slow

Source: Adapted from D. Watts, *The West Indies: Patterns of Development, Culture, and Environmental Change Since 1492* (Cambridge, UK: Cambridge University Press, 1987), p. 28.

Note: a. These are iron-rich soils, formed by the relative accumulation of iron through the gradual loss by leaching of other minerals.

canic soils included those of Montserrat before its recent volcanic eruptions; sugarcane plantations have thrived for centuries on limestone soils such as those of Barbados.

The Caribbean islands have in the past supported a rich range of flora and fauna. The distribution of plant species varies according to rainfall regime and altitude. Seasonal rainforest is the natural vegetation cover of most lowland areas of the West Indies below 660 feet in elevation, and it has been the principal focus of clearance. Precipitation increases with altitude in many locations, and with human clearance of natural vegetation for plantations, as well as other forms of agriculture, seasonal rainforest is frequently succeeded upslope by tropical rainforest.

Most remnants of Caribbean rainforest fall into the precipitation regime envelope depicted in Figure 7.1. Significant variation can be seen within this envelope, and this is reflected in a varying ability of the rainforest to recover from disturbance. As most Caribbean island areas are small in size, and many subareas exhibit a high degree of specialized plant habitat adaptation (e.g., Cockpit Country, Jamaica), the potential for species extinction is high.

Figure 7.1 Caribbean Tropical Rainforest Regime

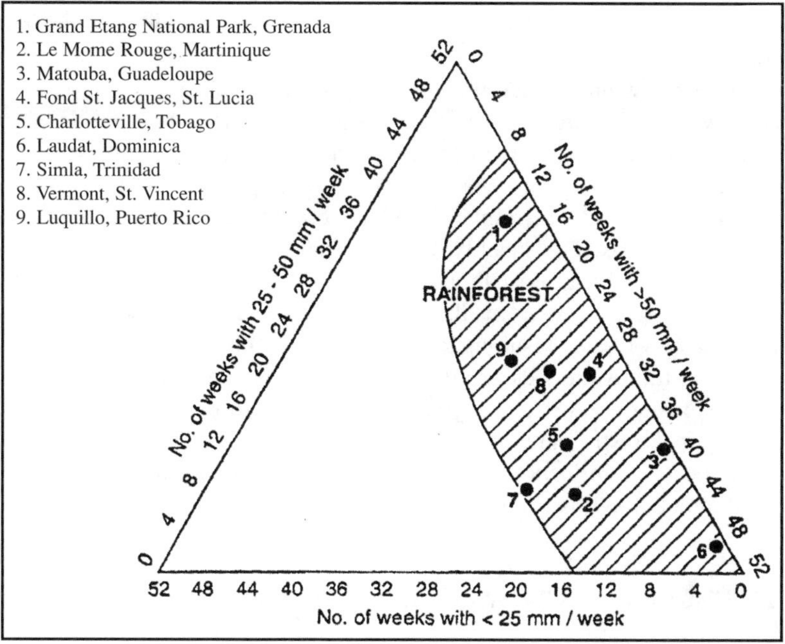

Source: L. A. Eyre, "The Tropical Rainforests of the Eastern Caribbean: Present Status and Conservation," *Caribbean Geography* 9, no. 20 (1998): 101–120.

The same may be said of Caribbean fauna. The island situation has given rise to a generally impoverished land-mammal fauna compared with adjacent South America. Only Trinidad, closest to the continental area, has a large range of species. But reptile fauna and native birds are more diverse, reflecting easier migration from island to island. Near-shore sea margins have in the past supported an immensely varied wildlife system, with large populations of fish, shellfish, and amphibia.

A notable consequence of the relatively warm seas that have characterized the Caribbean over at least the last 10,000 years has been the growth and nourishment of coral reef communities. Reef coral is still actively forming in some areas, but in many more the vitality of the coral has been progressively reduced by damaging effects Dead or severely damaged reefs are unfortunately no longer remarkable in the region as a tourist submarine excursion around Montego Bay on Jamaica's northern coast will readily testify. A consequence of this is reduced protection of the coastal zone from the effects of storm surges associated with hurricanes and tropical storms.

The most radical terrestrial influence on environmental change in the Caribbean over the past three and a half centuries has been the progressive destruction of natural vegetation (Watts 1987; Richardson 1992). Progressive deforestation, although focusing on the terrestrial environment, has led directly to the increased discharge of eroded soil particles in the coastal and near-shore zones with attendant reduction in vitality of coastal vegetation and reef communities.

More recently, human activities relating to increasing urbanization and tourism have focused primarily on the coastal zone. Throughout the insular Caribbean, significant degradation of this zone has been the result (see discussion below).

For the future, global climate models forecast regional precipitation decreases and increased seasonality, with regional rises in temperatures likely (Intergovernmental Panel on Climate Change 1992, 1995). This will affect terrestrial and marine ecosystems that have already been weakened by human action. In many ways, the resulting loss of soil and/or marine productivity will directly affect the livelihoods of farmers and fishermen alike, which in turn will lead to greater pressure, through rural-urban migration, on the social systems of regional towns and cities.

These negative influences on the Caribbean island environment will be discussed in detail in this chapter.

■ Historical and Recent Land Use Change

The introduction of sugarcane to Barbados in about 1640 triggered the large-scale clearance of native vegetation. By 1665 only isolated pockets of forest remained in Barbados (Watts 1987), and a similar process was under way on lowlands throughout the islands, fueled progressively by imported slave labor. Reports of accelerated soil erosion followed almost immediately (Richardson 1992). Native plant species were replaced to some extent by imported species such as breadfruit. Slave emancipation in the 1830s and 1840s exacerbated environmental deterioration in many cases. In Jamaica, for example, the freed slaves were forced to more marginal ground, often steeply sloping hillsides, where they persisted with the deleterious practices of fire clearance and clean weeding (Barker and McGregor 1988). The combination of preoccupation with cash crops on the best land, the intensification of domestic food production on more marginal land, and increasing population pressures brought many small-farmer systems throughout the Caribbean to the point of collapse. Inevitably, a drift away from agriculture has led to increasing urbanization.

Hillside agriculture and urban growth are linked by the increasing pressures on land as well as by increasing throughputs of mass and energy. In the case of hillside agriculture, this is seen in the growing transfer of sediment through terrestrial runoff from the slope to the near-shore zone, something that is likely to continue for some time. In the urban zone, pressures on space and amenities are leading to increasing urban hazards, such as flooding, slope failure, traffic congestion, and health risks such as local outbreaks of cholera and typhoid caused by the contamination of domestic water supplies.

Clearly, the ability to tackle these problems is partly one of economics—the cost-benefit equation of whether it is more expeditious to attempt to solve the problem or to live with it. In this context, it is becoming increasingly

Richard S. Hillman

The sign announces this area as a Green Area Restoration Project, Santo Domingo, Dominican Republic

apparent that attitudes toward land and the environment are major factors in whether or not environmental problems are perceived as such. In turn, such perceptions will influence whether problems are addressed and, if so, how they will be addressed.

As for agricultural land, some general points can be made on how Caribbean peoples perceive the land. First, there is a fundamental paradox, which is perhaps Caribbean-wide, in people's perceptions of "family land" (Besson 1987). On the one hand, family land is seen as scarce in relation to the dominant plantation sector. The reasons for this are long-standing, with roots in the accession of land by freed slaves during the transition from slavery (Besson 1987). The effect on an individual piece of land is often overuse. On the other hand, land is seen as an unlimited resource in light of the long-term role of land held by the family in respect of absent kinsfolk. This will often be manifested in voluntary nonuse of parcels in recognition of the rights of absent family members. Such idle land, widespread in some areas of Jamaica, for example, leads to underproduction. This perception of land, partly a protection for kinsfolk, may well maintain some land in a relatively undegraded condition in more traditional rural areas. The net effect, however, is more pressure on the land that is in regular use.

"The control of land signifies freedom and provides a partial buffer against external economic oscillation" (Richardson 1992:188). This would suggest that within the region land is primarily seen as an economic asset. However, there seems now to be a clear disjunction between agricultural land use (seen as traditional and unattractive) and the urban-centered tourist industry (seen as a more attractive economic proposition). The social implications include a drift toward an aging agricultural labor force as younger people migrate to the cities, as well as increased crime and prostitution in the cities as young people seek urban employment and housing.

Although these perceptions focus only on one aspect of a complex social process, these views of the value of land, if extrapolated to the wider Caribbean, imply the continuation of rural-urban drift. This has implications for the aging agricultural labor force in coping with an increasingly hostile environment, as well as for the increasing pressures on the already stretched urban areas. This also suggests that the continuing development of tourist-based activities will likely lead to the further diminution of indigenous and agriculturally based activities.

The Human Impact: Deforestation and the Environment

Demand for land has led to historic high rates of deforestation throughout the Caribbean (Lugo et al. 1981; Watts 1987). Ongoing and allegedly unsustainable rates of deforestation (e.g., an estimated rate of 3.3 percent per annum for Jamaica) were subsequently revised upwards to 5.3 percent per annum (Eyre 1987, 1996). It should be noted, however, that much of the speculation on rates of Caribbean deforestation has been based on partial analysis and on data of varying quality. Although large-scale deforestation has undoubtedly taken place in the past and is continuing (albeit probably at lower rates), accurate rates of contemporary Caribbean-wide deforestation have yet to be convincingly established.

Estimates of deforestation rates of thirteen islands in the eastern Caribbean from Puerto Rico to Trinidad, though varying enormously, indicate an annual deforestation rate of around 1.5 percent (Eyre 1998). Although this may not seem high compared to Jamaican deforestation, at present only 30 percent remains of the area capable of supporting rainforest (Eyre 1998; Table 7.2). This represents deforestation of some 70 percent (compared to the 1996 calculation of 67 percent of Jamaica's former forest cover lost).

Implications for Hillside Agriculture

Deforestation induces accelerated erosion due to a combination of steep slopes and high-intensity rainfall events, and although crops as they grow impart a progressively better protection against raindrop impact, fields are at their barest and most vulnerable when newly planted at the start of the rainy season. Hillside farming systems throughout the Caribbean are therefore char-

Table 7.2 Status of Rainforests of the Eastern Caribbean

	1	2	3	4
Puerto Rico	2,896	700	24	83
Saba	15	3	20	0
St. Eustatius	5	1	20	0
St. Kitts	28	20	71	0
Nevis	55	8	15	0
Guadeloupe	1,050	196	19	98
Dominica	751	342	46	30
Martinique	898	150	17	31
St. Lucia	579	189	33	0
St. Vincent	389	67	16	0
Grenada	180	39	22	49
Tobago	145	69	48	92
Trinidad	2,986	1,194	40	68[a]
Eastern Caribbean	9,977	2,978	30	34

Source: Adapted from L. A. Eyre, "The Tropical Rainforests of the Eastern Caribbean: Present Status and Conservation," *Caribbean Geography* 9, no. 20 (1998): 101–120.

Notes: (1) Area with tropical humid climate in sq. km.; (2) area in rainforest in sq. km.; (3) percentage of "suitable" area in rainforest; (4) percentage of rainforest in national parks and adequately protected reserves.

a. Categorization of "adequate" is dubious.

acterized by high rates of soil erosion and widespread land degradation (Watts 1987; Barker and McGregor 1988; Paskett and Philocette 1990; McGregor and Barker 1991; McGregor 1995).

The common spatial pattern of small and fragmented holdings, caused where landholdings are split among the heirs when a farmer retires from the land or dies and common practices such as fire clearance and clean weeding, coupled with population pressures, are a recipe for land degradation Practices such as fire clearance and clean weeding are a legacy from plantation management methods and have persisted despite many governments' efforts to ban the use of fire to clear land.

Systematic soil-erosion control schemes, such as those established in Jamaica through the Land Authority projects in the period 1950–1969, and through subsequent projects, have not proved to be effective (Edwards 1995). Among the principal reasons for these failures have been the lack of continuation funding; the breakdown of integrated systems of structures and waterways; the application of inappropriate control measures in inappropriate topographic locations; and the basic physical limitations of slope, soil, and climate.

Local factors also contribute to progressive deforestation, for example, the cutting of poles to support yam vines. In Jamaica alone, the annual requirement is at least 15 million new poles each year (Barker 1998). This particular requirement is driven by farmers' perception that yams are one of the crops most suited to cultivation on steeply sloping land; perceptions undoubtedly play a part in the overall failure to manage land appropriately. To cite one example from the Blue Mountains area of Jamaica, few farmers surveyed perceived soil erosion as a problem, despite having a good understanding of the process, and despite almost universal employment of soil conservation structures (McGregor and Barker 1991). Further, few perceived a direct link between soil erosion and declining yields, blaming a variety of factors from climate to the Jamaican government. A fundamental problem is rural poverty and the short-term planning horizons that it presents. Farmers have neither the time nor the financial ability nor the perception of the problem to plan on their own for a sustainable future.

The Human Impact: Urbanization and Ecology in the Coastal Zone

Contemporary Caribbean societies are strongly urban in character. Recent data indicate that the Caribbean is considerably more highly urbanized than the developing world and exhibits a higher urban proportion than the world as a whole (Potter 1995, 2000). More than 60 percent of the total population of the Caribbean resides in urban settlements, compared to a global urbanization figure of about 50 percent (McGregor and Potter 1997). The urban population of the Caribbean grew at around 2.4 percent per annum during the 1990s. Noticeably, levels of urban primacy—the phenomenon whereby more and more people are attracted to the national or regional capital city—are high, with 40–60 percent of national populations living in the primate capital. Indeed, the extension of a highly concentrated coastal-based "plantopolis" settlement pattern where patterns of settlement and transportation links are inherited from the original plantation distributions of location, transportation, and trade, due to the dictates of tourism and manufacturing activities, is a feature that presents a series of environmental challenges in Caribbean territories (Potter 1995, 2000).

Such high levels of urbanization and marked urban primacy are associated with urban housing and urban infrastructure problems. For example, in Jamaica more than 50 percent of the total population is now classed as urban, approximately half of which live in the Kingston metropolitan area alone. Growth rates in the decade 1982 to 1991 peaked at 2.3 percent per annum for Portmore, a commuter settlement near Kingston, and 1.9 percent per annum for the tourist-oriented Montego Bay (Thomas-Hope 1996). Substandard housing is a critical problem throughout the region, with inadequate sanitation and water supply, urban transportation, and waste disposal among the principal problems.

The Environmental Impact of Urban Development

The effects of urban development on the Caribbean environment are wide-ranging and widespread. They range from the effects of building on the coastal zone to the destruction of wetlands and the degradation of marine environments (Table 7.3). In particular, the expansion of tourism throughout the region has exacerbated many of the problems of water supply, traffic congestion, and building blight, as well as increasing the impact of social problems such as prostitution and petty crime.

The urban system is increasingly becoming unable to cope with the effects of increasing runoff, sediment, and waste. The urban area presents a more or less sealed surface, particularly as sediment and urban waste choke parts of the urban drainage system. Already significant areas of Kingston, Jamaica, flood during storms; and the road system increasingly becomes a temporary stream network with concomitant disruption of traffic. This problem is often at its most acute in squatter settlements, where drainage infrastructure is lacking. For example, the Four-a-Chaud area of Castries, St. Lucia, a squatter area constructed on reclaimed land adjacent to the waterfront, regularly floods during peak rainfall events.

In Jamaica the Kingston metropolitan area and Montego Bay both illustrate the pressures of urbanization on environmentally fragile areas, including reclaimed coastal lands liable to an increasing risk of flooding under condi-

Table 7.3 Some Environmental Problems Facing the Caribbean Region

Problem	Possible Cause
Declining ratios of arable land per capita	Urban growth
Unequal balance between agricultural production and consumption	Decline in domestic crops
Soil erosion, infertile land, cleared forests	Past and present land use
Forest usage for energy and manufacturing	Tourism; informal industry; foreign-owned industry
Limited water availability	Tourism; industrial development
Wetland degradation	Housing; industrial development; tourist developments; pollution
Overfishing and overhunting of rare species	Export industry; informal sector
Removal of sand from beaches	Urban construction; tourist developments
Pollution (lack of control and limited infrastructure)	Overpopulation; tourist industry; irregular housing; industrial development; informal sector
Degradation of marine environments	Tourism; industrial development
Degraded urban environments	Uncontrolled urbanization; inefficient resources; lack of basic services; poverty

Source: D. F. M. McGregor and R. B. Potter, "Environmental Change and Sustainability in the Caribbean: Terrestrial Perspectives," in *Land, Sea, and Human Effort in the Caribbean,* edited by B. M. W. Ratter and W-D. Sahr, Beiträge zur Geographischen Regionalforschung in Lateinamerika, no. 10 (Hamburg: Institut für Geographie der Universtat Hamburg, 1997), pp. 1–15.

Carolyn Watson

An open sewage canal, Cité Soleil, Haiti

tions of rising sea levels. Portmore, a rapidly growing coastal-zone suburb of Kingston, is particularly at risk, as some areas of urban expansion, built behind artificial barriers, are already below sea level; Portmore is situated in a tectonically active area with the associated risk of earthquake and tsunami damage. In light of the potentially increased storm-surge levels associated with the combination of more intense hurricane conditions and a progressively drowned protective coral reef, Portmore may be seen as a disaster waiting to happen.

The Marine Environment: Reefs and Near-Shore Fisheries

The southerly parts of coastal East Asia and the Caribbean are the two areas of the tropics where reefs are most at risk (Bryant et al. 1998). This is due to a combination of circumstances, including coastal development, marine-based pollution, overexploitation, and land-based pollution and erosion. More than 60 percent of the Caribbean's reef area is at medium to high risk, with risk being higher where onshore population concentrations are greatest (Jamaica, Haiti, much of the Lesser Antilles, and Tobago). Jamaica exhibits some of the worst degradation with storm damage from hurricanes, reef bleaching, and unchecked algal overgrowth all adding to the range of human-related sources of pollution. The reef in Montego Bay, despite its designation as a marine park in 1966, is the most seriously degraded, a reflection of the small size and unmanaged nature of the park. The Montego Bay Marine Park was reestablished in 1990, but the reef continues to be affected by poaching, pollution from the city and airport, and runoff and sediment from inland agricultural and building activities. The implications of this are reduced economic activity (e.g., fishing and tourism) and a higher potential for onshore storm damage.

Yet of the global reef area total of 367, the Caribbean region has 139 areas with protected-area status (totaling slightly more than 15,000 square miles), a greater regional coverage than anywhere except Australia's Great Barrier Reef (Bryant et al. 1998). There has, however, been criticism in the region of the degree to which parks (both marine and terrestrial) are in fact protected—leading to the designation "paper parks" by some, whereby protection exists in written legislation but where enforcement is weak or effectively absent.

Caribbean peoples have relied on the sea for food for centuries, but today stocks of all edible species are severely depleted. Some species, such as sea turtles, have been afforded conservation status, yet turtles are still widely available for consumption. Some ascribe reports of widespread fish kills in the region in 1998 to the effects of raised sea surface temperatures on shallow reef fish. But there are also hypotheses of waste contamination by cruise

UN Photo 146364, P. Teuscher

Fishermen of Dominica returning with a day's catch

ships, pathogens transported by the Orinoco River, and even Montserrat's volcanic activity (Caribbean Environment Programme 1999). These fish kills are affecting local fishermen, as consumption and tourist trade are down as a result of adverse media coverage.

Wetlands are a vital linkage between land and sea activities and have often formed an integral part of local indigenous (artisanal) fisheries (e.g., the Black River Morass in Jamaica; Johnson 1998) and are now under threat from a variety of exploitative and destructive practices. Moreover, much of the eastern Caribbean's coastal wetland areas are degraded, and in particular mangrove destruction has been significant. Of 195 sites investigated, 47 percent were seriously degraded, with the principal culprits being landfill and solid waste dumping; vegetation clearance (particularly unregulated cutting of mangrove and other species for timber or charcoal production); reclamation for agriculture; alteration of natural drainage patterns; and pollution by factory and domestic effluents (Bacon 1995). In addition, the delicate water and sediment balances of many eastern Caribbean wetland areas have been adversely affected by changes in land use, both agricultural and urban, within their catchments The highest-percentage degradation was shown by wetlands in Barbados (100 percent), St. Vincent (75 percent), and St. Kitts (63 percent; Bacon 1995). However, rehabilitation of wetland areas may be low-cost and effective, usually involving replanting of mangroves, strict management of exploitation, cleaning up of dumped wastes, and the reestablishment of natural flushing systems (Bacon 1995). Clearly, where these areas have been built upon to fulfill the demand for housing or tourist accommodation and facilities, such solutions are more problematic.

Tourism: Destroyer or Savior?

As for tourism, the official views of governments and tourist bodies frequently contrast with the views of environmentalists, researchers, and the media. There is no doubt that island governments see tourism as the savior of faltering economies or that the economic benefits of tourism have been offset by environmental degradation (see Table 7.3). The sustainability of tourism has frequently been called into question (e.g., France and Wheeller 1995; Pattullo 1996; France 1998). The prospects for introducing forms of ecotourism, whereby sustainable environmental considerations and strict conservation requirements are central themes of development as a viable alternative have received similarly mixed reviews (e.g., Weaver 1994; Woodfield 1998). The "hawking of heritage," ranging from museums of colonial artifacts and accounts of the slave trade and early plantation life to displays of traditional forms of livelihoods, is seen as a commercial expediency, often of a contrived nature (Potter 2000). The case study of the Jalousie Plantation Resort in St. Lucia, where development was permitted in an area of outstanding natural beauty and within a sacred Arawak site, is perhaps one of the more prominent of a number of controversial developments (Pattullo 1996; France 1998). Local politicians often play a role in such developments with the implication that environmental interests are taking second place to personal profit (Pattullo 1996)

The problems arising from coastal tourist development are many and include beach erosion, marine and coastal pollution, reef degradation, dumping of untreated sewage and other wastes, sand mining, and the destruction of wetlands and salt ponds. The market response to a degraded environment is often swift. For example, the southern coast of Barbados, where coastal erosion and sewage pollution have been significant, has suffered declining tourist numbers in recent years, despite measures being taken to stem erosion and the building of a new sewage plant. Yet the environmental lessons do not seem to have been fully taken on board. In Barbados, for example, the recent development of the Westmorland tourist resort has led to increased flooding risk along its coastal fringe; and proposals for a hotel and tourist complex at Graeme Hall Swamp, the island's largest inland water body, are on the table.

Although the attraction of tourism is understandable, the Caribbean nations' position from the early 1990s—of increasing debt, declining prices for their goods and raw materials, and the attack on traditional markets (driven in part by the U.S. government)—means that the environmental price has been substantial and requires addressing.

Climate Change and Caribbean Environments

The most likely future climate scenario for the Caribbean Basin projected by global climate models is one of regional precipitation decreasing up to 13.79 inches per decade (Intergovernmental Panel on Climate Change 1992, 1995), accompanied by a likelihood of increased seasonality and a tendency toward fewer, but more intense, rainfall events.

A rise in air temperatures, estimated for the Caribbean Basin to be in the range 1.5–3 degrees Celsius by 2060, would potentially lead to significant and wide-ranging changes in environmental conditions (Wigley and Santer 1993). For example, increases in sea surface and shallow water temperatures above a critical threshold of 30 degrees Celsius lead to significant increases in coral bleaching (Milliman 1993).

Coral Bleaching

Coral bleaching occurs when corals, under stress from rising sea surface temperatures, lose much of their symbiotic algae, which supply nutrients and color. The immediate environmental effect of coral bleaching is a reduction in the vitality of the coral. Severe or prolonged bleaching can lead to coral mortality. An add-on effect is the reduction of the protective effect of fringing coral reefs on Caribbean coastlines.

A significant number of incidences of coral bleaching in the Caribbean have been documented since the late 1980s (Bryant et al. 1998). A major event occurred throughout the tropics in 1998, ascribed by some to the El Niño event of 1997. In the Caribbean, the Belize reefs were the worst affected, though regionwide bleaching was reported. In a warmer world, the rate at which bleaching occurs is likely to outstrip the ability of coral to colonize cooler waters.

The concerns here are damage to one of the world's most complex ecosystems; losses of habitats and species; and the reduced ability of the reef to protect the onshore land from storm surges. The critical link here is the ability of the coral reef to grow fast enough to keep pace with the rising sea levels projected by global warming. An unhealthy reef unable to grow fast enough to keep pace with rising sea levels will become progressively drowned, and the degree of onshore protection from storm-surge waves will be reduced. It is too early to predict with any accuracy what will happen in the Caribbean Basin in this respect, but the present rate of reef degradation is clearly unsustainable.

Potential Influence on Hurricane Activity

A significant rise in sea surface temperatures above the critical threshold of 26 degrees Celsius in the western Atlantic will mean a greater probability of tropical storms deepening to hurricane status. It has been estimated that an increase in sea surface temperatures of 1.5 degrees Celsius in the region would lead to an increase in annual average hurricane frequency of about 40 percent (from about four per year to between five and six per year, based on data since the early 1900s (Shapiro 1982). The destructive potential of storms may also increase. It has also been estimated that an increase in sea surface temperatures of 1.5 degrees Celsius would increase the potential maximum hurricane wind by about 8 percent (Emanuel 1987).

Additionally, hurricane tracks may change due to the changing position of the weather systems associated with the Intertropical Convergence Zone (ITCZ), the zone of atmospheric turbulence where warm, moist tropical air meets cool subtropical air, in particular toward a more northerly penetration of the ITCZ. Areas such as the Leeward Islands and the Greater Antilles which lie to the north of a major hurricane track across the Caribbean Sea, may in the next few decades become more at risk from hurricane activity (Reading and Walsh 1995).

It must be said, however, that projected effects of regional warming are speculative (Intergovernmental Panel on Climate Change 1995). There are no clear trends as yet, and the data present a far from unequivocal picture (see Reading and Walsh 1995; Walsh 1998). Recent record-breaking hurricanes include Gilbert (1988), Hugo (1989), and Andrew (1992). The 1995 season was the most active season recorded since the 1930s, with eleven hurricanes and eight tropical storms recorded and with an estimated U.S.$7.7 billion in associated damage. In 1999 five tropical storms increased to hurricane level, including Lenny, the first big hurricane in more than 100 years to track from west to east across the Caribbean. Although missing the most populous islands, Lenny caused widespread damage on Anguilla, the Virgin Islands, St. Barthélemy, and St. Martin. These may be the precursors of changing patterns and intensities. Projections indicate that changes in the frequency, intensity, and trajectories of tropical storms and hurricanes are likely, but these are hard to predict.

Water Supply

A regional precipitation decrease will undoubtedly exacerbate existing water-supply problems throughout the region. Seasonal water deficits already exist, as witnessed by the example of the Mavis Bank area of Jamaica, an area of relatively intense hillside farming (Ministry of Agriculture, Jamaica, undated). This area, in common with much of the western Caribbean Basin, experiences two periods of moisture deficit annually (Figure 7.2). Although these are not at present a significant problem in a normal year, farmers' reports of drought conditions affecting the crop cycle have been more frequent in recent years.

Figure 7.2 Seasonal Water Deficits in a Jamaican Hillside Context (millimeters of rainfall)

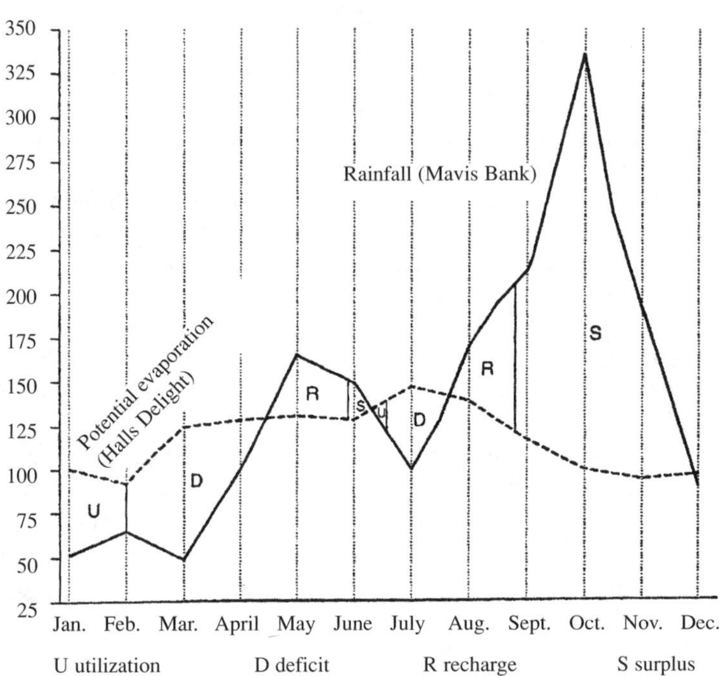

Source: Ministry of Agriculture, Jamaica, *Mavis Bank: Agricultural Development Plan* (Kingston, Jamaica: Ministry of Agriculture, undated).

A trend of increasing temperatures and decreasing rainfall will increase net moisture deficit, partly through increasing evaporation. In respect to the Mavis Bank example (Figure 7.2), the overall rainfall total may not change dramatically or may decrease. But the annual distribution may show lower dry season rainfalls (the period December to June), and therefore a more pronounced summer peak, and potential evaporation (the dotted line in Figure 7.2) will rise along with increasing temperature. The net result is likely to be a long dry period of moisture deficit from December to July or even August, as well as a much shorter single growing season.

Progressive loss of vegetative cover will also exacerbate this trend. A further factor in increasing evaporation rates is the projected increase of wind speeds. In addition to increases in upper-level winds associated with intensified tropical cyclone activity, increases in surface wind speeds are consistent with projections; trends in recent data from Jamaica and Trinidad and Tobago support this contention (Gray 1993).

Decreasing regional rainfalls will lower average stream flows as well as the amount of water available for recharging groundwater aquifer resources. Water-table levels will drop and increasing water supply problems will occur in urban and tourist areas. The potential for the intrusion of saline seawater into freshwater aquifers in the coastal zone will be increased, particularly where overabstraction of the freshwater aquifer is occurring due to urban expansion or increased demands from the tourist industry. If more freshwater is being extracted than can be replaced quickly enough by the natural flow of fresh groundwater from inland, then saltwater will seep in from the sea and contaminate the coastal groundwater supply.

Finally, a drier but stormier climate regime will lead, through increased surface runoff into stream channels, to more flash floods. This has implications not only for water supplies but also for risk scenarios associated with the urbanization of floodplain areas.

Sea-Level Rise

Sea-level rise associated with the expansion of ocean volumes and the melting of polar ice caps is a major threat to coastal lowlands in the Caribbean. This is especially critical for small island states, as they have high ratios of coastal lands to interior lands; much of the urban settlement and economic activities of island states in the Caribbean, including tourism, are focused on the coastal zone. Estimates of global sea-level rise indicate sea levels will be 19.685 inches higher by 2100, or somewhere in a range of 5.91–37.4 inches (Intergovernmental Panel on Climate Change 1995).

It has been estimated the sea level rises in the region at an average of 0.1182 inches per year, though considerable variation is evident throughout the Basin (Hendry 1993); the causes of this variation are not clear but are likely related to actual sea-level rise more so than any underlying vertical tectonic movements. Even this reduced estimate will inevitably give rise to significant effects in the coastal zone, where urban concentrations and the tourist industry are focused throughout the Caribbean region. Flooding, especially on reclaimed coastal lands, is a particular risk. Many of the beaches upon which tourism is dependent are likely to suffer significant erosion as wave and tidal forces react to the increasing depth of water in the near-shore zone.

Particularly at risk for economic losses will be locations with beaches and preexisting infrastructures. Not only are these already relatively well developed; they are prime targets for a combination of urban- and tourism-related expansion (e.g., Ocho Rios and Montego Bay in Jamaica, St. Lawrence/

Oistins in Barbados, Grand Anse in Grenada, Castries-Gros Islet in St. Lucia, and Condado Beach in San Juan, Puerto Rico).

Implications for Food Security

Projections are for increased seasonality, with reduced precipitation during dry periods, and possibly fewer but higher-magnitude rainfall events in wet seasons (Intergovernmental Panel on Climate Change 1992). Increased wind speeds are forecast, with attendant increased evaporation rates. This points to a tendency for longer periods of net moisture deficit in parts of the region. There is precedent for this, in that droughts have been recorded in the Caribbean Basin in the past and have caused significant crop failures leading to food shortages and "occasionally famine" (Watts 1995:6).

In addition to direct effects on crop yields and potential crop failure, the projected climatic conditions would cause accelerated soil erosion. This would occur particularly at the start of the wet season, through reduction of protection afforded to topsoil from the reduced biomass cover present during the intensified dry season. Thus, the climate-change projection will inevitably lead to land degradation on heavily used upland farming areas unless proactive steps are taken to protect upland watersheds.

Although climate changes on the scale proposed for the Caribbean region would have relatively little direct influence on crop growth patterns "as long as pests and diseases can be kept under control," increased risk of new, or increased existing, crop pests and diseases may be forthcoming (Watts 1995: 9). This might be controlled by vigilance and appropriate proactive measures. However, some crops grown successfully in the region could lose viability as the combination of reduced rainfall and increased temperatures affect germination probabilities and growth rates. In the absence of any research data, this urgently requires attention.

For tropical areas in general temperature increases of around 1.5 degrees Celsius would, in areas already close to marginality, increase rates of temperature-dependent evapotranspiration (moisture losses from the soil surface layers and from plant tissue) by 5–15 percent (Parry 1990). This would have an inevitable effect on yields unless compensated by local increases in rainfall. Regional increases in rainfall are unlikely in the Caribbean region for the foreseeable future, and yield declines seem inevitable without extensive irrigation systems, which in turn require much more careful water planning than is generally the case in the Caribbean at present.

Traditional staple crops, particularly those such as yams that are underground-rooting, are likely to survive the projected climate changes for the foreseeable future, though with the probability of declining yields. The more significant problem may lie with the developing structural dualism in agriculture manifested throughout the basin (see Barker 1993 for a discussion of the

Jamaican case). Better land is progressively given over to export monocropping, and crops grown for family consumption and the domestic market are becoming marginalized, that is, forced to less fertile or steeper lands. Although this may not in itself necessarily lead to greater risk from pests and diseases, it will almost certainly lead to greater risk in the event of more frequent drought conditions as well as to increases in the frequency and intensity of extreme events such as hurricanes.

With intense agricultural land use, the economic effects of extreme events will rise accordingly. For example, the effect of Hurricane Gilbert (1988) on Jamaica's export agriculture was devastating. The banana crop suffered virtually 100 percent losses, and more than 70 percent of Blue Mountain coffee was destroyed (Barker and Miller 1990). Hurricane Hugo (1989) destroyed virtually all banana production in Montserrat. Coastal low-lying areas are particularly vulnerable to storm surges and groundwater intrusion during hurricane events, causing coastal flooding and the saturation of agricultural land by saline seawater. Upland agriculture suffers significantly from the excessive landslide activity associated with high-magnitude events.

Sustainability and the Environment: Some Reflections

In examining the application of sustainable development in small Caribbean states, there is "an understandable and unavoidable tension everywhere between the demands of employment, improved wages and living conditions today and the environmental sustainability of economic policies implemented to achieve these demands" (Pantin 1994:10). In the Caribbean, even those who are sensitive to environmental issues have not yet found solutions to: the inherent problems of economic survival; the difficulty in assessing the environmental impact on natural resources of socioeconomic activities; and the ability to prevent or even mitigate environmental disasters in the region (Pantin 1994). A sustainable approach to development is of paramount importance in island states (Barker and McGregor 1995). At present, however, there are more questions than answers. For example, there is the question as to whether Caribbean ecosystems are inherently fragile or whether they are resistant to environmental change; and also whether the types of damage currently experienced in the Caribbean are more or less recoverable than the degradation being experienced in developed countries, such as large-scale industrialization and urbanization. The fact that the future of the Caribbean island states, due to their relatively small physical size and small economic turnover, is dependent on maintaining a balance between resource use and human needs makes an understanding of the relative resilience of Caribbean ecosystems all the more important.

From a historical perspective, current environmental problems in the insular Caribbean are a direct result of externally focused colonial trade and extraction policies (Richardson 1992). Centuries of change and development in the Caribbean region, including relatively rapid urbanization and economic activity, have altered the natural and human environments. Although most Caribbean islands are now independent, they are still subject, in varying degrees, to external economic dependency that is unlikely to change radically in the future (Thomas 1988; Deere et al. 1990).

However, it is noteworthy that Caribbean peoples are experienced and adaptable in shaping survival strategies, especially in the face of the plantation hegemony and legacy over access to land resources (Mintz 1985; Hills 1988; Hills and Iton 1983). Imposed upon the traditional means of earning a livelihood, the importation of Western models of development and recent economic restructuring agreements with the International Monetary Fund have presented new challenges to the people of the region in terms of survival, development paths, and sustainability.

Environmental degradation in the past was inextricably linked to European colonial settlement and associated plantation economies (Watts 1987; Richardson 1992). Yet the environmental crisis today can also be attributed to increasing poverty, economic restructuring, inappropriate industrial policy, rapid urbanization, and social deprivation (Lloyd Evans and Potter 1996). A fundamental issue is whether the environment should take precedence over economic development or vice versa. In a report on sustainable development in the region, the Economic Commission for Latin America and the Caribbean (ECLAC) stated that the prime objectives were the attainment of development and the sustainable management of natural resources and the environment and that the real challenge focuses on improving the standard of living for the majority of the population in a time of economic liberalization (ECLAC 1991). Under conditions of economic austerity, the tendency is to transfer natural resources into exports and foreign exchange earnings in order to improve living standards; environmental concerns are relegated to second place. Little, if anything, has changed since ECLAC's pronouncement.

Trying to make development sustainable assumes that it is possible to recognize what is unsustainable (Thomas-Hope 1996). If sustainability is concerned with meeting the needs of the present as well as those of future generations, then the Caribbean is replete with examples of unsustainable development. Table 7.3 highlights some human activities that are giving rise to environmental problems contributing to unsustainable development. The environmental impacts of coastal-zone developments, agricultural practices, urbanization, and tourism are critical aspects of development planning that need immediate attention.

Studies of Caribbean tourism illustrate contradictions surrounding environmental sustainability and provide numerous examples of negative environmental impacts and doubtful sustainable benefits. Coastal resources, including inshore fisheries, are radically affected by tourism in a number of ways, such as overfishing, reef mining, pollution, and reef degradation. However, much of the research on the impact of Caribbean tourism tends to be project-specific (and hence location-specific), and the broader national or regional perspective may be lacking. For example, the legacy of environmental degradation through colonial plantation agriculture in Antigua has continued in the modern period and is being replicated and exacerbated through shortsighted tourism developments that threaten the environmental integrity of the coastal zone (Lorah 1995). Similar issues have been raised by those concerned that ecotourism is becoming a clever marketing ploy rather than a genuine effort to develop a sustainable form of tourism (Cater and Lowman 1995; France and Wheeller 1995; France 1998 Woodfield 1998). The multiple appearance of tourism in Table 7.3 suggests that it is likely to be central to future regional sustainability because it impinges on many aspects of physical, economic, and cultural environments.

The nature of Caribbean food systems also illustrates the complexities and contradictions of sustainability in geographically small tropical islands (McElroy and de Albuquerque 1990; Spence 1996). The colonial period fundamentally established outward-focused agricultural economies devoted to export. Little has changed since independence to alter the economic orientation of commercial agriculture, though now the financial benefits may be more likely to remain in the Caribbean with the gradual increase in locally owned businesses. Concern about dependence on undiversified agriculture has persisted through several decades, resurfacing in the 1990s in relation to the survival of banana producers (Welch 1996; Grossman 1998). Yet efforts to increase yields and modernize agricultural production are fraught with new environmental problems as agricultural pollutants begin to have an impact on water supply and on marine ecosystems. Similarly, the study of decisionmaking by small farmers can highlight the multifaceted dilemmas of sustainability (Meikle 1992; Davis-Morrison 1998). How can the natural capital of land resources be conserved, sustaining the export food crops while at the same time producing a sustainable supply of domestic food for a growing domestic population? How can small farmers provide a decent standard of living for their families in the face of global trade liberalization and a renewed flood of cheap food imports into the region?

Generally speaking, discussion of sustainability issues connotes a medium- to long-term planning horizon, but high-magnitude natural disasters such as hurricanes, earthquakes, and volcanoes can have immediate disruptive effects on sustainability. Hurricanes such as Gilbert and Hugo brought entire islands to a state of emergency (see Barker and Miller 1990), and the effects of recent volcanic activity on Montserrat have been devastating to that island's survival. Though natural hazards have plagued the region for centuries, their impacts are likely to become more significant in the future as populations increase, as infrastructure becomes more developed and sophisticated, and as the environment becomes more degraded. Add to that trends such as global warming, which could have a severe impact in the insular Caribbean, widespread reef degradation, more violent patterns of hurricane activity, and subregional drought. Thus, hazards, whether natural or human-induced, also play a crucial role in the sustainability equation because of their unpredictable impacts on the resource base, land use, and human settlement.

Recommendations for policy and research emphasis in the search for sustainable development in the insular Caribbean have been made (see McElroy et al. 1990; Table 7.4). Realization of objectives will require progress on two basic issues: environmental damage control and habitat restoration; and breakthroughs in our understanding of potentially sustainable resource uses. However, such recommendations underscore the importance of social development in achieving these goals. For example, there is a need to channel investment into appropriate environmental education and training as well as the promotion of environmental awareness throughout society.

There is recognition that development strategies should focus on the social needs of the people while respecting the natural environment. In this respect, it is also important that any approach should be gender-sensitive, as women often undertake the primary role in environmental management (Dankelman and Davidson 1988; Braidotti 1994). Environmental conservation is often predicated on social inequality, especially on the basis of class, ethnicity, and gender; those in power drive their own agenda, sometimes to the detriment of others (Thomas-Hope 1996; Peake 1998). This demands the promo-

Table 7.4 Recommendations for Sustainable Development in the Caribbean

1. Agricultural policy should focus on small-scale diverse crop farms.
2. Small-farm orientation should promote agroforestry options.
3. Such small-farm focus would justify legal retention of agricultural resource use on criteria other than commercial viability.
4. Research required to determine ways to enhance local benefits of traditional tourism (applies also to ecotourism).
5. A regional institute is required to promote new technologies and to undertake assessments of their impacts.
6. New planning and user-friendly indices of environmental vulnerability are required.
7. Systems for promoting interisland transfer of resource management skills are needed.
8. Fostering of local specialists to gauge impact of international trends on insular economies is required.
9. External agencies and host governments must devise new ways to facilitate effective resource decisionmaking and policy implementation.

Source: J. L. McElroy, B. Potter, and E. Towle, "Challenges for Sustainable Development in Small Caribbean Islands," in *Sustainable Development and Environmental Management of Small Islands,* edited by W. Beller, P. d'Ayala, and P. Hein (Paris: UNESCO; Carnforth, UK: Parthenon, 1990), pp. 299–316.

tion of more sustainable and indigenous development programs, with empowerment as a major goal. Local environmental management will require community collaboration and the promotion of equity between different social groups (Lloyd Evans 1998).

The 1990s were characterized by the proliferation of nongovernmental initiatives in which environmental projects play a key role in mobilizing community development. There has been progress on three such projects in St. Lucia, and similar efforts have been documented even in crisis-torn Haiti (Conway and Lorah 1995; Maguire 1994). In many ways, such initiatives reflect a more enlightened and progressive attitude on the part of international, national, and regional power brokers, as well as genuine enthusiasm and involvement on the part of Caribbean peoples.

The most important resource in the Caribbean region is the human resource. In order to harness the true potential of people, Caribbean nations need to channel investment into education and training, the provision of basic needs, and creative employment opportunities (Lloyd Evans 1998). Education of the next generation and the promotion of environmental awareness throughout society must be given a central role in any future agenda. Caribbean peoples will determine the shape of sustainable development, whether it becomes a useful intellectual concept or an attainable human goal. Central to sustainability must be the future protection of the already degraded Caribbean environment.

■ Bibliography

Bacon, P. E. "Wetland Resource Rehabilitation for Sustainable Development in the Eastern Caribbean." In *Environment and Development in the Caribbean: Geographical Perspectives,* edited by D. Barker and D. F. M. McGregor, pp. 46–56. Kingston, Jamaica: University of the West Indies Press, 1995.

Barker, D. "A Periphery in Genesis and Exodus: Reflections on Rural-Urban Relations in Jamaica." In *The Geography of Urban-Rural Interactions in Developing Countries*, edited by R. B. Potter and T. Unwin, pp. 294–322. London: Routledge, 1989.

———. "Dualism and Disaster on a Tropical Island: Constraints on Agricultural Development in Jamaica." *Tidjschrift voor Economische en Sociale Geographie* (Journal for Economic and Social Geography), no. 84 (1993): 332–340.

———. "Yam Farmers on the Edge of Cockpit Country: Aspects of Resource Use and Sustainability." In *Resource Sustainability and Caribbean Development*, edited by D. F. M. McGregor, D. Barker, and S. Lloyd Evans, pp. 357–372. Kingston, Jamaica: University of the West Indies Press, 1998.

Barker, D., and D. F. M. McGregor. "Land Degradation in the Yallahs Basin, Jamaica: Historical Notes and Contemporary Perspectives." *Geography* 783, pt. 2 (1988): 116–124.

———. *Environment and Development in the Caribbean: Geographical Perspectives.* Kingston, Jamaica: University of the West Indies Press, 1995.

Barker, D., and D. J. Miller. "Hurricane Gilbert: Anthropomorphising a Natural Disaster." *Area* 22, pt. 2 (1990): 107–116.

Besson, J. "A Paradox in Caribbean Attitudes to Land." In *Land and Development in the Caribbean,* edited by J. Besson and J. Momsen, pp. 13–45. Warwick University Caribbean Studies. London: Macmillan, 1987.

Braidotti, R., ed. *Women, the Environment, and Sustainable Development: Towards a Theoretical Synthesis*. London: Zed Books, 1994.

Brookfield, H. C. "An Approach to Islands." In *Sustainable Development and Environmental Management of Small Islands*, edited by W. Beller, P. d'Ayala, and P. Hein, pp. 23–23. Paris: UNESCO; and Carnforth, UK: Parthenon, 1990.

Bryant, D., L. Burke, J. McManus, and M. Spalding. *Reefs at Risk: A Map-based Indicator of Threats to the World's Coral Reefs*. Washington, DC: World Resources Institute, 1998.

Bryant, R. L., and S. Bailey. *Third World Political Ecology*. London: Routledge, 1997.

Caribbean Environment Programme (CEP). "Caribbean Fish Kills." *CEP Newsletter* 14, no. 2 (1999): 9.

Cater, E., and G. Lowman, eds. *Ecotourism: A Sustainable Option?* Chichester, UK: Wiley, 1995.

Conway, D., and P. Lorah. "Environmental Protection Policies in Caribbean Small Islands: Some St. Lucian Examples." *Caribbean Geography* 6 (1995): 16–27.

Dankelman, I., and J. Davidson. *Women and the Environment in the Third World*. London: Earthscan, 1988.

Davis-Morrison, V. "The Sustainability of Small-Scale Agricultural Systems in the Millbank Area of the Rio Grande Valley, Portland, Jamaica." In *Resource Sustainability and Caribbean Development*, edited by D. F. M., McGregor, D. Barker, and S. Lloyd Evans, pp. 296–316. Kingston, Jamaica: University of the West Indies Press, 1998.

Deere, C., P. Antrobus, E. Melendez, P. Phillips, M. Rivera, and H. Safa, eds. *In the Shadows of the Sun: Caribbean Development Alternatives and U.S. Policy*. Boulder: Westview, 1990.

Draper, G., T. A. Jackson, and S. K. Donovan "Geologic Provinces of the Caribbean Region." In *Caribbean Geology: An Introduction*, edited by S. K. Donovan and T. A. Jackson, pp. 3–12. Kingston, Jamaica: University of the West Indies Publishers' Association (UWIPA), 1994.

ECLAC (Economic Commission for Latin America and the Caribbean). *Sustainable Development: Changing Production Patterns, Social Equity, and the Environment*. Santiago, Chile: United Nations, 1991.

Edwards, D. *Small Farmers and the Protection of the Watersheds: The Experience of Jamaica Since the 1950s*. Occasional Paper No. 3, University of the West Indies, Centre for Environment and Development. Kingston, Jamaica: Canoe, 1995.

———. "Protection of the Hillsides Occupied by Small Farmers in Jamaica: Lessons of History and Prospects for Public Initiatives." In *Resource Sustainability and Caribbean Development,* edited by D. F. M. McGregor, D. Barker, and S. Lloyd Evans, pp. 341–356. Kingston, Jamaica: University of the West Indies Press, 1998.

Emanuel, K. A. "The Dependence of Hurricane Intensity on Climate." *Nature*, no. 326 (April 2, 1987): 483–485.

Eyre, L. A. "Jamaica: Test Case for Tropical Deforestation." *Ambio* 16 (1987): 338–343.

———. "The Cockpit Country: A World Heritage Site?" In *Environment and Development in the Caribbean: Geographical Perspectives*, edited by D. Barker and

D. F. M. McGregor, pp. 259–270. Kingston, Jamaica: University of the West Indies Press, 1995.

———. "The Tropical Rainforests of Jamaica." *Jamaica Journal* 26, no. 1 (1996): 26–35.

———. "The Tropical Rainforests of the Eastern Caribbean: Present Status and Conservation." *Caribbean Geography* 9, no. 20 (1998): 101–120.

France, L. "Sustainability and Development in Tourism on the Islands of Barbados, St. Lucia, and Dominica." In *Resource Sustainability and Caribbean Development,* edited by D. F. M. McGregor, D. Barker, and S. Lloyd Evans, pp. 109–125. Kingston, Jamaica: University of the West Indies Press, 1998.

France, L., and B. Wheeller. "Sustainability Tourism in the Caribbean." In *Environment and Development in the Caribbean: Geographical Perspectives*, edited by D. Barker and D. F. M. McGregor, pp. 59–69. Kingston, Jamaica: University of the West Indies Press, 1995.

Gray, C. R. "Regional Meteorology and Hurricanes." In *Climate Change in the Intra-Americas Sea*, edited by G. A. Maul, pp. 87–99. London: Edward Arnold, 1993.

Grossman, L. S. *The Political Ecology of Bananas: Contract Farming, Peasants and Agrarian Change in the Eastern Caribbean.* Chapel Hill: University of North Carolina Press, 1998.

Hendry, M. "Sea-Level Movements and Shoreline Change." In *Climate Change in the Intra-Americas Sea*, edited by G. A. Maul, pp. 115–161. London: Edward Arnold, 1993.

Hills, T. L. "The Caribbean Peasant Food Forest: Ecological Artistry or Random Chaos?" In *Small Farming and Peasant Resources in the Caribbean*, edited by J. S. Brierley and H. Rubenstein, pp. 1–28. Manitoba Geographical Studies No. 10. Winnipeg: University of Manitoba, 1988.

Hills, T., and S. Iton. "A Reassessment of the 'Traditional' in Caribbean Small-Scale Agriculture." *Caribbean Geography* 1 (1983): 24–35.

Intergovernmental Panel on Climate Change (IPCC). *Climate Change 1992: The Supplementary Report to the IPCC Scientific Assessment*. Cambridge, UK: Cambridge University Press, 1992.

———. *Climate Change 1995: The Science of Climate Change*. Cambridge, UK: Cambridge University Press, 1995.

Johnson, A. M. "The Artisanal Fishery of the Black River Lower Morass, Jamaica: A Traditional System of Resource Management." In *Resource Sustainability and Caribbean Development,* edited by D. F. M. McGregor, D. Barker, and S. Lloyd Evans, pp. 390–404. Kingston, Jamaica: University of the West Indies Press, 1998.

Lloyd Evans, S. "Gender, Ethnicity, and Small Business Development in Trinidad: Prospects for Sustainable Job Creation." In *Resource Sustainability and Caribbean Development,* edited by D. F. M. McGregor, D. Barker, and S. Lloyd Evans, pp. 195–213. Kingston, Jamaica: University of the West Indies Press, 1998.

Lloyd Evans, S., and R. B. Potter. "Environmental Impacts of Urban Development and the Urban Informal Sector in the Caribbean." In *Land Degradation in the Tropics*, edited by M. J. Eden and J. T. Parry, pp. 245–260. London: Pinter, 1996.

Lorah, P. "An Unsustainable Path: Tourism's Vulnerability to Environmental Decline in Antigua." *Caribbean Geography* 6 (1995): 28–29.

Lugo, A. E. "Development, Forestry, and Environmental Quality in the Eastern Caribbean." In *Sustainable Development and Environmental Management of Small Islands*, edited by W. Beller, P. d'Ayala, and P. Hein, pp. 317–342. Paris: UNESCO; and Carnforth, UK: Parthenon, 1990.

Lugo, A., R. Schmidt, and S. Brown. "Tropical Forests in the Caribbean." *Ambio* 10 (1981): 318–324.

Maguire, R. E. "Sisyphus Revisited: Grassroots Development and Community Conflict in Haiti." *Caribbean Geography* 5 (1994): 127–135.

McElroy, J. L., and K. de Albuquerque. "Sustainable Small-Scale Agriculture in Small Caribbean Islands." *Society and Natural Resources* 3 (1990): 107–129.

McElroy, J. L., B. Potter, and E. Towle. "Challenges for Sustainable Development in Small Caribbean Islands." In *Sustainable Development and Environmental Management of Small Islands*, edited by W. Beller, P. d'Ayala, and P. Hein, pp. 299–316 Paris: UNESCO; and Carnforth, UK: Parthenon, 1990.

McGregor, D. F. M. "An Investigation of Soil Status and Land Use on a Steeply Sloping Hillside, Blue Mountains, Jamaica." *Singapore Journal of Tropical Geography* 9 (1988): 60–71.

———. "Soil Erosion, Environmental Change, and Development in the Caribbean: A Deepening Crisis?" In *Environment and Development in the Caribbean: Geographical Perspectives*, edited by D. Barker and D. F. M. McGregor, pp. 189–208. Kingston, Jamaica: University of the West Indies Press, 1995.

McGregor, D. F. M., and D. Barker. "Land Degradation and Hillside Farming in the Fall River Basin, Jamaica." *Applied Geography* 11 (1991): 143–156.

McGregor, D. F. M., and R. B. Potter. "Environmental Change and Sustainability in the Caribbean: Terrestrial Perspectives." In *Land, Sea, and Human Effort in the Caribbean,* edited by B. M. W. Ratter and W-D. Sahr, pp. 1–15. Beiträge zur Geographischen Regionalforschung in Latinamerika (Contributions to regional geographic research in Latin America), vol. 10. Hamburg: Institut für Geographie der Universtat Hamburg, 1997.

Meikle, P. "Spatial-Temporal Trends in Root Crop Production and Mobility in Jamaica." *Caribbean Geography* 3 (1992): 223–235.

Milliman, J. D. "Coral Reefs and Their Response to Global Climate Change." In *Climate Change in the Intra-Americas Sea*, edited by G. A. Maul, pp. 306–321. London: Edward Arnold, 1993.

Ministry of Agriculture, Jamaica. *Mavis Bank: Agricultural Development Plan.* Kingston, Jamaica: Ministry of Agriculture, undated.

Mintz, S. W. "From Plantation to Peasantries in the Caribbean." In *Caribbean Contours*, edited by S. W. Mintz and S. Price, pp. 127–154. Baltimore: Johns Hopkins University Press, 1985.

Pantin, D. *The Economics of Sustainable Development in Small Caribbean Islands.* Kingston, Jamaica, and St. Augustine, Trinidad: University of the West Indies Press. Centre for Environment and Development, University of the West Indies Jamaica, and the Department of Economics, University of the West Indies Trinidad, 1994.

Parry, M. L. *Climate Change and World Agriculture.* London: Earthscan, 1990.

Paskett, C. J., and C.-E. Philocette. "Soil Conservation in Haiti." *Journal of Soil and Water Conservation* 45 (1990): 457–459.

Pattullo, P. *Last Resorts: The Cost of Tourism in the Caribbean.* London: Cassell, 1996.

Peake, L. J. "Living in Poverty in Linden, Guyana, in the 1990s: Bauxite, the Development of Poverty and Household Coping Mechanisms." In *Resource Sustainability and Caribbean Development,* edited by D. F. M. McGregor, D. Barker, and S. Lloyd Evans, pp. 171–194. Kingston, Jamaica: University of the West Indies Press, 1998.

Potter, R. B. "Urbanisation and Development in the Caribbean." *Geography* 80 (1995): 334–341.

———. *The Urban Caribbean in an Era of Global Change*. Aldershot, UK: Ashgate Publishing, 2000.

Reading, A. J., and R. P. D. Walsh. "Tropical Cyclone Activity Within the Caribbean Basin Since 1500." In *Environment and Development in the Caribbean: Geographical Perspectives*, edited by D. Barker and D. F. M. McGregor, pp. 124–146. Kingston, Jamaica: University of the West Indies Press, 1995.

Richardson, B. C. *The Caribbean in the Wider World, 1492–1992*. Cambridge, UK: Cambridge University Press, 1992.

Shapiro, L. J. "Hurricane Climatic Fluctuations, Part II: Relation to Large-Scale Circulation." *Monthly Weather Review* 110 (1982): 1014–1023.

Spence, B. "The Influence of Small Farmers' Land Use Decisions on the Status of Food Security in Jamaica." *Caribbean Geography* 6 (1996): 132–142.

Thomas, C. Y. *The Poor and the Powerless: Economic Policy and Change in the Caribbean*. London: Latin American Bureau, 1988.

Thomas-Hope, E. *The Environmental Dilemma in the Caribbean Context.* Grace Kennedy Foundation Lecture 1996. Kingston: Institute of Jamaica and Grace Kennedy Foundation, 1996.

Walsh, R. P. D. "Climatic Changes in the Eastern Caribbean Over the Last 150 Years and Some Implications in Planning Sustainable Development." In *Resource Sustainability and Caribbean Development,* edited by D. F. M. McGregor, D. Barker, and S. Lloyd Evans, pp. 26–48. Kingston, Jamaica: University of the West Indies Press, 1998.

Watts, D. *The West Indies: Patterns of Development, Culture, and Environmental Change Since 1492*. Cambridge, UK: Cambridge University Press, 1987.

———. "Environmental Degradation, the Water Resource and Sustainable Development in the Eastern Caribbean." *Caribbean Geography* 6 (1995): 2–15.

Weaver, D. "Ecotourism in the Caribbean Basin." In *Ecotourism: A Sustainable Option?*, edited by E. Cater and G. Lowman, pp. 159–176. Chichester, UK: John Wiley, 1994.

Welch, B. *Survival by Association: Supply Management Landscapes of the Eastern Caribbean.* Kingston, Jamaica: University of the West Indies Press; and Montreal: McGill-Queens University Press, 1996.

Wigley, T. M. L., and B. D. Santer. "Future Climate of the Gulf/Caribbean Basin from the Global Circulation Models." In *Climate Change in the Intra-Americas Sea*, edited by G. A. Maul, pp. 31–54. London: Edward Arnold, 1993.

Woodfield, N. "The Role of Ecotourism in Grenada: A Marketing Ploy or a Step Towards Sustainable Development?" In *Resource Sustainability and Caribbean Development,* edited by D. F. M. McGregor, D. Barker, and S. Lloyd Evans, pp. 148–168. Kingston, Jamaica: University of the West Indies Press, 1998.

8

Ethnicity, Race, Class, and Nationality

David Baronov and Kevin A. Yelvington

In order to understand cultures other than our own, we must overcome preconceived ideas and stereotypes. The concepts used in this chapter, based on modern anthropological and sociological definitions, are designed to provide an objective approach to comprehending intuitive concepts such as ethnicity, race, class, and nationality.

Ethnicity may be best conceived of as a set of ideas concerning a group's real or imagined cultural links with an ancestral past. It suggests identification with a certain group based on cultural and historical traditions, including language and religion, and provides basic insights into the nature and origins of a group of people as well as explanations for their modern beliefs, behaviors, and accomplishments. Inherent in this concept is the notion that the members of a distinct ethnic group reflect some set of common characteristics that sets them apart from the broader society.[1]

With the conquest and colonization of Africa and the Americas in the fifteenth and sixteenth centuries, Europeans were for the first time developing sustained relationships with markedly different peoples and societies. Rationalizing and legitimizing their control required an ideological foundation based in a presumed superiority, prompting the creation of racial categories reflecting the idea that humankind is naturally divided into divergent physical and biological types. An array of characteristics was associated with each type, with an inherent hierarchy that reflected European superiority. The result was the division of the world's population into a fixed number of "pure" *races,* each representing bundles of traits (physical differences in skin color, hair, facial features, and the like) given differing values.

Scientists have demonstrated that humankind, in fact, cannot be neatly or meaningfully categorized into races. To begin with, there is no scientific reason to believe that people would conform to any racial ideal or so-called pure-blood model even if there were no miscegenation (mixing) between races. Even without miscegenation, the frequencies of genes responsible for the bundle of traits will change through time due to the forces of evolution. At least half of the world's population today displays bundles of racial traits not anticipated in the supposedly scientific traditional view of "the three races." Rather, they combine a number of physical traits thought to pertain to one race. The distribution of genes responsible for the bundle of traits is dispersed throughout the world. There are no sharp breaks between gene distributions, as one would find if the traditional view were correct. In fact, scientists have shown that there is much more genetic variation within groups regarded as races than exists among them. Race must be viewed, therefore, as socially constructed.[2]

Social class is a complex concept for which there are a variety of competing interpretations.[3] The idea of class reflects social power relations and is a critical determinant of access to social resources, social mobility, social status and acceptance, and social identity.

Importantly, various forms of social stratification can cut across class lines. Ethnicity and race are given further meaning within the context of social class and intersect with class in different ways. Often, a person's ethnic or racial identity may be a stronger determinant of social power than their class position. For example, ethnic and racial discrimination—such as that against Dominicans in Puerto Rico—cuts across class lines. At times, a person's ethnic or racial identity may be a determinant of class position, as was the case with those of African descent during the era of slavery and with East Indians and Chinese who came to the Americas as indentured laborers.

The multidimensional nature of social class—along with the influences of ethnicity, race, and nationality—provides avenues for strategic cross-class alliances as well as occasional intraclass conflict. Thus, social class must be understood as part of an ongoing, fluid process of contestation rather than as fixed, static, and unchanging categories. The control and distribution of social resources is the basis for a good deal of social conflict within the Caribbean and elsewhere. Understanding how social class, as well as ethnic-racial and national identity, shape this conflict is essential for an understanding of Caribbean society and culture.

Although nationality shares much with the concepts of ethnicity and race, there remains a crucial distinction. Discussions of ethnicity often center on a group's ultimate origins and how they have supposedly remained unchanged throughout the ages. *Nationality*, in contrast, reflects an ideology suggesting that there is a homogeneous and unifying cultural identity confined to geographically defined territories that is somehow able to overcome ethnic-racial differences within the population. In other words, regardless of the varied origins of different ethnic groups within a given society, there are certain characteristics common to the entire population. These commonalities uniquely define the people as a nation.[4]

This chapter will provide an overview of the nature of ethnicity, race, class, and nationality across Caribbean societies. In the process, it will shed light on how these concepts are interpreted and understood, as well as on how they have impacted the lives of those who reside in the region.

■ The Mix of Ethnicity, Race, Class, and Nationality Across the Caribbean

U.S. racial categories would be almost unrecognizable in much of the Caribbean and vice versa for persons in the Caribbean. In contrast to most of the Caribbean, where gradations of light or dark skin color, rather than pure racial types, tend to define racial identities, the U.S. tradition has been that a person with African or European descendants is either African American or white.[5] This is based on the so-called one-drop rule: one drop of African American blood makes one African American. The offspring of an African American and a white person (and the offspring of that couple and so on) has, by custom, been considered African American. This harkens back to earlier racist ideologies based on the fiction of pure racial blood lines.

Writing about Puerto Rico, Isar Godreau suggests that popular notions of ethnicity, race, class, and nationality can be characterized by what she calls *la semántica fugitiva* (slippery semantics; Godreau 2000). *La semántica fugitiva* refers to the indeterminacy and negotiation involved in everyday notions of ethnic-racial identity. There is often extensive use of indirectness and metaphor in everyday conversation. Rural Puerto Ricans, for example, often use descriptions for various degrees of rainfall as analogies for racial types. Thus, *aguacero* (hard rainfall) designates someone who is very dark skinned, and *lloviznas* (mild rainfall) refers to those deemed medium in skin color. *Opaco* (cloudy) denotes *trigueños bastante oscuro* (dark, wheat-colored people), that is, those with kinky hair but not completely dark skin (Gordon 1949:298).

La semántica fugitiva is reflected in the idea of *mestizaje* (*métissage* in French), meaning "miscegenation," or "race-mixing" as well as "cultural blending." An equivalent term is *creolization*. The word *creole* is taken from the Spanish word *criollo*, meaning "of local origin." Creolization in Caribbean popular culture extols a process of ongoing cultural and ethnic-racial blending. *Mestizaje* is coupled with the ideology of *blanqueamiento* (whitening). In the dominant belief system whiteness is given special value, representing and embodying European-derived culture. Whiteness becomes the aesthetic standard to which people aspire.

The larger point is, therefore, that ethnicity, race, class, and nationality (as manifested in the ideology of nationalism) are mutually constituting. Ethnic-racial identities influence social class by acting as a resource (or a liability) in securing social capital and prestige. Social class affects nationalism insofar as the privileged classes define and principally benefit from the dominant ideology of nationalism. Nationalism affects ethnicity and race in that those who are defined as white, mulatto, and so on—and the value accorded to each—in one nationalist context may not be so defined in another.

Historical Legacies

As Stephen Randall details in Chapter 3, the modern Caribbean rests on the bedrock of three formidable institutions: colonialism, the plantation system, and slavery. The legacy of colonialism for the Caribbean is evident today in the chorus of Dutch, English, French, and Spanish voices echoing across the region. When Europeans first reached the Caribbean they encountered a small collection of thriving Amerindian societies, which were almost totally eliminated as distinct cultural groups by the 1530s. European powers captured and either enslaved or slaughtered the indigenous Amerindian population and then set out to repopulate the newly claimed area with Europeans and African slaves.

For nearly the first two centuries of colonial rule in the Caribbean the entire region belonged to the Spanish Empire. The British, Dutch, and French did not arrive until the seventeenth century, but by the 1780s the French colony of St. Domingue (what would become independent Haiti) became the world's leading sugar producer, its plantations generating great wealth.

The defining feature of colonial rule and the plantation system in the Caribbean was slavery (Eltis 2000; Klein 1986, 1999; Shepherd and Beckles 2000). Over the 350-plus years of the Atlantic slave trade, as many as 10–12 million Africans were kidnapped from their homelands and forced to work as slaves in the Americas. Of these, it is estimated that roughly 40 percent reached the Caribbean. Another 40 percent were taken to Brazil; 16 percent landed in Spanish Latin America; and about 4 percent reached British North America (the colonies and later the United States). The category of slave was reserved by Europeans exclusively for persons of African descent. There were other forms of forced labor, however, and each was associated with a distinct ethnic-racial group. The *encomienda* system of forced labor was for Amerindians, whose spiritual salvation was entrusted to Christianizing Europeans. Indentured servitude was only available to Europeans (and later some Asians). Europeans sent their criminals and political prisoners to the Caribbean as unfree labor, although they were never slaves. After serving a definite period of indenture they were freed from service. Their masters had no claims of ownership over them or any of their offspring, as was the case for slaves.

Africans were kidnapped from across the span of the continent. Branding all slaves as Africans was therefore a convenient excuse for ignoring the significant ethnic-cultural differences among African peoples, who constituted as varied and distinct a population as existed on any continent. Table 8.1 illustrates the diverse regional origins of the Africans taken as slaves, though it cannot account for the full extent of the ethnic and cultural diversity of their societies. Table 8.2 provides additional details regarding the regional origins of Africans sent to major British colonies at the advent of the plantation system. Importantly, a slave's regional origins cannot be completely confounded with a slave's ethnic affiliation (called "nations" by slavers and planters at the time and later by the slaves themselves). Both tables portray a certain homogeneity in the regional origins of these slaves and provide clues as to the basis of the cultures of the Africans taken to these colonies.

Ethnic differences among Africans were not lost on the slave traders. Europeans made sharp distinctions between African ethnic groups as they related to the population's supposed temperament, tendency to rebel, health, work habits, and native intelligence—all critical factors for plantation productivity. The journals and correspondences of the planters are full of their reflections on these issues as well as their requests for specific types of Africans. An early scientific society centered in the bustling port and commercial center of Cap François, St. Domingue, called the Cercle des Philadelphes carried out detailed investigations into the lives of slaves. This did not, of course, stem from any humanitarian concern but from the interest in maintaining a profitable colonial economy. The Cercle undertook a general survey of agriculture in 1787 and sent out a questionnaire. Among its 250 questions, the survey asked slaveholders to identify which work suited which kinds of Africans and which Africans were the easiest to discipline (McClellan 1992).

A further concern related to African ethnicity was the fear of slave revolts. Planters avoided buying too many members of the same ethnic group for their plantations. It was reasoned that a common language and culture would facilitate planning and conspiracy. Indeed, a number of slave revolts across the Caribbean were led by one ethnic group or another. In the only completely successful slave revolt—the protracted and bloody war beginning in 1791 that brought about Haitian independence in 1804—Kongo soldiers, military tactics, and political ideology all played a role. Other slaves, rather than revolting, often formed maroon communities of runaway slaves. This was especially true in areas were the rugged terrain aided such escapes, as in Jamaica and Suriname.

Colonialism, the Plantation System, Slavery, and the European Notion of Whiteness

The lasting legacy of colonialism, the plantation system, and slavery has been the European fixation on race and the notion of *whiteness*. With colonial rule, multiple European ethnic identities soon began to fuse into a single white

Table 8.1 Estimates of Regional Distribution of Slave Exports to the Americas from Africa, 1662–1867

Years	Senegambia	Sierra Leone	Gold Coast	Bight of Benin	Bight of Biafra	West-Central Africa	Southeast Africa	Total	Annual Exports
1662–1670	3,232		12,174	23,021	34,471	9,695	91	82,684	9,187
1671–1680	5,842		20,597	22,753	24,021	15,794	309	89,316	8,932
1681–1690	10,834		15,333	71,733	21,625	32,760	5,392	157,677	15,768
1691–1700	13,376		17,407	103,313	12,115	30,072	190	176,473	17,647
1700–1709	22,230	34,560	31,650	138,590	23,130	109,780	0	359,940	35,994
1710–1719	36,260	6,380	37,540	138,690	51,410	132,590	0	402,870	40,287
1720–1729	52,530	9,120	65,110	150,280	59,990	179,620	0	516,650	51,665
1730–1739	57,210	29,470	74,460	135,220	62,260	240,890	0	599,510	59,951
1740–1749	35,000	43,350	83,620	97,830	76,790	214,470	0	551,060	55,106
1750–1759	30,100	83,860	52,780	86,620	106,100	222,430	0	581,890	58,189
1760–1769	27,590	178,360	69,650	98,390	142,640	266,570	0	783,200	78,320
1770–1779	24,400	132,220	54,370	111,550	160,400	234,880	0	717,820	71,782
1780–1789	15,240	74,190	57,650	121,080	225,360	300,340	0	793,860	79,386
1790–1799	18,320	70,510	73,960	74,600	181,740	340,110	0	759,240	75,924
1800–1809	18,000	63,970	44,150	75,750	123,000	280,900	0	605,770	60,577
1810–1815	19,300	4,200		34,600	33,100	111,800	8,700	211,700	42,340
1816–1820	48,400	9,000		59,200	60,600	151,100	59,600	387,900	77,580
1821–1825	22,700	4,000		44,200	60,600	128,400	43,200	303,100	60,620
1826–1830	26,700	4,900		70,500	66,700	164,400	58,100	391,300	78,260
1831–1835	27,400	1,100		37,700	71,900	102,800	3,000	243,900	48,780
1836–1840	35,300	5,700		50,400	40,800	193,500	99,400	425,100	85,020
1841–1845	19,100	200		45,300	4,400	112,900	20,300	202,200	40,440
1846–1850	14,700	700		53,400	7,700	197,000	66,700	340,200	68,040
1851–1855	10,300	300		8,900	2,900	22,600	12,800	57,800	11,560
1856–1860	3,100	300		14,000	4,400	88,200	11,300	121,300	24,260
1861–1865	2,700	0		2,600	0	41,200	2,700	49,200	9,840
1866–1867	0	0		400	0	3,000	0	3,400	1,700
Total	599,864	756,390	710,451	1,870,620	1,658,152	3,927,801	391,782	9,915,060	48,131

Source: Herbert S. Klein, *The Atlantic Slave Trade* (New York: Cambridge University Press, 1999), pp. 208–209.

Table 8.2 Distribution of the African Regional Origins of Slaves Arriving in Major British Colonies, 1658–1713 (percentage)

	Chesapeake	Barbados	Jamaica	Antigua	Montserrat	Nevis
Senegambia	34.2	5.3	5.4	2.5	21.8	8.9
Sierra Leone	0	0.8	0.5	3.0	0	5.0
Windward coast	0	0.2	0.4	0	0	2.9
Gold Coast	16.5	39.6	36.0	44.8	37.8	32.1
Bight of Benin	4.0	25.7	26.0	13.9	8.1	12.0
Bight of Biafra	44.0	13.4	11.5	32.3	12.6	24.7
West-central Africa	1.2	10.2	20.1	3.6	0	13.1
Southeast Africa	0	4.8	0.2	0	19.7	1.4
Number of slaves	7,795	85,995	72,998	8,926	2,037	14,040

Source: David Eltis, *The Rise of African Slavery in the Americas* (Cambridge, UK: Cambridge University Press, 2000), p. 245.

racial identity. The Spanish conquest of the Caribbean occurred at the time of the *reconquista* (the "reconquering" of Spain from the Moors) and the expulsion of the Jews from Spain. The resulting racial ideology was referred to as *limpieza de sangre* (purity of blood). Once introduced to the Caribbean, *limpieza de sangre* translated into a system of racial privilege in which whiteness stood at the top of an ethnic-racial hierarchy that put African and Amerindian physical features at the lowest end of the continuum. Within this system of racial privilege, race mixtures that occurred between pure races (and later mixed races) could be charted and—through precise mathematical computations—persons could be assigned differential rights and privileges. Table 8.3 indicates the profusion of racial terms (and their meanings) from eighteenth-century New Spain (Mexico).

As one might imagine, the resulting system of supposed racial types produced a confusing pattern of classification across the Spanish, British, French, and Dutch Caribbean territories. Indeed, a comparison of racial terms and categories on Spanish-, French-, and British-ruled islands at the time provides a clear illustration of the social construction of race. In this regard, a comparison of Table 8.4 and Figure 8.1 is instructive. Table 8.4 presents the exacting measures taken by elites in the French Caribbean to ascertain a person's precise degree of whiteness, whereas Figure 8.1 depicts similar efforts on the part of Jamaican elites.

Table 8.5, meanwhile, examines the 128 racial combinations and the (at least) eleven racial types identified by the Creole observer Médéric Louis Élie Moreau de Saint-Méry (1750–1819) in his three-volume *Description topographique, physique, civile, politique et historique de la partie Française de l'isle de Saint-Domingue* (Topographical, physical, civil, political, and historical description of the French part of the island of Saint-Domingue). The common thread running through all of these systems was the Caribbean elite's

Table 8.3 Racial Categories in Eighteenth-Century New Spain (Mexico)

1. Spaniard and Indian beget mestizo.
2. Mestizo and Spanish woman beget *castizo.*
3. *Castizo* woman and Spaniard beget Spaniard.
4. Spanish woman and black man beget mulatto.
5. Spaniard and mulato woman beget *morisco.*
6. *Morisco* woman and Spaniard beget *albino.*
7. Spaniard and *albino* woman beget *torna atrás* (turn away, as in "from white").
8. Indian man and *torna atrás* woman beget *lobo.*
9. *Lobo* and Indian woman beget *zambaigo.*
10. *Zambaigo* and Indian woman beget *cambujo.*
11. *Cambujo* and mulato woman beget *albarazado.*
12. *Albarazado* and mulato woman beget *barcino.*
13. *Barcino* and mulato woman beget *coyote.*
14. *Coyote* woman and Indian man beget *chamiso.*
15. *Chamiso* woman and mestizo beget *coyote* mestizo.
16. *Coyote* mestizo and mulato woman beget *ahí te estás* (there you are).

Source: Magnus Mörner, *Race Mixture in the History of Latin America* (Boston: Little, Brown, 1967), p. 58.

grave concern for determining a mixed individual's exact degree of proximity to (or distance from) whiteness.

The classic image of the ethnic, racial, and class structure of colonial Caribbean society during slavery is one of a pyramid. A small section at the apex represented whites. A thin band beneath this represented the mulatto population; the rest of society constituted the vast majority of African slaves. But this can be only a general, impressionistic guide. Ethnicity, race, and social class were never in perfect alignment, and often conflicts broke out within the top echelons of Caribbean society. The Haitian revolution provides a case in point. On the eve of the revolution, the "free people of color"—

Table 8.4 Some Terms Used in the French Caribbean for Race Mixtures and Degrees of Whiteness

Putative Ancestry	Term	English Equivalent	Reputed Degree of Whiteness
Offspring of white and black	*mulâtre*	mulatto	1/2 white
Offspring of white and *mulâtre*	*quarteron*	quadroon	3/4 white
Offspring of white and *quarteron*	*métis* or *octavon*	octoroon	7/8 white
Offspring of white and *octavon*	*mamelouc*	mustee	15/16 white
Offspring of white and *mamelouc*	*sang-mélé*	musteephino	31/32 white
Offspring of black and *mulâtre*	*griffe*	sambo	1/4 white
Offspring of black and *griffe*	*sacatra*	sambo	1/8 white
Offspring of black and *sacatra*	*marabou*	sambo	1/16 white

Source: Adapted from W. Adolphe Roberts, *The French in the West Indies* (New York: Bobbs-Merrill, 1942), p. 134.

Figure 8.1 Grades of Color in Early-Nineteenth-Century Jamaica

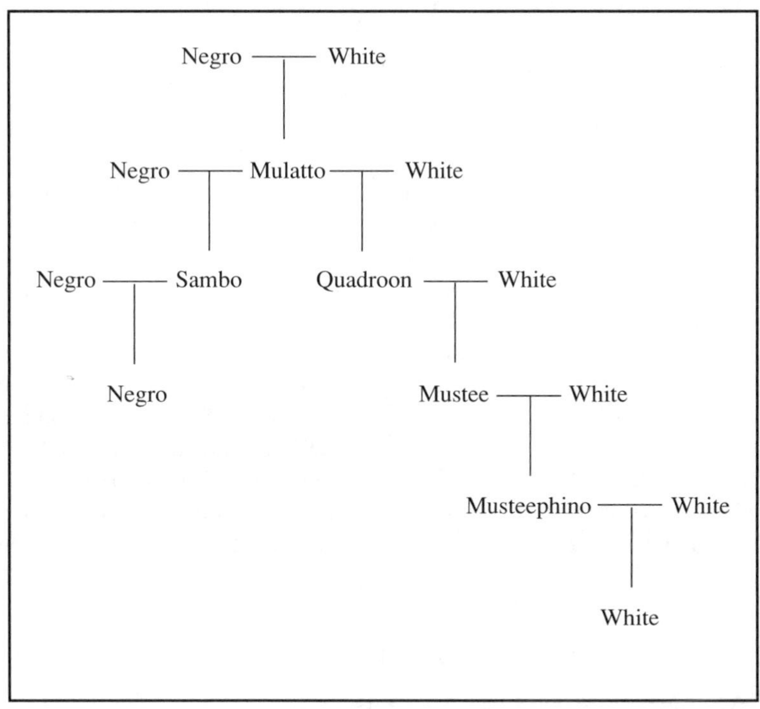

Source: Barry W. Higman, *Slave Population and Economy in Jamaica, 1807–1834* (Cambridge, UK: Cambridge University Press, 1976), p. 139.

Table 8.5 Racial Categories in St. Domingue, Late Eighteenth Century

Category	Parts White	Parts Black
Noir (black)	0	128
Sacatra	16	112
Griffe	32	96
Marabou	48	80
Mulâtre	64	64
Quarteron	96	32
Métis	112	16
Mamelouc	120	8
Quarteronné	124	4
Sang-mêlé	126	2
Blanc (white)	128	0

Source: Médéric Louis Élie Moreau de Saint-Méry, *Description topographique, physique, civile, politique et historique de la partie Français de l'isle de Saint-Domingue.* New Edition edited by Blanche Maurel and Étienne Taillemite (Paris: Société de L'Histoire des Colonies Françaises and Librairie LaRose, 1958 [1797–1798]), vol. 1, p. 100.

known as the *affranchis*—represented a small but influential portion of the overall population and in many ways were responsible for precipitating the revolution. Table 8.6 provides a breakdown of ethnicity and status in the colonies of Santo Domingo (the Dominican Republic) and St. Domingue (Haiti) at the end of the eighteenth century.

At the same time, there were profound class and status divisions within and across each segment of the social pyramid in St. Domingue that tended to mitigate the structural simplicity. For example, among whites there were *grands blancs* (high-status landowning whites), as well as *petit blancs* (lesser whites). Many *affranchis* owned slaves. There were also mulatto former slaves and well-to-do Afro-Haitians among the group of free coloreds, as they were called. The Haitian revolution avowedly upheld the power of Afro-Haitians. The resulting constitution of 1805 barred whites from owning property and equated the Haitian identity with "blackness"—a conscious effort to turn the colonial racial system privileging whites on its head. Despite such declarations, postrevolutionary power generally remained in the hands of an organized mulatto elite, and the division between this mulatto elite and the broader Afro-Haitian masses has plagued Haiti ever since. Following the revolution, mulattoes tended to exert significant economic and political control, whereas Afro-Haitians occupied the lower rungs of the social ladder.

The Aftermath of Colonial Rule and Slavery

As critical as slavery was for the development of ethnicity, race, class, and nationality across the modern Caribbean, the period immediately preceding and following the abolition of slavery has left an equally indelible mark (Scott 1985; Fraginals et al. 1985; Baronov 2000). The process of abolition itself was by no means uniform throughout the Caribbean. The competing colonial powers ended slavery at different times. The dramatic slave uprising and revolution in Haiti was far from the norm. More typical was the case of the British Empire. A combination of free-market forces and humanitarian

Table 8.6 Ethnicity and Status in Santo Domingo and St. Domingue at the End of the Eighteenth Century

	Santo Domingo (1794)	St. Domingue (1789)
Whites	35,000	40,000
Slaves	15,000–30,000	450,000
Free/mixed	38,000	30,000

Source: Anthony P. Maingot, "Race, Color, and Class in the Caribbean," in *The Americas: Interpretive Essays,* edited by Alfred Stepan (New York: Oxford University Press, 1992), p. 230.

interests eventually ended the slave trade in 1807, with slavery itself abolished by 1838. Cuba was the final holdout, maintaining slavery until 1886.

The paths following slavery with respect to the plantation system and the treatment of former slaves also differed significantly across the Caribbean. In many cases, slaves were initially forced into systems of apprenticeship (called *patronato* in Cuba). The purpose of apprenticeship—or so it was claimed—was to ease the transition for former slaves into their new lives. In fact, apprenticeship was primarily used to assist planters while they set about to replace slaves with new forms of coerced labor. Following apprenticeship, former slaves faced two basic options. They could continue to work on plantations under new structures of coercion, or, in areas where land was available, they could venture out and try to form independent peasant communities. Others occasionally migrated to other locations.

The immediate concern of planters on the eve of abolition was to maintain ready access to an easily coerced labor force. To resolve this dilemma a global network of forced labor migration was instituted. This enormous undertaking ferried huge numbers of workers from the distant reaches of the British, Dutch, Portuguese, and Spanish Empires to the Caribbean. Chinese and East Indian laborers represented the majority of workers forced to migrate. More than 125,000 indentured Chinese laborers came to Cuba, Guyana, Jamaica, and Trinidad. From 1838 to 1917 more than 400,000 East Indians were taken to Jamaica, Guyana, and Trinidad. Today East Indians comprise about 40 percent of the Trinidad and Tobago population and 55 percent of the Guyana population. More than 100,000 East Indians were sent to Martinique, Guadeloupe, and French Guiana. Another 35,000 went to Suriname, where they were joined by about 22,000 laborers from Java. Amerindians from the Yucatán were also sent to the Caribbean, along with a number of West African laborers and indentured workers from Madeira who wound up in Trinidad and Guyana. Thus, the end of slavery in the Caribbean resulted in one of the most ethnically and culturally diverse regional gatherings in the world.

In addition to the forced migration to the Caribbean there was a sizable amount of migration within the Caribbean. Migrants from Haiti as well as the British West Indies traveled to Cuba at the time of a sugar boom. Puerto Ricans crossed the Mona Passage to the Dominican Republic for similar reasons. Laborers from Curaçao moved to Suriname to work on the railway. This massive movement of labor flooded the Caribbean region and greatly reduced the bargaining power of former slaves. If former slaves refused to work, they were easily replaced. If former slaves refused to work under certain harsh conditions, they were threatened with the prospect of losing their job to an imported laborer. In addition, the forced global gathering of varying nationalities, ethnicities, and religions guaranteed a degree of internecine conflict that could effectively keep the powerless masses continuously divided.

■ Ethnic, Racial, and National Minorities in Caribbean Society

As follows from the Caribbean's unique history, few regions of the world today can match its cultural diversity. The ongoing migration into the Caribbean both before and since the end of slavery has created an extraordinary blending of peoples, languages, and faiths. As discussed, the long period of the slave trade and plantation system brought a diverse mix of African ethnic groups. The plantation system, of course, also brought European traders and planters from Spain, the Netherlands, England, Denmark, and France. The next wave of forced labor migration in the mid–nineteenth century brought people from China, India, and Portugal as well as additional laborers from western Africa and other parts of Central America and the Caribbean. Later waves of migration brought a still more diverse collection of peoples, including communities of Germans, Italians, Syrians, and Lebanese.

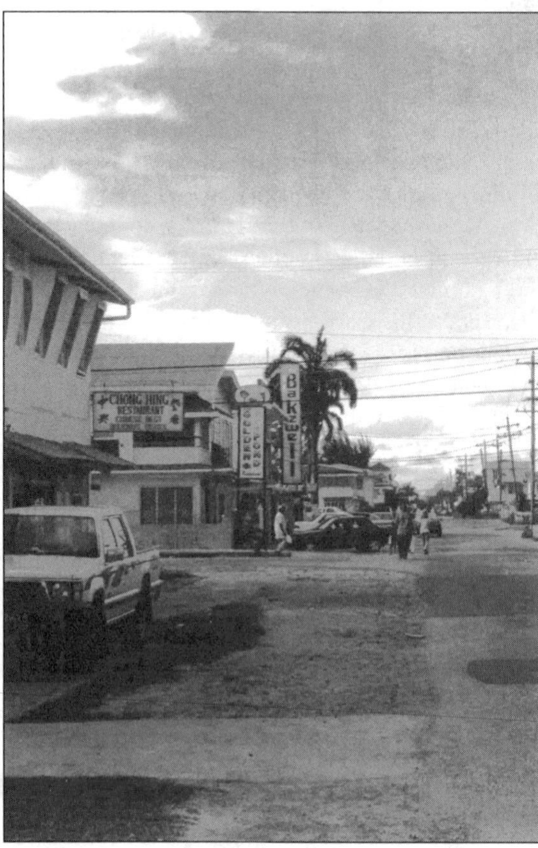

Chinese and Indian businesses in Georgetown, Guyana

Maureen Smith

By the end of the twentieth century the panorama of nationalities, languages, and religions across the Caribbean was staggering. Beyond the languages of the original colonizers (Spanish, English, French, Dutch, and their creole versions) one should not be surprised to hear Chinese, Hindi, Arabic, German, or Italian spoken throughout the region. Furthermore, as Leslie Desmangles, Stephen Glazier, and Joseph Murphy describe in Chapter 10, the region has communities of worship for every major world religion, including Hinduism, Islam, Buddhism, Judaism, and Christianity as well as a multitude of uniquely Caribbean syncretic religions.

The Afro-Caribbean population clearly represents the largest ethnic-racial group in the Caribbean. At the same time, though Afro-Caribbean peoples have achieved political power and prominence in many countries, they remain notably lacking among the region's social and economic elites. Thus, despite their declining numbers—as a percentage of the population—and dwindling political clout since the abolition of slavery, Caribbean whites continue to exert disproportional social, political, and economic influence. This is in large measure due to the enormous concentration of wealth and resources in the territories still under their control. In Martinique, for example, as late as eighty-seven years following abolition, in 1935, 3 percent of all landowners continued to own 61 percent of the cultivable soil. By the 1950s just five large corporations effectively controlled Martinique's agricultural production. The great majority of the island's wealth and strategic resources were controlled by Creole whites, referred to as *békés*. In 1960 estimates were that the *békés* held as much as two-thirds of the invested capital in the island.

The role of the white elite is complemented by that of the so-called trading minorities, which are ethnic-racial groups across the Caribbean who operate as merchants and traders. They facilitate intra-island trade and commerce as well as trade between the island and other regions of the globe. Because nearly all Caribbean islands rely heavily on export trade for economic survival, trading minorities occupy a powerful position with great influence over the daily lives of the masses in society. The potential for broad resentment and antiminority sentiment in the face of an economic downturn is a constant concern. The Chinese in Trinidad, Martinique, Guyana, and Jamaica are a case in point. Middle Eastern immigrants in Haiti, Trinidad and Tobago, and the Dominican Republic (such as Syrians and Lebanese) or Jews in Curaçao and Jamaica are additional examples.

In multiethnic societies such as Trinidad and Tobago, where there is social and economic competition among several groups, things can be especially complicated. Historically, Afro-Trinidadians and East Indians have lagged far behind whites, browns, and others. Table 8.7 looks at income distribution by ethnic-racial group in Trinidad and Tobago. Afro-Trinidadians and East Indians today each represent about 40 percent of the population. Following the oil boom of the 1970s and the expansion in state employment and entrepreneurial opportunities, Afro-Trinidadians and East Indians have made notable progress. A 1993 report on ethnic-racial business ownership, however, indicated that Afro-Trinidadians are virtually absent from the senior management of firms owned by whites, Syrians, Lebanese, Chinese, or East Indians (Centre for Ethnic Studies 1993). Thus, despite progress in closing the gap, the disparities remain sharp. In the early 1990s Afro-Trinidadian males earned U.S.$0.75 and East Indian males U.S.$0.64 for every dollar earned by males from other ethnic-racial categories. Female wages were U.S.$0.77 and U.S.$0.70, respectively, for Afro-Trinidadians and East Indians.

Lasting African Influences

As noted, the vast majority of Caribbean people trace their heritage to Africa. It is interesting to consider what this identity with Africa means to those in the Caribbean who also identify themselves as Martinicans, Jamaicans, Trinidadians, Cubans, Grenadians, Barbadians, and so forth. To begin, it is helpful to reiterate the danger of generalizing too greatly about the conditions that African slaves first encountered in the different slave societies of the Caribbean or about the mix of African ethnicities that were brought over. The only experience common to all was the brutal and barbaric treatment at the hands of Europeans. Based upon their enslavement and the forced mixture of African cultures, Caribbean slaves forged new folk traditions, belief systems, and sustaining ideologies. Sidney Mintz and Richard Price emphasize the significant ethnic heterogeneity of Caribbean slave populations. They have argued against any assumptions of historical connections between a single specific culture in West Africa and Afro-Caribbean cultures. "The Africans who reached the New World did not compose, at the outset, *groups*. In fact, in most cases, it might even be more accurate to view them as *crowds*, and very heterogeneous crowds at that" (Mintz and Price 1992:18).

What seem at first glance to be purely African cultural forms in the Caribbean are, in fact, better conceived of as broad cultural continuities. The

Table 8.7 Income Distribution in Trinidad and Tobago by Ethnic Groups, 1971–1972 and 1975–1976 (average monthly income, Trinidad and Tobago dollars)

Ethnic Group	1971–1972	1975–1976
Black	279	412
East Indian	240	454
Others	442	630

Source: Adapted from Jare Harewood and Ralph M. Henry, *Inequality in a Post-Colonial Society: Trinidad and Tobago* (St. Augustine, Trinidad: Institute of Social and Economic Research, University of the West Indies, 1985), pp. 64–65.

evolution of Afro-Caribbean culture has entailed the constant making and remaking of sociocultural practices and beliefs consistent with an ongoing cultural transformation and adaptation to the new Caribbean social reality. Some of the results of this dynamic process of continuity and change have been religious systems such as Santería (or Lukumí) in Cuba, Vodou in Haiti, the Orisha religion in Trinidad, and Myal and Kumina in Jamaica. Creole languages as well as various forms of dance, art, and music have also flourished within this unique cultural transformation. Table 8.8 details the mix of language influences shaping the modern Caribbean.

In this context, the image of Africa has become a potent symbol in Caribbean consciousness. It has been held up as the motherland or homeland by a variety of social movements at different times. The work of Jamaican Marcus Garvey (1887–1940) and his Universal Negro Improvement Association is a case in point. At its height in the 1920s, Garvey's association listed more than 1,000 branches internationally. Rastafarianism—known the world over for its association with reggae music—was born of this African-inspired social movement in Jamaica. In the 1930s Ethiopian Emperor Haile Selassie I was declared God on Earth by Jamaican preachers and their followers, prompting some Rastafari from across the Caribbean to try to enlist for war when Italy invaded Ethiopia in 1935 (Yelvington 1999).

■ Imagining the Caribbean Nation

In the Caribbean there are several ways of "imagining" the national community (Anderson 1983). It is perhaps best to view these competing versions as variations on a theme rather than as distinct and unrelated. What they have

Table 8.8 Caribbean Language Situations

Multilingual: Trinidad has standard and nonstandard forms of English, a French-based Creole, nonstandard Spanish, Bhojpuri, Urdu, and Yoruba. Suriname has Dutch, Sranan, Saramaccan, Ndjuka, Javanese, and Hindi.

Bilingual: St. Lucia, Dominica, and Grenada have standard and nonstandard forms of English and a French-based Creole. The Netherlands Antilles has Dutch and Papiamentu (with English and Spanish widely used).

Diglossia: In Haiti and the French West Indies, French and a French-based Creole exist but are kept relatively separate.

Continuum: Guyana, Antigua, Jamaica, Montserrat, and St. Kitts have different graded levels of language beginning with a polar variety commonly called "Creole" or "Patois" and moving through intermediate levels to a standard norm of English at the other pole.

Monolingual: Barbados, Cuba, the Dominican Republic, and Puerto Rico have a standard and a nonstandard form of European languages (English in the first case, Spanish in the others).

Source: Mervyn C. Alleyne, "A Linguistic Perspective on the Caribbean," in *Caribbean Contours,* edited by Sidney W. Mintz and Sally Price (Baltimore: Johns Hopkins University Press, 1985), p. 166.

in common is their genesis in eighteenth-century European conceptualizations of the state. In addition, nationalisms in the Caribbean revolve around the notion of a national culture. This is taken to mean a number of things, most especially popular forms of expression such as music (Manuel et al. 1995).

The extent to which dominant ethnic-racial groups are able to cast their vision as the accepted image of nationalism among the masses has far-reaching implications. Indeed, it is argued here that there are four essential frameworks for imagining the nation in the Caribbean: *mestizaje-créolité* (racial mixing/creolism), racial democracy, national race, and multiculturalism. This is not to suggest that any particular nationalist ideology is wholly subscribed to by all citizens or that it imposes a uniform pattern of social relations. For example, whereas anti-Haitian sentiment is the cornerstone of nationalism in the Dominican Republic, this is mitigated by ongoing cooperative relationships between Haitians and Dominicans in the border zones. In Trinidad and Tobago, the competition between Afro-Trinidadians and East Indians that typifies competing visions of the nation exists alongside bonds of kinship between members of each group.

Mestizaje-Créolité

Nationalism in many Latin American countries is characterized by the concept of *mestizaje* (Yelvington 1997). The concept of *mestizaje* revolves around the image of Amerindians and the offspring of Amerindians and Europeans who represent a unique and new ethnic identity. From this emerge two fundamental beliefs. Due to the lack of pure European ethnicity, the traditional European model of nationhood—built on a supposed European national character—is rejected. At the same time, attached to the claims of local ethnic distinctiveness are notions of backwardness and lack of civilization. Thus, ethnic-racial identities that form the ideological basis for nationhood in the European model are, in this case, treated as handicaps to be overcome. The ruling elites step in to argue that heterogeneous Caribbean ethnic-racial identities stand in the way of creating a harmonious and homogeneous nation. The project of national identity thus becomes inextricably linked to the interests of Caribbean ruling elites and is based largely on the elites' ability to construct a notion of nationhood around their ethnic-racial identity.

Certain contradictions are inevitable in this process. Contemporary Amerindian peoples are actively marginalized while—in recognition of the mixed ethnic-racial past—symbols of a noble pre-Hispanic Amerindian culture are recast as national characteristics. This process is exemplified by the case of Martinique, where leading intellectuals—such as Patrick Chamoiseau, Raphaël Confiant, and Jean Bernabé—promote a *créolité* cultural politics. These writers are often responding to the *négritude* (an idealogy extolling manifestations of blackness) of Aimé Césaire, a major Martinican thinker and

Thomas J. D'Agostino

Children of African descent in a barrio in Santo Domingo, Dominican Republic

politician. They promote the creole language, culture, and music as celebrations of a supposedly authentic Martinican culture and history. These *créolistes* attempt to present themselves as products of a historical process that resulted in a new creole culture. Herein lies the danger and the deception: national history becomes a tool of domination by elites.

The basic argument of the *créolistes* is that harmony rather than conflict characterized early Martinican society. It is claimed, for example, that the plantation—the site of the creolization process—was characterized by a relatively mild form of slavery as compared to elsewhere in the Caribbean. In Puerto Rico, Cuba, and the former French territories one also hears the argument that slavery was somehow more benign and that relations between slaves and masters were less onerous or objectionable than in other plantation societies such as Jamaica and the United States. It is easy to see how this fits with a nationalist project of *mestizaje-créolité*. Unlike in those countries colonized by the "cold" northern Europeans, there is no basis for modern ethnic-racial conflict because there was so little conflict in the past. We are, after all, one big, happy family united around common core values. Or so the story goes.

For all the claims of a harmonious and equal mix of cultural influences, European origins remain dominant. For example, the creole language is an integral component of national identity. For the *créolistes*, however, creole does not reflect the influence of African languages. Rather, modern creole is thought to have resulted from the dialects spoken by the early French colonists. This selective and creative reconstruction of Martinique's history has allowed elites to popularize a fictional account legitimizing and justifying their rule. Insofar as the *créolistes* have been able to position themselves as both heroic chroniclers of the "true" past and, coincidentally, as the very embodiments of a mythical, mixed ethnic-racial identity and tradition, they have been able to mask the self-serving effects of *francisation* (identification with French culture; "Frenchification").

Racial Democracy

Cuban nationalist José Martí (1853–1895) recognized the strong potential for ethnic-racial conflict within the revolutionary forces organized to overthrow Spanish colonialism during the Cuban war of independence (more commonly known as the Spanish-American War). As a result, he sought to unite Cubans with an ideology of nonracial nationalism. In his influential 1893 essay "Mi raza" (My race), Martí wrote, "Man is more than white, more than mulatto, more than black. Cuban is more than white, more than mulatto, more than black." There was an effort in the early twentieth century by many nationalist thinkers, of all ethnic-racial identities, to revive the work of Martí and to define the cultural essence of what it meant to be Cuban. As was the case in Martinique, harmony was emphasized over conflict. Both the *negristas* (the middle-class Afro-Cubans, mulattoes, and their white allies who proclaimed the national culture to be uniquely mulatto) and the Hispanicists emphasized the role of a Spanish-based creole culture where ethnic-race problems were minimal because Afro-Cubans, mulattos, and whites each shared this culture (Davis 1997).

This notion of ethnic-racial harmony has shaped Cuban nationalism for the past century—notwithstanding recurrent Afro-Cuban mobilizations against racism. Given the impact of twentieth-century U.S. interventions on ethnic-racial relations and nationalism in Cuba, Puerto Rico, Haiti, and the Dominican Republic, the language of racial democracy often also takes the form of anti-imperialism. Racial democracy—with healthy doses of anti-imperialism—became a central tenet of the Cuban national identity that framed the 1959 Cuban revolution. Fidel Castro has often referred to Cuba as a "Latin-African" nation. Because racial democracy emphasizes national cultural integration that idealizes ethnic-racial relations, there has been a tendency to soften the Afro-Cuban identity by presuming a mulatto or creole national cultural identity. Racial democracy precludes identification with specific ethnic-racial groups as a threat to national unity. Consequently, the postrevolutionary Cuban leadership has often come under criticism for its failure to effectively deal with the race issue.

A curious controversy erupted in Puerto Rico in 1997 when a new Barbie doll was introduced. The special Puerto Rican Barbie wore a colonial-tiered, lacy dress, evoking Spanish influence. It also featured an amapola flower both in the doll's hair and on the ribbon around her waist. This flower symbolizes the *jíbara* (a female peasant in the mountainous interior region). In Puerto Rico, the *jíbaro* (male peasant) plays a crucial symbolic role shaping national identity. Considered to possess the simple values and indomitable spirit of rural folk everywhere, the *jíbaro* also embodies the process of *mestizaje*-creolization. He is held to result from a mixture of the three races and cultures said to constitute Puerto Ricans: the Spanish colonizers, the Amerindians (or Taínos), and the African slaves. Yet the *jíbaro* is invariably depicted as white, effectively denying all but the most insignificant Amerindian heritage along with all traces of an African heritage.

Journalist Juan Manuel García Passlacqua argued that Puerto Rican Barbie was mulatto based on a popular vision of Puerto Rico as a *mestizo-mulatto* society. In a column in the *San Juan Star*, he lauded Puerto Rican Barbie's "mulatto complexion, her almond eyes, her thick nose, her plump lips, her raven hair and her most magnificently simple but gorgeous local folkloric dress." This tendency to treat the mulatto identity as the exclusive national image—at the expense of the Afro-Caribbean presence—is not unusual among nationalist writers (particularly males) in the Spanish-speaking Caribbean. As Arlene Torres has argued, "The crux of the matter is that Puerto Rico is *mulato* as a nation *cuando nos conviene* (when it is convenient to be so)" (Torres 1998:288). The ethnic-racial-nationalist implications of the controversy surrounding Puerto Rican Barbie are explored later in this chapter.

National Race

In the Dominican Republic, an Afro-Caribbean identity is commonly associated with Haitian lineage. If one is "truly" Dominican, one is not Afro-Caribbean; Dominican and Afro-Caribbean identities are mutually exclusive. National race, as an ideology of nationalism, tends to conflate nationality with ethnicity. In the Dominican Republic this has its roots in the dictatorship of Rafael Trujillo (1930–1961) and his anti-Haitian paranoia and prejudice. Although considered a mulatto himself—his maternal grandmother was Haitian, and he was consequently denied membership to the white elite's social clubs—Trujillo sought at every turn to valorize white civilization and culture. He instituted a policy of *hispanidad* (Spanishness), by which the national identity and culture of the Dominican Republic were rooted in a glorious European past. Roman Catholicism, Spanish literature, the conquistadors, and even the bullfight were upheld as the true legacy of the nation.

Trujillo's machinations were more than rhetorical. In the depths of the Great Depression, with sugar prices low and unemployment high, he ordered the security forces to massacre Haitian sugarcane workers. An estimated 20,000–30,000 Haitians were killed between October 2 and 4, 1937. Importantly, despite popular ideology suggesting that all Afro-Caribbean people in the Dominican Republic must be Haitian, not all Afro-Caribbeans were simply taken aside and slaughtered; steps were taken to distinguish Afro-Caribbeans who were Dominican from Afro-Caribbeans who were actually Haitian. Haitians were known to have difficulty pronouncing the word *perejil* (parsley). This follows from the fact that, within Haitian creole, the *r* sound is pronounced like an *l*. Based on this, Haitians were identified and killed (Yelvington 1997). This method of distinguishing Haitians from Dominicans testifies to the fact that Dominicans, at least at some level, recognize that there is such a person as an Afro-Dominican—a Dominican who is identical to a Haitian in appearance.

Although this episode represented an extreme form of racist nationalism in the Caribbean, virulent anti-Haitian sentiment remains a staple of Dominican politics. During the 1994 presidential election, Joaquín Balaguer, a multiterm president and Trujillo protégé, based much of his campaign on an appeal to voters based on anti-Haitian bigotry. It was argued that victory for his opponent, José Francisco Peña Gómez—the Afro-Dominican former mayor of Santo Domingo—would risk a tidal wave of Haitian immigration that could threaten the nation. Balaguer's campaign produced a video showing Peña Gómez attending a faith-healing ceremony that they tried to link to Haitian Vodou worship. A pamphlet was circulated characterizing Peña Gómez's election as part of a centuries-old Haitian plot to take over the Dominican Republic. Many Dominicans rejected Balaguer's racist appeals. Nevertheless, amid charges of fraud, the Central Elections Board eventually declared Balaguer the winner by a thin margin.

Multiculturalism

Things are somewhat different in the former British and Dutch colonies such as Jamaica, Guyana, Trinidad and Tobago, and Suriname. In these nations, nationalism and ethnic-racial identities intertwine in a manner that departs from the previously considered patterns. Nationalism here can be seen as part of a two-pronged process. First, multiculturalism is emphasized. National mottoes often reflect this orientation. Guyana refers to itself as the "Land of Six Peoples." Jamaica's national motto is "Out of Many, One People" and Trinidad and Tobago's is "Together We Aspire, Together We Achieve." In this respect, ethnic-racial differences and complementarity are both highlighted to prove and justify each group's indispensable contribution, authenticity, and citizenship.

Second, debates often emerge regarding which ethnic-racial group has historically contributed the most to the national culture, implying a right to certain social privileges. In this process, the Eurocentric social-status hierarchy is turned on its head. The formerly subordinate become the privileged while the formerly privileged become the scorned. A social-status hierarchy among ethnic-racial groups emerges in these societies along a continuum of so-called givers and takers. Europeans are at the bottom of the hierarchy, viewed as takers who benefited from society more than they contributed. Afro-Caribbeans and East Indians wage a never-ending contest to prove that they are the ultimate givers and that their group contributes the most to the nation. It is only fair—or so it is argued—that the biggest givers have the greatest say in the allocation of social and political resources.

From this upended social hierarchy a homogenizing synthesis emerges that conflates the concepts of nation, state, and ethnic-racial identity. As a result, the notion of *nonethnicity* is created wherein someone is either an authentic representative of a national culture (a Trinidadian or Jamaican, for example) or they are considered an "other" within a larger national setting. These others are portrayed as belonging to ethnic-racial groups that have retained their non-Trinidadian or non-Jamaican identity while continuing to reside in Trinidad or Jamaica. Afro-Caribbean and colored elites have developed a unique tactic, incorporating this inverted social hierarchy to anchor their privileged social position. This strategy—known as *Afro-Creole nationalism*—identifies national consciousness with images of Africa in a show of anticolonial zeal (Hintzen 1997). These elites celebrate various popular Afro-Caribbean cultural forms to identify with historical oppression and legitimize their views of national culture among the larger masses.

■ Contemporary Realities and Caribbean Migrant Communities

Today's Caribbean reality presents an intricate tapestry. Alongside the complex intersection of ethnicity, race, class, and nationality there is the growing phenomenon of migration that is creating a new web of transnational Caribbean communities (Basch et al. 1994). Dennis Conway reveals in Chapter 12 that the constant movement between the Caribbean and other lands is continuously reshaping Caribbean identities in new ways. This principle applies to few places more aptly than Puerto Rico. Returning to the earlier Puerto Rican Barbie controversy highlights key differences within Caribbean communities depending upon one's location within the larger diaspora.

Conflicting Puerto Rican Perspectives

In 1997 the Mattel Corporation introduced the new Puerto Rican Barbie as part of its Dolls of the World Collection. The doll's design and appearance raised a great many issues concerning an authentic Puerto Rican identity as well as the nature of Puerto Rico's relationship to the United States. Curiously, while Mattel had also introduced Mexican, Peruvian, Brazilian, and Spanish versions of Barbie—as well as the nonspecific Hispanic Barbie in the United States—none had generated as much controversy in the popular media as the Puerto Rican doll. Many objections centered on the doll's physical appearance and costume.

Puerto Rican Barbie wore a long white cotton dress trimmed with lace, pink ribbon, and floral adornments. Her skirt featured lace ruffles trimmed with a pink border. She also wore a wide pink ribbon around her waist, accented with an amapola flower that also adorns her long, wavy hair. Importantly, this flower symbolizes the doll's *jíbara* (female peasant) identity. The doll's accessories included earrings, a ring, and shoes.[6] There were complaints that Puerto Rican Barbie promoted a distinctly U.S. cultural vision of beauty—impossibly thin at the waist but full-bosomed—and that this can be damaging to the self-esteem and physical well-being of young girls in Puerto Rico. Company officials said the collection is mainly designed to introduce children in the United States to other cultures. Mattel later announced that it will give all Barbies a smaller bust and a bigger waist in future versions.

There were also objections to Puerto Rican Barbie's fair skin, long, flowing hair, and chiseled nose—as well as her colonial-era dress. Compared with the blue-eyed version, the doll seemed to have a darker complexion and wider nose. "We're using the Hispanic version of the Barbie doll for the Puerto Rican version," said a spokeswoman for Mattel.[7] "Of course it can't represent everyone in Puerto Rico since everyone is different," she admitted. Nonetheless, many argued that the doll represented an implicit message regarding social standards of beauty. "If you see the doll has lighter skin, then you see the implication that this is supposed to be prettier," said Roberta Johnson, professor of political science at the University of San Francisco. "Puerto Ricans have many different looks, so any Barbie would have a problem depicting the average woman."

The doll's physical appearance, in the wake of the extraordinary influence of U.S. popular culture exported to Puerto Rico, inevitably raises questions of identity along with deeper political concerns. "Puerto Rico has a history of [external] control that makes the people insecure about who they are," Johnson said. "A lot of people don't want to be consumed by the English-speaking country to the north." The Barbie package, for example, describes Puerto Rico as having been "discovered in 1493 by Christopher Columbus, who claimed it for Spain." This ignores Puerto Rico's original Amerindian inhabitants (the Taínos) and their contributions to Puerto Rican cultural identity. "I was insulted," said Gina Rosario, a school art director of Puerto Rican descent who lives in Alexandria, Virginia. "She looks very, very Anglo, and what was written [in the package's brief history of Puerto Rico] was very condescending—'The U.S. government lets us govern ourselves.' If you're going to represent a culture, do it properly—be politically honest," she said.

The Barbie episode underscored significant differences between Puerto Ricans living in Puerto Rico and Puerto Ricans living in the United States regarding cultural and national identity. For many in Puerto Rico, the doll was a welcome, if belated, attempt to valorize Puerto Rican culture. In the United States, Puerto Rican identity has different implications, and the very same symbols can generate alternative meanings. Ethnic-racial discrimination, social class, nationalism, and sexism all impact Puerto Ricans differently depending upon their location in the United States or in Puerto Rico. Negative media stereotypes and prejudice tend to hit Puerto Ricans living in the United States especially hard. Sensitivity to how Puerto Ricans are depicted—*and by whom*—means that U.S. Puerto Ricans feel a need to be in control of these representations and, based on this, have developed a heightened political consciousness.

Puerto Ricans in the United States have actively engaged in efforts to define and shape representations of Puerto Rican culture—to extol its virtues while confronting damaging stereotypes. Puerto Rican Barbie, with her Spanish colonial dress and Anglicized physical features, undermined these efforts. The contrasting receptions of Puerto Rican Barbie are also, in part, related to disagreements over Puerto Rico's political status. As Thomas J. D'Agostino explains in Chapter 4, Puerto Rico is currently a commonwealth of the United States, subject to U.S. law and jurisdiction, with limited self-governance and no voting representation in the U.S. Congress. Although those in Puerto Rico are closely divided in their support between statehood and the current commonwealth status, a clear majority of Puerto Ricans in the United States favor keeping the commonwealth status, strongly opposing Puerto Rico's annexation. "In Puerto Rico, the issue is recognition for this little island," said Angelo Falcón of the Institute for Puerto Rican Policy in New York City. "Over here, there's a real question of how we're presented." By contrast, writing for a Puerto Rican newspaper, García Passlacqua argued that what is important is that the doll "will help us explain ourselves, as we are, to all Americans."

The Growing Diaspora

Conflicting notions of authenticity and identity between Caribbean communities living in their country of origin and those living abroad are not unique to Puerto Ricans. Everywhere they settle, Caribbean migrant communities maintain transnational linkages with their homelands while forging new communities and identities in their adopted countries. The implications of such linkages are explored in greater detail by Dennis Conway in Chapter 12. Indeed, today London, New York, Amsterdam, Toronto, Miami, and Paris are home to many migrants, including second- and third-generation communities. Table 8.9 traces the path of significant Caribbean communities outside the region; Table 8.10 provides an overview of Caribbean migrants in the United States by country of origin.

This transformative migration experience has been well captured by many Caribbean writers' reflective (and quasi-autobiographical) works of fiction. The growing list of Caribbean migrant literature includes Samuel Selvon's *The Lonely Londoners* (1956), Paule Marshall's *Brown Girl, Brownstones* (1959), Julia Álvarez's *How the García Girls Lost Their Accents* (1991), and Cristina García's *Dreaming in Cuban* (1992). Each of these works attempts to understand the unique pressures and experiences shaping Caribbean migrant communities. For example, "La guagua aérea" (The flying bus) is a 1994 short story by Puerto Rican writer Luis Rafael Sánchez that has since been made into a film. The humorous story chronicles the initial period of air travel between San Juan and New York City in the 1960s and how such travel transformed the lives of both those leaving Puerto Rico as well as the family members who remained.

The role of nationalism often takes on heightened meaning abroad, where segregated communities sharpen national identities. The Washington Heights neighborhood of New York City is home to a large immigrant population from the Dominican Republic, and Haitians and those from the English-speaking Caribbean concentrate in Brooklyn. In Miami there is Little Haiti and Little Havana. While drawing distinctions between themselves and other Caribbean communities, Caribbean migrants also emphasize certain differences between themselves and host cultures and ethnicities. British West Indian migrants in Central America often proclaim the superiority of their British heritage over the local Hispanic traditions and Spanish language. In North America, Afro-Caribbean West Indians must learn to deal with everyday forms of racism. This is done, in part, by forming an insulating politics of blackness while attempting to differentiate themselves from non-Caribbean African Americans. Haitian youths in the United States, by contrast, often become "cover-ups," denying their Haitian heritage so as to avoid the strong anti-Haitian social stigma.

The status of Haitians contrasts strongly with that of Cuban immigrants. Haitians seeking to come to the United States typically are categorized as economic refugees. Those attempting to reach the United States by boat are, therefore, intercepted by the U.S. Coast Guard on the high seas and barred from entry. Cubans, by contrast, continue to benefit from Cold War–era poli-

Table 8.9 Caribbean Migrants in the Metropoles

Country	Year	Home Population	Migrants Living in the Metropolis	Metropolis	Migrants in the Metropolis as a % of Home Population
Puerto Rico	1980	3,196,520	2,014,000	United States	63
	1990	3,522,037	2,651,815		75
Suriname	1975	365,000	150,000	Netherlands	41
	1980	356,000	176,000		49
	1990	422,000	228,722		54
Martinique	1982	326,717	95,704	France	29
	1990	359,572	109,616		30
			175,200 (ancestry)		48.7
Guadeloupe	1982	328,400	87,024	France	26
	1990	386,987	101,934		26
			161,806 (ancestry)		42
Dutch Antilles	1990	248,000	75,722	Netherlands	30.5
Jamaica	1990	2,404,000	435,024 (ancestry)	United States	18
			685,024 (includes extralegal migrants)		28.5
			325,000 (ancestry)	United Kingdom	13.5
			1,010,024	United States and United Kingdom	42
Haiti	1990	6,349,000	289,521 (ancestry)	United States	4.5
			689,521 (includes extralegal migrants)		10.8
Dominican Republic	1990	6,948,000	520,151 (ancestry)	United States	7.4
			745,151 (includes extralegal migrants)		10.7
Cuba	1983	9,771,000	910,867	United States	9.3
	1990	10,500,000	1,053,197		10

Source: Adapted from Ramón Grosfoguel, "Colonial Caribbean Migrations to France, the Netherlands, Great Britain, and the United States," in *Caribe 2000: definiciones, identidades y culturas regionales y/o nacionales,* edited by Lowell Fiet and Janette Becerra (San Juan: Facultad de Humanidades Universidad de Puerto Rico, 1997), p. 64.

Table 8.10 Caribbean-Origin Populations by U.S. State, 1980 and 1990 (percentage)

State	Year	Puerto Rican	Cuban	Dominican	Jamaican	Haitian
New York	1980	49	10	79	54	60
	1990	41	7	69	44	39
New Jersey	1980	12	10	8	6	6
	1990	11	8	5	6	7
Florida	1980	5	59	4	13	19
	1990	9	64	7	22	37
Other	1980	34	21	9	27	15
	1990	39	21	19	28	17
Total population (in thousands)	1980	2,014	803	169	197	92
	1990	2,652	1,053	357	343	229

Source: Alejandro Portes and Ramón Grosfoguel, "Caribbean Diasporas: Migration and Ethnic Communities," in *Trends in U.S.-Caribbean Relations,* Annals of the American Academy of Political and Social Science, vol. 533, edited by Anthony P. Maingot (New York: American Academy of Political and Social Science, 1994), p. 61.

Note: Total Cuban- and Puerto Rican–origin population; foreign-born persons included for other countries.

cies that privilege Cuban refugees above others. At the same time, in sharp contrast to Haitians, Cubans in the United States overwhelmingly think of themselves as white. When the Cuban-orchestrated Mariél boatlift in 1980 sent thousands of Afro-Cuban and mulatto Cubans to the shores of South Florida, a decidedly hostile reaction awaited, and there was a general call for them to be sent back. In this respect, the so-called Cuban success story conceals significant ethnic-racial and class differences within the Cuban immigrant community. Cubans retain a strong preference for standard spoken Spanish in everyday life. At the same time, young Cuban Americans born in the United States continue to celebrate their cultural hybridism by extolling their command of Spanglish while proudly announcing their Cubanness—in a social context where it is convenient to do so—and emphasizing their linkages to an imagined homeland.

■ Conclusion

Just as 500 years ago the Caribbean was defined by the massive waves of migration into the region, today the Caribbean is notable for the ebb and flow of its peoples between the Caribbean and other regions of the former colonial empires. As new communities form and flourish within the diaspora, fresh identities and cultural patterns develop. Notions of ethnicity, race, class, and nationality are transported along with personal belongings to the new lands where these fluid and ever-changing concepts are, once again, socially constructed to fit the contours of the new environment. Thus, as soon as we think that we have grasped the essential truths of ethnicity, race, class, and nationality in the Caribbean, we inevitably discover a new metamorphosis leading to a richer, fuller description and meaning.

Although these concepts may be interpreted and understood in different ways across the Caribbean, the fact that ethnicity, race, class, and nationality continue to exert a profound influence on the lifestyles and expectations of peoples throughout the region is a common pattern that transcends political boundaries and cultural traditions.

■ Notes

1. Ethnic identity is seen by the people involved to draw from three principal spheres of influence: biological (or natural) factors; culture-bound traits; and otherworldly, sacred, or spiritual forces. Importantly, it is often held that there is a causal relationship between these factors, which combine to provide a real and cohesive basis of group identity. The particular weight given to each factor and the direction of causation vary significantly among different ethnic groups.

2. The characteristics of race differ according to which society we happen to be within. When a phenomenon has no universally agreed upon criteria for describing and defining it, we say it is "socially constructed." This means that race is constructed—it is given meaning—by people within individual societies. Therefore, when applying such concepts across cultures, we do not have the luxury of assuming standard meanings.

3. There are three predominant interpretations of social class to consider. The first—and the most common use in the United States—associates class position with personal income. The principal concern is how much money one has via salary or investments. The second interpretation of class emphasizes social status as a measure of class position. Social status revolves around a host of culturally shaped social values that grant higher or lower status to certain communities, occupations, or activities. The third interpretation of class associates class position with one's social role within a society's economic system. In this formulation, a person's social power is determined by one's relation to the production process.

4. This notion is captured by Benedict Anderson's concept of the "imagined community" (Anderson 1983). This is not to suggest that national identity is somehow dreamed up or fictitious. Rather, it implies that nationhood emerges as a widely accepted ideology among group leaders and members. *Community* is understood not in the sense of a small, face-to-face society. Rather, it flows from the notion of a physically dispersed group of persons who are somehow alike in fundamental ways and who could, therefore, form a community. Nationality is no less contested than ethnicity, race, or class. Indeed, especially in the Americas ethnic-racial pluralism confronts national ideals of homogeneity. Nationalism, therefore, supports dominant ideologies—promulgated by privileged elites—and tends to legitimate a particular configuration of social power.

5. In this regard, it should be noted that throughout this chapter we have substituted the term *Afro-Caribbean* (or *Afro-Haitian*, *Afro-Dominican*, etc.) for the racial category generally referred to as *black* in the United States. In this way, we are distinguishing between Afro-Haitians (or blacks in Haiti) and mulatto Haitians.

6. Mattel refused our request to include a photo of the Puerto Rican Barbie doll in this volume.

7. The information and quotes on the Puerto Rican Barbie controversy are from the following two newspaper articles: *Charlotte Observer*, December 30, 1997; and *New York Times*, December 27, 1997.

Bibliography

Alleyne, Mervyn C. "A Linguistic Perspective on the Caribbean." In *Caribbean Contours*, edited by Sidney W. Mintz and Sally Price, pp. 155–179. Baltimore: Johns Hopkins University Press, 1985.

Álvarez, Julia. *How the García Girls Lost Their Accents*. Chapel Hill, NC: Algonquin Books of Chapel Hill, 1991.

Anderson, Benedict. *Imagined Communities: Reflections on the Origin and Spread of Nationalism*. London: Verso, 1983.

Baronov, David. *The Abolition of Slavery in Brazil*. Westport, CT: Greenwood, 2000.

Basch, Linda, Nina Glick Schiller, and Cristina Szanton Blanc. *Nations Unbound: Transnational Projects, Postcolonial Predicaments, and Deterritorialized Nation-States*. Langhorne, PA: Gordon and Breach, 1994.

Centre for Ethnic Studies. *Employment Practices in the Public and Private Sectors in Trinidad and Tobago, Volume 2: The Private Sector*. St. Augustine, Trinidad: Centre for Ethnic Studies, University of the West Indies, 1993.

Curtin, Philip D. *The Atlantic Slave Trade: A Census*. Madison: University of Wisconsin Press, 1969.

Davis, Darién J. "*¿Criollo o Mulato?:* Cultural Identity in Cuba, 1930–1960." In *Ethnicity, Race and Nationality in the Caribbean*, edited by Juan Manuel Carrión, pp. 69–95. San Juan: Institute of Caribbean Studies, University of Puerto Rico, 1997.

Eltis, David. *The Rise of African Slavery in the Americas*. Cambridge, UK: Cambridge University Press, 2000.

Fraginals, M., F. Pons, and S. Engerman. *Between Slavery and Free Labor: The Spanish-Speaking Caribbean in the 19th Century*. Baltimore: Johns Hopkins University Press, 1985.

García, Cristina. *Dreaming in Cuban*. New York: Knopf, 1992.

Godreau, Isar P. "La semántica fugitiva: 'raza,' color y vida cotidiana en Puerto Rico" (Slippery semantics: "race," color and everyday life in Puerto Rico). *Revista de Ciencias Sociales* 9 (2000): 52–71.

Gordon, Maxine W. "Race Patterns and Prejudice in Puerto Rico." *American Sociological Review* 14, no. 2 (1949): 294–301.

Grosfoguel, Ramón. "Colonial Caribbean Migrations to France, the Netherlands, Great Britain, and the United States." In *Caribe 2000: definiciones, identidades y culturas regionales y/o nacionales* (Caribbean 2000: definitions, identities, and regional cultures and/or nationalities), edited by Lowell Fiet and Janette Becerra, pp. 58–80. San Juan: Facultad de Humanidades, Universidad de Puerto Rico, 1997.

Harewood, Jack, and Ralph M. Henry. *Inequality in a Post-Colonial Society: Trinidad and Tobago*. St. Augustine, Trinidad: Institute of Social and Economic Research, University of the West Indies, 1985.

Higman, Barry W. *Slave Population and Economy in Jamaica, 1807–1834*. Cambridge, UK: Cambridge University Press, 1976.

Hintzen, Percy C. "Reproducing Domination Identity and Legitimacy Constructs in the West Indies." *Social Identities* 3, no. 1 (1997): 47–75.

Hoetink, H. "'Race' and Color in the Caribbean." In *Caribbean Contours*, edited by Sidney W. Mintz and Sally Price, pp. 55–84. Baltimore: Johns Hopkins University Press, 1985.

James, C. L. R. *The Black Jacobins: Toussaint L'Ouverture and the San Domingo Revolution.* New York: Vintage Books, 1963.

Klein, Herbert S. *African Slavery in Latin America and the Caribbean.* New York: Oxford University Press, 1986.

———. *The Atlantic Slave Trade.* New York: Cambridge University Press, 1999.

Maingot, Anthony P. "Race, Color, and Class in the Caribbean." In *The Americas: Interpretive Essays*, edited by Alfred Stepan, pp. 220–247. New York: Oxford University Press, 1992.

Manuel, Peter, with Kenneth Bilby and Michael Largey. *Caribbean Currents: Caribbean Music from Rumba to Reggae.* Philadelphia: Temple University Press, 1995.

Marshall, Paule. *Brown Girl, Brownstones.* New York: Random House, 1959.

Martí, José. "Mi raza" (My race). In *La cuestion racial* (The racial question), pp. 25–29. Havana: Editorial Lex, 1959 [1893].

———. "Our America." In *Our America by José Martí: Writings on Latin America and the Struggle for Cuban Independence,* edited by Philip S. Foner and translated by Elinor Randall, Juan de Onís, and Roslyn Held Foner, pp. 84–94. New York: Monthly Review Press, 1977 [1891].

McClellan, James E. III. *Colonialism and Science: Saint Domingue in the Old Regime.* Baltimore: Johns Hopkins University Press, 1992.

Mintz, Sidney. *Caribbean Transformations.* Chicago: Aldine, 1974.

———. *Sweetness and Power: The Place of Sugar in Modern History.* New York: Viking, 1985.

Mintz, Sidney, and Richard Price. *The Birth of African-American Culture: An Anthropological Perspective.* Boston: Beacon Press, 1992.

Monge Oviedo, Rodolfo. "Are We or Aren't We?" *Report on the Americas* 25, no. 4 (1992): 19.

Moreau de Saint-Méry, Médéric Louis Élie. *Description topographique, physique, civile, politique et historique de la partie Française de l'isle de Saint-Domingue, avec des observations générales sur sa population, sur le caractère & les mœurs de ses divers habitans; sur son climat, sa culture, ses productions, son administration, &c. &c* (Topographical, physical, civil, political, and historical description of the French part of the island of Santo Domingo, with an overview of the character types and customs of its various inhabitants, as well as a study of its climate, its culture, its production, and its administrative system . . .). Philadelphia: The Author, 1797–1798.

———. *Description Topographique, Physique, Civile, Politique et Historique de la Partie Française de l'Isle de Saint-Domingue* (Topographical, physical, civil, political, and historical description of the French part of the island of Santo Domingo). New Edition edited by Blanche Maurel and Étienne Taillemite. Paris: Société de L'Histoire des Colonies Françaises and Librairie LaRose, 1958 [1797–1798].

———. *A Civilization That Perished: The Last Years of White Colonial Rule in Haiti.* Translated, edited, and abridged by Ivor D. Spencer. Lanham, MD: University Press of America, 1985 [1797–1798].

Mörner, Magnus. *Race Mixture in the History of Latin America.* Boston: Little, Brown, 1967.

Portes, Alejandro, and Ramón Grosfoguel. "Caribbean Diasporas: Migration and Ethnic Communities." In *Trends in U.S.-Caribbean Relations*. Annals of the American Academy of Political and Social Science, vol. 533, edited by Anthony P. Maingot, pp. 48–69. New York: American Academy of Political and Social Science, 1994.

Roberts, W. Adolphe. *The French in the West Indies*. New York: Bobbs-Merrill, 1942.

Sánchez, Luis Rafael. *La guagua aérea* (The flying bus). San Juan: Editorial Cultural, 1994.

Scott, Rebecca, *Slave Emancipation in Cuba*. Princeton, NJ: Princeton University Press, 1985.

Selvon, Samuel. *The Lonely Londoners*. New York: St. Martin's, 1956.

Shepherd, Verene A., and Hilary McD. Beckles, eds. *Caribbean Slavery and the Atlantic World*. Princeton, NJ: Markus Weiner, 2000.

Torres, Arlene. "La gran familia puertorriqueña 'Es prieta de beldá'" (The great Puerto Rican family 'is really really black'). In *Blackness in Latin America and the Caribbean: Social Dynamics and Cultural Transformations, Volume 2: Eastern South America and the Caribbean*, edited by Arlene Torres and Norman E. Whitten Jr., pp. 285–306. Bloomington: Indiana University Press, 1998.

Williams, Brackette F. *Stains on My Name, War in My Veins: Guyana and the Politics of Cultural Struggle*. Durham, NC: Duke University Press, 1991.

Yelvington, Kevin A. "Patterns of Ethnicity, Class, and Nationalism." In *Understanding Contemporary Latin America*, edited by Richard S. Hillman, pp. 209–236. Boulder: Lynne Rienner Publishers, 1997.

———. "The War in Ethiopia and Trinidad, 1935–1936." In *The Colonial Caribbean in Transition: Essays on Postemancipation Social and Cultural History*, edited by Bridget Brereton and Kevin A. Yelvington, pp. 189–225. Gainesville: University Press of Florida, 1999.

———. "Caribbean Crucible: History, Culture, and Globalization." *Social Education* 64, no. 2 (2000): 70–77.

9

Women and Development

A. Lynn Bolles

Understanding Caribbean women's significant contributions to overcoming the legacies of slavery and colonialism, as well as their role in the development of the modern Caribbean, provides a more complete vision than the popular images of sensuality and exoticism that have been attributed to Caribbean women throughout history. In order to enhance our understanding, this chapter analyzes the sociocultural context of Caribbean women; their early struggles during the colonial era; similarities and differences between the Hispanic and Anglophone Caribbean; continuing struggles in the twenty-first century; women in organized labor and the workforce; gender, class, and familial organization; the "independent" woman in the contemporary Caribbean; and women in the Organization of American States (OAS).

■ The Sociocultural Context of Caribbean Women

In the introduction to this book, Richard S. Hillman proposes an inclusive definition of the Caribbean region. The region, named after one of its indigenous groups, the Caribs, includes twenty-seven island and mainland territories, four major European language groups, countless vernaculars and dialects, and a myriad of races and cultures. Despite these differences, the people of the region have a shared identity—West Indian/Antillean/Caribbean—that results from a shared history. There is no denying that the Caribbean region experienced two of the most extreme forms of exploitation known in human societies: slavery and colonialism. Contact between Europeans and the indigenous populations almost eradicated the latter through warfare, forced labor, diseases, and genocide. As David Baronov and Kevin

Yelvington illustrate in Chapter 8, slavery and colonial oppression introduced two additional cultural systems—African and European—which, through the process of creolization (the blending of peoples and traditions), gave rise to particular complex social formations. Consequently, because of the legacy of slavery that marked free and nonfree on the basis of phenotype (skin color), Caribbean societies are highly stratified by race, color, class, ethnicity, and gender inequality (Barriteau 1998).

Contemporary Caribbean women are descended from the victims of the largest forced migration in modern history (arising from the enslavement of the African peoples) and of the coerced relocation of nineteenth-century indentured laborers, such as the East Indians. They are the survivors of European expansionism and its annihilation of Amerindians (Knight and Crahan 1979). In the Caribbean, however, one finds women with ethnic backgrounds from various regions of the world besides the predominant Africa and Europe. They include the Indian subcontinent, China, Lebanon, Syria, and other areas of the former Ottoman Empire.

For most island Caribbean societies, the Amerindian (namely, the Arawaks, the Taínos, and the Caribs) contribution to culture is reduced to a faint memory inscribed in archeological sites but is evident in some cultural traits such as language, place-names, home furnishings, and some food customs. However, the recognition and pride of Taíno heritage is resurfacing in certain quarters in the Dominican Republic and Puerto Rico, where festivals are held in commemoration of the Amerindian heritage (Davila 1997: 223–227). There are groups of Amerindians living in tropical forests in southern Guyana and Suriname. For contemporary Carib women from St. Vincent and their relatives, as well as the Garifuna from coastal Guatemala and Belize, their Amerindian culture continues into the twenty-first century (McClaurin 1996). There is no doubt that these indigenous groups paid a high price for their survival. Caribs who survived battles against the French and the English were forcibly removed and relocated. Britain moved Carib peoples beyond the tropics and even resettled a group in a northern colony (Nova Scotia, Canada). However, the Caribs did not go quietly. In 1650 the Caribs of Grenada allowed a French expedition from Martinique to buy extensive landholdings. A year later, hostilities resumed between the indigenous people and the French. Seeing their efforts had become futile, the last forty Caribs jumped to their deaths from a precipice on the extreme north of Grenada. They suffered this extreme sacrifice rather than submit to French rule (Ecumenical Program for Inter-Communication and Action 1982).

The East Indian population is the numerical majority in Guyana and is the largest ethnic group in Trinidad. Clearly, those societies exhibit critical cultural contributions from the subcontinent, both Hindu and Muslim. The vicissitudes of British colonial rule, the political economy, and immigration flows impacted the indentured populations. Many more men than women were conscripted, thereby skewing the demographics and altering cultural expectations for both men and women. Only when the male-female ratio evened out did the Hindu- and Muslim-prescribed roles of women and men become possible in the Caribbean. Gender constructs of the sending society weigh heavily on how Indo-Guyanese and Indo-Trinidadian women are viewed historically and how they are understood at present (Mohammed and Shepherd 1999).

Caribbean women of European descent are predominant in the Spanish-speaking countries of the Dominican Republic, Puerto Rico, and Cuba, although these societies are primarily *mestizo* (mixed race). *Mestizo* means that the majority of these societies reflect the sociocultural and racial context of creolization—the blending of two or more groups such as African, European, or Amerindian. Here, as in the rest of the region, class and color are fundamental indicators of a woman's social position. There are also Caribbean women of Chinese and Middle Eastern descent, among others, who have different ethnic and religious affiliations. Ironically, notwithstanding the creole nature of these societies, in the official census there are also categories of people designated as mixed (Yelvington 1995:22–23).

The majority of the women who live in the Caribbean, however, are of African descent. Furthermore, the sociocultural contributions of different African ethnic groups (e.g., Akan, Yoruba, Ibo, and Twi) in the early days were quite significant. Subsequently, language, music, religion, and other aspects of social organization contributed to the creolization process in all island and mainland territories (Manuel et al. 1995). In addition, the intensity of particular African ethnic cultural contributions is often most pronounced. For example, as Leslie Desmangles, Stephen Glazier, and Joseph Murphy show in Chapter 10, there are Trinidadian Yoruba songs, as well as religious practices of Kumina in Jamaica, Vodou in Haiti, and Santería in Puerto Rico and Cuba (Warner-Lewis 1979; Rey 1999). These cultural practices evolved within the context of slavery and the founding economic structures of the region.

During early colonization, white indentured servants could not follow the prescriptive norm due to their social status. Technically, these white women were not free. English, Irish, Welsh, and Scottish women contracted as indentured laborers to escape incarceration as political prisoners, prostitutes, and convicts; to avoid leading a life of abject poverty; and on their own accord (Shepherd 1999:20–39). However, after their time of servitude ended, those who remained in Barbados, Jamaica, or St. Kitts could become a part of the respectable class if they were lucky enough to find a mate to marry or to profit from their business acumen. Because they were white, they were aided in these endeavors by their color, as it was a major social marker for being free.

As time passed from the sixteenth to the seventeenth century, more African women were enslaved and brought to Caribbean colonies. These women satisfied two significant needs of these expanding sugar empires. First, there was the urgent necessity to replenish labor due to the high volume of production and high mortality rates among enslaved workers. African women who were familiar with agricultural work proved to be more than adequate workers in the sugarcane plantations. Subsequently, slave traders began to capture both men and women in Africa (Higman 1999:116).

By the close of the eighteenth century, the shift of the slave trade favored the number of women in the slave societies of the English-speaking Caribbean. For example, in Barbados there were consistently more women than men up until emancipation in 1834. In Jamaica, by 1827 women constituted more than half of the enslaved population (Higman 1999:116). Mature women hoed the soil, dug drains, cut and bundled canes, planted new canes, carried baskets of manure to the fields, and performed other physically demanding tasks. Younger women did lighter tasks such as weeding, tending cattle, and the like (Mathurin Mair 1975).

A second need was a secondary benefit for those who were not free and those who required a replenished workforce on their estates. By virtue of men and women together, the community of slaves made it possible for human nature to take its course, and needs of love and procreation brought children into the world. Given the structure of the slave society, however, these children were property and could be sold as a business transaction. Furthermore, white overseers, masters, and other slaves raped enslaved women. Power over the slave woman turned her own biology into a sexual-commodity object.

Children born to enslaved women assumed the social rank of their mothers—that of a slave. Some women who found themselves pregnant due to rape, or just despondent about their life as a slave, resorted to taking herbal remedies that induced spontaneous abortions. As historians have documented, women distraught over their life as slaves could not endure the thought that their own children would face a similar fate. Taking the right into their own hands, women ended potential life before it began. Incidences of infanticide were not uncommon. Guyanese poet Grace Nichols uses this imagery in her 1983 epic poem, "I Is a Long Memoried Woman," which depicts a slave mother throwing her newborn overboard during the Middle Passage and then committing suicide herself.

In 1765 an anonymously authored popular poem titled "The Sable Queen—An Ode" appeared in Jamaica (Bush 1990:11). The poem offered a positive image of brown and black women in glowing verse, remarking on their physical beauty and pleasing feminine attributes. With stanzas exclaiming the desirability of these beauties, the poem does not mention the circumstances that brought these women to the Caribbean. Clearly, these beauties were far away from their origins in African homelands. Furthermore, the poem never mentions that the majority of these pleasing, graceful women were enslaved or descendants of slaves. It also does not share with the reader that because of their status as slaves the exotic sable women were readily available to European men by any means of coercion or for a price affixed by her or her master. The Sable Queen was a most desired sexual commodity whether free or enslaved.

However, the sable beauties, whose bodies were objects of lust, were still enslaved or free women of color. By reason of their skin color, brown-skinned women occupied a social status far below that of European women. Consequently, the economic activities of the sable queens of the poem and the sable queens who labored in the sugarcane plantations all came to illustrate the multiple roles that women played historically in Caribbean societies. Neither type of sable queen, however, symbolized a dusky English rose put on a pedestal for all to admire and whose sole purpose was home and hearth. They were women whose lives and experiences were complicated because society denigrated any skin color but white—and that designation placed them into a different camp than the prescribed norm.

Following the Haitian revolution that freed the slaves of that country, the emancipation of peoples occurred at different times across the region. As Stephen Randall notes in Chapter 3, the British outlawed the slave trade in 1807 but did not emancipate its enslaved populations until 1838 after a five-year amelioration period. The Dutch (1863), Danes (1847), and French (1848) emancipated their populations at different times. This left the Spanish colonies as the only remaining practitioners of slave labor. As a colony, Puerto Rico emancipated its people in 1870, Cuba in 1886. However, these newly freed peoples were not members of independent countries. Haiti (1804) and the Dominican Republic (1844) functioned as autonomous nations following their respective emancipations, but as their histories tell us they continued to be constricted by neocolonial and island strife (Sagás 2000).

Dennis Pantin in Chapter 5 analyzes the economic impact of the sugar industry in Caribbean development. In this context, women, men, and children across the Caribbean carved out livelihoods under severe economic conditions resulting from the collapse of the international price of sugar. While creating new villages and urban settlements during this transition time, peoples' freedom in the Caribbean can be understood only within the ongoing neocolonial context. The aftermath of uneven social and economic development propagated by colonial administrations and the landed elite influenced the opportunities and living conditions available to peoples in Caribbean societies (Deere et al. 1990). More specifically, the social divisions of society (based on race and color, class and gender, and access to education and training) assigned black women to the low end of the socioeconomic ladder (Shepherd 1999:90).

■ Caribbean Women's Early Struggles

The pioneer work of the Jamaican feminist historian Lucille Mathurin Mair brought the unrecognized black woman into Caribbean history (Mathurin Mair 1975). The images about women found in conventional historical texts conveyed the idea that either the experiences of slavery and postemancipation life were homogeneous (essentially those of men), or that black women and men had different aspirations, needs, and functions in pan-Caribbean societies. Recent texts document female participation in resistance, in the development of culture and society, and in challenging male-centered, almost misogynistic interpretations of history (Shepherd et al. 1995; Shepherd 1999; Matos-Rodríguez 2001).

The new scholarship on Caribbean women analyzes the nature of surviving enslavement and various ways of living under colonial strictures. Since the mid-1970s Caribbean feminist history illustrates how an alternative view can bring people, especially women, and events into their proper light while providing a more inclusive vision of society. Women, as enslaved or free, across class, race, and ethnicities, used a range of cultural and social formations to tweak gender barriers. Abiding by prescribed gender norms and behavior, as well as adopting nontraditional roles, Caribbean women were instrumental in shaping the changes their societies underwent.

As Mathurin Mair comments, it is essentially awareness of oneself as a human being that makes the individual refuse to be reduced to the level of a non–human being in the way that slavery attempted (Mathurin Mair 1975:18). West African traditions of production, kinship, and family also supported the positive valuation of motherhood and the equality fostered by the estate labor force.

Conventional histories of slavery assert that women in slave society were more readily and firmly attached to white society. This interpretation suggests that black women accommodated more readily to slavery than their male counterparts (Patterson 1982). Presumably, a domestic slave woman's physical proximity to white men placed her in a contradictory position of devotion and betrayal. However, as the record of slave revolts in the British and French West Indies swells with accounts, there is no doubt that there was an outright rejection of slavery by peoples of African descent in the region. Furthermore, both men and women found many ways in their everyday lives to frustrate their masters. Planters needed the psychological and physical security of believing behavioral stereotypes of blacks to retain their own honor and power in slave society. Daily resistance on the part of women slaves was the response to this denigration. In fact, resistance to enslavement began from the moment of their capture, through the Middle Passage, and on to emancipation, which began with the Haitian revolution and continued to 1886, when Cuba finally freed its slaves.

As historian Barbara Bush argues, female insubordination took on various forms, including feigning illness, refusing to go to work, using abusive language (tongue lashings), leaving the estate without permission, losing articles of clothing from the master's laundry, withholding or using their sexuality for their own benefit, and using the slave codes in their own favor, especially concerning maternity rights (Bush 1990). Poignantly, one of the most powerful weapons in the hands of women cooks was their skillful use of poisons.

Other forms of resistance arose in the Caribbean as well. Maroons (from the Spanish *cimarrón*, or "runaway") were groups of people who escaped slavery and set up their own communities, usually in inaccessible areas such as swamps, forests, and mountains. Around 1769 in St. Domingue (the French form of Santo Domingo, early name of Haiti) a group of maroon women persuaded another group of women, who pounded grain and did other domestic chores, to join them. Although women refrained from running away in large numbers because of their kinship ties and children, it is now clear that they engaged in daily resistance and were often severely punished for these offenses against the planter class.

As the documents show, including the work by Barbara Bush, women on a daily basis caused more trouble than the men. According to contemporary histories written by men, few women seem to have taken part in the uprisings that plagued the Caribbean during the days of slavery (Higman 1999). Yet as Bush suggests, the absence of the names of female slaves from official records and contemporary accounts of slave uprisings and conspiracies does not constitute proof that they played no active part. Nanny, the legendary Jamaican windward maroon, provides an example of the role women played in their battle for freedom from slavery in the region.

Nanny was known by her own people and the British as an outstanding political and military leader. A junior British officer described her in the following way: "[She] had a girdle round her waist, with nine or ten different knives hanging in sheaths to it, many of which I doubt not had been plunged into human flesh and blood" (Mathurin Mair 1975:36). Legend also has it that Nanny slew captured English soldiers with impunity and that she had supernatural powers. Yet in 1739, when the British were finally defeated, they refused to recognize Nanny as the maroon leader during the signing of the treaty. Nonetheless, stresses sociologist Rhoda Reddock, Nanny figures prominently in Caribbean women's history because she led her people with courage and religious conviction and inspired them to maintain the spirit of independence that was their rightful inheritance (Reddock 1994).

It was only after the tremendous social, economic, and cultural change that took place in the nineteenth century (e.g., the Haitian revolution; the independence of the Dominican Republic; the emancipation in the English, Danish, Dutch, and French colonies; the rise of the peasantry; indenture; the wars of independence with Spain at the end of the century) that the region would be in a position to look for a female figure who could reclaim the spirit invoked by Nanny. One such figure is Doña Mariana Grajales de Maceo of Santiago de Cuba. Born a free woman of color in the early nineteenth century, Mariana was the mother of thirteen children, nine of whom lost their lives in

Cuba's independence wars (1868–1878), including the most famous, Antonio and José Maceo. Antonio Maceo (the Bronze Titan) has military standing that is likened to that of Toussaint L'Ouverture of Haiti's revolution. Caribbean historian Jean Stubbs remarks that Mariana—"the mother of Cuba"—has acquired legendary proportions akin to Nanny, "but the focus is on her status as a self-sacrificing mother, and not as a political or military leader" (Stubbs 1995:297)

Nanny and Mariana Grajales de Maceo each represent an aspect of womanhood that is fostered in the region. Each worked exceptionally hard to reach her own goals. Mariana nursed her sons, as well as other wounded soldiers, in the fight for independence. She lived in exile, and her own life was in jeopardy for decades. Nanny's status as a warrior-mother rekindles the heritage of the Akan peoples, who were prominent in the early enslaved populations. Nanny fought the battles but was denied recognition by the British because of her gender. Both women are now valued by their respective countries. One of the highest accolades bestowed to a Cuban mother is in the name of Mariana Grajales de Maceo. Nanny is Jamaica's only national heroine, and her visage appears on the Jamaican $500 bill.

■ Women in the Hispanic Caribbean

In general, the prescribed traditional roles of Hispanic women centered in the domestic arena of the home. Therefore, they had less visibility than their Anglophone counterparts in public life Women in parts of the Hispanic Caribbean, however, were exceptional. Thus, the similarity between them and their Anglophone Caribbean counterparts is significant (Safa 1995; McLaurin 1996).

The fact that women in Venezuela and the Dominican Republic have become politicians, business executives, and professionals, for example, appears to contradict the typical Latin American *machista* (male-dominated) culture. Yet movement toward sexual equality has been accomplished, in part, due to necessity. High divorce rates, widespread infidelity, rampant promiscuity that produced second families, large numbers of single teenage mothers, and male refusal of paternal responsibility have forced women to fend for themselves.

The tradition of *marianismo* (treating women as the Virgin Mary) has been resilient. Ironically, there is political currency inherent in having a mistress. Extramarital affairs, politically problematic in the United States, are a sign of power in the Caribbean, where *machismo* has yet to be completely overcome. Paradoxically, life in the extended family is considered sacrosanct. The system of *compadrazgo* (godparents—*padriños*—and distant relatives) is the norm despite the resultant nontraditional family structure. Another apparent inconsistency would be the popularity of beauty contests and cosmetics. But Caribbean women's preoccupation with glamour shows that professional success and equality are not incompatible with femininity.

Cuban women were active in the revolution. They also contributed to the literacy and health programs and today play an important role in professional and managerial life. Women occupy 28 percent of the positions in the Cuban government and 16 percent of those in the Dominican Republic, compared to the Latin American average of 15.4 percent. The U.S. and world averages are both 13 percent (Htun 1999:148–152).

Also, women's participation in the economy has increased dramatically. Although there is still a wage gap between women and men as well as significant problems in applying new laws recognizing the equal rights of women, illiteracy among women has decreased, and women constitute more than half of the students in primary, secondary, and university education. Women in the Hispanic Caribbean, therefore, have made much progress in overcoming historical obstacles and modern stereotypes.

■ Caribbean Women's Continuing Struggles

Early in the twentieth century, Caribbean women continued their struggles for equality and suffrage. Women played viable and assertive roles in

UN Photo 154387, Milton Grant

A women's group in La Vega, Dominican Republic

Puerto Rican politics, particularly after the Spanish-American War, whereby Puerto Rico came under the control of the United States. Combining politics and activities of the labor movement, women waged legal battles for suffrage and improved working conditions for both men and women. A major figure of the early twentieth century was Luisa Capietillo (1880–1922), a socialist labor organizer and writer. Literary scholar Edna Acosta-Belén tells us that Capietillo argued on behalf of equal rights for women and tried to raise the consciousness of workers (Acosta-Belén 1993). Challenging social conventions, Capietillo is remembered as being the first woman in Puerto Rico to wear slacks in public. Her writings placed her well ahead of her time, as she urged women to go forward and not shy away from social change. Likewise, Dominican novelist Julia Álvarez's *In the Time of the Butterflies* (1995) contributes to our historical knowledge of women's political engagement. The novel is based on the historical fact that three sisters participated in dangerous underground activities against Rafael Trujillo, the Dominican dictator. During thirty-one years of terror, Trujillo and his secret police tortured and murdered dissenters. The three sisters, immortalized by Álvarez, illustrate the range and depth of women's political commitment.

During the worldwide Great Depression of the 1930s, Anglo-Caribbean women were poised to reclaim the political spirit invoked by Nanny of the maroons. It is in the labor unions that the role of women is quite evident. The general strikes and worker insurrections, which blazed across the English-speaking Caribbean in the late 1930s, gave rise to two significant outcomes: (1) a more self-confident working class demanding its rights; and (2) trade union workers calling for the right to strike, for labor representation, adequate pay, and decent working conditions. The work situations had not improved since the days of slavery, which had ended 100 years earlier in the British territories. The trade unions, following British organizational structures, considered men as the primary workers, although they did recognize the fact that women constituted a major segment in the British West Indian labor force. During the strikes, there were women on the picket lines engaged in their own anticolonial struggle and exerting their right to self-determination. There were women who were fiscally responsible for those fledgling labor organizations—the early women trade union leaders (Bolles 1996). Yet these women are absent from much of the Caribbean historical literature.

One unique feature of the English-speaking Caribbean is the historically high incidence of female participation in the labor force. The organized labor activity of women trade union leaders in the Caribbean came about through the circumstances of their own work, life experiences, and the acknowledged deplorable working conditions of many others around them. Coming from a range of class backgrounds, the women came into the labor movement with the faith that their actions, together with those of others of like mind, would contribute to making their country a better place in which to live and work.

Like men in the labor movement, women trade union leaders continue to have a sense of collective consciousness: they recognize the benefits of collective action on behalf of the common good of working people. Once they were members of a trade union and their talents became apparent to those in leadership positions, or to their peers, these women took on responsibilities beyond mere membership. To this day, however, only a handful of women trade union leaders are included in the highest levels of decision-making in their organizations. Again, it is not a question of women's capabilities, but the nature of the deterrents put in their way, that impedes their progress.

Women trade union leaders have come from middle- and working-class backgrounds for the last fifty years of the labor movement's history (Bolles 1996). From the turn of the twentieth century to contemporary times, Caribbean women activist leaders have been able to carry out public political, social, and economic work on behalf of women, men, and children of their country, the region, and the world. Needless to say, additional factors in women's success include individual charismatic personalities, organizational skills, political savvy, and specific family histories. However, part of the success of Caribbean women leaders may be attributed to cultural cues that served their ancestors well—the ability to speak their minds, stand their ground, and use the most appropriate adaptive strategy available. For middle-class women this often meant upending their socialization.

Young middle-class women were not encouraged to move beyond the home by dictates of class position and colonial rule guided by local patriarchy. Across class lines, women's power was located at home. Female power seems to exist at a somewhat subterranean level, especially in regard to kinship and the family (Anderson 1986:320). In the workforce, women's power is severely curtailed, occupying gender-segregated activities and duties that confer low status (Bolles 1996). Organizations, with the exception of British expatriate wives' clubs and similar social welfare groups, did not question male domination or female subordination. Leadership and public speaking were male constructs that implied conduct unbecoming of a lady. Although public speaking became a critical asset for all women activists, it is the use of other skills that marked the talents of women leaders for improved quality of life and social change.

The following excerpts are from a collection of life stories of Commonwealth Caribbean women trade union leaders representing three generations. At age seventy-three, a member of the Barbados Workers' Union recalls how she joined the labor movement:

> They used to have meetings and all there in the market square and there'd be something with Toppin, the primer from The Advocate and all like that and I used to go and listen to these things and all like that so I knew about the union. So when the organizer came I was only too glad but then after I got in there then I got another reinforcement behind me, his nickname "Commisah," and he explained certain things and I talk with him and when I couldn't talk with Frank Walcott [CEO of the union]. (Bolles 1996:95)

A leader from the Jamaica Teacher's Association (JTA) states:

> Let us put it this way, from 1954 I recognized myself as a trade union person, having started to accept the responsibility to represent the teachers in council of the JTA. I think that 1966 when we had our first strike, running around Kingston and making sure that the schools were closed are things that I will never forget. (Bolles 1996:102)

Continuing the tradition, an Antiguan woman in her twenties remarks: "I am a person who believes in human rights and I saw I could make a difference" (Bolles 1996:103).

The outpouring of scholarship from the 1970s onward allowed researchers to critically examine archives and to engage in interdisciplinary study. It is in this vein that the analysis of women in the workplace has advanced beyond the basics of employment trends. Critical examination gives insight into the poor working conditions that continue to invade the lives of women across the Caribbean, despite the efforts of unionization and high labor force participation rates. As political scientist Luz del Alba Acevedo argues in "Feminist Inroads in the Study of Women's Work and Development," scholars must move their analyses beyond women's marginalization in the workforce and study the effects of "the feminization of the labor force and the economic inequalities inherent in a gendered hierarchical occupational structure in developing countries" (Acevedo 1995:70). If we examine the statistical evidence published by the United Nations Statistics Division, it demonstrates an increase in women's participation in the labor market (see Table 9.1). However, for a more complete vision we must simultaneously analyze the data on the gendered differences in part-time employment and unemployment (see Tables 9.2 and 9.3).

Labor-force participation rates for women have always been high within the English-speaking Caribbean, with some showing higher rates than others. The countries that have experienced severe fiscal problems, insertion into the global economy, and high unemployment rates in the formal sector have high percentages of women who are self-employed. Self-employment can include activities such as domestic work, market selling, as well as skilled work as seamstresses and high-tech consultants.

Table 9.1 Percentage Distribution of the Labor Force for Women and Men, by Status in Employment

Country	Wage and Salaried Workers		Self-Employed Workers		Contributing Family Workers	
	Women	Men	Women	Men	Women	Men
Antigua and Barbuda	83	78	15	20	1	1
Aruba	94	88	5	12	1	0
Bahamas	86	78	12	19	1	0
Barbados	90	83	9	16	0	0
Dominican Republic	65	47	31	48	4	5
Grenada	84	74	12	17	1	2
Guyana	53	52	44	38	—	—
Haiti	18	15	57	61	10	11
Jamaica	65	55	31	42	4	2
Netherlands Antilles	92	88	4	9	1	0
Puerto Rico	92	81	6	18	1	0
St. Kitts and Nevis	84	81	13	16	1	1
Trinidad and Tobago	77	72	16	24	6	2
U.S. Virgin Islands	88	83	4	11	0	0

Source: Percentage Distribution of the Labor Force by Status in Employment, United Nations Statistic Division, *The World's Women 2000: Trends and Statistics,* available online at http://unstats.un.org/unsd/demographic/ww2000/table5e.htm, accessed 2002.

Table 9.2 Percentage and Share of Part-time Employment for Women and Men

Country	% Part-time, 1990–1993		% Part-time, 1996–1998		% Women's Share, 1990–1993	% Women's Share, 1996–1998
	Women	Men	Women	Men		
Bahamas	14	11	15	11	53	52
Barbados	9	6	6	4	54	59
Jamaica	12	7	10	5	59	59
Suriname	32	8	24	8	66	61
Trinidad and Tobago	21	18	17	14	39	41

Source: Part-Time Employment, United Nations Statistic Division, *The World's Women 2000: Trends and Statistics*, available online at http://unstats.un.org/unsd/demographic/ww2000/table5b.htm, accessed 2002.

Table 9.3 Unemployment Rate in the Caribbean for Women and Men (percentage)

Country	Year	Women	Men
Antigua and Barbuda	1991	5.6	6.4
Aruba	1994	7.9	5.4
Bahamas	1998	9.6	5.9
Barbados	1997	17.8	11.3
Dominica	1997	27.2	19.6
Dominican Republic	1997	28.6	9.5
Grenada	1996	24.8	10.3
Jamaica	1999	10.3	15.8
Netherlands Antilles	1998	19.4	14.1
Puerto Rico	1999	9.6	13.2
St. Lucia	1997	23.8	17.7
St. Vincent and the Grenadines	1991	22.1	18.4
Suriname	1997	16.0	7.4
Trinidad and Tobago	1998	18.9	11.3

Source: Unemployment Rate, United Nations Statistic Division, *The World's Women 2000: Trends and Statistics,* available online at http://unstats.un.org/unsd/demographic/ww2000/table5a.htm, accessed 2002.

The United Nations Economic Commission for Latin America and the Caribbean (ECLAC) states that in absolute terms the number of Latin American and Caribbean peoples living in poverty hovers around 210 million. This figure is higher now than ever before. Of every 100 new jobs created between 1990 and 1995, eighty-four were in the informal sector (often self-employment). Young females under the age of twenty-five in Jamaica had the highest rate of unemployment. In places like Dominica, the overall female unemployment was 27.2 percent; 28 percent in the Dominican Republic; almost 25 percent in Grenada; and St. Lucia and St. Vincent and the Grenadines with around 23 percent each. In Jamaica, the minimum wage increased from $J30 (about U.S.$0.65) to $J45 (U.S.$1). At the current exchange rate of J$45 to U.S.$1, Jamaican workers earn less than U.S.$1 an hour if they work forty hours per week.

■ Gender, Class, and Familial Organization

Much of the social-science literature from the 1930s to the early 1970s stresses apparent differences between aspects of culture that are perceived as "European." Features designated as European (white or light-skinned, upper- or middle-class) are considered as the social "norm." Falling outside of this so-called norm are the African-based creole cultural systems of the majority. More than four centuries of European colonization resulted in the sociopolitical hegemony of the upper classes and accompanying derision of the cultures of the masses. Light skin color and middle-class status approximated the socially approved norm, whereas the African cultural patterns and dark skin of the black majority were cause for disparagement. In the case of Trinidad and Guyana, the Indo–West Indians were allotted a rank below that of Afro-Caribbeans; Chinese, Lebanese, Jews, and Portuguese were below whites.

Family forms were couched in ideal typologies. For example, decades of social-science research categorized West Indian family forms and household organizations in three patterns, listed here in descending order: nuclear family (wife, husband, children); common-law (nuclear without legal sanctions); and visiting unions (woman and children with a nonresident boyfriend or nonresident children's father (Mohammed and Perkins 1998). Research in the French and Dutch Antilles followed the British model, and studies in Cuba, the Dominican Republic, and Puerto Rico utilized the Spanish class-color specificities of *mestizo* culture.

Often, marriage was neither economically feasible (cost of a wedding, setting up a household) nor a given in the Caribbean reality of gender rela-

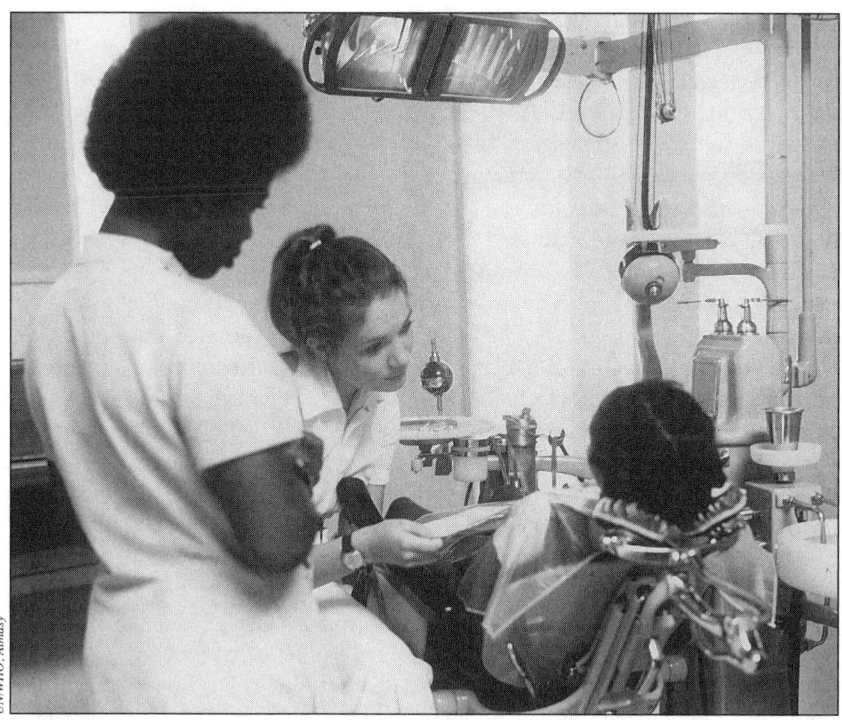

UN/WHO, Almasy

More and more Caribbean women are pursuing professional careers

tions. Indeed, having a child does not connote or necessitate the forming of a nuclear family. Therefore, the predominant Caribbean family forms stray from the ideal nuclear family. Within domestic organizations in the Caribbean, there is the prevalence of female-headed households, other variations in household structures, the double standard in mating relations, the normative experience of extramarital mating, and the commonplace acceptance of birth outside of wedlock (Mohammed and Perkins 1998).

As anthropologists Michael Horowitz (*Morne-Paysan: Peasant Village in Martinique*) and Miriam Salter (*The Caribbean Family: Legitimacy in Martinique*) remind us, the very notion of West Indianness refers primarily to peoples of African descent or of mulatto or *mestizo* origins. To a large extent, these terms exclude the Indian experience. This is particularly true in the discussion of family organization. The East Indian family structure was able to draw on its South Asian foundations when the ratio of men and women was less skewed. When there were twice as many men as women, there were a variety of relationships, none of which even came close to approximating traditional ones. Hindu and Muslim marriages were not legally sanctioned in Trinidad and Guyana until the mid–twentieth century. For those living primarily on sugar plantations, marital disputes and other domestic conflicts were settled according to Eurocentric family norms and values, usually by the estate manager. In contrast to subcontinent practices, couples resided with their paternal parents for only a few years, the father was no longer the sole trustee of family resources, and wives were given more say in family events. The caste system and caste endogamy (marrying within your own group by Hindus) was totally undermined. Arranged marriages within castes became impossible to attain (Mohammed 1995:39).

The domination of European constructs of gender-appropriate role, status, and proper place in society can be seen in the laws and policies enacted throughout the region in the twentieth century. For example, mass-marriage campaigns of the post–World War II period attempted to convince Jamaicans to transform common-law relationships into patriarchal legal marriages and enlisted churches, schools, the press, the radio, and welfare agencies in the effort (Smith 1962). This effort was also a remedy for another problem, as marriage would legitimize offspring who were deemed bastards under the law. Despite the media blitz, the mass-marriage campaign was a failure because of the popular economic requirements necessary for legal marriage, as well as the cultural acceptance of all children regardless of the circumstances of their birth. As a matter of fact, since the late 1970s, starting with Jamaica, most Commonwealth Caribbean governments have enacted a status-of-the-child law that finally put an end to questions of bastardy. This law states that a person cannot be held responsible for the consequences of his/her birth. In effect, illegitimacy is now a moot point, and all children are legitimate under the eyes of the law. In her text *Legitimate Acts and Illegal Encoun-*

ters (1994), Mindie Lazarus-Black studies how poor women, legally married or not, are taking their baby's father to court and demanding child-care payments because they are legal heirs to the man's property.

However, it was not the question of children that was viewed as a problem but the prevalence of female-headed households that concerned first colonial and now duly-elected governments. Furthermore, this situation, most prominent for poor and working-class women, dovetailed with increasing levels of social inequality.

Decades of detailed investigations by anthropologists and sociologists documented that Afro-Caribbean families did not represent disorganized or pathological adaptations to the conditions of slavery (Barrow 1996). Such a view resulted from looking at female-headed households in the Caribbean through middle-class European and/or U.S. eyes. For example, the model household of a family as two adults of the same generation, but different sexes, who are the biological parents of children with whom they live, rests in part on a gendered division of labor requiring a male breadwinner and a female homemaker, as well as on the belief that conjugal relations are more important than consanguineous ones. Eventually, feminist researchers challenged this notion of gender and family. The creole Caribbean family differs from this not only in reality but also in beliefs about what a family is and what is appropriate for its members to do. Anthropologists learned that, in attempting to understand both the economic support of households and children, and the performance of domestic responsibilities such as laundry, meal preparation, and child care, they could not assume that the boundaries of a dwelling define a family and what it does. Often, eating, sleeping, financial support, and child-rearing were shared among a network of male and female relatives and neighbors (Bolles 1996). However, research in the former Spanish colonies of Cuba, the Dominican Republic, and Puerto Rico shows the majority of households following a Eurocentric model, except for poor domestic units, which tended to be female-headed and whose members were of African descent (Brown 1975).

For subcontinent Indians, who were indentured laborers primarily in Trinidad and Tobago and Guyana, the organization of family did not resemble anything familiar to what was the norm in India. More men than women were indentured, and all lived in barracks on sugar estates. Sociologist Patricia Mohammed examined the life of Indian women who carried on wage labor on the estate and performed prescribed gender roles of cleaning, cooking, and washing for a spouse—and often barrack mates (Mohammed 1995). Only when the balance between males and females was finally established did the Indo-Caribbean peoples develop domestic units similar in structure to those in India (albeit nuanced differently for life in the Caribbean). Indo-Caribbean family structure became a catalyst for the revival of Indian culture in the West Indies. Pride over India's independence in 1947, and the arrival of Muslim religious preachers and artists, made family and religious ceremonies once again the center of Indian life. However, Indo–West Indian culture had evolved its own creolization due to influences of the wider society. Marriage was one of the first traditions to be compromised. Whereas parents' criteria for selection of marriage partners emphasized security, wealth, and family status, the younger generation looked for new and modern ways. The legally sanctioned nuclear family is still the most popular marital union, although common-law and visiting unions are becoming more prevalent than before. Young Indo–West Indians are also experiencing greater equality between spouses. A 1982 study noted that married women under the age of forty typically experience more autonomy than the generation of women before them.

The complexities of West Indian plantation life distorted the African heritage division of labor while, ironically, reinforcing it. For example, many mothers understood the cruelty of bringing children into slavery and resisted the master's encouragement to do so. The use of women as laborers in the fields beside men also revealed biases of color and gender; the majority of field slaves were black women. Although men and women labored equally in the field gangs, the chances of females doing any other task were slim (Mathurun 1975). Furthermore, there is a sharp division in the organization of household labor. Dorian Powell's 1984 study stresses the point that women perform a disproportionate amount of housework and usually carry the enormous responsibility of ensuring the survival of family members, a set of activities that Victoria Durant-Gonzalez calls "the realm of female responsibility." She states that a large proportion of women in the English-speaking Caribbean are "in charge of economics of producing, providing, controlling, or managing the resource essential to meeting daily needs" (Durant-Gonzalez 1982:3)

Anthropologist Helen Safa in *The Myth of the Male Breadwinner* (1995) conducted a comparative study of contemporary women, family, and factory work in Cuba, the Dominican Republic, and Puerto Rico. She notes that by the 1980s women had assumed more authority in the household than was culturally prescribed in the past, when they were employed in jobs outside the home. The additional authority does not necessarily come from their economic contribution but more from the fact that now there was more than one source of family income. It is not only the erosion of the man's role as the economic provider that is at issue; it is his ability and willingness to share this role with his wife. It makes for more equitable marital relationships. In Puerto Rico and the Dominican Republic, where male marginalization was most severe due to unemployment, the percentage of female-headed households was on the rise. As a matter of fact, 25 percent of all households in these countries were headed by women (Safa 1995:180). In contrast to the prevailing cultural patterns of male domination within families, the question is: Will these trends start to approximate marital patterns found in other areas of the Caribbean, or will new forms appear?

The "Independent" Woman in the Contemporary Caribbean

With the prominence of women heading households, we see the reality of the price of the inclusive concept of motherhood that pertains to the Caribbean. Because most Caribbean women are either employed in low-paying, low-skilled, and menial jobs or are unemployed, how can they fulfill all that is expected of them? The ideological support mechanisms found in the African-based traditional role of women in Caribbean societies prove to be invaluable cultural assets. Work—no matter how dead-end—has meaning and value for women. It not only meets their family responsibilities but also plays an important role in the development of women's self-image and the conception of "independent" womanhood (Bolles and D'Amico-Samuels 1990).

Independent is a word often used to describe West Indian women and how they carry out their responsibilities. Independence is a quality based on having one's own source of economic support—from employment, other income-generating activities, and, where possible, savings—while at the same time organizing and utilizing support from others (Barrow 1986). *Autonomy*, by contrast, implies exercising options while making decisions for oneself and having control over one's own destiny with no strings attached.

Independence, then, is not coterminous with female autonomy. Economic self-sufficiency is far beyond the grasp of most to whom the term *independent* has been applied in the Caribbean context. Rather than acting on behalf of a

Carolyn Watson

A women's literacy program, Jacmel, Haiti

single person, autonomy implies interdependence among a number of individuals. Autonomy is highly valued, and lifetimes are spent fulfilling obligations to others so as to reinforce that reciprocal support in time of need. Barrow says "one is considered foolish to refuse support from those who give, especially if they have a culturally prescribed obligation to do so" (Barrow 1986).

One mechanism used to preserve autonomy in the Caribbean is the maintenance of reciprocal relationships with the networks. Borrowing from Christine Barrow, there is an etiquette of network exchanges such that "independence," or at least the public image of it, is maintained. The most critical characteristic of successful network management is avoiding total dependence on one source of support, particularly a male partner. If a relationship endures over the years, the mate support tends to become secure. However, it can never be fully relied upon, because at any stage of marital union—whether visiting (where the man visits his girlfriend and perhaps their children), common-law (where a couple lives together), or points in between—the relationship can be temporarily or completely terminated. Therefore, Caribbean women's control over their lives is a function of their degree of economic autonomy, which includes the nature of their earning, spending, saving, property ownership, and the sexual division of money matters.

According to Barrow, female autonomy in the English-speaking Caribbean is encouraged from an early age, and education is emphasized as the means to get a good job. The major life-long strategy, then, to "cut and contrive," involves female networks that assist mothers, sisters, daughters and in-laws (children's father's female relatives) alongside income-generating activities. Although the notions of independence and autonomy are essential aspects of women's survival in the region, they should not be romanticized.

One of the developments that further exemplifies notions of interdependence, autonomy, women's employment, and the varied kinds of Caribbean households is the immigration of women of the region to the United States, Britain, and Canada. During the 1970s, the numbers of Caribbean women migrants from all areas of the region rose dramatically, changing the migration pattern from a male-dominated one to a female- and family-centered one. Telephones, accessible international air travel, and e-mail connect extended family to one another and allow for kin ties to be maintained across the miles. Sociologist Dwayne Plaza's 1997 research on "frequent-flyer grannies" describes how successful sons can facilitate travel plans for their mothers between Trinidad and Toronto. In the large enclaves of Miami and the Washington Heights neighborhood of Manhattan, Spanish is the dominant language and Cuban and Dominican cultural patterns are the norm (Grasmuck and Pessar 1991; Portes and Stepick 1993). Likewise in Little Haiti in Miami and in Brooklyn, New York, Haitian creole and Jamaican patois are the local vernaculars (Stepick 1998; Foner 2001). The movement and labor of women has made this transnationalism possible.

Women and the Organization of American States

The importance of gender issues has gained international attention, and Caribbean women are represented on the Inter-American Commission of Women (CIM), headquartered in Washington, D.C. Created by the Sixth International Conference of American States (Havana, 1928), the CIM acts as the Organization of American States advisory body on matters related to women in the Western Hemisphere and reports to the governments on the progress accomplished and the problems that need to be addressed, suggesting ways those problems can be resolved. Many high-profile women have been involved in CIM, including a variety of government ministers and legislative representatives from the 34 member states of the OAS. The CIM is directed by an executive committee comprised of seven members elected by an Assembly of Delegates. The committee for the period 2002–2003 includes members from Canada, the Dominican Republic, Guatemala, Nicaragua, Paraguay, the United States, and Venezuela.

The first meeting of the Caribbean region on Women in Politics, organized by the Network of Nongovernmental Organizations for the Advancement of Women of Trinidad and Tobago, was held in Port-of-Spain, Trinidad and Tobago, during May 11–13, 1998. Other meetings on women's issues, including a conference on sexual abuse, have yielded important data and policy recommendations.

Conclusion

Women of the region, whether poor or from the working or the upper classes, have been subject to inequities based on their gender. These gender inequities have historical precedents so pronounced that the resultant socioeconomic structures continue to impact every contemporary Caribbean country. Enslavement and its impact on the majority of African-descended women fostered the development of creole cultures. This slave system constructed social hierarchies of color and class and, in some areas, the indenture of immigrant workers. Surviving enslavement through various resistance strategies is the key to understanding postemancipation existence and life as colonial subjects. Across the region, women took action on behalf of themselves, their children, and men. Whether it was pursuing political activities, organizing labor, or making a living, Caribbean women worked against the odds. Still today, often they are denied access to resources (in relation to their class position), and their potential is minimized because they are not full participants in the development of their countries due to gender bias. Economic opportunities for women also do not mean the reduction of their domestic duties at home. However, those same domestic organizations provide support and strength to all members regardless of location—at home or abroad. As we learn more about the past, and the contributions women made to Caribbean life and culture, we will be better equipped to answer the questions posed by contemporary problems and those that may arise in the future.

Bibliography

Acevedo, Luz del Alba. "Feminist Inroads in the Study of Women's Work and Development." In *Women in the Latin American Development Process*, edited by Christine E. Bose and Edna Acosta-Belén. Philadelphia: Temple University Press, 1995.

Acosta-Belén, Edna. "Puerto Rican Women in Culture, History, and Society." In *The Puerto Rican Woman,* edited by Edna Acosta-Belén. New York: Praeger, 1986.

———. "Defining a Common Ground: The Theoretical Meeting of Women's, Ethnic, and Area Studies." In *Researching Women in Latin America and the Caribbean,* edited by Edna Acosta-Belén and Christine E. Bose. Boulder: Westview, 1993.

Acosta-Belén, Edna, and Christine E. Bose, eds. *Researching Women in Latin America and the Caribbean.* Boulder: Westview, 1993.

Álvarez, Julia. *In the Time of the Butterflies.* New York: Plume, 1995.

Anderson, Patricia. "Conclusion: WICP." *Social and Economic Studies* 35, no. 2 (1986): 291–324.

Barriteau, Eudine. "Theorizing Gender Systems and the Project of Modernity in the Twentieth-Century Caribbean." *Feminist Review* 59 (Summer 1998): 186–210.

Barrow, Christine. "Finding the Support: A Study of Strategies for Survival." *Social and Economic Studies* 35, no. 2 (1986): 131–176.

———. *Family in the Caribbean: Social and Economic Studies.* Kingston, Jamaica: Ian Randle Publishers, 1996.

Bolles, A. Lynn. *We Paid Our Dues: Women Trade Union Leaders in the Caribbean.* Washington, DC: Howard University Press, 1996.

Bolles, A. Lynn, and Deborah D'Amico-Samuels. "Anthropological Scholarship on Gender in the English-Speaking Caribbean." In *Gender and Anthropology,* edited by S. Morgen. Washington, DC: American Anthropological Association, 1990.

Bose, Christine E., and Edna Acosta-Belén, eds. *Women in the Latin American Development Process.* Philadelphia: Temple University Press, 1995.

Brown, Susan. "Love Unites Them and Hunger Separates Them: Poor Women in the Dominican Republic." In *Toward an Anthropology of Women,* edited by Rayna R. Reiter. New York: Monthly Review Press, 1975.

Bush, Barbara. *Slave Women in Caribbean Society.* Bloomington: Indiana University Press, 1990.

Cole, Johnnetta. *All American Women.* New York: Free Press, 1986.

Davila, Arlene. *Sponsored Identities.* Philadelphia: Temple University Press, 1997.

Deere, Carmen Diana, et al. *In the Shadows of the Sun: Caribbean Development Alternatives and U.S. Policy.* Boulder: Westview, 1990.

Durant-Gonzalez, Victoria. "The Realmot Female Responsibility." In *Women in the Family.* Cove Hill, Barbados: Institute of Social and Economic Research, 1982.

Ecumenical Program for Inter-Communication and Action (EPICA). *Grenada: The Peaceful Revolution.* Washington, DC: EPICA, 1982.

Foner, Nancy, ed. *Islands in the City: West Indian Migration to New York.* Berkeley: University of California Press, 2001.

Grasmuck, Sherri, and Patricia Pessar. *Between Two Islands*. Berkeley: University of California Press, 1991.
Green, Vera M. *Migrants in Aruba*. Assen, Netherlands: Van Gorcum, 1974.
Higman, Barry. *Writing West Indian Histories*. London: Macmillan Education, 1999.
Ho, Christine. *Salt-Water Trinnies*. New York: AMS Press, 1991.
Horowitz, Michael. *Morne-Paysan: Peasant Village in Martinique*. New York: Holt, Rinehart, and Winston, 1967.
Htun, Mala. "Women in Latin America: Unequal Progress Toward Equality." *Current History* (1999). Reprinted in *Global Studies: Latin America*, edited by Paul B. Goodwin. 9th ed. Guilford, CT: Dushkin/McGraw-Hill, 2000, pp. 148–152.
Johnson-Odim, Cheryl, and Margaret Strobel, eds. *Expanding the Boundaries of Women's History: Essays on Women in the Third World*. Bloomington: Indiana University Press, 1992.
Knight, Franklin W., and Margaret E. Crahan. "The African Migration and the Origins of an Afro-American Society and Culture." In *Africa and the Caribbean,* edited by Margaret E. Crahan and Franklin W. Knight. Baltimore: Johns Hopkins University Press, 1979.
Lazarus-Black, Mindie. *Legitimate Acts and Illegal Encounters*. Washington, DC: Smithsonian Institution Press, 1994.
Lewis, Oscar. *La Vida: A Puerto Rican Family in the Culture of Poverty*. New York: Random House, 1966.
Manuel, Peter, with Kenneth Bilby and Michael Largey. *Caribbean Currents: Caribbean Music from Rumba to Reggae*. Philadelphia: Temple University Press, 1995.
Mathurin Mair, Lucille . *The Rebel Woman in the West Indies During Slavery*. Kingston, Jamaica: Institute of Jamaica, 1975.
Matos-Rodríguez, Félix. *Women and Urban Change in San Juan, Puerto Rico, 1820–1868*. Gainesville: University Press of Florida, 1999.
Matos-Rodríguez, Félix, and Linda C. Delgado. *Puerto Rican Women's History: New Perspectives*. Armonk, NY: M. E. Sharpe, 1998.
McLaurin, Irma. *Women of Belize: Gender and Change in Central America*. New Brunswick, NJ: Rutgers University Press, 1996.
Mohammed, Patricia. "Writing Gender into History: The Negotiation of Gender Relations Among Indian Men and Women in Post-indenture Trinidad Society, 1917–1947." In *Engendering History,* edited by Verene Shepherd, Bridget Brereton, and Barbara Bailey. Kingston, Jamaica: Ian Randle Publishers, 1995.
Mohammed, Patricia, and Althea Perkins. "Freedom and Responsibility: New Challenges to Gender Relations in the Family." In *Gender and the Family in the Caribbean,* edited by Wilma Bailey. Kingston, Jamaica: Institute of Social and Economic Research, University of the West Indies, Mona, 1998.
———. *Caribbean Women at the Crossroads: The Paradox of Motherhood Among Women of Barbados, St. Lucia, and Dominica*. Kingston, Jamaica: Canoe Press, University of the West Indies, 1999.
Mohammed, Patricia, and Catherine Shepherd. *Gender in Caribbean Development*. Kingston, Jamaica: Canoe Press, University of the West Indies, 1999 rpt.
Moitt, Bernard. "Women, Work and Resistance in the French Caribbean During Slavery." In *Engendering History,* edited by Verene Shepherd, Bridget Brereton, and Barbara Bailey. Kingston, Jamaica: Ian Randle Publishers, 1995.
Momsen, Janet H., ed. *Women and Change in the Caribbean*. Kingston, Jamaica: Ian Randle Publishers, 1993.
Ortiz, Altagracia, ed. *Puerto Rican Women and Work: Bridges in Transnational Labor*. Philadelphia: Temple University Press, 1996.

Patterson, Orlando. "Persistence, Continuity, and Change in the Jamaican Working-Class Family." *Journal of Family History* 7 (1982): 135–161.
Plaza, Dwayne. "Frequent Flyer Grannies." Paper presented to the History of the Family Conference. Carlton University, Ottawa, Canada, May 15–16, 1997.
Portes, Alejandro, and Alex Stepick. *City on the Edge: The Transformation of Miami*. Berkeley: University of California Press, 1993.
Powell, Dorian. "The Role of Women in the Caribbean." *Social and Economic Studies* 33, no. 2 (June 1984): 97–122.
Reddock, Rhonda. *Women, Labour, and Politics in Trinidad: A History*. London: Zed Books, 1994.
Rey, Terry. *Our Lady of Class Struggle*. Trenton, NJ: Africa World Press, 1999.
Safa, Helen I. *The Myth of the Male Breadwinner*. Boulder: Westview, 1995.
Sagás, Ernesto. *Race and Politics in the Dominican Republic*. Gainesville: University Press of Florida, 2000.
Shepherd, Verene, ed. *Women in Caribbean History*. Kingston, Jamaica: Ian Randle Publishers, 1999.
Shepherd, Verene, Bridget Brereton, and Barbara Bailey, eds. *Engendering History: Caribbean Women in Historical Perspective*. Kingston, Jamaica: Ian Randle Publishers, 1995.
Slater, Mariam K. *The Caribbean Family: Legitimacy in Martinique*. New York: St. Martin's Press, 1977.
Smith, M. G. "Introduction: My Mother Who Fathered Me." In *West Indian Family Structure,* M. G. Smith. Seattle: University of Washington Press, 1962.
Stepick, Alex. *Pride Against Prejudice*. Boston: Allyn and Bacon, 1998.
Stubbs, Jean. "Social and Political Motherhood of Cuba: Mariana Grajales Cuello." In *Engendering History,* edited by Verene Shepherd, Bridget Brereton, and Barbara Bailey. Kingston, Jamaica: Ian Randle Publishers, 1995.
Warner-Lewis, Maureen. "The African Impact on Language and Literature in the English-Speaking Caribbean." In *Africa and the Caribbean,* edited by Margaret E. Crahan and Franklin W. Knight. Baltimore: Johns Hopkins University Press, 1979.
Yelvington, Kevin. *Producing Power: Ethnicity, Gender, and Class in a Caribbean Workplace*. Philadelphia: Temple University Press, 1995.

10

Religion in the Caribbean

Leslie G. Desmangles, Stephen D. Glazier, and Joseph M. Murphy

Vodou, Obeah, Santería, and Orisha are religions native to the Caribbean. For their devotees, these terms hold the keys to some of life's most profound concerns, but for many fans of Hollywood, they spawn in the imagination mysterious religious beliefs and practices related to destructive supernatural forces, zombification, cannibalism, and all sorts of religious wizardry. These popular notions are far from the truth, and an objective examination of these religions reveals that none of their beliefs and rituals confirms such views.

Caribbean religions are practiced by millions of people whose lives are affected profoundly by their teachings. Like other religions of the world, they give meaning to life, uplift the downtrodden, and instill in their devotees a need for solace and self-reflection. They also relate humans to powerful mythological divine beings believed to govern the universe. These demiurges are said to live in sacred abodes whose invisible "portals" can be opened with the proper rituals, allowing them to pass through to "visit" their devotees through spirit possession, an altered state of consciousness during which a person is believed to be "mounted" like a horse by a spirit. This invasion of one's body by a spirit is thought to displace temporarily the personality of the possessed, substituting instead the envisaged mythological persona of the spirit. Possession is therefore considered to be a most profound spiritual achievement, for it allows devotees to harbor powerful forces that manifest themselves to the members of a community in ritual performances. Moreover, it is a public commitment to the religion that heightens one's exercise of religious authority in the community. For these reasons, devotees wish to be possessed many times in their lives.

By extension, Caribbean religions also embrace an assortment of cultural elements: personal creeds and practices, including elaborate forms of folk medical practices, as well as systems of ethics transmitted across generations through proverbs, stories, songs, dances, and other forms of artistic expression. In short, if one important aspect of religion is to offer a unique dimension of experience that motivates the believers to interpret their whole lives by such experiences, then the Caribbean religions are more than religious phenomena. They are intrinsic parts of the cultures that they serve.

There are significant numbers of religions indigenous to the Caribbean, and scholars who study them usually include those of the Brazilian state of Bahia as well as those of the countries found on the northern coast of South America: Venezuela, Suriname, and Guyana. As Stephen J. Randall shows in Chapter 3, relatively long periods of colonial domination, a history of slavery and resistance to slavery, modes of production deriving from forced labor, and political and socioeconomic developments that resulted from these historical events are common experiences within the region.

■ Categories of Caribbean Religions

For theoretical purposes, Caribbean religions may be classified into several major categories (Simpson 1978:14). First we have the neo-African religions. These developed historically within the context of slavery and preserved a fair amount of African religious traditions, which have been combined with Roman Catholic beliefs and practices. They include Vodou in Haiti; Santería in Cuba, the Dominican Republic, and Puerto Rico; and Candomblé and Macumba in Brazil.

The second category includes the ancestral religions that have preserved fewer African traditions and derive from various forms of Protestantism imported to the Caribbean by Christian missionaries during the nineteenth century. These include Orisha in Trinidad and Grenada, the Kumina and Convince in Jamaica, the Big Drum in Grenada and Carriacou, and Kele in St. Lucia.

The third category includes the revivalist religions that are nineteenth- and twentieth-century phenomena and are related to charismatic Protestant movements imported from the United States. These encompass the Pentecostals, Baptists, Seventh Day Adventists, and Revival movements throughout the Caribbean; Shouters and Spiritual Baptists in Trinidad and Tobago, St. Vincent, Grenada, Guyana, and Venezuela; Shakers and Streams of Power in St. Vincent; Tie Heads (members of the Jerusalem Apostolic Spiritual Baptist Church) in Barbados and St. Lucia; Jordanites in Guyana; Spirit Baptists in Jamaica; and the Cohortes and Holiness movements (Pentecostal-derived groups) in Haiti.[1]

The fourth category emphasizes divination (the intuitive reading of one's future into an object) and folk healing through mediumship. These include

Myalism in Jamaica, revival movements in Jamaica, Espiritismo and the various spiritist sects in Puerto Rico, Umbanda in Brazil, and María Lionza in Venezuela.

The fifth category includes the religio-political movements that developed during the early part of the twentieth century and that address many issues related to neocolonialism and social and economic injustice. These include the Rastafari and Dread movements that originated in Jamaica (but which have become widespread throughout the Caribbean), as well as the newly introduced Nation of Islam from the United States.

A sixth category includes the religious traditions imported to the Caribbean from Asia such as the various Hindu sects of Trinidad and Tobago, Guyana, and Suriname. These sects were brought to the Caribbean in the nineteenth century with the arrival of thousands of indentured laborers to many parts of the Caribbean.

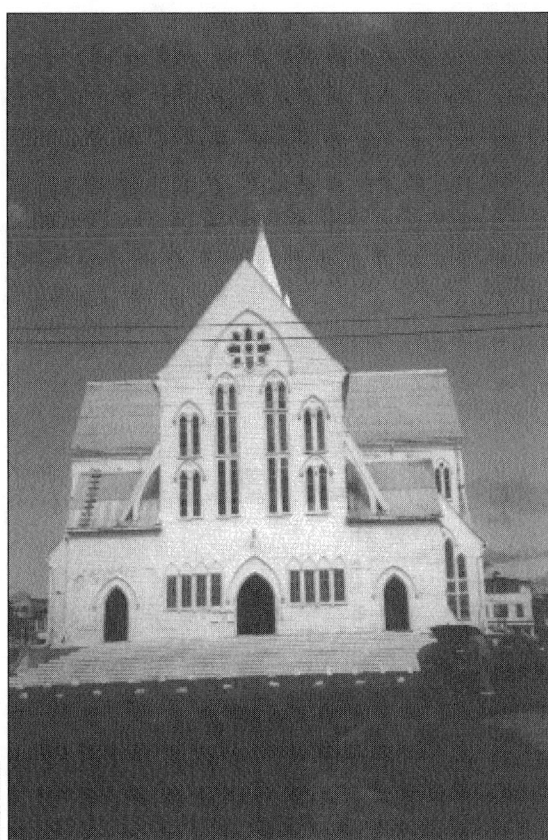

Maureen Smith

St. George's Cathedral, Georgetown, Guyana

The divisions that exist between these categories, however, are merely theoretical, for in reality they are not mutually exclusive but take diverse local forms in which the theology of some in one category may be included in the beliefs and practices of another. Moreover, European religions such as Catholicism in the Latin Caribbean and the Church of England in the Anglo-Caribbean were imposed on the indigenous population and imported African slaves. Although as one of the legacies of the colonial order they continue to occupy important social positions, especially among elite classes, Catholic and Anglican imposition contributed to the creation of hybrid or syncretic amalgamations for the vast majority, who incorporated their own beliefs into the dominant modes.

This chapter, therefore, focuses on Vodou, Santería, the Rastafari, and the Spiritual Baptists for the following reasons: their importance to the future direction of Caribbean religious thought in the region; the significant number of adherents who practice them; and because they exercise important influences on the lives of millions of Caribbean immigrants who are currently living abroad.

■ Working the Amalgam

Caribbean religions are amalgams of various religious traditions that originated in several continents: Africa, Europe, Asia, and the Americas. The blending of these traditions began with Christopher Columbus's arrival in the Western Hemisphere and with the establishment of the first European settlement on Hispaniola in December 1492, where the new settlers encountered a native population of Amerindians.

The Europeans' presence in the region in the years following the encounter of the two groups had profound effects on this native population. Consumed by their determination to discover gold reputed to exist on these islands, the Spanish conquistadors subjected the Indians to hard labor. The tyranny was so severe that merely fifteen years after the Europeans' arrival nearly four-fifths of the Amerindian population had perished. Various diseases imported from Europe, against which the Indians were not immune, decimated their numbers. Amerindian cultures might have disappeared completely because of centuries of suppression, but many traditions have survived to the present day. Taíno, Carib, and Ciboney "protector spirits" are included in the traditions of Brazilian Umbanda, Puerto Rican Espiritismo, and some of the regional practices of Cuban Santería.

The rapid decline in the Indian population necessitated a new source of labor, and Bartolomé de las Casas, an influential Spanish Catholic missionary who had become sympathetic to the Indians' mistreatment and had taken their plight before the Spanish crown, endorsed a plan to replace the Indians with African laborers.[2] Although no one is sure of the exact date the slave trade began to the Americas, some historical records indicate that it was as early as 1512, a mere twenty years after Columbus's arrival in the Caribbean, and that the number of Africans brought over totaled more than 12 million (Bastide 1971:5).

The Africans who came to the Caribbean as slaves originated in a variety of ethnic nations covering a wide region of West Africa. They brought with them their religious traditions, which they dyed into the fabric of the region's colonial life. In contacts with each other, they shared religious traditions and succeeded in fashioning religious amalgams that left an indelible mark on the cultures of the region and resulted in the continuity of Caribbean cultures with those of Africa.

The occurrence of African religious traditions varied throughout the Caribbean and depended on the particular ethnic mix of the African population, the historical circumstances of each country, the duration of colonialism, and the degree to which Europeans exercised a strong cultural presence. A prolonged European influence on a country's culture tended to decrease that country's ability to maintain many African traditions. For example, Haiti, where European colonial domination and cultural contact ended early with the slave revolution and independent statehood in 1804, managed to maintain many more African cultural and religious traditions than most of the other nations in the Caribbean whose colonial status lasted well into the twentieth century. Those nations' continuous cultural contact with Europe tended to abrade the African religious traditions.

But if African religious traditions survived in the Caribbean, it was largely due to maroonage. The word *maroon* derives from the Spanish *cimarrón*, a term used to designate a domesticated animal that had reverted to a wild state. The term soon came to be applied to the slaves who ran away from the plantations and gathered in the interior of the colonies to form secret societies known as maroon republics (Bastide 1971:51). The Africans who joined these republics probably congregated along ethnic lines, and thus the religious traditions in each republic depended upon the particular ethnic mix in each. The republics' theological diversity helps explain the local divergences in beliefs and practices that exist in Caribbean religions today. Depending on the geographic area, some emphasized particular African ethnic traditions and not others. Despite these ethnic divergences, however, the demographic distribution of Africans who came to each country in the Caribbean derived overwhelmingly from specific regions of Africa, and consequently the religious traditions of the more prominent ethnic groups prevailed over others. Thus, Santería in Cuba derives largely from Nigerian Yoruba beliefs and practices, whereas Haitian Vodou's theology derives from Dahomey (Benin) and Congo, the homelands of many Africans.

Despite similarities with African religions, Caribbean religions do not replicate those in West Africa. Environmental conditions, the historical contexts in the region, and the admixture of African religious and ethnic traditions represented in the Caribbean transformed African beliefs and practices permanently and made them different. Thus, Caribbean religions cannot be characterized as African religions but rather as African-derived religions whose beliefs and practices originated largely in West Africa.

An important aspect of Caribbean religions is how they incorporated Christian traditions in their theology. The degree to which Christianity was included within the theology of these religions differed from Catholic to Protestant colonies. By and large, the territories under British rule tended to be less syncretic than the Catholic-dominated ones (e.g., the French and Spanish colonies). Also, the period in which the systematic evangelization of Africans was undertaken by Protestants was much later and consequently was shorter than in the Catholic areas. Unlike the Catholic areas, where there were significant missionary efforts to convert slaves to Christianity, the British thought that Christianity was too sophisticated for Africans to understand and therefore considered slaves unfit for its practice. In Jamaica, for example, the Church of England (Anglican) did not make a conscious attempt to evangelize the slaves in any systematic way until the 1820s, shortly after the arrival of Moravian and Methodist missionaries from the United States. By contrast, the French began to convert the slaves to Christianity as early as the sixteenth century. The Code Noir (Black Code) of 1685 reiterated French efforts to convert the slaves, requiring all masters to have their slaves baptized by the local priests within eight days after arrival in the colonies.

Apart from the Anglican Church, which entrenched itself in the lives of the planters as early as the seventeenth century in the British colonies, Protestantism was not represented in the overwhelmingly Catholic Spanish and French Caribbean areas until the eighteenth century. The Protestant missions in the areas where Catholicism was the predominant religion were limited, the number of adherents relatively small. In these areas, Protestantism did not gain importance until the latter half of the nineteenth and the twentieth centuries with the arrival of missionaries from the United States. Among the major Protestant denominations, the religious groups that gained the most adherents were evangelical and conversionist in nature. These include Pentecostals, Baptists, Seventh Day Adventists, Jehovah's Witnesses, and, more recently, the Church of the Latter Day Saints (Mormons). The number of Pentecostals and Baptists today exceeds those of the other Protestant groups, perhaps because of their religious zeal and ardent recruitment of new members. In the case of Pentecostals and the Holiness groups, the possibilities of engaging oneself directly with the spirit world through spiritual trances and glossolalia (speaking in tongues) have traditionally been kindred to the African ritual styles entrenched in Caribbean society and might have contributed to the conversion of thousands of devotees.

Pentecostalism is a sect of Christianity that originated in the United States in 1906 with Charles Parkham (1872–1929), a zealous evangelist who led the Asuza Street Revival in Los Angeles, California. Pentecostalism's teachings are based on the story reported in the New Testament's Book of Acts in which it is said that after Christ's death and resurrection Christ's disciples gathered in a room; the Holy Spirit is believed to have descended on their heads, endowing them with the gift of grace and empowering them to preach the gospel, to prophesy, to heal the sick, and to speak in tongues (Acts 2:1–20). Pentecostals believe that the miracle at Pentecost can be reenacted in their lives today and that they can achieve a state of holiness by exercising spiritual self-discipline, by resisting the devil's temptations, and by being sanctified or baptized by the spirit. They are sanctified through trances in which the Holy Spirit is said to fill their minds and bodies, causing them to become glossolalic. Glossolalia is therefore a state of profound spiritual achievement that, like the apostles, makes it possible to receive revelations and to prophesy to the community, to heal the sick, and to interpret the dreams of fellow members. Baptists, Seventh Day Adventists, and Pentecostals believe in a literal interpretation of the scripture and emphasize the need to learn to know it by breaking the bible (reading the bible) daily. They are also millenarian and teach that the second coming of Christ and the last judgment are imminent and that one's hope for salvation and entrance into New Jerusalem derives from one's acceptance of Christ as savior, in the expiation

Richard Salter

The Mahaut Gospel Tabernacle Pentecostal church in Mahaut, Dominica of one's sins as well as those of others, and in the observance of a lifelong spiritual discipline.

Pentecostals and Baptists have left their mark on the religious lives of Caribbean peoples. The theology of these groups has inspired the formation of many religious sects throughout the Caribbean, many of which have combined traditional African ritualistic styles of worship with evangelical Protestant theology. The Africanness of these sects can be seen in the belief in ancestral reverence; in a style of worship that includes antiphonal calls and answers between leaders and congregants; in the hymns sung in rhythmical patterns accompanied by drums; and in the cadenced sways of the congregants' bodies. In short, much like African traditional religions, the Caribbean's Pentecostal and Baptist styles of worship use every possible visible and auditory vehicle to engage the congregants actively in their rituals. These rituals are danced out rather than conceived intellectually; they do not separate the mind from the body by merely leading a participant to high-flown intellectual exercises—they claim the entire person.

Because these religious groups are local cells independent of one another, it is difficult to determine their number, but there may well be no less than 100 different types of such movements in the Caribbean, each existing as a variation on a theme. But the most well known are the Tie Heads of the Jerusalem Apostolic Spiritual Baptist churches in Barbados; the Shouters and Spiritual Baptists in Trinidad; the various Cohortes and Holiness movements in Haiti and the Dominican Republic; the Shakers and the Streams of Power in St. Vincent; and the Native Baptists and Kumina sects in Jamaica.

Of late, Louis Farrakhan's Nation of Islam (the black Muslim movement) has come to play an important role in the lives of Caribbean peoples. Although there have been Muslims in the Caribbean for many decades, their numbers were relatively small. The Nation of Islam's recent success in the Caribbean can be attributed to several factors.

First, the evangelistic efforts of African American missionaries, or Caribbean nationals who were converted to the Nation of Islam and then returned to their homes from the United States, have had a profound effect on the religious lives of Caribbean peoples. Second, its appeal is its unique theology as well as its emphasis on socioeconomic objectives. More precisely, it couches socioeconomic teachings in theological language by calling for social justice and an end to poverty, as well as by affirming the need for equal opportunities for all persons of color. Third, the Nation of Islam teaches that all blacks possess a common spirit deriving from their shared historical experiences; they are the descendants of Africans who were severed from their kin groups and from their cultures and who were brought to the Americas as slaves by whites. Slavery was an institution that was supported by the Christian church, and thus it would seem incongruous for the descendants of slaves to commit themselves to a religious faith that subjugated their ancestors and continues to oppress them even today. Finally, the Nation of Islam fosters a pan-African spirit of racial solidarity and identity among blacks in the Americas. It can also be seen as an awakening of a spirit of nationalism and anticolonial sentiments common among many emerging nations whose citizens seek to find their rightful places among other peoples of the world.

It is difficult to ascertain the exact number of Muslims in the Caribbean. There are few mosques, and the growing number of Friday-evening worship services are informal ceremonies held, for the most part, in devotees' homes and places of business; local communities often have no membership rolls that indicate the exact number of devotees.

Hinduism also plays an important role in Caribbean culture. Although there are small communities of Hindus throughout the Caribbean, the largest concentrations live in Trinidad, Guyana, and Suriname. The religious presence of Hinduism in the Caribbean can be explained historically. After the emancipation of slaves in 1838, British colonizers imported indentured laborers from colonies in other parts of the world. These included China, various parts of Africa, and Ireland, but the majority came from India. As indentured servants they committed to working in the sugarcane fields for a period of two years, after which they could return to their homeland or stay in the Caribbean. If they decided to stay, they could either continue to work on the same plantation, be reassigned to another, or embark in an independent commercial venture of their own. Approximately 70 percent remained in the Caribbean (Lai 1993:136). The importation of indentured laborers spanned

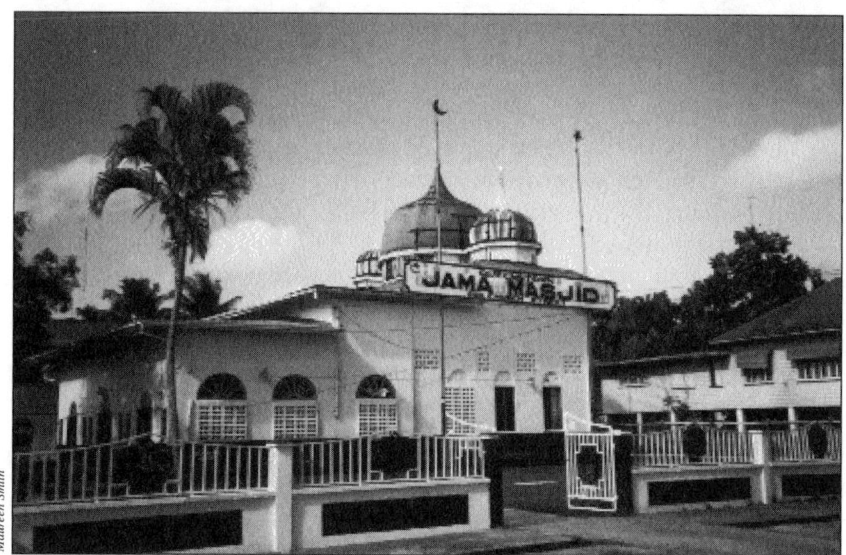

Maureen Smith

The Queenstown Jama Masjid mosque in Georgetown, Guyana

the period between 1838 and 1910 with a brief interlude between 1848 and 1851 (Brereton 1974:26). During that period, it is estimated that as many as 143,000 East Indians came to Trinidad. Additional numbers were brought to Suriname, Guyana, Martinique, and Guadeloupe.

East Indians who came to the Caribbean belonged to various social castes. Nearly 15 percent were Brahmins who were highly trained priests from northern and northwestern India. Their presence left an indelible mark on the countries in which they settled. In the 1890s their descendants formed the East Indian Association, the first Indian organization in Trinidad that sought to maintain Indian cultural traditions. It also addressed many of the social and economic issues related to the Indian community. Later, in the 1950s, a new organization was formed, the Sanatan Dharma Maha Sabha, to strengthen Indian national life in Trinidad and standardize Hindu worship. It eventually created a commission that supervised some sixty primary and secondary schools and promoted the teaching of Hindu cultural and religious traditions among Indian youths. Despite some success in safeguarding Indian traditions, Hinduism in Trinidad (as in the rest of the Caribbean) cannot be said to be an Asian religion that has been transplanted. Through the years, it has evolved differently in the Caribbean than its counterpart in South Asia. It developed new myths, as well as rituals and festivals (such as the annual Holi Pagwa) that bear few resemblances to those of India; they are original to the region.

In short, Caribbean religions may have derived from various continents, but they are creole creations that have been shaped by centuries of unique socioeconomic, political, and cultural factors. Many are hybrid in that they combined religious traditions from elsewhere and have taken divergent forms locally. Despite their differences, however, they reflect many common characteristics.

The first commonality concerns devotees' outlook on the nature of faith. Devotees may think of religion strictly in practical terms. For them, faith does not consist of a self-surrender to mysticism or to complicated theological debates. Religion is a way of life, and one's faith must satisfy actual needs and answer some profound existential questions. As the description of Santería will show later in this chapter, the spirits must serve as founts of wisdom that address practical matters of life.

Second, these religions maintain religious calendars, with feast days that require devotees' attendance at special ceremonies in the temples or in sacred places. Ceremonies are officiated by powerful priests and priestesses who constitute loosely organized local hierarchies that exercise an extraordinary authority in their respective communities.

Third, except for Spiritual Baptists, Caribbean religions maintain neither theological nor ecumenical centers for the training of leaders—no presses, no editorial staff, no publications. Thus, leaders receive no formal training but learn skills from other practitioners through inheritance or social contacts. New religious leaders establish their authority in communities through knowledge of the theology of the religions, a public commitment to the faith (as in the case of Pentecostals in the ability to prophesy), and the manifest sincerity of their religious fervor.

It is not unusual to find that within a small area two religious centers maintain differing myths and rituals. As discussed later in this chapter, there have been some attempts to create training centers and establish a universal creed among Spiritual Baptists of Trinidad, but such efforts have been largely unsuccessful to date. Because these religions have no clearinghouse and no established orthodoxy, it is difficult to document their beliefs and practices in a comprehensive way. Our task becomes even more difficult when one considers the multiplicity of theological details, which vary widely from one region to another. Still, it is possible to discover the internally consistent systems that exist in individual religious centers.

What follows, therefore, is not intended to portray the universal beliefs and practices of Caribbean peoples. Rather it is a description of the most commonly held beliefs and practices by the devotees of three religions native to the Caribbean.

■ Vodou

Vodou is the religion indigenous to Haiti. The word *Vodou* derives from *vodu* or *vodun* in the Fon language of Benin on the western coast of Africa and means "deity" or "spirit." Thus, Vodou relates the life of its devotees to thousands of incommensurable spirits called *lwas* (from a Yoruba word for "spirit"), who govern all of life in addition to the entire cosmos. *Lwas* are believed to not only manifest themselves in nature but also to reveal themselves through the bodies of devotees in spirit or trance possession. Moreover, like many religions of the world, Vodou is a system of beliefs and practices that provides explanations for the most profound questions related to human existence. It provides an explanation for death that is treated as a spiritual transformation, a portal to the sacred world beyond where productive and morally upright individuals, perceived by devotees to be powerful ancestral figures, can exercise significant influences on their progeny by possessing them. In short, it is an expression of a people's longing for meaning and purpose in their lives.

The theology of Vodou was born on the sugar plantations of the French colony of St. Domingue (the French form of Santo Domingo, early name of Haiti). Little is known about the slave communities on the island during that period, but it is evident that they were critical in preserving African religious traditions. Glimpses from the colonial writings that survive note that the practice of Vodou was made unlawful among the slaves; consequently they observed their rituals in secret and at night, presumably to avoid interference by police. Because slaves' religious meetings sometimes served to incite bloody insurrections that threatened the social and political stability of the tiny colony, colonial masters feared them. Planters were instrumental in the creation and enforcement of laws that made it illegal to practice Vodou in the colony.

Moreover, the brutal treatment of slaves caused thousands to flee plantations to become maroons in the interior. Scholars consider maroonage in St. Domingue to have had far-reaching effects on Haitian history that can be seen in two ways: first, it was instrumental in fostering the slave rebellion that liberated Haiti from French rule in 1804; and second, it contributed to the preservation of whole enclaves of African religious traditions that shape Vodou's theology today. These included, among others, the traditions of Dahomey (modern-day Benin), Congo, Zaire (currently known as the Democratic Republic of Congo), Angola, and Nigeria. No one knows how many maroon communities existed in St. Domingue, but it can be estimated that their numbers multiplied to several hundreds by the eve of the Haitian revolution at the end of the eighteenth century. They probably varied widely politically, socially, theologically, and organizationally.

Most Africans imported to the colony were agricultural and pastoral peoples whose mythologies functioned to establish an intimate mystic relationship with the land. St. Domingue's economic history of social oppression altered African religious traditions permanently, making Vodou a religion exclusive to the Americas. Many of the African spirits were adapted to the new milieu. Ogun, for example, the Nigerian spirit of ironsmiths and other activities associated with metals such as hunting and warfare, took a new persona in colonial St. Domingue. He became Ogou, the military leader who led phalanxes into battle against oppression and who continues to inspire those who challenge oppressive political regimes in Haiti.

The majority of Europeans who came to St. Domingue were Roman Catholics who regarded Vodou as an aberration and sought to extricate it from colonial society. They were quick to enact a number of edicts such as the Code Noir making it illegal for the slaves to practice African religions openly. The severity of such laws drove African rituals underground. To circumvent interference in their rituals by masters, slaves learned to overlay African practices with the veneer of Roman Catholic symbols and rituals. They used symbols of the church in their rituals as white masks over black faces—veils behind which they could hide their African practices. Médéric Louis-Elie Moreau de St.-Méry, an eyewitness of Vodou during the eighteenth century, reported that makeshift altars and votive candles concealed the Africanness of their rituals (Moreau de St.-Méry [1797] 1958, vol. 1:55). The presence of these symbols prompted the slaves to use them in these rituals; the inclusion of prayers revering the Catholic saints also caused them to establish a system of correspondences between African gods and Catholic saints. These latter consisted of a system of reinterpretations in which symbols associated with gods in African mythology were made to correspond to similar symbols associated with the saints in Catholic hagiology. For example, the Dahomean snake deity Damballah was made to correspond with St. Patrick because of the Catholic legend about St. Patrick and the snakes of Ireland. Such correspondence was achieved in the case of many saints, for which there were corresponding Vodou names. In effect, the slaves were successful in creating what is known as a symbiosis (Desmangles 1992:8). The word *symbiosis* as used here has a different meaning from that of the biological sciences, where it refers to the living together of dissimilar organisms in a mutually beneficial relationship. Etymologically, symbiosis is from the Greek *sun* (with) and *biós* (life, life together with). In the ethnological sense, symbiosis is the spatial juxtaposition of diverse religious traditions from two continents that coexist without fusing with one another. Like the tiny parts of a stained-glass window juxtaposed to form a whole, parts of the Vodou and Catholic traditions are juxtaposed in space and in time to constitute the whole of Vodou.

The encroachment of Vodou practices on Catholic theology was embarrassing for church clerics, who from time to time launched vehement campaigns against fetishism in Haitian society. It was in this spirit that in 1896, 1913, and 1941 the church conducted its antisuperstitious campaigns that burned and destroyed hundreds of *ounfòs* (Vodou temples) and ritual paraphernalia throughout the country. The 1941 campaign, termed Operation Cleanup, included the publication of a catechism in the form of a pamphlet that circulated widely among Haitians and was taught in the churches as well as public and parochial schools. Like many such documents, it was written in the traditional question-answer format, the goal being to encourage Catholics to renounce their superstitious practices, abandon the veneration of the *lwas* and ancestral spirits, and renew their vows with the church.

These attempts to eradicate Vodou had little effect, for Haitians continued to practice the two religions simultaneously and maintain allegiance to both in parallel. An often quoted Haitian proverb is that one must be Catholic to serve the Vodou *lwas*. The truth of that statement illustrates the distinctions in the roles that each religion plays in Haitian society. It also illustrates what seems logical to Vodouists: that the world is governed by the godhead and the *lwas* (and, by extension, the Catholic saints), who can be represented in two corresponding forms. The priest, in his celebration of the mass, functions as a point of contact with the impersonal godhead. Haitians regard the Catholic priest as the conduit through which believers can gain access to the sacred world; in his role as the sole dispenser of grace, the Catholic priest stands at the crossroads between the sacred and the profane worlds. By contrast, the

Vodou *oungans* (priests) and *mambos* (priestesses) establish contact with personal yet mysterious spirits who reveal themselves to their servants in trance possession. Moreover, unlike the Catholic priest, they are not conduits through which the possessed can have contact with the world of the spirits, for each Vodou believer in the Vodou ceremonies has gained direct access to the *lwas*' world through trance possession.

The Concepts of the *Lwas*

When Vodouists speak of the *lwas* (and, by extension, the Catholic saints), they group them into families, or nations, called *nanshons*. The nomenclatures used to designate most of these *nanshons* correspond to the names of geographical areas or of ethnic nations of West Africa from which they originated. Each *lwa* has its own persona by which it can be distinguished from another, and each *nanshon* possesses its own characteristic ethos that demands of its devotees corresponding attitudes. There are generally held to be seventeen *nanshons* of *lwas*, but most Haitians know only a few by name. They include the Wangol (from Angola), Rada (or Arada), Petro, Ginen (from Guinea), Congo, Nago (or Anago), and Ibo. Of these, the Rada, Petro, and Congo *nanshons* are by far the best known in present-day Haiti. Rada's name derives from Arada, the name of a prominent kingdom in Dahomey (modern-day Benin) during Haiti's colonial period. Similarly, the Congo *lwas* originate in the Bakongo region of West Africa, which provided thousands of slaves to Haiti during the colonial period. The name Petro derives from Dom Pedro, a legendary figure who was reportedly the maroon leader of a slave insurrection in the eighteenth century. Significantly, the *nanshons* no longer designate place-names but merely characterize categories, or what Vodouists think of as families of *lwas*.

Many of the Rada *lwas* have Petro, Ibo, and Congo counterparts. As if their images were inverted as they reflect each other in a mirror, the personae of the Rada *lwas* become reversed in the Petro *nanshon*. In designating the Petro *lwas*, Vodouists use the Rada name for each *lwa* and add epithets, such as Je-Rouge (Red-Eye) or Dantò to designate their Petro or Congo affiliations. For example Rada's Ezili, the beneficent *lwa* of love in Vodou, becomes Ezili Je-Rouge in her Petro affiliation, a destructive and offensive spirit who can cause harm to recalcitrant devotees.

Despite the notable differences in the *lwas*' personae and functions in the various *nanshons*, Vodouists do not understand these differences to represent two distinct divine entities, the one symbolizing beneficence and the other maleficence. Rather they believe that the personalities and the functions are attributes of the same being. This belief corresponds to what may be thought of as the coincidence of opposites, which means that the envisaged mythological personality of each *lwa* in each nation is expressed in its diametric opposition in another *nanshon*. In effect, a *lwa* is a manifestation of Bondye (from the French *bon dieu*, meaning "good lord") who is the Gran Met (Grand Master), the godhead who governs the universe. But Bondye chooses to manifest himself in opposing ways in different *nanshons*. In spirit possessions, the *lwas* present themselves in the bodies of their devotees by turns, or even simultaneously, as beneficent and terrible, creative and destructive. Although a *lwa*'s personae appear to oppose one another, they are nevertheless reconciled (or rather transcended) by Bondye's vital cosmic power, which fosters the forces of good and evil. In short, a *lwa*'s personae are merely different faces of the same being, envisaged in West African and not in Christian terms; as in much of West Africa, the godhead is considered much too impersonal to be approached directly; he can merely be invoked in rituals through less hallowed spirit media.

Concepts of the Self

Vodouists believe that the human body is a manifestation of Bondye, who is its creator. It contains a spirit that derives from the divinity but is constituted of several compartments, characterized by their psychic functions. In some ways, the Vodou notion of the compartmentalized self is analogous to Sigmund Freud's description of the theoretical divisions of the human psyche. The first compartment of the human spirit is the *gwo bon anj* (literally, "the big good angel"), a life-force, the source of divine energy that is implanted in the human body and is associated with the act of breathing itself, which is a manifestation of life. The *gwo bon anj* is not breathing itself but is an internal source of energy that ensures the movement of the thoracic cavity when a person breathes. It is also the source of dynamic energy from which derives physiological movement: the beating of the heart, the flow of blood throughout the body, and the movements of the body itself. That energy is the very divine life-force that is inherent in the body, which serves as its shell.

The second compartment of the human spirit is the *ti bon anj* (literally, "the little good angel"), the ego spirit that is identified with personality, is manifested in one's deportment and facial expressions, and is displaced in spirit possession. The third compartment is the *mèt tèt* (literally, "the master of the head"); it is the manifestation of a guardian *lwa* who has protected a person from danger throughout his or her life. It is also the *lwa* who has been the subject of service and spirit possession for that person.

At death, a special ritual called *desounen* (the uprooting of life) is performed near the body shortly after death by the *oungan* or *mambo*. It extracts these compartments of the spirits from the body and dispatches them to their respective abodes: the *gwo bon anj* and the *mèt tèt* to Ginen, the underworld where the spirits of the dead live; the *ti bon anj* to heaven (because of the Catholic influence); and the body to the navel of the earth, where it will disintegrate and never rise again. The Vodou cycle of funerary rites constitutes an elaborate set of observances performed by members of the family that last an entire year after a person's death.

As in Africa, ancestral spirits exercise authority over the living. In Ginen, they join the community of the living dead, ruled by Gede, the *lwa* of death and the ruler of the underworld. In time, they are thought to acquire a sacred wisdom that allows them to observe the community of the living, to see far into the future and into the past, and to guide the living in their daily round of life. That is why the community contacts them in times of trouble or when it needs guidance at any significant impasse. Because ancestral spirits exist in the sacred world, they are considered to be demigods.

Spirit Possession

Trance possession and its apparent dissociative state of consciousness have been the subjects of much literature. Seen through the distorted lenses of popular literature, spirit possession has been described as the manifestation of demons that reveal themselves in the bodies of host victims, resulting in temporary mental and behavioral disorders. Exorcisms were reported to be means of extricating demons from the bodies of possessed individuals. In psychology, spirit possession was described in earlier studies as the product of psychopathology that included dissociation, changes of movements and vocalization, imaginal states, amnesia, and hallucinations. Such behaviors were thought falsely to express psychotic or hysterical traits among shamans and other religious specialists in their flights from reality. The exchange of one's personal identity for another was also construed as the result of multiple personality disorders that required clinical attention.

More recent studies of trance possessions have disputed such claims and have recognized their widespread presence throughout the world. Erika Bourguignon's research on possession belief of some 488 societies worldwide reveals that 74 percent of their peoples believed that spirits could occupy their bodies and affect their personalities directly (Bourguignon 1973). *Possession* can be defined as an altered state of consciousness in which the self is experienced as disembodied and replaced by a supernatural entity. During possession, Vodouists believe that the body becomes a vessel in which a *lwa* resides or that the body becomes a horse that is being ridden by that *lwa*.

The possessed embody the mythology of the community by enacting the events that surround the lives of the *lwas*. By assuming the envisaged mythological personae of *lwas*, the possessed reenact the mythology of the community in the context of the rituals. Moreover, the temporary surrender of one's identity to that of a supernatural entity, and the alternate behavior that accompanies such experiences, are pursued by persons who long for a transcendent experience whereby they embody a spirit.

Possession is one of the elements that characterizes Vodou as a democratic religion. Indeed, it is a means by which a devotee can experience firsthand a direct engagement with the spirit world; it is an important part of a ceremony because it is through the body of a devotee that a spirit can act and share its wisdom with the community. It is also through the same medium that the members of the community can share their concerns with the embodied spirit. Thus, possession is a quintessential spiritual achievement in a believer's religious life, because it is a public commitment to the religion and is a testimony to religious fervor. In short, one of the most important functions of Vodou rituals is the opportunity for spirits to communicate with devotees and to hear devotees' concerns.

In ceremonies, Vodouists use every sensory means at their disposal to invoke the spirits, to petition them to visit the temple, and to invade the bodies of devotees in spirit possessions. Depending on the *nanshon*, each of the personae of the *lwas* has its own songs, its own dances and drum rhythms, as well as its own symbols. These symbols are known as *vèvès*—geometric, Kabbala-like traceries that symbolize the personae and the functions of the *lwas*. In the *peristil* (the section of the temple in which Vodou ceremonies are held) the *oungan* traces a *vèvè* for every *lwa* as each is being invoked in the ritual. As the community sings and dances to the rhythmic music of a *lwa*, the *oungan* uses corn flour, which he places in a dish held in his left hand. Grasping some of the flour with the thumb and the forefinger of his right hand, he carefully sifts it onto the floor of the *peristil*, meticulously drawing a *vèvè* for each *lwa*. Vodouists believe that these visual and auditory media summon the *lwas* to leave their abode and to possess their devotees.

Thus, the *nanshon* in Vodou does not primarily designate the historical origin of the *lwas* but presents the personae of the *lwas* as well as the characteristic attitudes with which the devotees approach them. In their Rada, Petro, and Catholic characterizations—at least in the way such characterizations are manifested in the possessed devotees—the *lwas* appear as beneficent and maleficent, and devotees act out the personae as the community envisages them in the local mythology. Through such manifestations, the community is able to recognize not only which *lwa* has come to visit it in the peristil but also which *nanshon* is represented. In a sense, the living depiction of the *lwas'* personae in the bodies of devotees replaces the literary and artistic vehicles upon which mythologies of other cultures, including those of Christian Europe, often rely for the portrayal of their deities. In Haiti, one does not come to know the *lwas* by merely observing or imagining them through the myths but by *becoming* them.

In conclusion, Vodou constitutes a set of beliefs and practices related to powerful spirits (and, by extension, Catholic saints) who enter every aspect of life. The *lwas* deal with illnesses and come to the assistance of their devotees through spirit possession and are expected to impart their wisdom in very practical ways. In effect, Vodou, like African traditional religions, is not a religion in the Western sense in which one may or may not choose to identify with a system of thought. Vodouists do not think of believing as identifying with a system of thought or with the community that affirms such a system. Spiritual reality cannot be the subject of scientific investigation but is based on what to Vodouists is self-evident: the entire cosmos is filled with the presence of incommensurable spiritual forces whose awesome power no one can escape and who are forever active in human lives.

Santería

Santería is a Cuban religious tradition that originated among the Yoruba peoples of West Africa and has since spread around the world. Santería (meaning "way of the saints" in Spanish) reminds us that African traditions in the Caribbean developed through an oppressive encounter with European colonialism. Nearly 1 million African men, women, and children were enslaved and carried to Cuba to work on sugar plantations, where they earned enormous profits for European landholders and venture capitalists. In the midst of the systematic atrocities of a society built on slave labor, many Africans in Cuba were able to find power and healing in the religious traditions brought from their homelands. The Yorubas in Cuba paralleled their clandestine rites to African spirits with those of the Catholic saints supported by the colonial ethos. And so the tradition came to be called Santería, a way of venerating Yoruba spirits likened to Catholic saints.

Two events at the end of the eighteenth century brought over Yoruba people in large numbers to Cuba. First, the successful revolution in Haiti ended European control of the most lucrative sugar plantations in the world. Liberated Haitians turned to subsistence farming, and European investors were forced to look elsewhere to realize large profits from enslaved labor. Second, the West African empire administered from the Yoruba city of Oyo disintegrated due to a series of challenges from without and within. Fulanis from the north, Dahomeans from the west, and rival Yoruba city-states pulled the empire apart, and the Yorubas were plunged into years of war. From the late eighteenth century through the first decades of the nineteenth century, perhaps as many as 1 million Yorubas displaced by these wars were sold along the slave coast of West Africa and carried to the Americas.

The European demand for sugar, the loss of Haitian slave labor and plantations, and the ready supply of enslaved Yorubas led to the rapid development of the sugar industry in Cuba. Hundreds of thousands of Yorubas cleared, planted, and harvested sugar on hundreds of new plantations. The large and rapid influx of people sharing Yoruba language and culture established Yoruba ethnicity as a permanent part of Cuba's cultural mosaic. They came to be called Lucumi after an old name for Oyo. Today those who would emphasize this heritage in their religion will speak of *la religión lucumi* or *la regla lucumi*.

The development of Santería (*la religión lucumi*) was greatly enhanced by the formation of ethnic mutual-aid societies called *cabildos*. In the cities and towns of Cuba, Lucumi—enslaved and free—were able to join together for mutual benefit, protection, and recreation. The *cabildos* assisted the infirm, buried the dead, held accounts for the purchase of members' freedom, and venerated the spirits of Yorubaland. Out of the leadership of the Lucumi *cabildos* came the lines of initiation that sanction Santería priesthood today.

The Lucumi tradition recognizes two categories of interdependent priesthood: those of Orula, the patron of divination; and those of individual spirits called *orichas*. The priests of Orula are called *babalaos* (the fathers of the mystery) and are extensively trained to divine for devotees by means of an ancient oracle named Ifa. By the random fall of specially prepared palm nuts,

Richard S. Hillman

A *curandero* shop in Santo Domingo, Dominican Republic, with provisions for religious ceremonies

the *babalao* can interpret the destiny of individuals and groups and develop their relationship to the multitude of *orichas* who empower life. Devotees will seek out the services of a *babalao* for advice in securing the power of the *orichas* to meet the challenges of life: for health, for security, for love.

The other category of priest is called *iyalocha* (mother of the *oricha*, if a woman) and *babalocha* (father of the *oricha*, if a man). The often-used Spanish equivalents are *santera* and *santero,* respectively. These people have been consecrated to the service of a particular *oricha*, though they may be authorized to pass on the priesthoods of many other spirits as well. They have received the power of the *orichas* "in their heads" and so may at times embody the presence of the *orichas* for other devotees. Each *iyalocha* or *babalocha* is free to establish her or his own spiritual house (*ilé*) and thus conduct ceremonies independently as well as cooperatively with other houses. *Iyalochas* and *babalochas* who initiate others into their houses are addressed as *madriña* (godmother) and *padriño* (godfather) and are expected to be treated with great respect by their godchildren.

The business of a Santería house carries many of the same functions as the nineteenth-century Lucumi *cabildos*. Godchildren gather for mutual aid and recreation, yet the principal feature of a contemporary house is the organization of the cycle of ceremonies for the *orichas*. Ceremonies may be held for the initiation of new members; anniversaries of initiation; further advanced initiations for priestesses and priests; ceremonies of petition and thanksgiving to the *orichas* for special intentions; and the annual feast days of the spirits. Santería has inherited its calendar from the colonial authority of the Roman Catholic Church and so celebrates its calendar feasts on the days of the *oricha*'s Catholic equivalent.

The analogy of the *orichas* with Catholic saints is imperfect but useful in understanding Santería theology. The *orichas* proceed from one almighty God (*aché*) who has delegated and divided his power among them. Through the currency of this divine *aché*, the *orichas* may be petitioned for help in securing early success and heavenly wisdom. The *orichas* are powerful, invisible entities who move at the source of the energies of the world. Each *oricha* is the "owner" of a particular cluster of energies that can be seen in natural phenomena such as rivers, fire, wind, or iron. These energies also give rise to the personalities of the *orichas* so that Ochún, for example, who is the *oricha* of the river, is manifested as a life-giving, sensuous woman; and Changó, *oricha* of thunder and lightning, is a bold warrior-king. Each *oricha* has hundreds of stories that detail its exploits and explain its powers and avenues of approach. And each *oricha* is venerated with special stones, herbs, beads, colors, foods, rhythms, and songs appropriate to it.

A life with the *orichas* usually begins with a critical problem in an individual person's life: an illness; an errant lover; a lost job. He or she might consult a *babalao* or *iyalocha* to determine if an *oricha*'s aid might be effective in meeting the crisis. The proper oracles would be consulted and a solution offered that would involve a sacrifice appropriate to the *oricha* whose power is most suited to the resolution of the problem. A sacrifice may be a very simple one of candles lit and prayers said; if the oracles so prescribe, however, there are much more elaborate undertakings involving the preparation of special foods and the cooperation of the entire community. At its most lavish, a Santería sacrifice might require the services of many highly trained priests and priestesses, professional musicians who have mastered the vast musical repertoires of the *orichas*, and the accumulation of costly foods and live animals for ritual slaughter.

As the ceremonial exchanges with the *orichas* and with the community grow, it is likely that a particular *oricha* will begin to assert itself as the individual's patron or patroness. Once divination has determined the identity of this *oricha*, the individual will be called to the Santería priesthood through a lengthy ordination ceremony called *asiento* (seating) in Spanish and *kariocha* (*oricha*-crowning) in Lucumi. Here the individual and the *oricha* form an irrevocable bond in which the *oricha* is enthroned or seated in the "head," or deepest personality, of the individual. The newly made priest now bears the responsibility to represent his or her *oricha* at the ceremonies of the community. With the *oricha* in his or her head, the newly made priest may act as a medium for the *oricha*, losing his or her own personality in the rhythms of the drumming and dancing and manifesting the personality of the *oricha* patron or patroness. Thus Ochún and Changó, for example, are seen to actually appear at ceremonies, manifested through the service of their human priestly mediums. The *orichas* may speak with the community to admonish, prophesy, and heal. The appearances of the *orichas* through the bodies of devotees are greeted with reverence and joy by the congregation and are the dramatic highpoint of Santería's ceremonial life.

The vibrant idioms of Santería ceremonial life have crossed over into Cuban popular culture in many ways. The rhythms of the sacred drums have been adapted to recreational dances like mambo, rumba, and cha-cha. Many of the gestures and steps of these dances have their origins in the attitudes of the *orichas* when they manifest through their human mediums. Cuba's socialist government has sponsored Afro-Cuban culture as an authentic expression of the island's independent creole identity, the most notable product being the internationally recognized Conjunto Folklórico Nacíonal, which presents dance performances on *oricha* themes. In the 1990s the government began subsidizing prominent *santeros* and *santeras* and facilitated their meeting with foreign devotees in order to instruct and initiate them. Of course with foreign seekers comes much-needed hard currency, yet the governmental interest in this kind of commerce underscores the visibility and influence of Santería in Cuban life. Cuba has become famous for its Santería and point of pilgrimage for seekers and tourists alike. When Pope John Paul II came to

Cuba in 1998 the government made every effort to deemphasize the extent of Catholicism in the nation, and many officially sanctioned publications proclaimed Santería as the religion of the Cuban people. Again the strategic value of such support is apparent, yet the central role of Santería in representations of nation is clear as well.

The fame of Santería owes a great deal to what might be called the second diaspora of the religion: the great exodus of Cubans from the island after the socialist revolution of 1959. Among some 1 million Cuban emigrants were priestesses and priests of Santería. They established thriving houses in Puerto Rico, Venezuela, and, in particular, the United States. Although estimates of the numbers of practitioners and priests are difficult to determine, it is very likely that they number in the hundreds of thousands and that there are many more devotees of the *orichas* in the United States than in Cuba. The religion was often the primary agency for the aid of poorer Cuban emigrants, offering networks for health services, legal aid, and dispute arbitrations.

The way of the *orichas* spread very quickly among non-Cubans in the United States, notably among African Americans seeking to integrate black nationalism with an authentic African worldview. In the large cities the religion has been taken up by Dominican, Colombian, and Mexican Americans and by others as well. The energy, creativity, and resources of these new communities of the religion have led to the formation of international organizations dedicated to fostering dialogue and cooperation in an emerging world religion.

The religion faces a host of challenges as it extends beyond the Caribbean to the international arena. The very name Santería is often seen by many practitioners as both parochial and tied to a colonial ethos that the religion heroically resisted. Now, independent of colonial attitudes and persecution, the religion might stand on its own in the company of other world traditions. Alternative names might be Yoruba (recognizing the African ethnic origins of the tradition) or Lucumi (demonstrating the importance of the religion's development in Cuba) or perhaps simply Oricha (respecting the spirits venerated). Regardless of the label, the tradition is engaged in the difficult process of developing systems of authority and of sanctioning priesthood and canonizing texts. As the religion continues to grow, particularly among populations only distantly aware of Cuba (or even the struggle for justice among communities abroad), the leaders of the religion will have to adapt to new meanings and initiatives. The religion is represented at hundreds of Internet sites that disseminate information far beyond the influence of the most conscientious and dedicated elders.

Afro-Cuban religion is one of dynamic aesthetics, spiritual depth, and heroic resistance to oppression and despair. It is one of the great contributions of the Caribbean to the world and a model for intercultural worlds of the future.

■ The Rastafari and the Dread

The Rastafari and the Dread are religio-political movements and are twentieth-century phenomena. They address issues of social and economic justice among blacks in Jamaica and elsewhere in the world and oppose the social ills as well as the institutions that perpetuate such ills. The Rastafari express their resistance to the established order in theological terms, in that they have a millenarian orientation. Their members believe that they are destined to return to Ethiopia, which they envision as the promised land.

Historically, the Rastafari movement began in Jamaica in the early part of the twentieth century. Its theology derives from a long tradition of redemptive religious movements in Jamaica. As early as 1784, an American slave named George Liele (also known as George Sharp, the surname of his owner in Savannah, Georgia) founded one of the first Baptist churches in Jamaica. After his owner's death, he was placed in the service of one Colonel Kirkland, who manumitted him in 1783. In the same year, Kirkland emigrated from the United States to Jamaica and took the young George Sharp with him. It was there that he changed his name to George Liele and began to evangelize and convert the slaves who worked on the plantations in and around Kingston and Spanish Town. Later in life he reflected on the early days of his ministry in Jamaica by observing that he "began, about September 1784, to preach in Kingston, in a small private house to a good, smart congregation," which he formed with "four brethren from America . . . and the preaching took very good effect with the poorer sort, especially the slaves" (Barrett 1974:113).

The significance of Liele's church to the history of religion in Jamaica is its name. He called it the Ethiopian Baptist Church, and it later was renamed the Jamaican Baptist Church. The reference to Ethiopia had symbolic value and derived meaning from various biblical passages in which the word *Ethiopian* is used interchangeably with *Nubian* and *Cushite*. In the Bible, the word *Cushite*, from the Hebrew *cush*, means "black skin" or "burned skin." In the Bible, *cush* was translated by the Greek term *ethiop;* thus, in modern times *Ethiopia* became *Africa* ("land of the burned-skin people"), and most Rastafari today equate these terms and use them interchangeably. There are many biblical passages that depict the Cushites; two are important to this discussion. Some passages describe the Cushites as noble and valiant warriors, whereas others allude to them as a poor and exiled people who were "led naked and barefoot, their buttocks shamefully exposed" to the world (Isaiah 19:21). It may well be that the term *Ethiopia* as Liele used it would have a double meaning: it would have referred to the slaves' self-image as a poor and oppressed people living in an estranged land, and, like the Rastafari today, it would have been used as a metaphor for social protest and resistance.

The virtues of Ethiopia or Africa as holy places continued to be extolled in Jamaican religious thought in the latter half of the nineteenth century and at the beginning of the twentieth century, especially during the period of the Great Revival (1860–1920). This period saw the meteoric rise of scores of religious movements such as the Convince and the Kumina (or Pukumina) mentioned earlier in this chapter, the Revival bands, and different forms of spiritual healing cults called Myalism, which stressed ancestor reverence and spirit possession and had a millenarian or utopian vision of the world. An important feature of millenarianism is its salvific message of redemption, in which the current world and its forces of evil will be destroyed by cataclysmic events brought by supernatural intervention, followed by the establishment of a new world in which there will be a radical reversal of the current order. In this new world, the first will be last and the last will be first. The mighty and wicked rulers will be destroyed, and the meek and the oppressed poor will rule the new kingdom to come. One of these movements during the Great Revival was the Native Baptist (or Bedwardite) Church, which became significant during the early part of the twentieth century.

The Native Baptist Church was founded by Alexander Bedward around 1891. Born of slave ancestry in 1859, Bedward was reared in the spirit of the Great Revival and lived on the Mona estate, the current site of the main campus of the prestigious University of the West Indies. As a young man, he is said to have had a vision in which a spirit gave him the gift of healing and he was later anointed as the incarnate Christ on Earth. He claimed that the end of the world was near and that he would ascend to heaven, taking his followers in the sky with him. Shortly after their ascension, cataclysmic disasters would destroy the world after which the earth would be renewed. A New Jerusalem would be established on the earth, and the meek and downtrodden would be redeemed. The mighty would be brought down and would become subservient to the poor and the meek.

There exist some parallels between the Native Baptist teachings and those of the Rastafari. First, the Native Baptists believed in the spiritual efficacy of fasting. The Rastafari say that fasting cleanses, sanctifies, and prepares one to face the spiritual struggles in the maintenance of one's faith in an alienating environment. Second, the Native Baptists, like the Rastafari today, believed in the regenerative power of the sun—a symbol of strength and fertility—and often formed bands of devotees who went on sacred excursions through the night to greet the rising sun. Third, the Native Baptists called upon the powers of God to crush the whites, whom they saw as the incarnate of the Pharisees and Saducees in the New Testament, and believed that Bedward's prophecy would come to pass, that is, white civilization would eventually be destroyed. Looking forward to our discussions of Garveyism and the Rastafari, there is an important distinction in regard to race between the Rastafari and Garveyism, on the one hand, and Native Baptists on the other. Despite the fact that Bedward taught that white civilization would be destroyed, he regarded whites as superior to blacks but that blacks' oppression, like the redeeming quality of Jesus's suffering, would serve as a means to their eventual redemption. In the end, blacks would become superior by replacing whites in the new kingdom to come. In contrast, the Rastafari (as well as Garveyism) believed in the superiority of blackness and affirmed that God was black and not white (Chevannes 1994:109).

The Native Baptists' millennial visions were carried well into the 1920s and were instrumental to the emergence of Garveyism and the subsequent rise of the Rastafari movement in Jamaica. Marcus Garvey was born in a Roman Catholic family in the Parish of St. Ann in Jamaica on August 17, 1887. His father was a proud man who traced his ancestry to the early maroon freedom fighters who had battled the British army in Jamaica for nearly a century. The young Marcus heard stories of great maroon heroes like Cudjoe and Quaco; reflecting on his youth later in his life, he noted that these stories had a profound effect on him.

Very early in life Garvey became aware of the problems of inequality, poverty, and social injustice in Jamaican society. After the emancipation of the slaves in the early 1830s, there emerged three social classes in Jamaica: the wealthy white elite who were usually descendants of British slave owners; a relatively small middle class of black Jamaican professionals; and, at the bottom, a large number of blacks who were so poor that they lived below a minimum standard of subsistence. The majority blacks were uneducated, with little hope of ever improving their lot. Many of them were unemployed, and those few who did work received low wages. Between 1910 and 1914, Garvey tried relentlessly to expose the plight of poor blacks before the Jamaican authorities. He visited Panama and England to evaluate the social and economic conditions of the large numbers of Jamaicans in these countries and discovered that they were equally poor there as well. He returned to Kingston and founded the United Negro Improvement Association (UNIA) in 1914. The goal of this organization was to lobby for the cause and improve the lot of poor Jamaicans. In 1916 he moved the UNIA's headquarters to New York City, where he thought his work would be more effective, far from the intimidation of Jamaica's British colonial government. He worked with black Protestant ministers and members of their churches in New York, preaching at Sunday morning services about the work of the association. He also struggled with the rank and file in government over issues related to higher wages, civil liberties, the granting of political rights (including universal suffrage), and the ownership of land among the disenfranchised.

The UNIA's focus might have been secular, but Garvey's speeches echoed many of the religious themes found in the earlier revivalist movements in Jamaica. He declared that blacks were the chosen people of God and that they had been forced to live in the diaspora against their will when their ancestors were brought over as slaves. For more than 300 years they had been subjected to white racism, social oppression, abject poverty, and economic exploitation. Black people's devils were therefore whites who set a course for the future with the creation of corrupt civilizations that would eventually meet their own demise. Blacks in the Americas should therefore look to Africa, from where a king would rise; he would be a long-awaited messiah who would liberate them from oppression. Just as blacks here looked with hope to Africa, so, too, "princes would come out of Egypt," and Ethiopia would be the first of all African nations to "soon stretch out her hands unto God" (Psalm 68:31). To Garvey, the kingdom of heaven was to occur on Earth and would entail the repatriation of all blacks to Africa. Although Garvey did not actively undertake blacks' return to Africa, his writings and speeches (published in the *Negro World*, the official newspaper of the UNIA) inspired significant numbers of them to return there. Garvey was a persuasive and eloquent orator, and his articulation of these issues and his personal struggles over these questions undoubtedly set the stage for the millenarian theology of the Rastafari.

The Rastafari emerged in Jamaica shortly after 1930, the year that Haile Selassie became emperor of Ethiopia. His enthronement was covered widely by the international press, not only because of the ostensive opulence that surrounded it but also because of the new monarch's flamboyant titles. He was to be known as Ras Tafari, that is, the "King of Kings and Lord of Lords, the Conquering Lion of the Tribe of Judah." He also claimed to be the 225th descendant in an unbroken succession that originated with King David and the Queen of Sheba.

The emperor's celebrated enthronement caused many poor Jamaicans to remember Garvey's prophecy about Ethiopia as well as the use of language by the Ethiopian Baptists. For the Rastafari, the term *Ethiopia* became the "land of the blacks," the long-awaited promised land, and the emperor himself the messiah. According to the Rastafari, all blacks in the Americas were the reincarnation of the ancient Israelites and could also be likened to the dispersed Jews in the Diaspora. As Jah's (God's) chosen people, the Rastafari believe that they should make a vow to separate themselves from whites.[3] The Rastafari believe that God is black, as were Adam and Eve, Christ, all the prophets, and all the great religious figures of the Bible. Blacks are therefore superior to whites because they were the chosen people of God.

Since the time that Europeans came to the Americas, they have transported blacks there and forced them to live in a society that whites created. The Rastafari regard white civilization as Babylon, that is, a world that is abysmally corrupt and evil, one that is therefore not worthy of their participation. They believe that God allowed blacks to be exiled in the Americas as slaves because of their past transgressions and those of their ancestors but that the advent of the invincible emperor was a sign that their sins had been expiated and that the end of their suffering was near. Like the ancient city of Babylon, the world of whites was hopeless hell and would be destroyed. That destruction then will open the way for God to enact His covenant with His people and ensure their safe and final passage to Ethiopia—the promised land. They believed that the emperor who was God became manifest in the flesh to ensure their safe repatriation to Ethiopia and that he was working out the details with the leaders of the nations of the world. Following their repatriation, blacks would have their revenge; a new order would be established—the reversal of the social order—where whites would become subservient to blacks.

Yet like other Caribbean religions, not all the Rastafari sects hold these tenets or give the same interpretations. Indeed, since the death of Haile Selassie in 1974 many have placed less emphasis on the movement's otherworldly millennial dream and have insisted that deliverance would come not from the outside but internally, that is, from within Jamaican society. For them, Ethiopia is a symbol of religious unity and racial identity. It is also an international symbol that unites all blacks of the world under one common banner of hope in the face of white oppression.

Since the 1950s the Rastafari have tended to live in close-knit religious communities that simulate the organizational structures of traditional African compounds. This communal setting prompted clearer formulations of Rastafari theology: the elaboration of symbols and ritual forms; the popularization of ritual music and drumming; and the designation and observances of religious festival days. The long sessions of theological debate (known as reasonings) among the men are occasions to identify key biblical passages that underlay their theology and substantiate the relations between their beliefs and the world's current state of affairs.

During this period the Rastafari developed peculiar notions of what they consider "natural" and thus in keeping with the biblical tradition (Chevannes 1994). These notions have affected the Rastafari lifestyle in profound ways. The wearing of beards and dreadlocks, something that already existed in the movement, did not gain importance until the 1950s. The Rastafari allude to several sources for keeping their hair untouched and natural. Some cite the biblical passage in which one who takes a holy "vow of separation [referring to their separation from the whites] no razor shall come upon his head," but should "let his locks of hair hang by the side of his head" (Numbers 6:9). Others, like the Dread, emphasize the long suffering of the "people of God" in a "strange land." Dreads wear natural locks that symbolize tears resulting from the sorrow that they experienced through centuries of oppression, injustice, and deprivation. Others would argue that Rastafari thought emphasizes that which is natural and untouched, that the growing of locks and beards manifests that belief, and that they assume a natural physiognomy that was given to mankind at creation—one that is neither cosmeticized nor sculptured by human hands. Still others would claim that the locks and their unkempt appearance opposed the establishment and thus symbolized their categorical rejection of Babylon. Such emphasis on the natural also underlies Rastafaris' strict dietary rules.

The Rastafari believe that the killing of an animal for human consumption does nothing more than promote death, for killing the animal removes from it the life-giving power of Jah that resides within it. Thus, the meat that is cut off from a dead animal is unfit for human consumption because it does not withhold Jah's life-force. In contrast, a flower may continue to bloom even after it has been severed from its stem; a fruit will continue to ripen even after it has been cut from the tree; and a grain removed from the plant continues to hold within it the power of regeneration when it is planted into a fertile ground. The Rastafari follow a vegetarian diet that incorporates dairy products. They believe that a vegetarian diet is sacred, for it allows one to derive from nature Jah's life-sustaining force.

The use of ganja, or marijuana, which is so important to the reasonings, took an important place in the 1950s as well. According to the Rastafari, the most common reason for using the sacred plant is related to a biblical passage in which, during the sixth day of the creation, God declared that he made the grasses and all vegetation for mankind's enjoyment (Genesis 1:29). The Rastafari also believe that ganja is a holy weed that can promote visions that allow them to obtain a clearer vision of Jah. In effect, the use of ganja is a sacramental act that infuses within the body the sacred power of the spirit as it derives from nature. It also opens the mind to the will of Jah and allows for miraculous and unexpected revelations from the Almighty.

Throughout the 1950s and 1960s, many Rastafari communities established themselves in the urban centers of Jamaica, and their members became overtly critical of whites, entrepreneurs, and black Jamaican police officers, whom they regarded as traitors of the race. They were particularly critical of the established clergy for its lack of moral integrity and its service to two masters: God and Satan. During this period, militant Rastafari sought to create rapid changes in Jamaican society and incited violent civil disturbances in Kingston that threatened socioeconomic and political stability. In effect, these disturbances might not have been as threatening as they were perceived by Jamaican authorities, but the aura of mystery that surrounded their communal lifestyle, their conscious decision not to participate in Jamaica's national life, and the dreadlocks (which many perceived as bordering on the grotesque and the savage) engendered a profound fear of them among many Jamaicans. The Jamaican government undertook a detailed study of the Rastafari, undoubtedly to allay the fears of its citizens. Released after a relatively long inquisition into their beliefs and lifestyle, a favorable report (and the first of its kind) was published about the movement (see Augier et al. 1960).

Today the militancy of the Rastafari can be seen in their opposition to many aspects of contemporary society that they perceive as Babylon. It includes the hegemony of the West and the mighty arm of its multinational corporations. For this reason, they do not participate in Jamaica's national life.

But their withdrawal from society has ironically rendered a service to Jamaican culture, for their emphasis on blackness has stimulated a new sense of identity among Jamaicans (Barrett 1977). Terms of endearment, forms of address (such as "Brother," "Sister," and "Rastaman"), as well as the customary greeting ("peace and love"), which they use among themselves, have awakened among black Jamaicans a sense of communal attachment to a common culture that transcends social class. The Rastafaris' rejection of Jamaican society has necessitated a need to create new artistic venues that have been embraced by the very culture that they rejected. These art forms have made significant contributions to the development of Jamaican popular culture. In the domain of music, the use of the *akete* drum and its music has contributed to the development of reggae. The Rastafari have also written scores of poems and essays and have produced sculptures and paintings that symbolize various aspects of their theology. They also called for an awareness of the black African heritage well before it became fashionable in the late 1960s.

It is art—and especially the reggae music as popularized by Bob Marley and others—that has contributed to the international reputation that the Rastafari currently enjoy. Since the late 1960s Rastafari culture has spread to many parts of the world, and many communities have been formed in urban centers throughout the world. Not all of these are religious communities, however, for many have adopted the hair style, the diet, the secular use of ganja, and the sense of communal identity without the religious dimension central to the movement. In effect, the Rastafari are probably the most culturally and internationally diffused of all the Caribbean religions. The appeal is not merely the music or various art forms but the universal message that befits the current conditions of the contemporary world. The Rastafari decry the economic exploitation of the poor by the wealthy and the social and political oppression of the downtrodden by the mighty.

■ Spiritual Baptists

The Spiritual Baptists of Trinidad are part of a rapidly expanding international religious movement with congregations in St. Vincent (where many Trinidadian Spiritual Baptists claim their faith originated), Trinidad and Tobago, Grenada, Guyana, Venezuela, London, Toronto, Los Angeles, and New York City. In addition, there are a number of similar religious movements on other Caribbean islands whose rituals parallel those of Spiritual Baptists (i.e., the Tie Heads of Barbados, the Jordanites of Guyana, and the Spirit Baptists of Jamaica). An important consideration is that many Spiritual Baptists do not consider these others to be a part of their religion and seldom participate in joint worship services, pilgrimages, missions, and other activities with members of these other groups. They do, however, maintain close and active ties with brethren in St. Vincent, Guyana, Grenada, Venezuela, the United States, Europe, and Canada.

Like other religions of Caribbean origin, Spiritual Baptist membership is predominantly black, and—like many other Afro-Caribbean groups—the Spiritual Baptists seem to have started out as a religion of the oppressed. In recent years, however, congregations in Trinidad have attracted membership among middle-class blacks, as well as sizable numbers of wealthier East Indians, Chinese, whites, and individuals of mixed heritage. Although some Spiritual Baptist leaders take great pride in their multiethnic congregations, it is possible to overplay the influence of other ethnic groups. The Spiritual Baptist faith is still overwhelmingly a black religion, with Asians and whites representing less than 5 percent of all adherents. Recent membership in Trinidad and Tobago has fluctuated between 10,000 and 12,500.

Many Trinidadians confuse Spiritual Baptists and followers of the African-derived Orisha movement.[4] They assume that Spiritual Baptist and Orisha rites are identical. Members of these two faiths, however, do not share this confusion. A large percentage of Spiritual Baptists condemn Orisha rites as heathen worship. Orisha devotees, for their part, assert that the Spiritual Baptists copy their ideas and try to steal their power. On occasion, Spiritual Baptist leaders have picketed Orisha centers prior to Orisha ceremonies.

Another complicating factor is that a growing number of Spiritual Baptist leaders are also involved in the Kabbala. The influence of Kabbala was noted briefly by George Eaton Simpson who, conducting fieldwork in the 1960s, remarked on Spiritual Baptists' widespread use of the Sixth and Seventh Books of Moses (Simpson 1966). Simpson's sources (who were mostly from churches along the Eastern Main Road) did not provide him with much information about Kabbala. It is in the nature of Kabbala to be secretive, and many of Stephen Glazier's sources, at least two of whom were heavily involved in Kabbala, were from the same geographical area as Simpson's sources (Glazier 1991). Because Kabbala rites are private and not readily shared, ethnographic research in this area did not open up prior to the pioneering work of Kenneth Lum starting in 1986.

Kabbala rituals are similar to those of American and Latin American spiritualism and Puerto Rican Karedicismo. A major difference is that during Kabbalistic séances spirits from the other side communicate exclusively via a series of alternating short and long taps, which are simultaneously transcribed and translated by a medium. Kabbalistic rites are usually performed apart from Spiritual Baptist worship, most often in private homes. Sometimes, however, Kabbala tappings are embedded within regular Spiritual Baptist worship. In 1999 Glazier noted Kabbala being performed amid Sunday morning services in Arima and Maraval. In both cases, Kabbala spirits communicated as part of a healing ceremony that was conducted by a Spiritual Baptist shepherd and nurse in the right-hand corner of the church. The paramount leader served as medium. Hidden behind a lace veil, the paramount leader transcribed the tappings. His interpretations were given in a private consultation at the conclusion of worship.

It should be emphasized that Kabbala has never been a part of Spiritual Baptist worship in some Trinidadian churches. Kabbala may be unknown among Spiritual Baptists on other Caribbean islands. It is practiced in neither St. Vincent nor New York City but is widespread among Spiritual Baptists in Trinidad. Séances are conducted so unobtrusively that only the initiated recognize what is taking place. To the uninitiated, the tapping of a shepherd's crook on an earthen floor (like pounding pews, ringing bells, and clapping hands) is simply taken as another aspect of Spiritual Baptist musical expression. This is exactly the intention of Kabbala operators and one reason Spiritual Baptist services are considered such a good cover for Kabbala rites.

Orisha rites, many of which are conducted outdoors in crowded residential areas, are not as secretive. Drumming and possession, which are the major components of Orisha rites, are public and highly visible. In examining the relationships between Spiritual Baptist churches and Orisha centers, four distinct types of organizations may be discerned: Spiritual Baptist churches with Orisha connections; Spiritual Baptist churches without Orisha connections; Orisha centers with Spiritual Baptist connections; and Orisha centers without Spiritual Baptist connections. These distinctions reflect ways in which members of these religions think of themselves. Are they, for example, Spiritual Baptists who also "do" Orisha work, or followers of the Orisha who also "do" Spiritual Baptist work?

Members of all four types of organizations may also sponsor Kabbala rites, but Kabbala is most common among Spiritual Baptists who maintain close connections with Orisha and least common at Orisha centers without Spiritual Baptist ties. Of course, there are also many Kabbalists in Trinidad who do not participate in either Spiritual Baptist or Orisha rites.

Spiritual Baptists as well as devotees of Orisha combine beliefs and practices from a variety of religious traditions. A major difference is that Spiritual Baptist rituals are directed to their version of the Holy Trinity, whereas Orisha rites are directed toward and incorporate African-derived deities. Spiritual Baptists profess that they are Christians. This is not to imply that Spiritual Baptists do not acknowledge the power of the Orisha. They believe strongly in the power of African deities but do not believe that such deities should be venerated. A frequent assertion is that Spiritual Baptists do not fear the Orisha because Christ gives them power over Orisha.

Although they practice separate traditions, Spiritual Baptists and Orisha devotees are interrelated on a number of levels. Their memberships overlap, and perhaps 90 percent of all Orisha devotees in Trinidad and Tobago also participate in Spiritual Baptist services; perhaps 40 percent of all Spiritual Baptists also participate in African-derived religions. Of course, there are degrees of participation. Not all leaders in the former religion are necessarily officials in the latter and vice versa.

Close associations between Spiritual Baptist churches and Orisha services are unique within the Caribbean. Participants in other African-derived faiths—like Cuban Santería and Haitian Vodou—maintain ties with the Catholic Church; for example, the first step in serving the Haitian *lwa* is a Catholic baptism. Spiritual Baptists, however, are the only Protestant group in the region that serves as an institutional base for an African-derived religion. The relationship between Orisha devotees and Spiritual Baptist churches could be described as symbiotic. Spiritual Baptists maintain permanent buildings, whereas most Orisha devotees do not. Spiritual Baptists meet twice a week, whereas Orisha feasts are held only once or twice a year. Thus, Spiritual Baptist churches provide a convenient location for Orisha devotees to organize feasts and plan their activities and are also a setting for opening prayers for Orisha ceremonies.

For Spiritual Baptists, the most central and controversial rite is mourning. Mourning ceremonies, Spiritual Baptists claim, make their religion distinct from all other religions in the world. The Spiritual Baptist concept of mourning has a very different meaning compared to many other religious traditions. Among Spiritual Baptists, it does not relate directly to physical death and bereavement but is an elaborate ceremony involving fasting, lying on a dirt floor, and other so-called deprivations, although contemporary rites give greater emphasis to symbolic deprivation than actual physical deprivation.

Like African initiation, death-symbolism is apparent in mourning rites, but the ritual's central role has always been to remind mourners of human frailty and the imperfection amid life. Spiritual Baptists say that they participate in mourning ceremonies for a variety of reasons—to cure cancer, to see the future, or to communicate with the deceased. On a more mundane level, mourning enables Spiritual Baptists to temporarily escape family obligations, gives them an opportunity for fellowship, and even provides the possibility of weight loss (though fasting is no longer encouraged, some mourners find it easy to diet within the context of the ceremony). For many, it is a vision quest; an attempt to discover the "true" self in relation to God the Father and God the Holy Ghost. The major stated goal of mourners, however, is to discover one's true rank within a twenty-two-step church hierarchy. Every Spiritual Baptist is expected to mourn often, and every Spiritual Baptist desires to advance within the church hierarchy.

Many Spiritual Baptists complain that the mourning ceremony has been radically misinterpreted by outsiders. Rather than emphasize deprivations (visual, sleep-related, dietary), these Spiritual Baptists see the rite as a time of meditation—like a Catholic retreat. As noted above, Spiritual Baptist leaders frequently take it upon themselves to make mourning rites less demanding. And in recent years (since, say, the early 1980s) most ceremonies in the majority of churches have been abbreviated from three weeks to one week to three days. Mourning rites are no longer uniform for all participants. Older mourners may be assigned a full-time nurse (this is a spiritual rank, but very often nurses have had some medical training) for the entire duration of the rite. Leaders are expected to assess the health of each potential participant and adjust the rite accordingly. Greater care is taken in terms of diet (only the prohibition on salt remains; all other food restrictions are left to the discretion of the individual leader). Those who want to observe a strict fast are encouraged to do so at home.

Lastly, mourners are no longer anonymous. In the past, mourners in the chamber were given numbers and referred to as "Mourner number 1," "Mourner number 2," and so on throughout the rite. This underscored the loss of individuality associated with death. Now, senior mourners, especially those of higher ranks, are referred to by name during the ceremony. This represents an abrupt departure from prior practices.

As noted, mourning is believed to have curative powers, and because so many individuals enter the rite in an unhealthy condition, occasionally participants die during the ceremony. Deaths may prompt a routine government inquiry and perhaps a lawsuit. This has happened seven times since the mid-1970s. In government inquiries, the government attempts to determine whether poor diet and damp conditions in the mourning room could have been contributing factors to mourners' deaths. Government officials assert that Spiritual Baptist leaders should refuse participation to mourners believed to be too weak to withstand the rigors of the ceremony.

Leaders defend themselves by claiming that they take every possible precaution to ensure a mourner's physical survival but point out that their primary responsibility is for the spiritual survival of the mourner. According to Spiritual Baptist ideology, mourning rituals are believed to have been spiritually effective even if the mourner dies. Religious interpretations seem to have prevailed. No Spiritual Baptist leader has been indicted as a result of a government inquiry.

Most lawsuits have been settled out of court. One case that did make it to court was later dismissed because it could not be shown that the mourner died as a result of the ceremony (she died almost two years later, in a traffic accident). All cases were brought by members of mourners' immediate families and were unsuccessful because other mourners (the only witnesses) refused to testify against the spiritual leaders who had directed the ceremonies.

Without exception, Spiritual Baptist leaders interpret attempts to scrutinize the mourning ceremonies as an assault on religious freedom. Leaders who do claim religious persecution make much of a 1917 ordinance (the Shouters Prohibition Ordinance) introduced in the Legislative Council of Trinidad and

Tobago banning shouting, bell ringing, and other components of Spiritual Baptist worship. The ban on shouting remained in effect from 1917 to 1953. Similar ordinances were introduced and passed on other islands of the British West Indies, most notably on Jamaica, Grenada, St. Kitts, and St. Vincent.

A number of sources stressed that the Trinidad ban lasted longer and was more rigorously enforced than on other islands. But leaders who do not believe that the Spiritual Baptist faith has been subjected to persecution point out that the ban was sporadically enforced and that it did little to slow the spread of the Spiritual Baptist religion. For example, the Belmont church, alleged to have been the target of the original ordinance, continued to conduct weekly services throughout the period of the ban. It has been alleged that in five instances Spiritual Baptist leaders were fined (in 1940, 1941, and 1945; see Thomas 1987). This has not been verified; however, it is possible to discern evidence of governmental interference and censorship of Spiritual Baptist practices in calypsos composed during the 1930s and 1940s. One source cites Growling Tiger's 1939 calypso tune "What Is a Shouter?" (Rohlehr 1990). The lyrics reflect attitudes of the time:

> The Shango, of course, is quite disagreeable
> For the drum is miserable
> But the Kookoo and goat and nice white rice
> I mean the rum and the coffee is nice
> But the Shouters is a husband, children, and wife
> And they livin' miserable, a corrupted life
> If is that they call civilization
> It's a disgrace to my native land.

A persistent theme in Spiritual Baptist sermons is that the faith has made great progress in the face of adversity, and the period of the ban is likened to the Ancient Israelites' forty years in the wilderness.

A number of dramatic changes have taken place among the Spiritual Baptists since the mid-1970s. The most dramatic changes relate to the roles of women within the faith. When Glazier began fieldwork, Spiritual Baptist women were not permitted to occupy the same ritual space as men. In 1976 about 26 percent of the churches Glazier attended observed separate seating for males and females (males on the right, females on the left). Today this practice has largely been abandoned.

In the past, Spiritual Baptist women were expected to direct their attentions toward a raised platform at the center of the church (known as the center pole) while men conducted church services from a raised platform (the altar) near the front of the church. Women never spoke from the altar platform but addressed their concerns to the congregation in the form of a prayer kneeling at the center pole. Only uninitiated men, women, and children gravitated toward the center pole. All men—even non–Spiritual Baptist men—were encouraged to speak from the front when asked if a woman was ever allowed to stand on the altar. The response was that women were allowed up there only to dust and mop (Glazier 1991).

Although many churches still do not allow women to preach from the front altar, some larger suburban churches encourage low-ranking males to make their comments from the center pole and higher-ranking females to preach from the front of the church. Women have become much more prominent in denominational affairs. There are now two female bishops. In addition, two females serve as faculty members at the Spiritual Baptist theological seminary (the Southland School of Theology in La Brea, Trinidad).

A most intriguing change pertains to the decorative use of clocks in Spiritual Baptist churches. Clocks are and have been standard ritual paraphernalia in Spiritual Baptist worship since the 1940s. As an apocalyptic group, Spiritual Baptists are acutely aware of the fleeting passage of time. As a this-worldly religion, Spiritual Baptists understand time on earth as the only time when one is able to make supplication to God the Father, who determines one's fate after death. Spiritual Baptists seem little concerned with details of the afterlife. Neither heaven nor hell are topics of intense speculation. But when you die—they assert—the "book is sealed" (i.e., there is nothing more one can do).

In the 1970s most churches possessed two or more clocks that were prominently displayed. There was always a clock on the wall behind the altar, and usually another in the back of the church positioned so as to be seen from the pulpit. In the past, few of the clocks were in working order. Operating clocks were either set several hours fast or ran several hours slow. In the 1990s some churches began to purchase and display accurate clocks.

In sermons and other public pronouncements, Spiritual Baptists put a great deal of emphasis on punctuality. Almost every sermon begins with the assertion "my time will be short and I will keep my message brief on account of the hour." Having issued this disclaimer, however, most speakers feel free to exceed their allotted time. Although regular Spiritual Baptist services are not supposed to last more than three hours, many services extend more than five hours. It is frequently stressed that Spiritual Baptist services should begin and end on time, but one does not have to attend many services to learn that this is not always the case. Such *temporal elasticity* has been noted as a characteristic of Trinidadian social life, but Spiritual Baptists are not merely following local conventions. Temporal elasticity has a theological rationale as well: Spiritual Baptists envision themselves in the midst of a great battle between secular time and sacred time; it is a battle in which sacred time must reign triumphant.

The 1990s ushered in a period of increasing respectability and visibility for the faith. In 1996 a general conference of Spiritual Baptist bishops and leaders was held at the Central Bank Auditorium in Port-of-Spain, Trinidad, one of the nicest, best-equipped conference facilities in the Caribbean. Not coincidentally, the Central Bank Auditorium was selected by the bishops because it was seen as a center of political and economic power. Several speakers (Spiritual Baptists and non-Baptists) began their talks by remarking, "Who would think that the Baptists be here?" Senator Michael Ramsharam and other dignitaries were invited to address the conference. Future Prime Minister Basdeo Panday was also said to have been in the audience. Panday was instrumental in establishing a national holiday in honor of the Spiritual Baptists.

The proceedings of this conference have been published under the title "Call Him By His Name, Jesus: Spiritual Baptists: Christians Moving into the 21st Century."[5] They have been widely distributed in local bookstores as well as throughout the Caribbean by the World Council of Churches. The proceedings contain the full texts of all bishops' remarks as well as questions and comments from the floor. It is a remarkable document. Most notable is Archbishop Alexander Murrain's address calling for: a new cathedral with a library for researchers who want to make a history of the Spiritual Baptist faith; establishment of a trade school to help Spiritual Baptists get better jobs; and a Spiritual Baptist park that will serve as a pilgrimage site for Spiritual Baptists in the Caribbean and throughout the world.

The day of the repeal of the Shouters Prohibition Ordinance in 1953 has been designated as a national holiday in Trinidad and Tobago, and Spiritual Baptists have been granted land to establish an open space—a national memorial park—and to build a Spiritual Baptist cathedral and a trade school. Spiritual Baptist leaders were given their choice of a number of properties. What is of interest, however, is the land they were offered but did not choose. They did not pick a major Spiritual Baptist church like the archbishop's seats in Belmont or Laventille; they did not choose a prominent pilgrimage site like Maracas Bay or Maracas Falls; they did not choose a wilderness area. They chose instead to locate their open space and cathedral at the confluence of two major arteries: the Uriah Butler Highway (the main road to San Fernando and the south) and the Priority Bus Route (which parallels Eastern Main Road to Arima). This is considered prime commercial property and was desired by a number of developers. Earlier, McDonald's had made an unsuccessful bid for the site.

The church has also established a governing body, the Council of Elders, with headquarters on Saddle Road in Maraval. The headquarters are located in an expensive residential area on the main road to Moka golf course and the beach. The headquarters themselves are in a modest house that is in disrepair, but its highly visible sign on a high-traffic road underscores Spiritual Baptist obsessions with location, location, location.

A number of Spiritual Baptist bishops have openly stated that they would like to see Spiritual Baptists become more like the other churches. They pursue their goal with a zeal that would have surprised even chroniclers of rationality in religious organizations like Max Weber (1960) and Ernst Troeltsch (1960). To become more like the other churches, a seminary (the Southland School of Theology) has been established for training ministers. Unlike prior generations of Spiritual Baptist leaders, it is hoped that these ministers will qualify for ordination and be legally entitled to marry and bury parishioners. A sore point among many Spiritual Baptist leaders is that members of their congregations must look elsewhere for weddings and funerals because Spiritual Baptist ministers are seldom licensed. Ordination, however, may not have the anticipated impact. Funerals for Spiritual Baptists are usually held in Catholic, Anglican, or Pentecostal churches. A complicating factor is that families arrange for funerals to take place in the family's home church, and unless other family members are Spiritual Baptists, they will be unlikely to hold their funerals in Spiritual Baptist churches.

A comprehensive Spiritual Baptist ministers' manual was published in 1993. Its 238 pages include detailed instructions for conducting dedication of infants, baptisms, and mournings as well as a suggested order of worship and a list of appropriate hymns and scripture passages for each juncture of the service. For a religion that prides itself in following the spirit, it seems ironic that such a manual should exist at all. But it should be added that the manual does accurately reflect Spiritual Baptist practices—even if in a somewhat stifled way.

It is extremely difficult to gauge the impact of these proposed changes on rank-and-file believers. Thus far the impact has been minuscule. The Southland School of Theology has no full-time students; the Spiritual Baptist ministers' manual is rarely consulted; and construction has yet to begin on the park, the trade school, and the cathedral. The majority of Spiritual Baptist churches remain small and lack a solid financial base. For the average church member, things continue pretty much as before.

■ Caribbean Religions in the Diaspora

Since the 1950s many Caribbeans have migrated to other places, notably to other parts of the Caribbean as well as Central America, the United States, Canada, and the United Kingdom. As Dennis Conway shows in Chapter 12, living in the diaspora they inhabit many of the world's largest cities. Despite the stresses of urban life and the lingering suspicions by outsiders of Caribbean religions as mere superstition and devil worship, Caribbean peoples have managed to maintain their religious beliefs and practices abroad. Among some 1 million Cuban emigrants who settled in various parts of the world, many of whom fled after the socialist revolution in 1959, were priestesses and priests of Santería. They established houses in Puerto Rico, Venezuela, and the United States and they continue to wield considerable authority over the peoples whom they serve. Although estimates of the numbers of practitioners and priests are difficult to determine, totals could run as high as in the hundreds of thousands, with many more devotees of the *orichas* in the United States than in Cuba. The religion continues to play an important part in peoples' lives in the diaspora and is often the primary agency assisting poorer Cuban emigrants with health services and legal aid.

In the case of the Spiritual Baptists, the church has sent missionaries abroad in recent years. Several churches have opened among West Indian communities in London and Toronto. Among all of the new churches in the diaspora, perhaps the greatest growth has been in churches in Canada, Europe, and the United States. For example, St. Peter's Spiritual Baptist Church in Brooklyn claims to have more than 2,000 members, and two Spiritual Baptist churches in Toronto claim more than 1,000 members each. The New Jerusalem Spiritual Baptist Church outside London claims more than 200 members.

Haitians also have recreated their religious traditions in the diaspora. They have established *ounfòs* as well as communities that approximate those of the African *lakou* (rural courtyard) that managed to survive throughout Haitian history. In Haiti, a *lakou* is an area in which are gathered five or six extended families who live in separated dwellings, sometimes with one house that serves as a temple. The members of the *lakou* gather around the home of a patriarch or a matriarch, a spiritual leader who is regarded by the members of the *lakou* as the link between the secular world of the *lakou* and the sacred world of the *lwas*.

The *lakou* as a social institution has waned considerably in Haiti since the 1950s. Job opportunities and prospects for better education in towns have resulted in the emigration of the *lakous*' younger members to the cities and have engendered the gradual disintegration of the rural *lakous*' infrastructure. But it has reemerged among Haitians in the diaspora. The *house systems* are analogous to the *lakous;* they consist of an entire building in which several families live in individual apartments but share domestic and financial resources. They gather around a priest or priestess, whose apartment often combines living quarters and a temple.

In the context of rituals, most of the paraphernalia used are readily available in most large cities in the diaspora. Even pilgrimages are reproduced. For example, All Souls' Day in the church's liturgical calendar (November 1) nearly corresponds to Halloween in North America, the day consecrated to the souls of the dead in the Catholic liturgical calendar and in the Santería and Vodou calendars. Similarly, July 16, the day devoted to the Virgin Mary in the

Catholic liturgical calendar, is reserved for Ezili in Vodou and Ochún in Santería. On that day, many Haitians in New York make pilgrimages to the Lady of Mount Carmel Church; those in Canada will go to St. Anne de Beaupré near Quebec.

Perhaps one of the single most significant aspects of Caribbean religions in the diaspora is their multiethnic character. Ritual participation is open to members of cultural and ethnic groups from other parts of the world. This is especially true of the Rastafari, whose religious ideology and social message have had widespread international appeal, resulting in the creation of Rastafari communities in different parts of the world. In the case of Santería, as among the Spiritual Baptists and Vodou, the names of the spirits spread very quickly among nonnationals in the United States, notably among African Americans seeking to integrate black nationalism with an authentic African worldview. The emphasis on Africa and African cultures by the Rastafari has been particularly appealing to African Americans in the United States. In larger U.S. cities, Santería is practiced by Dominican, Colombian, and Mexican Americans, as well as others. The energy, creativity, and resources of these new communities have led to the formation of international organizations dedicated to fostering dialogue and cooperation in an emerging world religion. The participation of other cultural and ethnic groups will undoubtedly change these religions, for their members may incorporate their own cultural and religious traditions—a factor that may change the character of Caribbean religions in the diaspora as well as distinguish Caribbean religions in the diaspora from counterparts in the Caribbean. It may well be that Caribbean religions' traditions, for the second time in history, will become theologically diverse. And like the religion of the maroon republics during the period of slavery, the ethos of the theology of each religious center in the diaspora will depend upon its demographic composition and the theological inclination of its leader.

■ Conclusion

Caribbean religions are similar to African religious traditions but are different in other ways; they developed in a distinct cultural context far from Africa. Two major differences: Caribbean religions are multicultural to the core, and they derive their traditions from various regions (including Africa, Europe, and the Americas). African beliefs and practices within Caribbean religions provide a commonly shared experience in a cultural context in which the combinations of African religious elements varied according to the preeminence of the religious traditions of a particular ethnic group or the theological inclinations of local religious specialists.

African and Caribbean religions are dissimilar in that they developed in two different environments, each of which produced its own characteristic theological blending: the Catholic and the Protestant. Religious amalgamation, however, occurred in different ways and was facilitated through a system of reinterpretations whereby Christian traditions were translated in terms of African religious beliefs and practices.

Throughout their history, Caribbean religions have exhibited an extraordinary resilience that has made it possible for them to survive in the most adverse social situations throughout their history in the Caribbean and in the diaspora. Local autonomy has also permitted ritual and theological innovations by leaders. Such innovations have facilitated successful translocation into the most arduous socioeconomic and environmental conditions in the diaspora.

Notes

1. Baptists are to be distinguished from Spiritual Baptists in the Caribbean. Henceforth in this chapter, the terms *Spiritual Baptists* or *Spiritual Baptist Church* will be used to distinguish between the two religious organizations.

2. Several days before las Casas died in 1566, he recognized that slavery was wrong, that war was unjustifiable, and that the annexing of Indian land by Europeans was unscrupulous. He condemned all the European governments for transporting slaves from Africa.

3. This term is a shortened but endearing version of Jaweh (or Yaweh), God's name in the Hebrew Bible.

4. Note the change in orthography from *oricha* used in the context of Santería. Both terms have the same connotation in both religious traditions.

5. These proceedings appear in Stephen D. Glazier, "Changes in Spiritual Baptist Religion, 1976–1990," in *Ay Bobo: Afro-Caribbean Cults: Identity and Resistance,* Tell I: Kult, edited by Manfred Kremser (Wien: Institut fur Volkerkunde der Universitat Wien, 1996), pp. 107–114.

Bibliography

Augier, Roy, M. G. Smith, and Rex Nettleford. *The Rastafari Movement in Kingston, Jamaica.* Mona, Jamaica: University of the West Indies, 1960.

Barrett, Leonard. *Soul Force: African Heritage in African American Religion.* Garden City, NY: Doubleday, 1974.

———. *The Rastafarians: Sounds of Cultural Dissonance.* Boston: Beacon Press, 1977.

Bastide, Roger. *African Civilisations in the New World.* New York: Harper/ Row, 1971.

Birth, Kevin. *Any Time Is Trinidad Time.* Gainesville: University Press of Florida, 1999.

Bourguignon, Erika. *Religion, Altered States of Consciousness, and Social Change.* Columbus: Ohio State University Press, 1973.

Brandon, George. *Santería from Africa to the New World: The Dead Sell Memories.* Bloomington: Indiana University Press, 1993.

Brereton, Bridget. "The Experience of Indentureship, 1845–1917." In *Calcutta to Caroni: The East Indians in Trinidad*, edited by John Gaffar La Guerre. London: Longman Group Limited, 1974.

Campbell, Horace. *Rasta and Resistance: From Marcus Garvey to Walter Rodney.* London: Hansib Publishing, 1985.

Chevannes, Barry. *Rastafari: Roots and Ideology.* Syracuse: Syracuse University, 1994.

Courlander, Harold. *The Drum and the Hoe: Life and Lore of the Haitian People.* Berkeley: University of California Press, 1960.

Desmangles, Leslie G. *The Faces of the Gods: Vodou and Roman Catholicism in Haiti.* Chapel Hill: University of North Carolina Press, 1992.

Encyclopedia of African and African American Religions. Edited by Stephen Glazier, Hans Baier, Leslie Desmangles et al. New York: Routledge, 2001.

Garvey, Amy Jacques. *The Philosophy and Opinions of Marcus Garvey, of Africa for Africans.* Dover, MA: Majority Press, 1986.

Glazier, Stephen. *Marchin' the Pilgrims Home: A Study of the Spiritual Baptists of Trinidad.* Salem, MA: Sheffield, 1991.

Homiak, John. "From Yard to Nation: Rastafari and the Politics of Eldership at Home and Abroad." In *Ay Bobo: Afro-Karische Religionen*, edited by Manfred Kremsner. Vienna: WUV-Universitatsverlag, 1995.

Lai, Walton Look. *Indentured Labor, Caribbean Sugar: Chinese and Indian Migrants to the British West Indies, 1838–1918.* Baltimore: Johns Hopkins University Press, 1993.

Lindsay, Arturo, ed. *Santería Aesthetics in Contemporary Latin American Art.* Washington, DC: Smithsonian Institution Press, 1996.

Lum, Kenneth. *Praising His Name in the Dance: Spirit Possession in Spiritual Baptist Faith and Orisha Work in Trinidad, West Indies.* Amsterdam: Harwood Academic Publishers, 2000.

McCarthy-Brown, Karen. *Mama Lola: A Vodou Priestess in Brooklyn.* Berkeley: University of California Press, 1991.

Moreau de Saint-Méry, Médéric Louis-Elie. *Description topographique, physique, civile, politique et historique de la partie française de l'isle de Saint-Domingue* (Topographical, physical, civil, political, and historical description of the French part of the island of Santo Domingo). 3 vols. Paris: Société de l'Histoire des Colonies Françaises, 1958 [1797].

Murphy, Joseph M. *Santería: An African Religion in America.* Boston: Beacon Press, 1988.

Rohlehr, Gordon. *Callypso and Society in Pre-Independence Trinidad.* Published by the author, 1990.

Schuler, Monica. "Myalism and the African Religious Tradition in Jamaica." In *Africa and the Caribbean: The Legacies of a Link,* edited by Margaret Crahan and Franklin Knight. Baltimore: Johns Hopkins University Press, 1979.

Simpson, George Eaton. "Baptismal, Mourning, and Building Ceremonies of the Shouters in Trinidad." *Journal of American Folklore* 79 (1966): 537–550.

———. *Black Religions in the New World.* New York: Columbia University Press, 1978.

Thomas, Eudora. *A History of the Shouter Baptists in Trinidad and Tobago*. Tacarigua, Trinidad: Calaloux, 1987.

Troeltsch, Ernst. *The Social Teaching of the Christian Churches*. New York: Harper and Row, 1960.

Weber, Max. *The Sociology of Religion*. Glencoe, IL: Free Press, 1960.

Zane, Wallace W. *Journeys to the Spiritual Lands: The Natural History of a West Indian Religion*. New York: Oxford, 1999.

11

Literature and Popular Culture

Kevin Meehan and Paul B. Miller

Literature functions in the Caribbean, as elsewhere, as a documentary source that reveals the cultural patterns and social history that make up a civilization. Representative segments of every major cultural zone in the world—Amerindian, African, European, and Asian—have intermingled in the Caribbean, and this richness is reflected in the range and diversity of literature from the region. At the same time, because artists express their unique understanding of the world through literature, and audiences come to share this understanding through reading, listening, and responding, literary texts also shape the history and culture of a given place as much as they reflect it.

Previous chapters have explored particular aspects of Caribbean reality, past and present. In this chapter, we look at traditions of verbal expression worked out over many centuries. In referring to specific writers and works, we introduce a series of creative tensions characteristic of Caribbean cultural identity. These tensions, which we view as sources of vibrant creativity in the Caribbean, include writing versus popular oral expression; the interplay of multiple languages; the dynamic of domination, resistance, and struggle for autonomy; the clash between individual island and collective regional identity; and the conflict between a desire to establish home and identity in the Caribbean, on the one hand, and the force of movement, displacement, and exile on the other. These tensions recur from the period of Amerindian settlement to the present day and allow us to examine diversity within the Caribbean as well as the common threads that suggest a unified regional culture.

■ Indigenous Cultural Patterns

Caribbean cultural history is often treated as if it began in 1492 with the arrival of Christopher Columbus off the shore of Guanahani, an island in the Bahamas that Columbus renamed San Salvador. As Stephen Randall reveals in Chapter 3, even scholars sympathetic to the idea of indigenous cultural influences in the region note pessimistically the near-total destruction of Taíno and other Arawak populations within one generation, and the eventual military defeat of the Caribs in the 1790s, at which point British forces deported survivors from former Carib strongholds in the eastern Caribbean to Honduras and Belize.

Despite genocidal treatment at the hands of European colonists, however, native Caribbean peoples survive today in the islands of Dominica and St. Vincent and in greater numbers in mainland coastal settlements from Belize down to Guyana, Suriname, and French Guiana. Native culture is active in the fullest sense, and recent years have seen events such as the reunion of Carib communities in Honduras and St. Vincent; a renaissance in the formal study of indigenous songs, stories, dance, architecture, and foodways; growing participation by Caribbean natives in indigenous peoples' movements worldwide; and publication of poetry in Caraib, Arawak, Trio, and Wayana (native languages spoken in Suriname). The currency of such poetry is suggested by a Trio song inspired by the sight of a low-flying airplane:

> *Jësinaewa ëhtëkëeirë / jekanawaimërë serë/jarëtono jarëtono mëëre jënëtono mëëre / Jepananakirii jesautotao tïrïkë* (Weep and wail / for this is the giant canoe, / the cannibals are coming to get you; they're coming to eat you up. / Let's put some salt on him, the *pananakiri* [maneater] says). (Jones 1998:511)

Here, the singer depicts airborne outsiders as man-eaters, thus reversing the usual association of Caribbean natives with cannibalism and savagery. Even when it is not articulated in indigenous languages, modern Caribbean expressive culture abounds with references to native civilization, ranging from the choice by rebel slaves in the former French colony of St. Domingue (the French form of Santo Domingo, early name of Haiti) to reclaim the Taíno word *ayiti* (meaning "mountainous land") as the name of their independent country, to the recurring emphasis on Carib ancestry by the Antiguan writer Jamaica Kincaid, to the Cuban luthist Barbarito Torres's recent declaration in the song "Soy hijo del Siboney" (I'm a son of the Siboney). Such examples are not isolated, and they make it clear that the necessary starting point for any exploration of Caribbean literature is the native Amerindian legacy.

Settlement

Even though native cultures in the archipelago did not reach the level of development seen in Maya, Inca, and Aztec societies, which boasted urbanization, monumental architecture, advanced technology, writing and sciences, and so on, it still is important to view the region as settled at the time of the European incursion. Native arrivals began around 10,000 B.C. with the migration of people from Florida and the Yucatán. These were nomadic hunter-gatherers who lived mostly in the larger islands (latter-day Jamaica, Cuba, Hispaniola, and Puerto Rico) and who became known as Siboney. Much later, during the first century A.D., a second wave of natives moved into the archipelago from the Amazon Basin on the South American mainland. Agriculturally oriented, this second group was directly descended from the Galibi tribe in Guyana. As they blended with the Siboney and came to dominate the islands culturally and politically, members of this second wave were known collectively as Ahuruacos, or Arawaks, a word that means flour-eaters and identifies them with cassava, their main staple food. Subcultures developed at the local level, giving rise to other group names such as Lucayo, Kaketios, Ciguayo, Igneri, and—most numerous in the larger islands—Taíno.

Five centuries before the arrival of Europeans, a third wave of indigenous settlers known as the Caribs moved up from the south. Traditionally viewed as more warlike than the Arawaks, Caribs destroyed most of the male population in the smaller islands of the eastern and southern Caribbean and subjugated the surviving Arawak women. This history of conquest is the reason most often cited to explain the fact that Carib men spoke one language while the women spoke an entirely different language among themselves—one based on the preexisting speech of the Arawaks (Fouchard 1988:41–44). Over time, Carib settlements reached as far north and west as Cuba and Hispaniola, though in the larger islands the pattern was one of coexistence with Taíno inhabitants. Hispaniola (the island that today is Haiti and the Dominican Republic) was, at the time of Columbus's arrival, divided into six *cacicats* (provinces), each one presided over by a *cacique* (chief). Two provinces were Taíno, two Carib, and two mixed Carib-Taíno.

A Template for Regional Culture

Hispaniola is a microcosm of the linguistic and cultural features of native Caribbean civilization. At least three languages were spoken: Carib was split into two branches along gender lines, whereas Taínos spoke their own unique language known as Marcorix. Together, these languages contributed vocabulary that describes important aspects of Caribbean flora (*cassava, guava, calabash*) and fauna (*lambi*, *coqui*, *agouti*), climate (*hurricane*), and material culture (*hammock*).

Although the three languages were distinct, Carib and Taíno people developed important shared features that allow us to speak of a unified or coherent culture of expressive arts. Stone carvings and paintings appear in caves, grottos, and hillsides, throughout Hispaniola and the entire archipelago from Jamaica to Trinidad. And though scholars still debate the precise meaning of these petroglyphs, there is general agreement that the inscriptions are sacred in nature and form part of a fully developed religious practice. The primary tenets of this religion, which was Taíno-Arawak in origin but found Carib adherents as well, revolved around veneration of spirits—referred to variously as *zemi, chemi, cimi,* or *semi*—that reside in the visible world (e.g., in stones, trees, and rivers). Some anthropologists and literary historians have argued that these petroglyphs are the work of an elite group of priest-historians, or *bovites*, and that we should consider such inscriptions the first example of Caribbean writing (Fouchard 1988:37–39, 79–81).

Popular verbal arts found expression in the songs of talented singers known as *sambas*. The cultural equivalent of medieval European troubadours or modern-day calypsonians, the *sambas* composed song-poems known as *areitos*. Examples of *areitos* include love songs, elegies, prayers, and war songs (Fouchard 1988:83–84).

Anthologies of Haitian and Dominican literature often begin with *areitos* such as "The Farewell to Racumon," "The War Song of Caonabo," and "The War Song of Cacique Enrique," none of which can be attributed to a specific composer. The sixteenth-century chronicler Gonzalo Fernández de Oviedo described in detail the music and dance of the Taínos in Hispaniola:

> These people had the good and gentle way of commemorating things past and ancient, which was in song and dance, and they called [*sic*] *areito*. . . . And as their joy and happiness would grow, they would at times join hands and at others go arm-in-arm, and, forming a circle, or ring, of them—man or woman—would take the initiative to lead, and would take certain steps forward and back. (Carpentier 1979:24)

Without question, though, one *samba* did emerge from the indigenous tradition to achieve almost mythological acclaim. This is Anacaona, the Taíno poet-queen. Named from the Taíno words for flower (*ana*) and gold (*caona*), she ruled over the *cacicat* of Xaragua, which had its capital at Yaguana, near the present-day Haitian city of Leogâne. Not only were Anacaona's songs known throughout the island; she was a multimedia performer and patron of the arts who included pantomime and large-scale choreographed pageants with her music and words. She also sponsored lavish feasts to mark seasonal changes and special affairs of state, and it was at one of these feasts marking a visit by the Spanish viceroy Nicolás de Ovando in 1503 that the Taíno hosts were massacred by their Spanish guests and Anacaona was hung from a post outside the smoking ruins of her city.

Sadly, such violence typified the dominant European response to native Caribbean civilization throughout the region. Despite the resulting disruption of indigenous cultural patterns, even this cursory examination reveals that native expressive arts contain many of the same characteristics—multilingualism, the coexistence of elite-based writing and popular-based oral performance genres, and lavish seasonal festivals—that also shape the scene of contemporary Caribbean literature.

The Early Colonial Era: Material Changes and Cultural Adaptation

Written literature in the region draws many of its distinctive images, themes, and political paradoxes from the diplomatic correspondence, travelogues, and histories produced during the first three centuries following 1492. Written for the most part (though not entirely) by Europeans, these texts are important documents in the ongoing project of creolization, or cultural adaptation. Although this adaptive process is comprehensive in scope, we are most concerned with literary aspects of creolization. Often what creolization boils down to from a literary perspective is the refashioning of languages—and, in some cases, the invention of entirely new languages—in order to make them capable of registering the unique social reality of the Caribbean.

Diplomatic Correspondence

The first three centuries of colonial writing in the region can be framed effectively by two texts, Christopher Columbus's "Letter of Columbus on the Discovery of America" (1493) and Toussaint L'Ouverture's "Letter to the French Directory" (1796). Written in April 1493 to the Spanish treasurer, Columbus's letter precedes the publication of his journals and is the first piece of commentary on the Caribbean to appear in Europe. It sets forth in uncanny detail many of the stock images that continue to characterize the region. The climate is Edenic, and Columbus is surprised to find trees that are "green and flourishing" despite having arrived at a time when a European would expect the onset of winter (Columbus 1892:3). Columbus offers a prospectus of the vast natural resources available as a return on the royal investment, including gold, spices, cotton, chewing gum, aloes wood, and "as many slaves for the navy, as their majesties will wish to demand" (Columbus 1892:11). This account establishes the logic of imperial control over Caribbean wealth and resources and shows already the presence of a strongly ingrained assumption that material and human wealth would inevitably flow out of the region. Writing about native inhabitants, Columbus alternates between celebrating the Taíno as noble savages who, for example, "go always naked, just as they came into the world," and depicting Caribbean society as tainted by underdevelopment, ignorance, and superstition (Columbus 1892:4). "They firmly believe," Columbus writes of the Taíno, "that all strength and power, and in fact all good things are in heaven, and that I had come down from thence with these ships and sailors" (Columbus 1892:6). In another passage, which might be seen as the first attempt to record native Caribbean speech, Columbus notes that the Taíno repeatedly proclaim his arrival with the phrase "Come, come and you will see the celestial people" (Columbus 1892:7). In this initial rendering of Caribbean reality, allegations of native ingenuousness underwrite the magical aura ascribed to the region and help to secure the idea of Caribbean dependency on European military, political, economic, and cultural power.

Writing at the other end of the colonial era, and providing a sharp contrast to Columbus, is Toussaint L'Ouverture, a former slave who, during the 1790s, became the preeminent military and governmental leader of St. Domingue, which was the wealthiest French sugar colony and forerunner of the modern nation of Haiti. Toussaint's words reveal that official documents, even in the colonial era, could also voice the aspirations of African and mixed-race Caribbeans for dignity and freedom, thus challenging the assumption of dependence on European control. Penned in November 1796 during the height of the Haitian revolution (1791–1804), Toussaint's "Letter to the French Directory" denounces the scheme of white plantation owners to reinstate slavery, which the French government had abolished by decree in 1794. Adopting the rhetoric of patriotism and revolutionary ideals (liberty, equality, and brotherhood), Toussaint warns the French authorities that former slaves who fought to secure their freedom were willing to die in order to preserve it. While proclaiming loyalty to the "sublime morality" of republican France, Toussaint declares himself a "better father" to the people of the colony than the white planters (L'Ouverture 1989:197, 198). Toussaint's letter suggests that the model for effective leadership is a parent-child relationship, thus echoing the legacy of Columbus and setting the stage for critiques in twentieth-century Caribbean literature of patriarchal and patronizing leadership. At the same time, Toussaint's authoritative address and striking reference to the Caribbean colony as "my country" announce a note of radical Caribbean autonomy and bring colonial writing to the very brink of nationalism.

Travelogues and Histories

Between Columbus and Toussaint, regional expression gradually took shape in a steady stream of histories and travelogues. Initially, these documents were primarily in Spanish, including Columbus's *Diarios* (Diaries, 1493, 1498, 1503); *Brevíssima relación de la destruyción de las Indias* (Short account of the destruction of the Indies, 1542) and the multivolume *Historia de las Indias* (History of the West Indies, 1552) by Bartolomé de las Casas; *Historie del S. D. Fernando Colombo* (Fernando Colon's history of Santo Domingo, 1571) by Columbus's son; and later commentaries such as *Historia geográfica, civil y política de la isla de San Juan Bautista de Puerto Rico* (Geographic, civic, and political history of the island of San Juan Bautista de Puerto Rico, 1788) by Iñigo Abbad y Lasierra and *Viaje a La Habana* (Trip to Havana, 1844), by Condesa de Merlín, among many others.

About a hundred years after Columbus, other Atlantic trading nations—the Netherlands, France, and England—began to challenge Spanish control of the islands, and we can see a corresponding rise in travel writing and histories in other European languages. Though the Dutch were the first to pose a serious threat to Spanish dominance over trade in metals, spices, agriculture, and captive Africans, their literature is comparatively slight in the early colonial period. Even so, two of the inaugural documents in the second wave of colonial historiography, Gaspar Ens's *Indiae Occidentalis historia* (West Indian history, 1612) and Jean de Laet's *Nieuwe Wereldt ofte Beschrijvigne van West Indien* (The New World, or the description of the West Indies [Old Dutch], 1625), are from Dutch writers.

Three monumental French travelogues—*Voyages aux isles de l'Amerique, 1693–1705* (Voyages to the islands of America, 1693–1705) by Jean Baptiste Labat, *Voyage a Saint-Domingue, pendant les annees 1788, 1789 et 1790* (Voyage to St. Domingue during the years 1788, 1789, and 1790) by François Alexandre Stanislaus de Wimpfen, and *Description topographique, physique, civile, politique et historique de la partie francaise de l'isle Saint-Domingue* (translated as A civilization that perished: The last years of white colonial rule in Haiti, 1797) by M. L. E. Moreau de St. Méry—and two histories—*Histoire Général des Isles . . . dans l'Amerique* (translated as Jean-Baptiste DuTertre on the French in St. Croix and the Virgin Islands, 1654) by Jean-Baptiste DuTertre, and *Histoire philosophique et politique des établissements et du commerce des européens dan les deux Indes* (Philosophical and political history of the settlements and trade of the Europeans in the East and West Indies, 1770) by Abbé Guillaume-Thomas-François Raynal—span the era from the mid–seventeenth through the late–eighteenth centuries and chronicle the rise of plantation society in Martinique, Guadeloupe, and St. Domingue. While English-language commentary on the Caribbean began in 1530 with Richard Eden's translation of *The Decades of Peter Martyr*, a Spanish text dealing with Columbus, the British travelogue tradition exploded in the eighteenth and nineteenth centuries with works like Edward Long's *History of Jamaica* (1774), Bryan Edwards's *The History Civil and Commercial of the British West Indies* (1793), and a cluster of volumes by British women travelers, most notably *Lady Nugent's Journal of Her Residence in Jamaica* (1801–1805).

Histories and travelogues provide details about the life of pirates, planters, and petty clerks while offering important, though often hostile, accounts of indigenous culture and, in later centuries, descriptions of the culture of enslaved Africans who, by the seventeenth century, formed the majority population throughout the islands. From a literary perspective, the history and travelogue tradition is significant in five ways. First, colonial texts chart the emerging plantation political economy. In their depictions of the changing regional landscape, historians and traveloguists establish images of gardens and houses that return in the belletristic fiction and poetry of later centuries as emblems of European domination.

Second, histories and travelogues serve as compendia of early literary efforts such as "The Sable Venus," "The Repentant Sailor," and Francis Williams's "Ode," all of which appear in Long's *History of Jamaica*. Williams's verse, composed in Latin in 1759 to honor the Jamaican governor George Haldane and considered by many anthologists to be the first example of poetry by a native of the region, contains several lines that refer to the poet's own status as a black Jamaican, including "Minerva forbids an Aethiop to extol the deeds of generals," and "Nor let it be source of shame to you that you bear a white body in a black skin" (quoted in Boxill 1979:32).

Third, documentary writing by Europeans, even though it is typically hostile to enslaved storytellers, musicians, dancers, and religious leaders, nevertheless provides accounts of popular culture among Africans and Caribbean-born captives of African descent. Moreau's writing on St. Domingue and Long's on Jamaica, for example, contain the first important descriptions of Vodou and Myal, respectively. As Leslie Desmangles, Stephen Glazier, and Joseph Murphy discuss in Chapter 10, both Vodou and Myal are popular religions based on ancestor reverence, spirit possession, and group empowerment; their fully developed rituals focused resistance against the plantation regime and became foundations for national culture in the nineteenth and twentieth centuries.

Fourth, the extensive use of documentary genres anticipates important regional forms such as the slave narrative in the nineteenth century and testimonial narrative in the twentieth century. Finally, Caribbean histories and travelogues have provided grist for literary artists who use these forms as templates for novelistic writing beginning with Aphra Behn's *Oronooko, Or the Royal Slave* (1688) and Daniel Defoe's *Robinson Crusoe* (1717), stretching down to contemporary works by Wilson Harris, Edouard Glissant, Maryse Condé, Rosario Ferré, Edgardo Rodríguez Juliá, and numerous others.

■ The Nineteenth Century: Toward Cultural Autonomy

The success of the Haitian revolution in 1804 inaugurated a new phase in the cultural history of the Caribbean. Whereas writing in the three previous centuries had been produced mostly by Europeans who identified very little with the region, from 1800 on Caribbean literature has been written more and more often by Caribbean people themselves seeking to fully define and celebrate Caribbean settings and identities.

And whereas writers in the early colonial era (pre-1800) were generally hostile to popular culture manifestations, Caribbean writers since then have increasingly sought to narrow the distance between written and popular culture. Indeed, the closer we get to the present moment, the more Caribbean writers see themselves in sympathetic dialogue with, and in many cases as products of, popular culture in all its complexity. The challenge of linking creative writing with popular songs, tales, dances, and so on is more characteristic of twentieth-century Caribbean literature and will be addressed in other sections of this chapter. Here, the focus is on Caribbean writing from the nineteenth century, in particular the contribution of romantic poetry, prose romances, novels, and documentary genres—all of which are linked to the central historical dynamics of abolishing slavery and solidifying independent national identities throughout the region.

Romantic Poetry and Prose

Weakened by the impact of the Napoleonic Wars in Europe, Spain began to lose control over its American empire in the 1810s. The wave of independence movements that swept across South America under the initiative of Simón Bolívar passed through the Caribbean as well. During a period of exile from the mainland, Bolívar penned the famous "Letter from Jamaica" (1814) advocating an integrated, independent Latin America. He subsequently sought refuge in independent Haiti and received money, arms, and a printing press from Haitian President Alexandre Pétion. In 1821 Spanish colonists in the eastern part of Hispaniola declared the formation of the Dominican Republic. Independence sentiments were brewing as well in Cuba and Puerto Rico, though in all three islands the struggle for national liberation would occupy the better part of the century and would be, in many respects, an unfulfilled quest.

Along with the political and economic aspects of nation-formation, Caribbean people faced the cultural challenge of unifying groups divided by racial, class, and other antagonisms into a coherent national community. Writers struggled against isolation, censorship, and (particularly in the case of white Caribbean writers) their own racial chauvinism. Despite such obstacles, writers found numerous ways to play their part in initiating the process of unification. The Cuban poet Plácido penned "Despida a mi madre" (Farewell to my mother) hours before being executed in 1844 for his part in an independence plot. Plácido was a mulatto who had been abandoned at birth by his white mother, and his final words reach out across the color line with a message that combines revolutionary conviction and antisentimental feelings:

"*moro en la gloria, / Y mi plácida lira á tu memoria / Lanza en la tumba su postrer sonido* (I calmly go to a death that is glory-filled, / My lyre before it is forever stilled / Breathes out to thee its last and dying note)" (Plácido 1959:294).

Plácido's great successor at the end of the century is José Martí, who reanimated the themes of national reconciliation and Cuban autonomy. But whereas Plácido adopts the style of romanticism to convey his message, Martí's *Versos Libres* (Free verses) and *Versos Sencillos* (Simple verses) bring Spanish Caribbean poetry to the brink of modernism. Martí's lines are unrhymed, he employs a variety of meters other than the traditional ten-syllable foot, and his poetry focuses on symbols and objects in the world—for example, a *rosa blanca* (white rose) offered as a token of universal solidarity—in contrast to romantic writers' emphasis on exalted individual states of consciousness at odds with limiting social conditions.

Martí's contemporary in the Dominican Republic is Salomé Ureña de Henríquez. Recognized, like Martí, as the *musa de la patria* (national poet), and the author of an epic volume celebrating Anacaona, Ureña is most well known for lyric poems such as "A la patria" (To the homeland), "A Quisqueya" (To Quisqueya), and "La fe en el porvenir" (Faith in the future) that combined romantic nationalist fervor with an emphasis on positivism and ideals of rationality and progress. Ureña also evinces romantic style by exploring intimate emotions in poems such as "Melancolía" (Melancholy), "Angustias" (Anguish), "Tristezas" (Sadness), and "Amor y anhelo" (Love and desire).

Even more than poetry, the prose romance stands out as a key literary contribution to the development of nineteenth-century national culture, particularly in the Spanish-speaking countries. In addition to providing a birth-of-the-nation story, national romances usually feature ideal character types who represent the major divisions in a given society. When depicted as lovers whose desire reaches across such divisions, the characters' stories help consolidate national communities by imaginatively moving toward resolution of social conflict. Although typically associated with texts such as Anselmo Suárez-Romero's *Francisco* (1839) and Cirilo Villaverde's *Cecilia Valdés* (1839) from Cuba, and Manuel de Jésus de Gálvan's *Enriquillo* (1882) from the Dominican Republic, the national-romance genre also appears in Haiti, where the prose tradition begins with Emeric Bergeaud's *Stella* (1859). Interestingly, where Spanish Caribbean national romances present stories of romantic coupling, *Stella* uses the courtship theme to frame a story of fraternal strife in which two brothers, Romulus, a mulatto, and Remus, a black, vie for the affections of Stella, a white woman who symbolizes the spirit of the French Revolution transplanted in Haiti. In Bergeaud's text, resolution comes not from erotic coupling but rather from the brothers' reconciliation.

Interwoven with the national question—sometimes enhancing and sometimes impeding the push toward independence—was the fight to abolish slavery. Suárez-Romero's *Francisco*, for example, is a proabolition story whose ideal characters play out a love triangle that includes Dorotea, a tragic mulatto, Francisco, a noble black man too refined for the harsh regime of Cuban slavery, and Ricardo, a supremely bestial white planter. Against a real-life backdrop of constant slave revolts and fear that Cuba would become a second Haiti, Suarez-Romero depicts his enslaved lovers as docile martyrs, yet even this was too much for Spanish censors, who suppressed the novel for decades.

In the English-speaking islands, there is a parallel stream of novels that address the problem of slavery and its abolition. Typically, texts such as the anonymously authored *The Adventures of Jonathan Corncob* (1787), *Montgomery, or The West Indian Adventurer* (1812, 1813), *Hamel, the Obeah Man* (1827), and *Marley, or the Life of a Planter in Jamaica* (1828), as well as J. W. Orderson's *Creoloana* (1842), do not follow the prose romance pattern but instead adopt formulas such as the picaresque (*Bildungsroman*). Nineteenth-century nationalist and abolitionist fiction is written almost exclusively by European sojourners or Caribbeans of European descent, and one thing these texts share is a tendency—inherited from the historians and traveloguists—to represent plantation society from the point of view of white planters, even when depicting the brutality of the system and presenting calls to reform or dismantle it.

Documentary Genres

The voices of native Caribbean writers of color emerge primarily through documentary writing during the nineteenth century. Although their chosen genres and points of view on Caribbean society are very different from the European-authored texts, nonfiction writers such as Juan Francisco Manzano, Mary Prince, Jean-Baptiste Philippe, and J. J. Thomas are equally immersed in the social currents of abolition and nationalism. One of the most important texts in nineteenth-century Cuban literature is Manzano's *Autobiografía de un esclavo* (Autobiography of a slave, 1835). Born into slavery, Manzano, against the interdictions of his owners, teaches himself to read and write and escapes with the assistance of the del Monte group, an alliance of mostly white abolitionist thinkers and writers. With the proceeds from his own writings, Manzano purchases his own freedom, and at the behest of Domingo del Monte he writes a denunciation of slavery. His autobiography narrates a relatively pleasant childhood as a privileged, well-dressed slave belonging to a wealthy mistress. However, this carefree youth is in stark contrast to his adolescence and early adult life, when ownership is transferred to a new mistress, under whom he suffers continual torture and sadistic treatment. Manzano's *Autobiography* can be considered a founding text in Cuban writing, insofar as it laid the groundwork for combining a personal testimonial expression with a rhetorical denunciation of an inhumane institution that earned for both the genre and the author a lasting and universal appeal. Editions of Manzano's *Autobiography* in both the original Spanish and in translation are still printed today; and it seems clear that the text that marks the modern renaissance of the testimonial genre, Miguel Barnet's *Biografía de un Cimarrón* (Biography of a Maroon), was inspired by Manzano's title.

Building on the tradition of Olaudah Equiano, whose best-selling autobiography, *Equiano's Travels* (1789), included lengthy firsthand accounts of slavery in the Caribbean, Mary Prince's *The History of Mary Prince, a West Indian Slave, Related by Herself* (1831) exposed the slave experience from a black woman's point of view for the first time. Appearing in Britain precisely at the moment when the debate over abolition was reaching a climax, Prince's narrative went through three editions in one year. It caused an uproar in the press, the courts, and Parliament in the years immediately preceding the passage of an emancipation bill in 1834.

Apart from this historical and political significance, *The History of Mary Prince* is an important literary document for at least four reasons. First, it conveys a pan-Caribbean sentiment in the sense that Prince moves throughout the islands, from her birthplace in Bermuda to Turks Island and, finally, Antigua before moving to England in 1828. Each place—even the hideous salt mine in Turks Island—is described vividly and invested with great emotional attachment.

Second, the author's final destination is England, and in her expressions of nostalgia for the family and places left behind, as well as the realization that only outside the Caribbean is it possible to gain freedom and a public voice, Prince anticipates the predicament and sentiments of émigré writers from later generations. Third, her narrative casts typical Caribbean themes of displacement, hardship, resistance, and verbal wit within the framework of a woman's story. Not only does this make clear how racialized violence and the fight against it are, for black women, waged over sexuality; it also lays the groundwork for discussing a tradition of women's writing in the Caribbean.

Finally, even though Prince's story is filtered through the mediating figures of a British woman scribe and an abolitionist editor, and even though this fact raises the problem of authentic voice, idiomatic Caribbean expressions nevertheless break through. For example, Prince spent many days in the stocks as punishment for her verbal rejoinders to white Antiguans, and when she protests against excessive bondage with the complaint that the British in the Caribbean "moor them up like cattle," Prince takes an important step toward discovering a distinctive Caribbean voice in writing.

In a Trinidadian context, Jean-Baptiste Philippe's *Free Mulatto* (1824) defended the position of free persons of color by asserting that "the colored population of Trinidad have the same civil and political privileges with their white fellow-subjects." Though Baptiste did not go so far as to call for the emancipation of enslaved blacks, his appeal challenged the regime of color prejudice that, he claimed, had worsened when the island passed from French to British rule in 1802. Thomas's *The Theory and Practice of Creole Grammar* (1869), and *Froudacity, or West Indian Fables Explained* (1889), continue the development of Trinidadian cultural identity in the period after emancipation. Like Philippe (and Prince, for that matter), Thomas begins both books as a protest against a particular form of British imperialism, but each title ultimately impresses the reader less as a protest against colonial tyranny than as an affirmation of the Caribbean self. Particularly in the final section of *Creole Grammar*, which contains a long list of Creole proverbs, we can see the author's love for and appreciation of vernacular expressions like *même baton qui batte chein noèr la pé batte chein blanc la* (the same stick that beats the black dog can beat the white). Such expressions, Thomas claims, "prove that the Africans are not, after all, the dolts and intellectual sucklings some would have the world believe them. . . . These applications are usually so truthful and ingenious that they are worth volumes of comments and laboured definitions" (Thomas 1989:121). While the political drama of decolonization plays out more fully in the twentieth century, it is clear from all of the nineteenth-century documents that the cultural struggle toward independence was well under way and that the voices of Caribbean majority populations were beginning to surface in literary texts.

■ The Early Twentieth Century: Literary Movements, Vernacular Writing, and Cultural Unification

The first four decades of the twentieth century are characterized by an increasing confluence of popular and elite cultural activity.

Popular Culture and the Rise of Caribbean Literary Movements

In the wake of emancipation, which came in the 1830s for English-administered islands, the 1840s for French territories (Napoleon had reinstated slavery after the 1794 emancipation), the 1860s for Dutch, and the 1870s and 1880s for Spanish, changing economic structures resulted in the arrival of new populations from outside the region, including indentured labor from India, China, and Java, and free rather than slave labor from Africa. Britain also effected population transfers between various islands to manage labor crises and social unrest. Against the backdrop of such restructuring, Caribbean societies felt more than ever the shaping force of popular songs, dances, public speaking styles, and religious practices.

Sacred culture was pivotal in decisive moments of social upheaval, including the Haitian slave revolt, which started with a Vodou ceremony presided over by Boukman and an unnamed woman priestess. Jamaica, too, had a history of militant uprisings being kicked off by religious leaders, including the so-called Sam Sharpe Rebellion in 1831 and the Morant Bay Rebellion in 1865, which were inspired by Baptist ministers Sam Sharpe and Paul Bogle, respectively.

Secular popular culture also grew in scope throughout the latter nineteenth century. For example, carnival celebrations in Trinidad assumed much of their modern form during the period 1840–1900 and combined the dances of preemancipation French Creole slave society (especially the calinda song form and dance style), with national dances brought by groups of liberated Africans after emancipation, songs and dances of Anglophone migrants from Barbados and elsewhere, and the seasonal festivities of the old planter class that had traditionally celebrated with concerts, dancing, and picnics from Christmas until Ash Wednesday. Trinidadian carnival synthesized all these elements into an ensemble of marching bands, stickfighting, verbal boasting, and satiric songs (Rohlehr 1990:1–42). Even when carnival became a vehicle for expressing social strife, as in the famous Canboulay riot of 1881, it came closer than anything else to encompassing all strata of island life. Although the evolution of Trinidadian carnival is unique, it does indicate the potential of popular culture throughout the region to integrate societies that had been fragmented and divided under plantation slavery.

At the same time that popular practices were stamping their imprint on Caribbean societies, elite groups were emerging everywhere in the region to form salons and little reviews between 1900 and 1940. Thomas MacDermot, editor of the *Jamaica Times,* created the All Jamaica Library publishing series from 1905 to 1909; H. G. DeLisser edited Jamaica's principal newspaper, *The Gleaner,* from 1904 until his death in 1944 and issued annual editions of *Planter's Punch* beginning in 1920; Esther Chapman founded the *West Indian Review* in 1934, O. T. Fairclough launched *Public Opinion* in 1937, and Edna Manley directed *Focus*, a cultural spin-off of *Public Opinion*, beginning in 1943. All these journals appeared in Jamaica, which (with the possible exception of Haiti) witnessed the greatest quantity and quality of literary activity in the region before 1940 (Cobham-Sander 1981:64–108). Alfred Mendes, C. L. R. James, Albert Gomes, and others formed the Beacon Group in Trinidad, where they produced two journals, *Trinidad* and *The Beacon.* Jacques Roumain and others founded the indigenous movement as well as numerous journals such as *La Revue Indigène* (The indigenous review), *La Relève* (Relief), and *La Trouée* (Opening) in Haiti; in Cuba the *Revista de Avance* (Advance review), Gustavo E. Urutilla's column Ideales de Una Raza (Ideals of a race) in the Havana daily *El Diaro de la Marina*, and the Club Atenas salon all helped to organize literary culture and promote the efforts of poets Nicolás Guillén, Regino Pedroso, and others.

Self-consciously literary in a way that had very little precedent (the Domingo del Monte salon that produced Suárez-Romero and Villaverde in nineteenth-century Cuba is perhaps the only earlier example), these elite groups sought to codify and analyze popular culture and to develop distinctive literary expressions based on popular forms, including songs, proverbs in creole, and animal tales featuring Anancy the Spider, Compère Lapin (Br'er Rabbit), Frog and Scorpion, and more. In the poem, "L'atlas a menti" (The atlas lied), which appeared in a 1927 issue of *La Revue Indigène*, Haitian writer Philippe Thoby-Marcelin summons the folkloric character of Bouqui. Though typically depicted as a dull-witted peasant who falls prey to the sly trickster Ti Malice, Marcelin's Bouqui speaks completely in creole and becomes an icon of inassimilable resistance, exclaiming to the other figure depicted in the poem, an alienated, French-speaking Haitian schoolboy:

> *Dèhiè mônes gains mônes / HEIN? / Et lan cate-là / Blancs-yo fait Haiti piti/con-ça* / (Behind the mountains are more mountains / EH? / And that's how / the foreigners make Haiti so small / with their maps).

Similar experiments with writing poetry based on popular speech can be found in texts such as *Motivos de son* (Son motives, 1930), *Songoro Cosongo* (1931), and *West Indies, Ltd.* (1934), by Guillén in Cuba; *Tuntun de pasa y grifería* (1937) by Luis Pales-Matos in Puerto Rico; and *Constab Ballads* (1912) and *Songs of Jamaica* (1912) by Claude McKay, who published these volumes of dialect poetry in Jamaica with encouragement and support from MacDermot and others before moving to the United States and eventually becoming associated with the Harlem renaissance school. Within the same milieu of salons and little reviews, Caribbean prose writers were developing fictional equivalents of dialect poetry. Such efforts ranged from, on the one hand, the work of Mendes, James, and DeLisser, all of whom embedded creole-voiced characters within standard (i.e., British) English narration, to, on the other hand, creative renderings of folk storytelling presented entirely in dialect. Examples of this latter type of writing appeared in the 1930s under the signature Wona in the Jamaican-based *West Indian Review*.

Viewed in a larger social and political perspective, the literature generated by the salons and little reviews points in three ways to intensifying anticolonial dynamics throughout the region. First, by deliberately promoting the incorporation of popular speech in written literary expression, these writers—even when they adhered to European or North American ideas of cultural excellence—enhanced literary creolization as a process of autonomous cultural development.

Second, salons, little reviews, and the movements associated with them addressed explicitly and implicitly the relationship of intellectuals and masses, as, for example, in the fiction produced by the Trinidadian writers of the Beacon Group. James and Mendes both project a hierarchical concept of this relationship by granting more authority to their frame narrators, who represent the observing Caribbean intellectual and whose standard English creates distance from working-class, dialect-speaking characters. Even here, though, such depictions produce a sort of freeze-frame image of divisions in society. Reproducing intellectual elitism this way in print did not in itself solve the problem of social stratification, but it could and in some cases did open up the possibility of critical awareness and the search for alliances among writers and mass groups.

Third, the by-product of thinking about such alliances was typically movement toward a more unified national culture and heightened resistance to outside domination. The tone of such resistance ranged from extreme anti-U.S. sentiments in Haiti, where U.S. Marine forces had occupied the country beginning in 1915, to the more conservative desire to achieve cultural autonomy (rather than outright independence) expressed by Jamaican writers associated with the Jamaica Poetry League, *Planter's Punch*, and *West Indian Review*, with other islands and movements falling somewhere in between these two poles. Particularly as a strong labor movement developed in the 1930s, and as mass strikes broke out on island after island in the years preceding World War II, critical responses to literary experiments helped intellectuals to understand sympathetically and collaborate with popular movements, thus ameliorating some of the fragmentation and stratification in Caribbean society.

■ The Mid–Twentieth Century: The Dialectic of Exile and Nationalism

The two decades from the end of World War II to the mid-1960s mark a period of unprecedented breakthroughs in the writing, publishing, and worldwide reception of Caribbean literature. Ironically, it was the very experience of exile and migration out of the region that resulted in writers like Aimé Césaire, Mayotte Capécia, Edouard Glissant, Joseph Zobel, Alejo Carpentier, Una Marson, Louise Bennett, Samuel Selvon, V. S. Naipaul, George Lamming, Wilson Harris, and Derek Walcott gaining exposure to printing presses, theaters, radio stations, and other cultural resources located in metropolitan centers like London and Paris. National culture, then, seemed to reach its highest pitch precisely at the moment when Caribbean people, writers included, were leaving the islands in unprecedented numbers.

The dialectic of exile and nationalism was prompted in part by economics, particularly the lack of opportunities at home and the need to enlist Caribbean labor in the rebuilding of war-devastated European countries. In part, too, there was political fallout from a United Nations postwar mandate to dismantle colonial empires. This mandate created a feedback loop that quickened the progress toward regional autonomy that had been made by oil workers, miners, and farm labor during the strikes and agitation of the 1930s. In addition to political and economic developments, there were, as in the previous century, important cultural factors in the push toward nationalism. Even in cases such as Martinique and Guadeloupe, where the end of colonial status did not lead to national independence, cultural nationalism still supplied one of the major premises for moving beyond old-style colonialism.

Negritude

As a matter of cultural history, the literary outburst across the Caribbean that helped articulate nationalist consciousness featured new movements such as Negritude in the Francophone societies, *negrismo* in Cuba and Puerto Rico, *Wie eége sanie* (Our own things) for Sranan-Togo writers in Suriname, and the Caribbean Artists Movement for Anglophone writers based in London. An important part of the literary infrastructure for such movements was the consolidation of journals and reviews. Negritude, for example, is often described as having sprung from the group of Caribbean and African writers who met as students in Paris and collaborated on the journal *Etudiant Noir* (Black student) (1934). Poetry volumes by two members of this group quickly followed. *Pigments* (1937), by Guyanese poet Leon Gontran Damas, and *Cahier d'un retour au pays natal* (Notebook of a return to my native land) (1939), by Martinican poet Aimé Césaire both denounce the French idea of colonialism as a civilizing mission. Damas and Césaire focus instead on the political violence of the slave trade—"How many of ME ME ME / have died / SINCE THEN / since they came that night" writes Damas in "Ils sont venus ce soir" (They came that night) (*The Negritude Poets* 1989:45)—the psychological violence of identity crises experienced by colonial subjects (*Dans cette ville inerte, cette foule désolée sous le soleil, ne participant à rien de ce qui s'exprime, s'affirme, se libère au grand jour de cette terre sienne* (In this inert town, this desolate throng under the sun, not connected with anything that is expressed, asserted, released in broad earth daylight, its own) writes Césaire in *Cahier* (Césaire 1983:36–37), and positive reevaluations of African past and Caribbean present.

With the founding of *Présence Africaine* in 1948 as a quarterly journal and printing press located in Paris under the direction of the Senegalese editor Alioune Diop, Negritude was able to consolidate itself as a transcontinental movement of black intellectuals. Composed of Caribbean figures such as Césaire, Damas, Frantz Fanon, Edouard Glissant, Jacques Stephen Alexis, René Depestre, and (somewhat later) Maryse Condé, and African figures such as Leopold Sedar Senghor, David Diop, Tchicaya U Tam'si, Jean-Joseph Rabérivelo, and Jacques Rabémananjara, *Présence Africaine* issued its review, published books by writers associated with the group, and sponsored important international meetings dedicated to promoting the goal of decolonization and recognition of African culture as a civilizing presence globally. Although Negritude as an ideology has for the most part been supplanted by newer concepts such as Caribbeanness and creolization, its importance as a cultural and political catalyst in the Caribbean cannot be overstated.

The Caribbean Artists Movement

Among English-speaking Caribbean writers from the same generation, the infrastructure of journals and literary movements was somewhat more dispersed than in the case of Negritude. Toward the end of the period we are considering here, however, a nucleus of writers and artists formed in London under the banner of the Caribbean Artists Movement. The foundations for a movement began in the 1940s with establishment of the creative journals *Bim* (1942), edited in Barbados by Frank Collymore, and *Kyk-over-al* (1945), edited in Guyana by A. J. Seymour, along with the scholarly review *Caribbean Quarterly* (1948), published by the University of the West Indies, which regularly featured creative writing along with analytic pieces on regional history, politics, and culture.

Unlike earlier Caribbean-based journals that had short runs, these reviews appeared steadily throughout the 1950s and 1960s, as did *Caribbean Voices* (1946), a BBC radio series that began as "the brainchild of the Jamaican poet Una Marson" (Cobham-Sander 1981:102). Broadcast out of London under the direction of Henry Swanzy, this show featured interviews and readings of creative works and is credited in accounts by George Lamming, V. S. Naipaul, and others as providing another important outlet for émigré writers.

In 1966, New Beacon Books, a store managed by Trinidadian poet and labor activist John La Rose, became the focal point for the Caribbean Artists Movement. The various projects born in the context of this movement included theoretical discussions of creole culture, "which is born in the West Indies and which contains non-European forms in large numbers" (Elsa Goveia, quoted in Walmsley 1992:97), conventional literary responses—La Rose also operated a printing press, New Beacon Press, that published many new volumes of poetry and prose—artistic forays into new media, exploration of new venues for art exhibits, poetry readings and conferences, Marina Maxwell's Yard Theatre in Jamaica, and numerous other developments designed to ensure that "Caribbean art, particularly its revolutionary new forms, would reach and activate a new range and generation of people" (Walmsley 1992:305).

The Caribbean Artists Movement typifies the dialectic of exile and nationalism because from its exiled grounding in London it reached deliberately back to inspire and conspire with specific local projects in Trinidad,

Guyana, Jamaica, the United States, and Canada. It thus summed up the cultural nationalist efforts that had been accumulating for a generation among displaced and itinerant Caribbean writers while also signaling a move beyond nationalism in the directions of pan-Caribbean regionalism and strengthening diasporic sensibilities.

A Boom in Caribbean Novels

The history of the first two postwar decades has been presented through the framing moments of Negritude and the Caribbean Artists Movement, both of which were poetry-centered to a large extent. It is important to note before continuing, though, that this period of intense nationalist ferment is most remarkable in literary terms for the unprecedented number of excellent Caribbean novels published across the board in French, Spanish, and English. Cuba and the Cuban revolution was an especially creative force for the novel in the 1960s. Alejo Carpentier, who had led the way into the well-known boom in Latin American fiction with *El reino de este mundo* (The kingdom of this world, 1949), published *El siglo de las luces* (Explosion in a cathedral) in 1962. Carpentier was followed by other Spanish Caribbean writers. José Lezama Lima published his astounding and controversial epic *Paradiso* in 1968, and Reinaldo Arenas's *El mundo alucinante* (The hallucinatory world, translated as The ill-fated peregrinations of Fray Servando, 1965) predated and anticipated many of the techniques of so-called magical realism. Another classic of the boom, *Tres tristes tigres* (Three trapped tigers, 1967), was written by a Cuban author-in-exile, Guillermo Cabrera Infante.

An important Puerto Rican writer from the period is Pedro Juan Soto, who, along with hosts of musicians from the island who went on to forge the salsa style, lived in New York and was one of the first Puerto Rican writers to incorporate this migratory and multilingual experience into his writing. His works include *Spiks* (1956) and *Usmaíl* (U.S. Mail, 1959). Many Caribbean critics also claim the great novel *Cien años de soledad* (One hundred years of solitude, 1968) by Nobel laureate Gabriel García Márquez as a Caribbean novel because the mythical city of Macondo is located on the Caribbean coast.

In French, Haitian writer Jacques Roumain published *Gouverneurs de la rosée* (Masters of the dew, 1944), which is still the definitive attempt to depict Haitian culture in terms of the peasant majority. Haiti traditionally has been rich in literary production, and Roumain's novel was followed by numerous efforts to explore national culture and history, including Jacques-Stephen Alexis's *Compère Général Soleil* (Comrade General Sun, 1955), *Les arbres musiciens* (The musician trees, 1994), and *L'Espace d'un cillement* (The blink of an eye, 1957); and Marie Chauvet's *La Danse sur le volcan* (Dance on the volcano, 1959) and *Fonds des nègres* (Black valleys, 1960). In Martinique, Mayotte Capécia's *Je suis Martiniquaise* (I am a Martinican woman, 1946) and *La negresse blanche* (The white negress, 1948); Joseph Zobel's *Diab'-la* (The devil, 1946) and *La Rue Cases-Nègres* (Black Shack Alley, 1950); and Edouard Glissant's *La lézarde* (The ripening, 1959) and *Le quatrième siècle* (The fourth century, 1964) all deal with the dilemmas of colonization, racial awakening, and historical consciousness.

Among Anglophone writers, H. G. DeLisser's *Jane's Career* (1914) and A. R. F. Webber's *Those That Be in Bondage* (1917) show some concern with defining local culture in Jamaica and Guyana, respectively. But the real run in cultural nationalist novels might be said to have begun in the 1930s with Claude McKay's *Banana Bottom* (1933), Alfred Mendes's *Pitch Lake* (1934) and *Black Fauns* (1935), and C. L. R. James's *Minty Alley* (1936). During the postwar period, the list of novels that imagine, define, and celebrate the contours of specific island settings is impressive and includes, in Trinidad, Ralph DeBoissiere's *Crown Jewel* (1952) and *Rum and Coca Cola* (1956), Samuel Selvon's *A Brighter Sun* (1952) and *Turn Again, Tiger* (1958), and V. S. Naipaul's *The Mystic Masseur* (1957), *The Suffrage of Elvira* (1958), *Miguel Street* (1959), and *A House for Mr. Biswas* (1961); in Jamaica, V. S. Reid's *New Day* (1949), Roger Mais's *The Hills Were Joyful Together* (1953), *Brother Man* (1954), and *Black Lightning* (1955), John Hearne's *Voices Under the Window* (1955), *Strangers at the Gate* (1956), and *The Land of the Living* (1961), Andrew Salkey's *A Quality of Violence* (1959), Sylvia Wynter's *The Hills of Hebron* (1962), and Orlando Patterson's *The Children of Sisyphus* (1964); in Barbados, George Lamming's *In the Castle of My Skin* (1953), *Of Age and Innocence* (1958), and *Season of Adventure* (1960); and in Guyana, Edgar Mittleholzer's *Corentyne Thunder* (1941), *A Morning at the Office* (1950), *Children of Kaywana* (1952), *Kaywana Blood* (1958), and *Thunder Returning* (1960), Jan Carew's *Black Midas* (1958), *The Wild Coast* (1958), and *The Last Barbarian* (1961), and Wilson Harris's *Palace of the Peacock* (1960), *The Far Journey of Oudin* (1961), *The Whole Armour* (1962), and *The Secret Ladder* (1963). The foregoing list ranges widely in terms of narrative approach, emphasis on particular social groups (black, white, colored, East Indian, peasant, worker, planter, merchant, etc.), and projection of physical settings (Guyanese novels, for example, tend to convey a strong sense of the immense South American landscape that is absent in fiction set in the more limited physical space of islands). What they all share, however, is an affirmation of some aspect of local Caribbean reality.

■ The Late Twentieth Century and Beyond: The Dialectic of Return and Disillusionment

Inspired by political developments such as the birth of the West Indies Federation (1958) and the ousting of U.S.-backed dictators in Cuba (1959) and the Dominican Republic (1961), many writers, artists, and intellectuals were returning to the region, literally as well as symbolically, even before the wave of national culture reached its peak in the mid-1960s. Perhaps inevitably, the idealism of homecoming clashed with the reality of enduring social divisions, political corruption, and economic dependence. Against a historical backdrop that included the breakup of the West Indies Federation in 1962 due to interisland rivalries, increasing restraints on free expression in Cuba after 1968, continuing problems of brutal dictatorship in Haiti and the Dominican Republic, and nagging dissatisfaction about the dependent status of Puerto Rico and French Caribbean territories, Caribbean literature from the past three decades has continued to express the desire for autonomy. At the same time, writers have posed radical questions about lingering barriers to full integration and liberation within single islands and the region as a whole.

If the previous period was shaped by a dialectic of exile and nationalism, the most recent decades have been shaped by a new dialectic of return and disillusionment. The complexity of this dynamic is evident in "The Spoiler's Return," a poem by the Nobel laureate Derek Walcott from his 1981 collection *The Fortunate Traveller*. Set in Port-of-Spain, Trinidad, "high on this bridge in Laventille" (Walcott 1992:432), Walcott adopts the persona of Spoiler (Theophilus Phillips), a calypso king in 1953 and 1955, deceased in 1960, who was renowned for surreal, Kafkaesque lyrics featuring brain transplants, space travel, and irretrievable bank deposits (Rohlehr 1990:464–474).

Thematically, the poem follows in the calypso tradition of biting social critique, as Spoiler, upon his return from the grave, surveys the spectacle of postindependence decay. Objects singled out for commentary include unscrupulous business elites described as "sharks with shirt-jacs, sharks with well-pressed fins / ripping off we small-fry with razor grins," murderous politicians "who promise free and just debate / then blow up radicals to save the state" (a reference to the 1981 assassination of historian and labor organizer Walter Rodney in Guyana), the once-popular Trinidadian prime minister, Eric Williams, whose disdain for the people is captured with the line "those with hearing aids turn off the truth," and finally the general apathy that Spoiler attacks with the prediction that "all you go bawl out, 'Spoils, things ain't so bad.' / This ain't the Dark Ages, is just Trinidad" (Walcott 1992:433–434).

Against this scene of social decay, Spoiler's ghost becomes the perfect vehicle for protest, denunciation, and renewal with the claim, "I decompose, but I composin still" (Walcott 1992:432). Stylistically, Walcott embeds his social critique in the rhyming couplets utilized by calypsonians, signaling a primary identification with popular form. At the same time, he skillfully suggests a wider literary linkage by having Spoiler claim kinship with classical and neoclassical satirists Martial, Juvenal, and Pope, as well as his notoriously dyspeptic compatriot, V. S. Naipaul, whom Walcott-Spoiler dubs "V. S. Nightfall" (Walcott 1992:433).

The Influence of Popular Forms: Music, Film, and Drama

Walcott's immersion in calypso rhythms and rhetoric is indicative of a much broader process in the most recent decades of Caribbean literature, which is an intensification of links with popular cultural forms. Walcott's contemporary and peer, Kamau Brathwaite, has incorporated the faster rhythms of calypso as well as the slower Dread beats of reggae in his numerous volumes of poetry. In *History of the Voice* (1984), Brathwaite has theorized the practice of basing poetry on vernacular speech (including song), suggesting that the fundamental meter of Caribbean speech is dactylic in contrast to the iambic meter of British English (Brathwaite 1984:17). A younger generation of performance, or dub, poets has taken the linkage with music even farther. Artists such as Linton Kwesi Johnson, Michael Smith, Oku Onoru, Mutabaruka, and Binta Breeze have produced records and CDs on which they chant and sing their verse with backing from top-flight musicians. In prose writing, too, music has often been used in recent years to signal cultural resistance and recovery from cultural alienation. In Rosario Ferré's "Maldito amor" (literally, "cursed love," translated as "Sweet diamond dust," 1986), the title is taken directly from a nineteenth-century Puerto Rican composition and reflects the tortured interwoven histories of rich, poor, black, and white; the final vignette uses the clash between gangs favoring salsa and rock to symbolize rival political stances. Liliane Dévieux's heroine, in the short story "Piano-Bar" (1988), recovers a sense of her Haitianness and Caribbeanness by dancing to Dominican merengue and listening to "Haiti chérie," which evokes "the waves and undulations of the sea of the Antilles, the contours of our island, the bulging shapes of our mountains" (Dévieux 1991:74).

Cinema, as well as music, has had a significant impact on popular and literary culture in the contemporary Caribbean. Cuban film, throughout the postrevolution era, has set consistently high standards both in quantity and quality. The work of Tomás Gutiérrez Alea, in particular, has been influential far beyond the local scene. His films range from *Memorias del subdesarrollo* (Memories of underdevelopment, 1968), *La muerte de un burócrata* (Death of a bureaucrat, 1966), and *Guantanamera* (1996), which offer biting critiques of intellectuals and bureaucratic absurdity, to *La última cena* (The last supper, 1976), a historical drama depicting a slave revolt on a colonial plantation, to *Fresa y chocolate* (Strawberry and chocolate, 1993), a comedy addressing the problem of homophobia and censorship. As elsewhere in the world, Caribbean cinema has included film versions of literary classics, including *El otro francisco* (1975, dir. Sergio Giral), a brilliant commentary on Suárez-Romero's 1839 novel *Francisco*; *Sugar Cane Alley* (1983, dir. Euzhan Palcy), a faithful rendering of Joseph Zobel's coming-of-age novel *La Rue Cases-Nègres;* and *The Orchid House* (1994, dir. Horace Ové), a six-hour miniseries for BBC based on Phyllis Shand Allfrey's novel. In one celebrated instance, the adaptation process worked in reverse, with Michael Thelwell's excellent novelization of the Jamaican cinema classic *The Harder They Come* (1972, dir. Perry Henzel).

Caribbean drama has also felt the impact of modern-day movements toward vernacular language and popular audiences. There has been a definite—though sporadic—arthouse theater scene in the region from the time of colonial St. Domingue down to the contemporary period with plays by Derek Walcott such as *The Sea at Dauphin* (1954) and *Ti Jean and His Brothers* (1958), as well as works by Aimé Césaire such as *La tragedie du Roi Christophe* (The tragedy of King Christophe, 1963) and *Une tempêste* (A tempest, 1970). René Marqués (1929–1979) is Puerto Rico's most well known playwright (as well as an important essayist); his *La carreta* (The oxcart, 1953) was another groundbreaking work that examined the conditions leading to the mass exodus of Puerto Ricans to New York. More recent decades, though, have seen the emergence of popular theater projects, beginning with Yard Theatre (mentioned above in the context of the Caribbean Artists Movement), Marina Maxwell's effort to produce theater by, for, and about the poor in Kingston, Jamaica. Also in Jamaica, drama has been used with great effectiveness as a tool of popular education and women's development by the Sistren Theater Collective. The success of Sistren extends not only to workshops on women's health, economic empowerment, and sex roles but also to video productions and a crucial volume of testimonial writing, *Lionheart Gal: Life Stories of Jamaican Women* (1987).

These significant developments in music, film, and drama, along with written literature produced in response to such popular forms, represented another attempt on the part of writers to work through the dialectic of return and disillusionment. Even as the experience of returning to the region has confronted artists and intellectuals with troubling examples of political and business leaders disconnected from the suffering majority, a large part of the creative response has been to push recent Caribbean writing ever closer to the majority voices by incorporating and responding to popular cultural forms.

The Achievement of Caribbean Women Writers

Unquestionably, the modern era is one in which women writers increasingly have come to define the field of Caribbean literature. The emergence of women (one is tempted to call it a *reemergence*, given the historical prominence of Anacaona, Prince, Ureña, Marson, Bennett, Rhys, and others) is a phenomenon witnessed across the language groups. Recent anthologies of Caribbean women's writing like *Creation Fire*, *Green Cane and Juicy Flotsam*, *Her True-True Name*, and *The Whistling Bird* represent the transnational trend by including, in English-language publications, work from Francophone writers such as Mayotte Capécia, Marie-Thérèse Colimon-Hall, Marie Chauvet, Maryse Condé, Jacqueline Manicom, Simone Schwarz-Bart, Jan J. Dominique, and Edwidge Danticat (the latter two are Haitian writers who compose and publish primarily in English). Anglophone women writers include Erna Brodber, Michelle Cliff, Ramabai Espinet, Beryl Gilroy, Merle Hodge, Jamaica Kincaid, Velma Pollard, Olive Senior, and Jan Shinebourne. From the Hispanophone Caribbean, Julia Álvarez, Judith Ortíz Cofer, Rosario Ferré, Cristina García, Nancy Morejón, and Ana Lydia Vega have all published important, well-received works. Among Caribbean women writers from Suriname, the Netherlands Antilles, Aruba, and the Netherlands, key figures include Cándani, Thea Doelwijt, Chitra Gajadin, Trudi Guda, Nydia Ecury, Ellen Ombre, Astrid Roemer, Johanna Schouten-Elsenhout, and Bea Vianen.

Distilling any collective features out of such a diverse group of artists is practically impossible, but a few broad-brush comments may be useful for purposes of summing up the achievement of women writers in the Caribbean. Most important, perhaps, is that as a group women writers challenge many of the thematic concerns that have become thought of as canonical in Caribbean writing. Women have not always enjoyed access to the material resources—such as academic scholarships—that allowed earlier generations of men to leave the region and experience what George Lamming called "the pleasures of exile." This is not to say that women have *not* traveled or that they have *not* contributed to the literature of exile and diasporic Caribbean living. There is, however, a marked emphasis on transforming immediate local reality, and this different focus is significant enough to challenge the exile-return dynamic that has defined so much of male-authored Caribbean writing from the twentieth century.

Caribbean women also present serious challenges to the way male writers have thematized liberation and the quest for national autonomy. Women in classic Caribbean nationalist texts are often presented as marginal figures, passive objects, and helpmates, whereas men take the active roles in shaping history; not surprisingly, perhaps, women writers counter this tendency and place their women in more central and active roles. Also, whereas male-authored tales of freedom struggle are often presented as externalized, filial rebellion modeled on the Caliban-Prospero conflict taken from Shakespeare's *The Tempest*, women writers often focus on internal states as the locus for freedom struggle, and they emphasize filial reconciliation with empowering ancestral traditions as much as rebellion against tradition.

■ Conclusion

Caribbean literature at the turn of the twenty-first century is vibrant and charged with the legacy of centuries—if not millennia—of intensive cultural adaptation to the material, political, and economic conditions of the region. Political domination and socioeconomic exploitation by first-world powers and their local agents continue to structure cultural activity, as has been the case since 1492. Perhaps writers everywhere deal with social problems born of alienation and disillusionment like poverty, unemployment, and violence. Such problems, however, are particularly intense in the Caribbean. The resulting question of whether or not to commit one's art to social struggles is embraced by some—and rejected by others—but the pervasive urgency of the engagement question is a distinctive quality of Caribbean writing.

The tension between exile and return, or living a nomadic versus a locally rooted life, is one characteristic feature of the Caribbean experience that may have abated somewhat. The most recent generation of literary artists contains a significant number of writers such as Julia Álvarez, Merle Collins, Edwidge Danticat, Junot Díaz, and others whose work moves back and forth between pieces set in the Caribbean and others set in a diasporic milieu. These writers' responses to dislocation echo the work of earlier migrant voices stretching back to Mary Prince (at least), but the sense of binationalism and growing comfort with diasporic living evident in recent works arguably resolves some of the anxiety and polemics that have traditionally marked the issue of a Caribbean writer's physical location. Even the Cuban experience, which for decades was marked by a binary ultimatum characterized by exile or insularity, *gusanos* (traitors) or revolutionaries, Miami or Havana, has now become a much more flexible and dispersed arrangement so that dozens of writers and artists come and go freely between the island and other destinations throughout the world. Cristina García's *Dreaming in Cuban* (1992), for example, narrates many passages back and forth between the island, South Florida, and New Jersey; each of the characters is in fact obsessed or preoccupied with his or her own private and diasporic idea of Cuba.

It is the capacity to reflect the region in all its kaleidoscopic diversity that defines Caribbean literature more than any other quality. Earlier periods have seen an emphasis on European, African, and East Indian cultural influences, and although those elements continue to be explored as aspects of Caribbean cultural identity, the present moment includes new developments such as the depiction of a Chinese Jamaican legacy (Patricia Powell's *The Pagoda,* 1998). As Surinamese literature becomes more widely disseminated through translation, English-language readers will be exposed to the growth in Javanese Caribbean writing, as well as literature in Sranantongo, the language of the maroon Bush Negroes, and writing in no less than four indigenous languages.

Fortunately for students and teachers interested in assimilating this vast field of literature, the contemporary period has also seen the Caribbean emerge as one of most important arenas of literary and cultural criticism. The professionalization of literary studies through the University of the West

Indies has produced a generation of first-rate critics and anthologists, including Carolyn Cooper, J. Michael Dash, Mervyn Morris, Kenneth Ramchand, Gordon Rohlehr, Elizabeth Wilson, and many others. There is also a pattern in the Caribbean of creative writers providing superb criticism. Literary figures including Antonio Benitez-Rojo, Kamau Brathwaite, Patrick Chamoiseau, Maryse Condé, Edouard Glissant, Wilson Harris, George Lamming, Sylvia Wynter, and others have produced some of the most provocative and lucid critical commentaries available.

Again and again, in recent decades, critical discussions have returned to the idea of Caribbeanness as creolization. For Kamau Brathwaite, creolization refers to the "unplanned, unstructured, but osmotic relationship" that arises among various cultural traditions in a given island society (Brathwaite 1974:6). Jean Bernabé, Patrick Chamoiseau, and Raphaël Confiant define *créolité* in similar terms as "the *interactional or transactional aggregate* of Caribbean, European, African, Asian, and Levantine cultural elements, united on the same soil by the yoke of history" (Bernabé et al. 1990:889). Creolization, critics emphasize, is a process of historical accretion, something one comes to understand through the work of historical recovery.

A useful concluding example explains both accretion and recovery as the keys that unlock Caribbeanness. This anecdote comes from Frank Martinus Arion, a multigenre writer from Curaçao, who explains how his efforts to track down the origins of the Great Curassow, a bird that symbolizes the island, opened up all the layers of colonial and precolonial history leading back to the Arawakan name for the bird, *pauwi*. After stopping the host of a radio show on animals in a Curaçaoan parking lot to show him an illustration of the bird, Arion writes, the two friends engage in the following conversation:

> "Are you in a hurry?" he asked at last.
>
> "No."
>
> "Let's go to my ranch then. I have a pair of them. Never knew this was the bird you were after. Had them all along. Got the hen from a doctor of Venezuelan descent. The cock from a lady when she heard I had a hen. Tremendously beautiful birds. They call them something like 'culo blanco.'"
>
> "Right. Pauwí culo blanco. Crax alector. Great Curassow. Black Curassow. Kòrsou Grandi. Pauwís. Powisi. Pauwili. Pauwiezen. Great Curaçao." I threw the groceries in his car and started for the Caribbean. (Arion 1998:452)

■ Bibliography

Abbad y Lasierra, Iñigo. *Historia geográfica, civil y política de la isla de San Juan Bautista de Puerto Rico* (Geographic, civil, and political history of St. John the

Baptist Island of Puerto Rico). Rio Piedras: Universidad de Puerto Rico, Editorial Universitaria. 1st ed. Madrid, 1788.
Arion, Frank Martinus. "The Great Curassow or the Road to Caribbeanness." *Callaloo* 21, no. 3 (1998): 447–452.
Bernabé, Jean, Patrick Chamoiseau, and Raphaël Confiant. "In Praise of Creoleness." *Callaloo* 13, no. 2 (1990): 886–909.
Boxill, Anthony. "The Beginnings to 1929." In *West Indian Literature*, edited by Bruce King. London: MacMillan, 1979.
Brathwaite, Kamau. *Contradictory Omens: Cultural Diversity and Integration in the Caribbean*. Mona, Jamaica: Savacou Publications, 1974.
———. *History of the Voice: The Development of Nation Language in Anglophone Caribbean Poetry*. London and Port-of-Spain, Trinidad: New Beacon, 1984.
Bush, Barbara. *Slave Women in Caribbean Society, 1650–1838*. Kingston, Jamaica: Heinemann, 1990.
Carpentier, Alejo. *Música en Cuba* (Music in Cuba). Havana: Editorial Letras Cubanas, 1979 [1946].
Césaire, Aimé. *The Collected Poems*. Translated with introduction and notes by Clayton Eshleman and Annette Smith. Berkeley: University of California Press, 1983.
Cobham-Sander, Rhonda. "The Creative Writer and West Indian Society: Jamaica, 1900–1950." Ph.D. diss. St. Andrews, Scotland: University of St. Andrews, 1981.
Columbus, Christopher. "The Letter of Christopher Columbus on the Discovery of America." New York: Trustees of the Lennox Library, 1892.
Dévieux, Liliane. "Piano-Bar." In *Green Cane and Juicy Flotsam: Short Stories by Caribbean Women Writers*, edited by Carmen C. Esteves and Lizabeth Paravisini-Gebert. New Brunswick, NJ: Rutgers University Press, 1991.
Du Tertre, R.P.J.P. *Histoire Generale des Antilles Habiteés par les François* (General history of the Antillean French). Paris: T. Jolly, 1667, 1671.
Espinet, Ramabai, ed. *Creation Fire: A CAFRA Anthology of Caribbean Women's Poetry*. Toronto: Sister Vision; and Tunapuna, Trinidad: CAFRA, 1990.
Fouchard, Jean. *Langue et littérature des aborigènes d'Ayiti* (Language and literature of the natives of Haiti). Port-au-Prince, Haiti: Editions Henri Deschamps, 1988.
Goveia, Elsa. *A Study of the Historiography of the British West Indies to the End of the Nineteenth Century*. Washington, DC: Howard University Press, 1980.
Green Cane and Juicy Flotsam: Short Stories by Caribbean Women, edited by Carmen C. Esteves and Lizabeth Paravisini-Gebert. New Brunswick, NJ: Rutgers University Press, 1991.
Her True-True Name: An Anthology of Women's Writing from the Caribbean, edited by Pamela Mordecai and Betty Wilson. Portsmouth, NH: Heinemann, 1989.
Jones, Francis R., trans. "Kunawaraku's Song About Man-Eating Strangers." From a Dutch translation by Cees Koelewijn. *Callaloo* 21, no. 3 (1998): 511.
L'Ouverture, Toussaint. "Letter to the French Directory, 11/15/1796." In *The Black Jacobins: Toussaint L'Ouverture and the San Domingo Revolution,* by C. L. R. James. New York: Grove, 1989.
The Negritude Poets: An Anthology of Translations from the French, edited by Ellen Conroy Kennedy. New York: Thunder's Mouth, 1989.
Philippe, Jean-Baptiste. *Free Mulatto*. Edited by Selwyn R. Cudjoe. Wellesley, MA: Calaloux, 1996.
Plácido [pseudonym of Gabriel de la Concepción Valdés]. "Despida á mi madre" (Plácido's farewell to his mother). Translated by James Weldon Johnson. In *The Book of American Negro Poetry*, edited by James Weldon Johnson. New York: Harcourt Brace, 1959.

Prince, Mary. *The History of Mary Prince, A West Indian Slave, Related by Herself.* Edited by Moira Ferguson. Ann Arbor: University of Michigan Press, 1993.

Rohlehr, Gordon. *Calypso and Society in Pre-Independence Trinidad.* Tunapuna, Trinidad: Gordon Rohlehr, 1990.

Schomburg, Arthur A. "My Trip to Cuba in Quest of Negro Books." *Opportunity* (February 1933): 48–50.

Sistren with Honor Ford Smith. *Lionheart Gal: Life Stories of Jamaican Women.* Toronto: Sister Vision Press, 1987.

Thomas, J[ohn]. J[acob]. *The Theory and Practice of Creole Grammar.* Introduction by Gertrude Buscher. London and Port-of-Spain, Trinidad: New Beacon, 1989.

Walcott, Derek. *Collected Poems, 1948–1984.* London and Boston: Faber and Faber, 1992.

———. *Dream on Monkey Mountain and Other Plays.* New York: Farrar, Straus, and Giroux, 1970.

Walmsley, Anne. *The Caribbean Artists Movement, 1966–1972: A Literary and Cultural History.* London and Port-of-Spain, Trinidad: New Beacon, 1992.

The Whistling Bird: Women Writers of the Caribbean. Edited by Elaine Campbell and Pierette Frickey. Boulder: Lynne Rienner Publishers, 1998.

12

The Caribbean Diaspora

Dennis Conway

International migration is one of the Caribbean region's most fundamental demographic processes, contributing to the population diversity that characterizes the contemporary small societies of this region. After the decimation of its indigenous peoples—some would characterize it as a genocide—following their encounter with early Spanish adventurers, the Caribbean was peopled largely by waves of immigrants from Europe and Africa with smaller proportions from Asia. Colonial conquests; mass movements from the Old World to the Americas; mass enslavement and forced migration; indentured recruitments; selective streams of influential or distinctive minorities; and significant return flows, counterstreams; and interregional transfers characterize the migration history of the region. The Caribbean was, therefore, settled by immigrants, and the subsequent Caribbean diaspora in part grew out of these early mobility patterns.

Old World movements beget New World movements. African and European diasporas were reformed to become Caribbean diasporas. There were substantial reversals in this transition as Caribbean diasporas crossed the Atlantic once again, with European colonial mother countries as their focus. Eventually, these ties to Europe, though persisting to this day in some Caribbean societies, would give way to ties to North America (both Canada and the United States). Other destinations in the Western Hemisphere would also host Caribbean immigrants and international circulators, both within the Caribbean and on the Central American isthmus. The Caribbean diasporas gradually became widespread and multilocal in their nature. As these systems evolved, the island home society remained the constant hub, but the widening net of dispersed streams often changed the circuits from bipolar linkages—as between island and mainland, or between small island and large neighbor—to multiple island-to-island links and multiple island-to-mainland enclave networks. Although early paths became well trodden and so traditional that they were entrenched in many a country's social memory, new international paths were constantly being added as opportunities arose elsewhere.

Changes also occurred in the character of the streams within the networks. Notably, the last quarter-century has witnessed significant changes in the dynamics of Caribbean diasporas. Emigration (relatively permanent movement) as well as return migration have increased in importance. International movements within the region, as well as extraregional international moves, have drawn a more complex map of the diasporas than the commonly accepted models of Caribbean–to–United States movements would predict. International circulation (temporary, reciprocal, and cyclical movement) also has become a common adaptation to the socioeconomic crises the region's peoples face. Refugee flights, as a distinct category of international movers—fleeing persecution, economic hardship, even environmental destruction—might be smaller in volume, but their size betrays their significance in the political and economic affairs of impacted Caribbean countries, not to mention their impact on host North American and European societies. Transnational multilocal networks of migrants, families, and an ever-widening circle of kin have become entrenched systems of interchange that link communities in the Caribbean, Europe, and North America. These networks facilitate the exchange of people, goods, information, ideas, cultural traditions, and material benefits among far-flung diasporas. For many, the Caribbean world has grown to incorporate Caribbean communities in Toronto, Montreal, New York, Miami, Amsterdam, London, and Paris into a wider pan-Caribbean socializing network. The diasporas have become multilocal circuits of interchange, whereas they were once bidirectional emigrations with accompanying counterstreams of returnees.

A complete history of Caribbean diasporas would have to detail the interisland patterns of human movements of aboriginal people during the preencounter era, as well as the international mobility patterns of the next 500 years. However, a more modest agenda is proposed for this chapter. First, a brief historical account of the patterns of immigration and settlement of the region will demonstrate how mobility and its accompanying external influences gave each Caribbean territory its own cultural mosaic. Also demonstrated are the importance of immigration and emigration in the crosscurrents of interisland interdependence, as well as how the exchange of people within the region contributes to a common Caribbean experience. Eventually, and in large part as a response to the declining fortunes of national economies and ecologies, colonial neglect, and growing destitution of the masses, emigrations and wide-flung diasporas gradually overtook immigration as the most significant demographic force. The second part of the chapter, therefore, takes up this more recent period of transformation, and illustrates the complexity of today's Caribbean diasporas as their accompanying transnational networks affect the migration options of many people differently and as the movers and stayers in turn affect their home societies, their mainland enclave communities, and the family networks that sustain these transnational mechanisms.

■ The Encounter with Europe: Domination of the Caribbean

The initial encounter between Europeans and Caribbeans in 1492 ushered in the first of a series of immigrant waves that would fundamentally influence the Caribbean's demographic trajectory. Claiming sovereignty over the newly discovered territory, the Spanish crown enlisted the services of adventurers such as Christopher Columbus to aid colonization. For political and religious reasons, only Spanish citizens qualified as immigrant colonists—*conquistadores* (conquerors), *encomenderos* (those to whom Indians were entrusted), or *hacendados* (landowners). However, the importance of these immigrants lay more with their power, authority, and influence than with their numerical size. Although their population size continued to increase, albeit modestly, the numerically dominant Amerindian populations suffered calamitous declines. The causes were many: European-introduced diseases and epidemics, the destruction of indigenous systems, enslavement, and mass deportation to the New Spain mainland (Mexico). All too soon, the declining indigenous populations prompted the colonizers to seek new, replenishable sources of labor from across the oceans. They recruited yeoman farmers from Iberia, bought slaves shipped from Africa, and recruited indentured servants from other parts of their colonial empires.

For the Portuguese in Brazil, Dutch managers served their masters and developed sugarcane plantations, and later they were invited to British West Indian islands to improve technology and profits. Toward the end of the sixteenth century, an active slave trade was fostered. The Spanish operated their system directly from Africa to licensed ports in the Americas such as Santo Domingo, Veracruz, and Cartagena. The British, active in the slave trade and the intensive use of slave labor, trafficked slaves to their West Indian plantation colonies from West African ports. The French and Dutch colonists and planters also relied on the large-scale trading of slaves; as many as 12 million Africans were transported across the Middle Passage against their will—a forced transatlantic diaspora of lasting significance. Other parts of the respective colonial empires were continually being scoured for indentured labor or domestic servants, but this phase of forced importation of Africans brought about changes in regional population concentrations that would persist to the present day: the demographic dominance of Afro-Caribbean racial majorities. Just about all the Caribbean islands, regardless of European colonial ties, experienced a similar Afro-Caribbean racial transformation. Cuba was profoundly transformed, as was St. Domingue (the former French colony that became independent Haiti). Small islands like Barbados and Antigua soon had Afro-Caribbean majorities of 90 percent, and even among the larger West Indian islands, like Jamaica, an Afro-Caribbean majority emerged. Puerto Rico and the Dominican Republic, in contrast, did not experience such a dramatic racial transition.

Throughout the fifteenth and sixteenth centuries the slave trade and the plantation economies were so profitable that other European colonial powers successfully challenged Spanish hegemony. Buccaneers and privateers plundered the Caribbean's Spanish Main. As Stephen Randall shows in Chapter 3, French and British navies fought pivotal battles, armies built strategic fortifications and enlisted the services of indigenous militias, and politicians traded the dominions, haggling over terms that kept the colonial administrations in a constant state of insecurity. The island archipelago of the Lesser Antilles was one such battleground; the Caribbean coast of Central America was another region of British colonial expansion and mercantile control. Earlier recruitment of European yeomanry to settle and farm these possessions at first relied on land and property enticements, then arranged deportations and persecution of religious minorities. These efforts brought several ethnic minorities—Welsh Royalists, Dutch Jews, Syrians (Levantines), and Madeiran Portuguese—to the region. When plantations demonstrated their profitability, however, buying easily replaceable labor from Africa proved to be the Caribbean's answer.

Producing sugarcane with slave labor, the plantation economies of the French, British, and Dutch colonial possessions in the Caribbean became profitable. Enormous profits accrued to the European colonialists, to slavers, the planters, the crown governments and administrations, and the merchant classes. This agricultural industry flourished for the next 150 years, but most of the generated capital left the islands to promote commerce and industrialization in the imperial heartlands and to support political careers in Europe. Not surprisingly, the environmental consequences of this wholesale transformation of small-island landscapes to cultivable acreages were dramatic. As Duncan McGregor discusses in Chapter 7, eventually (and inevitably) many of the smaller islands' ecological systems became seriously degraded. There was, however, plentiful land for plantation expansion elsewhere in the Caribbean, and newer development in Trinidad, the British and Dutch Guianas, Santo Domingo, and Puerto Rico consolidated the need for more African slaves. Although Great Britain outlawed the slave trade in 1807 and called for the abolition of slavery in 1834, Caribbean plantations still needed labor. With many of the former slaves intent on moving off the plantation or off the island, if necessary, the newer plantations of the Guianas and Trinidad were able to recruit them, thereby initiating interregional migration streams from small islands to these larger territories (Richardson 1983). The plantations, however, needed more labor than could be provided by such interregional mechanisms.

Following the abolition of slavery, and after a brief experimentation with apprenticeship arrangements, plantation owners and island administrations turned to the recruitment of indentured laborers to solve their labor shortages. The region therefore experienced another wave of mass immigration, this time from Asia. China was the largest source region, followed by India. Chinese men and, later, women were brought into Cuba and several British territories (including Jamaica, British Guiana, and Trinidad) to work as plantation laborers. Although mainly recruited for field labor, many of the Chinese who took up their indenture option to remain rather than be repatriated gravitated to urban commerce, such as dry goods, laundries, and restaurants. Approximately 500,000 East Indians (so they were called) undertook indentured contracts to work on the plantations of Trinidad, Jamaica, and British Guiana. Remaining behind were approximately 150,000 East Indians in Trinidad, 21,500 in Jamaica, and 240,000 in British Guiana. Later, but under similar indenture contractual arrangements, 20,000 Hindustanis (also from India) and 30,000 Javanese (from the Dutch colony of Java) were brought to the new plantation estates in the coastal lowlands of Dutch Guiana. Unlike the Chinese, most East Indian laborers stayed in rural surroundings after their indentured contracts expired, some continuing to serve as plantation workers while others formed a small farmer sector.

However, indenturing wasn't the only labor recruitment strategy. There was continued recruitment of immigrant minorities from Southern Europe and the European imperial homelands. In the Spanish colonies of Cuba, the Dominican Republic, and Puerto Rico, administrations and planters encouraged white immigration from Europe, in large part fearing the loss of cultural dominance and the demographic threat of the African-Caribbean racial majority.[1] Elsewhere among British possessions, there were attempts to attract former slaves from North America, and some colonization by free Africans was promoted and accomplished.

Seventeenth-century British colonization of the Atlantic Caribbean coast of the Central American isthmus also established enclave dominions in an area that would subsequently come under North American corporate control. The British encouraged their own settlers to exploit the forest and land resources in places such as British Honduras (Belize), Bluefields (in Nicaragua), and the Bay Islands off Honduras. Elsewhere along the Mosquito Coast of Nicaragua, the British allied with the native Indians in their conflicts with the weak Spanish administrators, trading firearms and even setting up British-educated puppet monarchs, who declared loyalty to the British crown. When the Central American republics gained political independence in the 1820s, Britain retained control of British Honduras, challenged the sovereignty of their republican claim over the Bay Islands and the Mosquito Coast, and generally supported British colonial enclave communities via commercial linkages. Later in the early nineteenth century, a more successful challenge to this British control would come from an independent United States (Sunshine 1985).

The eighteenth century witnessed the genesis of international connections between the Caribbean and the U.S.–North American mainland, both in terms of capital investment circulating and people migrating. At the very beginning of the plantation era, the demise of white yeoman small farming in the West Indies had prompted the more adventurous to emigrate to the North American mainland colonies to start again. Later, some successful planters expanded their family properties to start mainland plantations. For example, Barbadian planters settled and prospered in South Carolina, and Barbadian merchant families established links with Baltimore. Louisiana–St. Domingue (Haiti) connections were entrenched from these earliest colonial beginnings, and migration and circulations between Cuba, St. Domingue, and Louisiana further enmeshed Caribbean and Gulf Coast societies in a common cultural heritage: part creole, part Hispanic, part Acadian. The triangular trade of sugar, manufactured goods, foodstuffs, timber, cotton, and tobacco, which involved merchant houses with interests in Britain, its North American colonies, and the Caribbean, cemented transnational and transatlantic mercantilist linkages, served planter's interests, and furthered interconnections, thereby deepening and entrenching the dependent relations of the Caribbean with external forces and influences. The wealth that was created in the region was always circulating out of it, and the region's people were to respond likewise as conditions worsened.[2]

■ Caribbean–North American Circulations, 1880–1970

Turmoil in the financial sector, including the failure of many banks in London, New York, and Boston during the financial depression of the 1880s, left many planters bankrupt and brought about wrenching structural changes in several small islands, among them St. Vincent and Tobago. Between 1880 and 1924 all of the Caribbean's plantation economies became severely depressed; local populations suffered deepening impoverishment as a result. Several colonial administrations advocated or permitted safety-valve emigration, though few actually legislated this politically sensitive policy. Voluntary emigration and circulation was an option taken up by the more fortunate. Wealthier traders and businessmen fled the hard times using the improved steamship services to New York, with Jamaicans, Barbadians, and Trinidadians emigrating to New York and Boston. Others moved with the help of their ethnic networks to havens in less-hard-hit Caribbean territories. Emigration to the colonial homeland for the more privileged elite classes was always an option, and sons and daughters were duly shipped off to be educated in European institutions, as befitting their social station in life.

International circulation via short-term labor contracts was the only available opportunity for the impoverished masses in the British West Indies. The Colonial Office and local administrations no longer viewed these possessions as good investments now that sugarcane was losing the competition with homegrown European beet sugar. The Asian economies of the British Empire promised much more, so the West Indies was basically neglected. Not surprisingly, British West Indian contract labor was recruited all over the Western Hemisphere, especially in Central and South America. U.S. business interests were expanding in the hemisphere, and labor was much in demand. British West Indian men and women circulated, labored, and succumbed as they helped construct the Panama Canal. Between 1900 and 1914 some 60,000 Barbadians labored in Panama, and one estimate states that 20,000 died between 1906 and 1912. As many as 121,000 Jamaicans labored in Cuban sugar fields and factories between 1902 and 1932. Thousands of Leeward Islanders—Kittians, Antiguans, Nevisians, Montserratians—traveled as so-called deckers for temporary jobs in the U.S.-owned sugar industry in the Dominican Republic. U.S. Virgin Islanders and Bahamians circulated to Miami in the first decade of the twentieth century, helping to build a gateway metropolis in Florida. Middle-class Jamaicans, Barbadians, Trinidadians, and wealthier small-islanders circulated to West Indian communities in New York and Boston, with considerable emigration occurring as the return circuit was postponed indefinitely, the intended repatriation forgone in favor of staying in their adopted country. The diasporas were becoming embedded and the networks entrenched in the social fabric of the islands.

The 1924–1940 period was one of continued hard times and limited opportunities for the Caribbean masses. The Caribbean economic state remained grim, and there was another crash in world sugar prices in 1921. Coincidentally, anti-immigrant (i.e., nativist) sentiments were heightened in the United States, in large part due to the massive influxes of new immigrants (from Italy, Greece, other Southern and Eastern European regions, as well as China) that the country had experienced during the preceding two decades. Accordingly, the U.S. National Origins Act of 1924 (the Johnson-Read Act) promulgated a discriminatory national quota system for Asians and Caribbean peoples—limiting the number of immigrants from any country to an annual quota based on the number of nationals already in residence in the United States in 1920. Elsewhere in the Caribbean Basin, restrictive immigration legislation in Venezuela, Cuba, and the Dominican Republic also discriminated against previously welcomed black visitors. Repatriation was encouraged, and Haitians, Jamaicans, and small-islanders returned to swell the ranks of the unemployed masses back home. The only labor opportunities available in the region were in oil-related industries in the Netherlands Antilles (Aruba and Curaçao) and Trinidad. Small-islanders from places like Grenada, Barbados, Antigua, and St. Kitts circulated to that employment opportunity. Other small-islanders continued patterns of circulation wherever they could find opportunities: interisland trade and commerce, working passages and joining the merchant marine, often as not relying on networks provided by previous emigrants.

With U.S. entry into World War II, there were burgeoning labor needs as U.S. men went off to war, and the agricultural sector and industries needed boosts in output; this started another international labor recruitment drive. *Braceros* (manual laborers) were recruited from Mexico as farm labor, and Caribbean cane-cutters joined this program. For many of the unemployed in the Caribbean, circulation via short-term labor contracts to the United States was again possible under the U.S. War Manpower Act, although the door quickly slammed shut again in 1952. In addition, World War II also saw many colonial regiments "doing their duty" in the European theater, and the mobilization of these war veterans would soon lead to a restructuring of colonial ties, to the growth of radical social movements, and to the onset of decolonization.

Predictably, the post–World War II period (1945–1965) was one of mass emigration from Caribbean colonies to a variety of European metropoles: Britain, France, and the Netherlands. There was emigration with an intention to return from the British West Indies to British cities initiated by massive recruitment schemes to staff service industries and administrations in the 1950s. Thousands of West Indians emigrated, exercising their right to take advantage of employment and educational opportunities in Great Britain. Some of the smaller Windward and Leeward Islands experienced depopulation and aging during this mass emigration; Montserrat lost almost 10 percent of its people, and Carriacou, a ward island of Grenada, lost 20 percent of its residents (Lowenthal 1972). Many intended to return, and some did return to their Caribbean homelands upon retirement, but significant numbers stayed. The influx of "New Commonwealth" immigrants from the West Indies, from Pakistan, and from India gradually aroused racist sentiments and fears, however. Eventually and abruptly this alien immigration was terminated in 1962. The restrictive and discriminatory Commonwealth Immigration Act effectively stemmed the flow. Smaller numbers of Caribbean people of color also emigrated from French *départements d'outre mer* (overseas departments) like Guadeloupe, Martinique, and French Guiana to France and from the Netherlands Antilles (islands such as Aruba, Bonaire, Curaçao, and St. Maarten) and Dutch Guiana to the Netherlands. These streams were selective circulations, that is, emigrations of elites and youths from the small professional and middle classes among colonial societies.

In North America, a similar colony-to-metropole diaspora sprung to life as Puerto Ricans sought opportunities on the mainland. The rapid development plan for Puerto Rico (Operation Bootstrap) involved a massive restructuring of the island's agricultural sector. It embraced a modernization strategy of industrialization-by-invitation, and the ensuing rapid industrialization and urbanization in Puerto Rico were accompanied by mass circulation between the island and U.S. metropolitan centers, particularly New York City and Spanish Harlem. Between 1955 and 1970, approximately one-third of the Puerto Rican population moved off the island, perhaps as many as 70 percent heading for New York City. By 1970 more than 1 million Puerto Ricans had moved to the mainland, with New York City, Miami, and Chicago hosting substantial enclave communities. Many moved back and forth between the island and their adopted city, attempting to achieve the best of both worlds—culture and identity in the former; money, material wealth, and skills in the latter (Ellis et al. 1996; Lowenthal 1972).

Cuban links to the U.S. mainland also strengthened during this period. A coup by Fulgencio Batista in 1952 prompted a stream of exiles to flee to Florida, where they set up an expatriate political base. Between 1951 and 1959 approximately 10,000 Cubans became permanent U.S. residents, but this influx was swamped by the historic exodus following Fidel Castro's ascension to power in 1959. Between 1959 and 1962 the exodus of middle-class Cubans accompanied the consolidation of Castro's regime. Approximately 1 million Cubans fled, with two-thirds heading for the U.S. mainland.

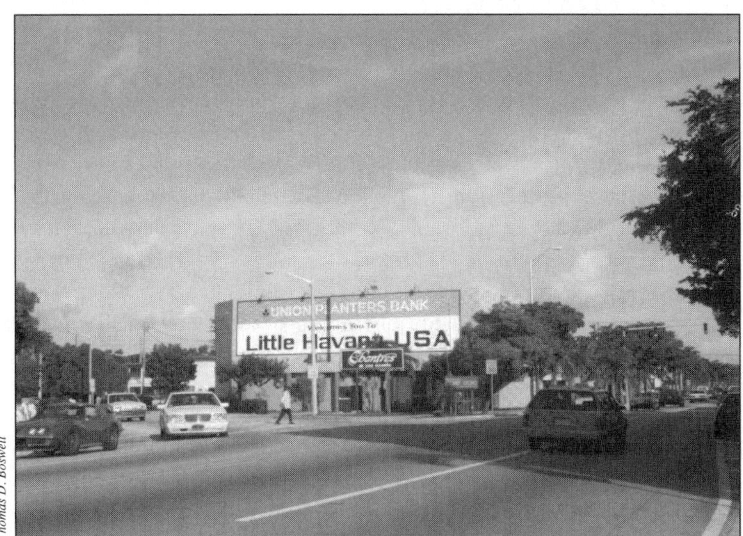

Thomas D. Boswell

The entrance to Little Havana, Miami, Florida

A significant minority moved to Puerto Rico, where they soon formed a powerful immigrant business class. Miami and New York were the main destinations for these political refugees, and gradually, as their domestic power consolidated, the Cuban presence in Miami strengthened. Later, exiled Cubans moved to this Latino city, and Miami's Cuban community constituted more than 60 percent of the total Cuban American population (Boswell and Curtis 1984). For other Caribbean hopefuls in the region, the Immigration and Nationality Act of 1952 (the McCarran-Walter Act) reaffirmed the 1924 discriminatory quota system; it wasn't until 1965 that Caribbean people—other than Puerto Ricans and Cubans—would be able to seek overseas opportunities in the United States.

A watershed moment for international mobility was the 1965–1970 transition, dictated by fundamental changes in U.S. immigration policy and practices by McCarran-Walter and subsequent amendments. Additionally, this point in time signaled the fundamental restructuring of Latin American and Caribbean economic fortunes that ensued in the 1970s and persists to the present day. This chapter closes, therefore, with an examination and illumination of the latest phase in the development of complex Caribbean diaspora networks, where regional, hemispheric, and transnational mobility is bringing about significant demographic and cultural transformations of what were distinctive cultural milieus.

■ Caribbean Diaspora Networks, 1970s to the Present

Prior to the 1970s the Caribbean was first a region of significant immigration, then selective emigration streams, and then continued interregional immigration. Initially, European imperial powers received immigrants from their colonies, but eventually North American hegemony held sway. As already mentioned, emigration from the British West Indies during the 1955–1961 period was considerable; perhaps as much as 6 percent of the islands' population left for the imperial homeland—150,000 Jamaicans, 19,000 Barbadians, and some 8,000 from the small islands of St. Kitts and Nevis, Dominica, Grenada, and St. Lucia. This was matched in succeeding decades by increased immigration and residence in the United States, in large part because of the longer duration of entry that country afforded to Caribbean petitioners. In particular, greater numbers of Trinidadians, Guyanese, and Antiguans moved to the United States in the 1970s compared to the United Kingdom during the peak entry period (1955–1961), many of them choosing New York City as their Caribbean "home away from home" (Table 12.1).

The globalization of the world's economic order in accordance with market principles, which began in the 1970s, continued through the 1980s and

Table 12.1 Comparison of Caribbean Immigration to the United Kingdom (1955–1961) and to the United States (1965–1985)

Origin	1960 Population	Total Emigration to UK 1955–1961	Immigration to United States 1965–1971	1972–1978	1979–1985	1980 Population
Barbados	232,085	18,741	9,400	14,089	14,534	249,000
British Guiana/ Guyana	558,769	7,141	7,700	26,708	58,107	759,000
Jamaica	1,609,814	148,369	79,000	88,740	139,244	2,053,000
Trinidad and Tobago	825,700	9,610	30,000	44,267	27,397	1,055,000
Leeward Islands						
Anguilla	N/A	N/A	N/A	866	704	N/A
Antigua	54,060	4,687	N/A	4,033	9,823	65,000
Montserrat	12,167	3,835	N/A	1,422	1,029	12,000
St. Kitts and Nevis	56,693	7,503	N/A	4,443	8,756	44,000
Windward Islands						
Dominica	59,479	7,915	N/A	2,510	4,673	74,000
Grenada	88,617	7,663	N/A	5,260	7,398	93,000
St. Lucia	86,194	7,291	N/A	2,559	5,109	115,000
St. Vincent and the Grenadines	80,705	4,285	N/A	3,039	5,075	98,000
Total	3,664,283	227,040	126,100	197,936	281,849	4,617,000
% population		6.2 (1960)				6.1 (1980)

Sources: Ceri Peach, *West Indian Migration* (London: Oxford Univresity Press, 1968); U.S. Immigration and Naturalization Service (INS), *Annual Reports of the Immigration and Naturalization Service* (Washington, DC: Department of Justice, 1964–1968); and INS, *1994 Statistical Yearbook of the Immigration and Naturalization Service* (Washington, DC: Department of Justice, 1994).

1990s, and is still imposing neoliberal policies today, brought about these changes in population trends. Wholesale indebtedness, recessions, increasing polarization of classes, and declines in standards of living, among other things, were the structural realities that the region suffered during this time. This prompted more diasporas, more transnational circulation, and the formation of more multilocal networks. Emigration has again replaced immigration as the region's defining demographic process, although interregional immigration is not an unknown problem for a few small islands (e.g., the Cayman Islands and the Bahamas) whose economic fortunes have held up.

There has been continued economic hardship for many, further exacerbated in some islands by outbreaks of civil unrest and violence, as well as by natural disasters and ecological calamities, which have initiated several streams of refugees. International circulation and temporary movements to neighboring or more distant places have become a common strategy for many regardless of their skill levels, and well-entrenched networks facilitate such sojourning patterns. There has also been a widening of opportunities for more educated and highly skilled Caribbean people. They have taken advantage of opportunities in time-honored ways, drawing upon their flexibility, their resourcefulness, their initiative, and even their cultural capital (e.g., musical and athletic talents) to seek livelihoods in other parts of the Caribbean, in North America, in Europe, and farther afield in the globalizing marketplace for skilled professionals. How this evolution of the Caribbean diasporas came to become a more firmly based hemispheric network incorporating North American communities with their Caribbean counterparts is the final piece of the story.

Three major immigration policy changes in the mid-1960s heralded this new era. First, restrictive legislation in Britain effectively "slammed the door" to that country's Commonwealth Caribbean immigrants in 1961. Then, in 1962, new Canadian immigration legislation removed racial discriminatory biases for entry requirements, opening another route to North America for Commonwealth Caribbean immigrants. In the United States, the 1965 Immigration and Nationality Act replaced the race-biased national origin–led entry system and established a set of seven preference categories, with family reunification as the underlying objective. Later, in 1976, the U.S. Congress established a preference for Western Hemisphere countries, allocated ceilings for individual countries, and enacted favorable conditions for entry of relatives and family of U.S. residents. Then, the 1978 and 1980 amendments to the Immigration and Nationality Act extended the entry ceilings of this preference system. This was the opportunity exploited by would-be Caribbean emigrants.

Well-established Caribbean communities in Miami, New York, Boston, Washington, D.C., New Jersey, and Hartford, Connecticut, provided family- and kin-based networks and links to support U.S.-bound migration. Temporary trips (circulations) between island homes and mainland enclaves were open to many Jamaicans, Trinidadians, and Barbadians, among others; six-month sojourns using visitor visas became a common practice. Also beginning in the mid-1960s, there was a steady flow of professionals and youths from the Dominican Republic to New York City; this rapidly grew to mass circulation and emigration between island and city. By 1980 a net estimate of Dominicans residing on the U.S. mainland was 400,000, most in the Washington Heights area of New York (Grasmuck and Grosfoguel 1997; Morrison and Sinkin 1982).

Prior to the 1970s professional advancement, alienation with island society, and acclimatization to metropolitan ideals and standards of living (often inculcated while being educated abroad) had encouraged emigration of a self-selected group of highly educated individuals from the middle and elite classes, either to regional metropolitan countries or to Canada and the United States. The emigration of these groups of voluntary exiles (émigrés) was sometimes emulated by middle-class professionals—Trinidadian and Jamaican nurses, for example, who were recruited by agencies or by others already established in New York City or Toronto's health sectors—and sought better opportunities in Canada and the United States, where they could practice their professions (Henry 1990). Indeed, such flights of Caribbean human capital have always constituted a "brain drain" that the national economies have had difficulties withstanding. Ideas for "redraining the brains" (i.e., reversing the emigration flow of scarce professionals) are not to be taken lightly, and return migrants need to be encouraged to come back to fulfill social obligations to Caribbean societies that helped educate them (Henry 1990).

In the 1970s this brain drain of émigré professionals translated into mass flights from the deteriorating conditions and political unrest brought about by mismanaged and often repressive regimes during the late 1960s and 1970s. During François "Papa Doc" Duvalier's regime in Haiti in the 1960s, almost three-quarters of the middle (i.e., professional) classes fled to French Canada. It was not until the 1970s that this exodus was followed by flights of small-business operators and peasants. These lower-class Haitians not only went to French Canada; they also transited through the Bahamas to Miami or found their way to the Caribbean communities in Brooklyn (Conway and Cooke 1994). Later, political unrest continued to plague the country, even after Jean-Claude "Baby Doc" Duvalier fled into exile in 1986, and successive U.S. administrations attempted (rather unsuccessfully) to establish a democratic regime in that troubled and impoverished country. The result was continued pressure to emigrate, and South Florida was the destination for an influx of Haitian boatpeople that was unfairly depicted by the media as an "invasion." The unfortunate refugees generally were not well treated by immigration authorities.

Cubans, by contrast, had to wait several years after the early-1960s mass exodus before the Castro regime relaxed its emigration restrictions and allowed more to leave. Immediately, Cuban Americans in Florida initiated a comprehensive airlift of Cuban refugees, and this private-sector transport effort continued until 1973, with some 300,000 persons fleeing to Miami and elsewhere in the United States. During the remainder of the 1970s, the exodus became a trickle, with many fleeing the island via intermediate countries such as Mexico, Spain, Venezuela, and Jamaica. Then, in April 1980, aspiring émigré Cubans received another window of opportunity, and for five months a flotilla of small boats ferried more than 100,000 people between Mariél in Cuba and Miami. However, these "Marielitos" were not treated as preferentially as their forerunners. Among them was a sizable group of Cuban prisoners, of whom some 5,000 had been released with significant criminal records (Boswell and Curtis 1984). This criminal stigma colored the U.S. public's assessment of the Marielitos.

To the growing anti-immigration lobby in the United States, Cubans were no longer distinguishable from other invasions of colored foreigners from the Caribbean, Latin America, and Africa. Many of the hard-core criminals among the Mariél refugees received severe treatment and were incarcerated in high-security U.S. federal penitentiaries. Despite the growing negative feelings directed at this latest wave of Cuban émigrés, Cuban refugees continued to receive preferential treatment by U.S. immigration authorities because they were fleeing a communist regime. By contrast, many Haitians claiming political refugee status were not treated as well, and throughout the 1980s they were uncritically assessed as economic refugees and therefore didn't qualify for refugee admission. It wasn't until 1996 that U.S. President Bill Clinton's administration mandated that all refugees (including Cubans) were to be treated similarly by the U.S. Immigration and Naturalization Service.

Illegal entry and sojourns in neighboring Caribbean countries increased in importance and in volume from the mid-1970s onward. Many sought opportunities in other Caribbean countries that were experiencing relative prosperity due to tourism, the oil industry, or continued colonial support. In addition to attracting professionals from within the region, the tourism and oil industries provided opportunities for the less-skilled as they parlayed agricultural backgrounds into work in construction, repair, and maintenance. This continued a long-held tradition in many stagnant rural communities in the Caribbean, which uses intraregional migration as a means to escape impoverishment in declining agricultural sectors at home while retaining home ties and the promise of return. Well-established paths emerged within and throughout the Caribbean, and current circulation and migration trajectories follow such routes. Nevisians and Kittitians transit to Antigua, St. Thomas in the U.S. Virgin Islands, and elsewhere; St. Lucians transit to Barbados, to Trinidad, and elsewhere. The Grenadian-Trinidad circuit is well entrenched, and Vincentians who also go to Trinidad appear in appreciable numbers in New York City. Dominicans, by contrast, have chosen neighboring Martinique and Guadeloupe as their preferred transit, and some find their way on to Paris and Europe via those islands. Sometimes, routes include ports of call in San Juan, Puerto Rico, Miami, New York, or Toronto, metropolitan locales that may be terminals or transits. Retaining the widest set of options possible, Caribbean migrants anticipate or at least do not reject the possibility of returning to their Caribbean home. While in the United States, many prefer to retain their original citizenship. Others take U.S. citizenship to sponsor further migrations of family members.

In the United States, passage of the 1986 Immigration Reform and Control Act granted amnesty to 2 million unauthorized alien residents and refugees, particularly Haitians, Dominicans, and Cubans. Eventually, through the early 1990s they would be granted green cards and permanent residency status. Not surprisingly, the lost decade of the 1980s witnessed the largest volumes of visiting and resident entries to the United States from the Caribbean of any decade in the twentieth century. In 1990 amendments to the Immigration and Nationality Act increased admission quotas for highly skilled young women and men in undersupplied occupations, such as nursing and medical technology, which opened the door to the recruitment of health services technicians and practitioners, scientists, and even athletes from the Caribbean. Still, unauthorized entries troubled U.S. officials; the differential treatment of specific streams of refugees (such as the Haitians and Cubans) troubled civil rights groups; and the downturns of the Californian economy from the mid-1980s onward aided and abetted anti-immigrant rhetoric. The 1990s were to become a decade in which anti-immigrant sentiment and political positioning in California, and to a lesser extent in Florida, heightened tensions and fomented restrictive immigration policies. In 1996 there was a reversal of U.S. immigration policies, with Congress passing the Illegal Immigration Reform and Immigrant Responsibility Act, which enforced the rapid deportation of "criminal" resident aliens; enacted higher penalties for overstayers; restricted legal immigrants' access to welfare programs and some of their benefits; and increased surveillance at the Mexico border. Yet the decade would end with less punitive provisions in place as well as a mobilization of Latino voters in California that effectively reversed that state's anti-immigrant stance. Increases in recruitment of highly skilled immigrants were proposed and enacted, and security at the Mexico border was couched more within the war on drugs than illegal immigration.

For Caribbean hopefuls, however, the same mechanisms used in the 1980s and 1990s are still in play. Haitians were perhaps the only Caribbean people whose journeys and visits to the United States were limited or curtailed. Those from the Dominican Republic continued to visit New York, and the Washington Heights area became even more firmly identified with that Caribbean society. Similarly, Crown Heights in Brooklyn was the West Indian area where Labor Day in Brooklyn was celebrated with a Carnival procession, including residents from all over the Caribbean. After 1996 Cuban refugees no longer enjoyed the privileged status they had enjoyed with previous administrations, but the hardships during the post-Soviet period continued to encourage Cuban defections and refugee flights, with *balseros* (those fleeing on rafts) choosing the most dangerous means of crossing.

Elsewhere, visiting patterns (i.e., nonimmigrant entries) to the United States from all over the region continued to be substantial. With the exception of Haitians, the numbers of unauthorized illegal overstayers in the United States from the majority of Caribbean societies were not excessive when compared to Canadians, Salvadorans, Guatemalans, and Mexicans. New York, Miami, New Jersey, Boston, and even Los Angeles had vibrant Caribbean enclave communities where U.S.-based families extended welcomes to their Caribbean-based kin.

In Canada, Toronto's multicultural mosaic also had Caribbean enclaves, and Montreal and Quebec City both sustained a distinctive Haitian community. North American–Caribbean ties remained strong, and the multicultural presence of Caribbean communities in several North American cities certainly has enlivened their transnational environments. New York City is home to the largest concentrations and most numerous mix of nationalities. In addition, for several groups New York City remains the major destination, with 50 percent or more residing there, including Barbadians, Dominicans, Grenadians, Guyanese, and Vincentians (Table 12.2). Still, Caribbean peoples represent about 1 percent of the resident populations of Canada and the United States (Table 12.3). North American–Caribbean migration circuits and networks remain firmly embedded.

■ Conclusion

International circulation, temporary sojourning, and repetitive mobility have emerged as dominant and common patterns throughout the Caribbean. Extraregional diasporas have fostered overseas enclave communities in North America, and growing numbers of households and families have a transnational flexibility for living between two worlds. All this contributes to the cosmopolitan nature of the Caribbean. These diasporas also consolidate regional and metropolitan networks and links. Intraregional movements have long held sway as traditional paths for job searches, for marriages, for visiting, and for short-term target-earning. Some of these internal paths serve as transit stations for eventual journeys to Europe and North America, but some of these waystations retain Caribbean migrants (e.g., Puerto Rico's growing concentration of Dominicans, Antigua's retention of Kittitians, and Guadeloupe's retention of Haitians and Dominicans (from neighboring Dominica).

Table 12.2 New York City's Share of Legal Resident Admissions from Selected Caribbean Countries, 1990–1994

Origin	1990/1991 Population	U.S. Admissions 1990–1994	New York City 1990–1994	New York City/U.S. (%)
Antigua	64,000	3,874	1,201	31.0
Bahamas	255,000	4,356	187	4.3
Barbados	257,000	5,480	3,101	56.6
Belize	187,000	9,071	1,159	12.8
Cuba	10,628,000	61,178	1,008	1.6
Dominica	86,000	3,944	748	19.0
Dominican Republic	7,110,000	222,178	110,140	49.6
Grenada	91,000	4,543	2,575	56.7
Guyana	795,000	48,138	30,764	63.9
Haiti	6,486,000	102,380	14,957	14.6
Jamaica	2,366,000	99,346	32,918	33.1
St. Kitts and Nevis	40,000	3,435	641	18.7
St. Lucia	133,000	3,336	895	26.8
St. Vincent and the Grenadines	114,000	3,649	2,057	56.4
Trinidad and Tobago	1,236,000	35,024	15,878	45.3
Other Caribbean	—	3,794	1,159	16.0

Sources: New York City, Department of City Planning, "The Newest New Yorkers, 1990–1994: An Analysis of Immigration to NYC in the Early 1990s" (New York: New York City Department of City Planning, 1996); U.S. Immigration and Naturalization Servie (INS), *Statistical Yearbook of the Immigration and Naturalization Service* (Washington, DC: Department of Justice, 1994).

Far from being a simple safety valve or a demographic exodus caused by the lack of employment opportunities at home, the surplus of young people (and their unmet needs), and the complex patterns of short- and long-term international movements of emigration (displacement) and circulation (temporary, reciprocal movement) cement Caribbean societies with several North American metropolitan societies in a complex system of transnational interdependence. Short-term visiting appears to be one option to permanent residency; repetitive visits maintain the connections; and living a multilocal life has become a common survival strategy. Emigration continues to be a tradition for many islanders, too. Migration is more than ever a livelihood strategy in Caribbean societies, at home and abroad. Such a transnational life brings a multiplicity of identities to the fore, and there appears to be a growing pan-Caribbean consciousness in the cosmopolitan enclave communities of certain North American gateway metropoles—New York City, Miami, Toronto, and Montreal, in particular. Pan-Caribbeanism is being fostered by cross-cultural marriages, a widening and intertwining of Caribbean family networks, and the growing maturity of many Caribbean societies. Moreover, the further incor-

Table 12.3 Populations from the Caribbean Who Immigrated to Canada and the United States, 1990–1991 (by country of origin)

		Population from the Caribbean (thousands; as part of the census)		
Origin	1990/1991 Census Count	Canada, 1991	United States, 1990	Percentage That Lives Outside the Country in the Americas
Antigua	64,000	2.0	—[a]	3.01
Bahamas	255,000	1.1	21.6	8.19
Barbados	257,000	14.8	43.0	18.43
Belize	187,000	1.0	30.0	14.19
Bermuda	61,000	1.7	—[a]	2.78
Cuba	10,628,000	1.8	737.0	6.58
Dominican Republic	7,110,000	2.8	347.9	4.92
Grenada	91,000	4.7	17.7	20.09
Guyana	795,000	66.1	120.7	19.38
Haiti	6,486,000	39.9	225.4	3.95
Jamaica	2,366,000	102.4	334.1	15.58
Puerto Rico	3,783,000	0.2	1,200.0	24.10
St. Lucia	133,000	1.8	—[a]	1.37
St. Vincent and the Grenadines	114,000	—[a]	2.1	5.64
Trinidad and Tobago	1,236,000	49.4	115.7	12.00
Total		289.7 (1.04%)	3,195.2 (1.25%)	

Source: Pan American Health Organization (PAHO), *Health in the Americas,* Vol. 1 (Washington, DC: PAHO, 1998).

Note: a. Under 50 persons.

poration of these microstates into a globalizing new world order, where North American and European values and cultures themselves compete, change, or resist, has also contributed to the emergence of this consciousness.

Remittances—the flow of hard currency and in-kind transfers of material goods by migrants to families back home—have grown to become an essential financial input to Caribbean families of all classes. Commonly they are used to purchase needed goods—food, medicine, clothes, and the like—and consumption use is of considerable importance. In addition, however, remittances are important—and increasingly so—for both investment and savings; also, in many small states there are substantial constraints on alternative productive uses of remittances. Contrary to earlier opinions, remittance flows appear to be sustainable over long periods with little indication of remittance decay over time. Though remittances are primarily used for consumption, there is also substantial investment in economic activities and in the well-being of others, some of which enables the perpetuation of the migration-remittances nexus (Connell and Conway 1999; Portes and Guarnizo 1991).

Transnational Caribbean migrants provide their families at home and abroad with an extended range of options for various forms of familial, personal, and community development. Most important, remittances promote the development of human capital and growth of social and cultural capital stocks in local communities, with investments transferred at the appropriate scale (and scope) of effectiveness, that is, the household level (Connell and Conway 1999).

The Caribbean's many diasporas have matured and evolved to become embedded multilocal networks in which an adherence to one national identity is less adaptable than a transnational identity; having multiple identities is a more flexible response to today's uncertainties. Caribbean people continue to demonstrate their flexibility, their creativeness, and their fortitude despite the intractable social and economic problems they and their societies have faced since their incorporation into the colonial world in the fifteenth and sixteenth centuries.

Notes

1. See Chapter 8 for further discussion of attitudes toward race, ethnicity, and class.
2. Chapter 5 contains an analysis of Caribbean economic patterns.

Bibliography

Boswell Thomas D., and James R. Curtis, *The Cuban-American Experience*. Totowa, NJ: Rowman and Allanhand, 1984.

Connell, John, and Dennis Conway. "Migration and Remittances in Island Microstates: A Comparative Perspective on the South Pacific and the Caribbean." *International Journal of Urban and Regional Research* 24, no. 1 (1999): 52–78.

Conway Dennis. "Conceptualising Contemporary Patterns of Caribbean International Mobility." *Caribbean Geography* 2, no. 3 (1988): 145–163.

———. "Caribbean International Mobility Traditions." *Boletín Latino-Americano y del Caribe* 46, no. 2 (1989): 17–47.

———. "The Complexity of Caribbean Migration." *Caribbean Affairs* 7, no. 4 (1994): 96–119.

Conway, Dennis, and Tom Cooke. "Non-White Immigration, Residential Segregation, and Selective Integration into a Restructuring Metropolis, New York City." In *Social Polarization in Post-Industrial Metropolises,* edited by John O'Laughlin and Jurgen Frederichs. Berlin and New York: De Gruyter and Aldine Presses, 1994.

Díaz-Briquet, Sergio. *International Migration Within Latin America and the Caribbean: An Overview*. Staten Island, NY: Center for Migration Studies, 1983.

Ellis, Mark, Dennis Conway, and Adrian J. Bailey. "The Circular Migration of Puerto Rican Women: Towards a Gendered Explanation." *International Migration* 34, no. 1 (1996): 31–58.

Glick-Schiller, Nina, Linda Basch, and Cristina Blanc-Szanton. *Towards a Transnational Perspective on Migration: Race, Class, Ethnicity, and Nationalism Reconsidered.* Annals of the New York Academy of Sciences, vol. 645. New York: New York Academy of Sciences, 1992.

Grasmuck, Sheri, and Ramón Grosfoguel. "Geopolitics, Economic Niches, and Gendered Social Capital Among Recent Caribbean Immigrants to New York City." *Sociological Perspectives* 40, no. 3 (1997): 339–363.

Guengant, Jean-Pierre, and Dawn I. Marshall. *Caribbean Population Dynamics: Emigration and Fertility Challenges.* Barbados: Conference of Caribbean Parliamentarians on Population and Development, 1985.

Hatton, Timothy J., and Jeffrey G. Williamson. *Migration and the International Labor Market, 1850–1939.* London and New York: Routledge, 1994.

Henry, Ralph. "A Reinterpretation of Labor Services of the Commonwealth Caribbean." Working Paper No. 61. Washington, DC: Commission for the Study of International Migration and Cooperative Economic Development, 1990.

———. "Cooperation in Human Resource Utilisation in the Commonwealth Caribbean." *Bulletin of Eastern Caribbean Affairs* 16, no. 1 (1990): 25–28.

Hondagneu-Sotelo, Pierrette. *Gendered Transitions: Mexican Experiences of Immigration.* Berkeley, Los Angeles, and London: University of California Press, 1994.

Kritz, Mary M. "International Migration Patterns in the Caribbean Basin: An Overview." In *Global Trends in Migration: Theory and Research on International Population Movements*, edited by M. M. Kritz, C. B. Keely, and S. M. Tomasi, pp. 208–233. Staten Island, NY: Center for Migration Studies, 1981.

Lowenthal, David. *West Indian Societies.* New York: Oxford University Press, 1972.

Morrison, Thomas K., and Richard Sinkin. "International Migration in the Dominican Republic: Implications for Development Planning." *International Migration Review* 16, no. 4 (1982): 819–836.

New York City, Department of City Planning. "The Newest New Yorkers, 1990–1994: An Analysis of Immigration to NYC in the Early 1990s." New York: New York City Department of City Planning, 1996.

Pan American Health Organization (PAHO). *Health in the Americas*, 1998 ed., vol. 1. Washington, DC: PAHO, 1998.

Peach, Ceri. *West Indian Migration.* London: Oxford University Press, 1968.

Portes, Alejandro, and Luis E. Guarnizo. "Tropical Capitalists: U.S.-Bound Immigration and Small-Enterprise Development in the Dominican Republic." In *Migration, Remittances, and Small Business Development: Mexico and Caribbean Basin Countries,* edited by Sergio Díaz-Briquets and Sidney A. Weintraub. Boulder: Westview, 1991.

Potts, John. *The World Labor Market: A History of Migration.* London: Zed Books, 1990.

Proudfoot, John. *Population Movements in the Caribbean.* New York: Negro Universities Press, 1970.

Richardson, Bonham C. *Caribbean Migrants: Environmental and Human Survival on St. Kitts and Nevis.* Knoxville: University of Tennessee Press, 1983.

Russell, Sharon S., and Michael S. Teitelbaum. *International Migration and International Trade.* World Bank Discussion Paper No. 160. Washington, DC: World Bank, 1992.

Simmons, Alan. *International Migration, Refugee Flows, and Human Rights in North America: The Impact of Free Trade and Restructuring*. New York: Center for Migration Studies, 1996.

Stalker, Peter. *The Work of Strangers: A Survey of International Labour Migration*. Geneva: International Labour Office, 1994.

Sunshine, Catherine A. *The Caribbean: Survival, Struggle and Sovereignty*. Washington, DC: Ecumenical Program on Central America and the Caribbean, 1985.

U.S. Immigration and Naturalization Service (INS). *Annual Reports of the Immigration and Naturalization Service*. Washington, DC: Department of Justice, 1964–1968.

———. *1994 Statistical Yearbook of the Immigration and Naturalization Service*. Washington, DC: Department of Justice, 1994.

13

Trends and Prospects

Richard S. Hillman and Andrés Serbin

In one way or another, each chapter in this book has established the importance of understanding the Caribbean region as a whole. Despite linguistic, geographic, and other dissimilarities, common experiences and challenges compel an integrated approach to contemporary problem-solving. Global trends, moreover, require policymakers in the Caribbean to recognize the logic of regional integration as a means to achieve political and economic development.

This logic is compelling for insular microstates that individually are weak compared to the larger, more powerful states with which they must interact. Caribbean nations are similarly at a disadvantage with regard to market agents, such as transnational corporations, international financial organizations, and private banks. Also, there has been a dilution of the strategic importance of the region since the end of the Cold War. Caribbean countries are no longer viewed as objects of the East-West rivalry and therefore cannot play one side against the other to their own benefit.

Although regional integration increasingly has been recognized as a serious option for the Caribbean, difficult obstacles inherent in intergovernmental dynamics and international relations have stultified its full realization. An interesting new trend, however, has emerged as a potential catalyst for the promotion of modifications in intergovernmental and international initiatives that would support political, economic, and social development in the whole Caribbean region. Transnational civil society, formed by nongovernmental organizations (NGOs) and networks, old and new social movements, and professional and academic associations, often transcends the domestic sphere extending to regional and global levels in its initiatives, agendas, and demands.

Transnational civil society—through the pressure, advocacy, and influence of regional and global nongovernmental networks—can act as a regulating (and potentially correcting) mechanism for the actions of nation-states and the international market. These networks address social issues and promote increased participation of social actors in decisionmaking processes. In this regard, transnational civil society, still in its incipient and formative stage, is beginning to assume an important role in the regional integration processes. Especially in the Caribbean, it is developing an unexpected regional leadership in promoting an intersocietal integration process while contributing to the advancement of the process of regionalism where intergovernmental initiatives and social actors are converging, although with difficulties and obstacles.

■ The Intergovernmental Dynamic

The Association of Caribbean States (ACS), founded in Cartagena, Colombia, in 1994, crystallized the idea of a greater Caribbean by bringing together fourteen of the fifteen countries from the Caribbean Common Market and Community (CARICOM, a Caribbean economic community), the Central American countries, the Group of Three (G-3) countries (Colombia, Mexico, and Venezuela), Cuba, the Dominican Republic, and Guyana. Associate members include Aruba, the Netherlands Antilles, and France (representing French Guiana, Guadeloupe, and Martinique). This intergovernmental initiative was promoted, within the framework of the Economic Commission on Latin America and the Caribbean proposals for open regionalism, by the English-speaking members of CARICOM on the recommendations of the West Indian Commission as well as by the G-3 countries.

The ACS was founded due to the acceleration of subregional and regional integration processes in the Western Hemisphere. This rationale implied the search for expanded economic relationships for the insular Caribbean states, a politically and socially stabilized region for the G-3 countries, and the development of a common platform for negotiations with the United States and Canada aimed at a speedier and smoother entry into the North American Free Trade Agreement (NAFTA). The long-term goal is entry into the Free Trade Area of the Americas.

However, the inclusion of Cuba and the dependent territories, associated states, and overseas departments of European countries created difficulties for the ACS. Obstacles included U.S. pressure on the Cuban government; complex negotiations regarding the distinctive status of the British-associated states and territories (the British Virgin Islands, the Cayman Islands, the Turks and Caicos, Montserrat, and Anguilla); the situation of Aruba and the federation of the Netherlands Antilles as members of the kingdom of the Netherlands; and the status of the overseas departments of Guadeloupe, Martinique, and French Guiana as French territories.[1]

These difficulties exist alongside others. These include the internal negotiations leading to the establishment of a secretariat in Port-of-Spain, Trinidad; the appointment of a secretary-general (Ambassador Simón Molina Duarte of Venezuela); the definition of the budget and contributions from member countries; and the formulation of regulations, procedures, and internal rules. All have absorbed a great deal of the energy and available time in the ACS in the years since its creation (especially in negotiations in the technical and ministerial meetings and in the creation of different commissions). But these are not the only reasons explaining the lack of progress. The dynamic of hemispheric integration and the interrelationships among diverse actors of the greater Caribbean also have caused delays.

At the hemispheric level, the polarization between NAFTA and the Common Market of the South (Mercosur) has had an impact on many of the problems experienced by the ACS. Mexico's membership in NAFTA, along with its active involvement in the political and institutional forging of the ACS, have generated expectations among countries in the region. Some of them hoped to use their closer links with Mexico in the ACS as a bridge to NAFTA. Also, they would like to counteract the negative impact of Mexican membership in NAFTA on the Caribbean Basin Initiative, launched by the United States in the early 1980s. Despite its influence in the formation of the ACS, Mexico has chosen to give more priority to NAFTA and to developing closer economic relations with its North and Central American partners.

Venezuela signed a free-trade agreement with CARICOM in 1991 as part of its active Caribbean policy. However, the administrations of Presidents Rafael Caldera and Hugo Chávez gave priority to relations with Brazil and Mercosur. Colombia also signed a similar agreement with CARICOM but then deepened its relations with Mercosur.

These trends have resulted in the deceleration of the free-trade agreements and integration processes that were initiated in the 1990s. In this context, the Dominican Republic, which (with Haiti and the CARICOM countries) is a member of CARIFORUM (an ad-hoc organization that groups the Caribbean beneficiaries of the Lomé convention with the European Union), offered to act as a "bridge" in building a "strategic alliance" between the countries of Central America and the Caribbean in the framework of the ACS in 1997 (Ceara Hatton 1997). Nonetheless, this strategic alliance will have to overcome many obstacles on both sides.

The Central American countries are advancing toward closer relations with Mexico and their traditional trading partner, the United States. At the same time, they are taking steps to deepen the integration of the isthmus through increased intraregional trade and a proposed political union. Banana production and the existence of export quotas for entry of that product into the market of the European Union continue to be a point of friction between CARICOM and Central America, exacerbated by the recent dispute within the World Trade Organization between the United States and the European Union.

There may be points of convergence. There is a need to establish a common position in response to the growing limitations of the Caribbean Basin Initiative, particularly in terms of competition from Mexican products in NAFTA. After a CARICOM–Central American meeting in Georgetown, Guyana, in 1998, however, the initiative for a strategic alliance received a cold reception. It was noted in the final declaration as being of "great interest" but without any specific steps or commitments taken to achieve it (Byron and Girvan 2000).

Also, full Cuban incorporation in the region remains problematic. The Cuba factor continues to reflect the inertial effects of the Cold War despite Cuba's membership in CARICOM and CARIFORUM (with official observer status). However, there was a renewed dynamic of increasing relations among the insular Caribbean countries in 1999. This was closely associated with the CARICOM strategy to widen insular Caribbean interaction and consolidate the CARICOM integration process. Representatives of Cuba and the Dominican Republic have been attending CARICOM meetings, Haiti has become a full member, negotiations regarding Cuba–Dominican Republic–CARICOM free-trade agreements have advanced, and relations between Cuba and the Dominican Republic are deepening, with both countries actively engaged in the Regional Negotiating Machinery focused on the post-Lomé negotiations with the European Union (Ceara Hatton 2000).

The regional geopolitical picture and the difficulties that stand in the way of the development of the ACS are complicated by disagreements over the agenda of the regional grouping. Although the meetings of the ACS council of ministers (Port-of-Spain, Trinidad, August 1995; Havana, Cuba, December 1996; Cartagena, Colombia, November 1997; Santo Domingo, Dominican Republic, April 1999; island of Margarita, December 2001; and Belize City, Belize, November 2002) have focused on issues of tourism, transport, and trade, no significant advances have been made. The Trinidad-Guyana proposal at the 1996 Havana summit for a regional free-trade agreement has met with indifference or reticence from other countries, especially Mexico.

There has, however, been discussion within the ACS on the approval of tariff preferential agreements among member countries.[2] And progress has been made in important issues for the greater Caribbean, such as studies on sustainable tourism, coordination of transportation initiatives, as well as ACS special committees—especially the committee on natural disasters and catastrophes (Ceara Hatton 1997; Byron 1997).

After long delays, government representatives finally established in 1999 a set of rules for the recognition and informal participation of social actors in the ACS. The Regional Coordination of Economic and Social Research (CRIES), a broad-based network of NGOs and research centers, was thereby admitted to the ACS. Although CARICOM approved a social charter on the initiative of the Caribbean Policy Development Center—an umbrella organization for different island NGOs—formal consultative status has not yet been granted to social actors.[3]

■ Transnational Civil Society

Since the early 1990s civil society has formed regional social networks by promoting intersocietal integration and by developing a dialogue with organizations involved in subregional integration (Serbin 1997). For example, the Civil Society Charter for the Caribbean Community recently was approved by CARICOM (Jácome 1999; Byron and Girvan 2000; Yanes 2000). Another example is the Caribbean Policy Development Centre (CPDC), which seeks

> to help NGOs in the Caribbean to understand where and how policies are made and how they affect our daily lives; to share information about these policies; to build the confidence and ability of Caribbean people to influence public policy; to work constructively with governments to design and support policies that benefit and improve the lives of Caribbean people; and to work together to change policies that do not benefit Caribbean people. (*CPDC Bulletin* 1996:8)

Central American initiatives have experienced problems but affected the restructuring of the Civil Society Consultative Committee of the Central American Integration System after the impact of Hurricane Mitch (Yanes 2000). The present composition of this consultative committee includes a group of twenty Central American organizations from across the region.[4]

Paralleling these initiatives, CRIES was formed in 1982.[5] According to the organization, the CRIES strategy is based on two fundamental premises:

> First, any solution for the major social and economic problems of the region's countries and territories necessarily has to pass through a regional project of Greater Caribbean integration. This project can only be built with the active participation of all the sectors of regional civil society. (CRIES 1997)

Since 1997 CRIES has actively promoted a program for the participation of civil society in the integration process by organizing workshops, conducting studies, and using a specific strategy to intensify the dialogue between regional governments and actors from civil society. In this framework, CRIES, together with the Venezuelan Institute of Social and Political Studies (INVESP), actively promoted the Forum of Greater Caribbean Civil Society.

■ The Forum of Greater Caribbean Civil Society

The creation of the forum began with a regional project on the sociopolitical agenda of integration, initiated by INVESP in 1995.[6] The project's original purpose was to identify the social actors involved in the regional integration process and their regional agendas, as well as to contribute to design mechanisms for participation by such actors in regional decisionmaking (INVESP 1996).

In the framework of this project, a first regional conference was held in Caracas in 1996, with the backing of the Latin American Economic System. A broad spectrum of representatives from NGOs, businesses and trade unions, and intergovernmental organizations from the greater Caribbean attended. During the conference, a proposal to organize the Forum of Greater Caribbean Civil Society was discussed, based on a 1996 study by Alvaro de la Ossa. The proposal gained support in successive workshops in 1996 and 1997 held in Guatemala, Caracas, and Barbados with political and academic actors and NGOs and was included in the extension of the INVESP project to the whole of Latin America and the Caribbean. Representatives of Mercosur and the Inter-American Development Bank attended one of these meetings.

In May 1997 the CRIES general assembly elected a new board (with a balanced representation from the insular Caribbean, Central America, and the G-3 countries). A mandate was approved that outlined a strategic program. The Regionalism and Civil Society program was designed to match the technical and academic capacities of CRIES to the needs and demands of the greater Caribbean civil society.

After the 1997 annual conference of the Caribbean Studies Association in Barranquilla, Colombia, the Colombian foreign minister and the ACS secretary-general invited regional academic networks and organizations to participate in the meeting of the ACS council of ministers to be held in Cartagena. The invitation explicitly mentioned the role played by CRIES in promoting a regional view of the greater Caribbean. Objections to the participation of civil society in the ACS, however, were based on the argument that no regulation had been approved as to the recognition and admission of social actors into the organization.

Nevertheless, the activities of the first Forum of Greater Caribbean Civil Society opened in Cartagena on November 23, 1997, with delegates representing more than 800 NGOs, social movements, and academic organizations. During the three days of the forum, a series of general documents were discussed and approved.[7] The decision to make the forum a permanent body was legally validated through a constitutive act. The executive committee was confirmed in its functions and given a two-year term. Its mandate was to proceed with the arrangements for future meetings, foster research, organize information workshops, develop an education campaign, and support the work of committees. New committees were created to deal with issues of labor, education, science, and technology. A committee was also appointed to present the conclusions of the forum to the ACS council of ministers.

The presentation of the forum's conclusions to the ACS set a precedent not only for the greater Caribbean but also for the entire Western Hemisphere. The forum highlighted the dialogue between the civil society of the greater Caribbean and the ACS; the urgent need for the joint development of the region; and the importance of avoiding exclusion in regional decisionmaking. On the initiative of regional civil society with the support of several governments, the first step was taken on intergovernmental and intersocietal initiatives for integration in the greater Caribbean.

A series of workshops and the second forum (Bridgetown, Barbados, 1998) and third forum (Cancún, Mexico, 1999) were the result of intensive regional work promoted by CRIES, INVESP, and other regional NGO networks. As a result of this process the ACS council of ministers (Panama, 1999) admitted CRIES as a regional social actor. This allows CRIES to participate at the council meetings and to work, on a consultative basis, with the different ACS committees in promoting a regional social agenda that is based on the conclusions of the debates at the Civil Society Forum of the Greater Caribbean. The election of professor Norman Girvan as ACS secretary-general at the Panama meeting opens the door to the increased participation of NGOs and academics in the regional integration intergovernmental scheme. However, the official recognition of the forum is still pending at the ACS, notwithstanding the fact that the application was submitted by its executive committee in 1998.

■ The Future

These trends, as well as the discussions contained in each chapter of this book, lead to the conclusion that existing political and economic structures in the region continue to experience debt, widespread domestic poverty, unemployment and crime, illegal migration, illicit narcotics trafficking, corruption, and social malaise. Although transnational civil society can begin addressing these problems, the best hope is for consulting with and lobbying existing political institutions. Meetings and workshops are the beginning of a process that could lead to greater cooperation for eventual regional integration.

If the past is prelude, the region's evolution as a crucible of many civilizations, its unique amalgamation of peoples and cultures, its beauty, and its potential will produce important contributions. The evolution, however, has been tortuous and will probably continue to present difficulties in the near future.

We have seen the impact of location, population trends, resource availability, and the environment on economic development and the people in the

Caribbean. The legacies of colonialism, plantation life, and slavery that persist in influencing contemporary realities have created challenges for political development. Different political, social, and economic institutions have converged in similar patterns of patron-clientelism, elite dominance, and creole fusion. Although many development strategies and economic programs have been tested, none appears to have mitigated the effects of dependency or general structural weakness. Regional integration offers hope, but the long history of external intervention in the region and populist-inspired nationalism have had negative influences on cooperative policies. Moreover, there are crucial issues regarding the ecology of the region, the natural assets and liabilities inherent in economies (many dependent on tourism) affected by hurricanes, depletion of coral reefs, and other forms of environmental degradation and pollution. Patterns of race, ethnicity, class, and gender are problematic as well as promising. Although these socially constructed concepts are often used to rationalize and legitimize disparities in status and wealth among different groups, the relative absence of ethnic and racial violence can be attributed in large part to the integrative creole model inherent in the multicultural societies of the Caribbean. This dynamic is illustrated in the politicized nature of much of the literature and popular culture. Finally, the geographical diversity and impact of the Caribbean diaspora are essential parts of this equation.

Hopefully, the creation and consolidation of the ACS and the civil society initiatives constitute significant steps toward the convergence of governmental and nongovernmental efforts to integrate the greater Caribbean. These steps must go well beyond the predominantly economic (and often purely commercial) dimension by including a broad spectrum of social, political, environmental, and cultural issues.

In essence, the process may depend on the capacity of the ACS to overcome its own organizational and political difficulties. There is a need for a legitimate interlocutor, especially for the social sectors that are excluded and marginalized from the benefits and the decisions related to the greater Caribbean integration process. In order for the forum to represent the interests of the greater Caribbean's civil society, it is necessary to articulate the needs and objectives of domestic social organizations and movements in each country (Duncan 1997; Jácome 1999). It will also be necessary to develop closer links with movements and organizations that are promoting regional and global agendas.

Progress also depends on overcoming the political, organizational, and financial weaknesses plaguing regional organizations and networks, as well as overcoming the memory of integration attempts that have faltered in the past. It is crucial that there be continuous dialogue with regional governments and intergovernmental organizations to build equitable, participative, and sustainable development in the Caribbean. Although civil society has the potential to play a vital role in the representation of popular interests, ultimately national governments must implement policies that address the region's endemic problems and fulfill the expectations of its people in order to ensure the future stability of the Caribbean region.

■ Notes

1. This is a situation that has been generating difficulties in the ACS. At present, France has associate status as the representative of its Caribbean overseas departments; in the Dutch Caribbean, the Netherlands is a member with observer status, the Netherlands Antilles has associated status, and Aruba has postponed its application for permanent membership. The United Kingdom joined the ACS as an observer, leaving to its associated states and territories the decision whether and how to join the ACS.

2. As noted by one scholar:

> It could have considerable symbolic and practical importance. First it would provide tangible evidence of the existence of the ACS as a trade grouping and help to draw the attention of the business community to the opportunities for trade within the Caribbean Basin. Secondly, the CPT [Caribbean preferential tariff] provides for asymmetrical reductions based on differential levels of development among the member states. Acceptance of asymmetry by the larger ACS states could have a "spill-over" effect on the WTO [World Trade Organization] and the FTAA [Free Trade Area of the Americas] negotiations. It would establish a precedent that the small economies of CARICOM and Central America could use in pressing for special and differential treatment for countries that are less developed, or small and vulnerable. (Girvan 2000:6–7)

3. The twenty-one-member organizations of the Caribbean Policy Development Center, based in Barbados, include: Afrika Hall, Barbados; Association of Development Agencies and Association of National Development Agencies, Belize; Association of Caribbean Economists, Jamaica; Caribbean Association of Feminist Research and Action, Trinidad; Caribbean Conservation Association, Barbados; Caribbean Conference of Churches, Trinidad; Caribbean Organisation of Indigenous Peoples, Guyana; Caribbean Human Rights Network, Barbados; Centre of Studies of America, Havana; Economic Research Center for the Caribbean, Santo Domingo; Caribbean Network for Integrated Rural Development, Trinidad; Eastern Caribbean Popular Theatre Organisation, St. Vincent; Women and Development Union, Barbados; and Windward Islands Farmers Association, St. Vincent (*CPDC Bulletin* 1996).

4. See Rojas (1997:4) for a list of members.

5. CRIES maintains close links with the Caribbean Policy Development Center and the Iniciativa Civil para la Integración Centroamericana and is constituted by the following organizations: Association for the Advancement of Social Sciences, Guatemala; National Foundation for Development, Institute for Economic and Social Development of El Salvador; Salvadorian Programme of Development and Environment Research and TENDENCIES, El Salvador; Documentation Centre of Honduras, National Research and Studies Centre, and the Team of Reflection, Research, and Communication, Honduras; Centres of Research Studies and the Research Centre of the Atlantic Coast, Nicaragua; Training Centre for Development, Ecumenical Research Department and the Central American Foundation for Integration, Costa

Rica; Panamanian Center of Studies and Social Action, Training and Social Development Centre, Justo Arosemena Latin American Studies Centre and the Research and Teaching Centre of Panama, Panama; Centre of Studies of America, Cuba; Centre of Research and Economic and Social Training for Development and Haitian Group of Research and Pedagogic Action in Haiti; Economic Research Center for the Caribbean, Research Center for Feminine Action and the Centre of Research and Social Promotion, Dominican Republic; Caribbean Policy Development Centre and the Women and Development Unit, Barbados; Society for the Promotion of Education and Research of Belize; Association of Caribbean Economists, Consortium Graduate School of Social Sciences, and the Institute of Social and Economic Research, Jamaica; Center for the Studies of Puerto Rican Reality, Puerto Rico; Caribbean Network for Integrated Rural Development, Trinidad; Mutual Support Forum, Mexico; Institute of Political Studies and International Relations, Colombia; and the Venezuelan Institute of Social and Political Studies.

6. INVESP has been a member of CRIES since 1990. INVESP was elected to chair the board of CRIES in May 1997. The other elected representatives are from the National Foundation for Development of El Salvador; Advancement of Social Sciences in Guatemala; the Mutual Support Forum of Mexico; and the Institute of Social and Economic Research, University of the West Indies, of Barbados and Jamaica.

7. The documents are available in a volume published by INVESP/CRIES in 1999.

■ Bibliography

Acta Constitutiva de la Asociación de Estados del Caribe (Constitutive Act of the Association of Caribbean States), Cartagena de Indias, July 1994.

Byron, Jessica. "The Association of Caribbean States: New Regional Interlocutor for the Caribbean Basin?" Paper presented at the Fifth Conference of the Association of Caribbean Economists, Havana, November 30–December 2, 1997.

Byron, Jessica, and Norman Girvan. "CARICOM/CARIFORUM: integración regional y los temas del comercio internacional" (CARICOM/CARIFORUM: regional integration and the themes of international commerce). In *Anuario de la Integración del Gran Caribe 2000* (Greater Caribbean integration annual report 2000). Caracas: Nueva Sociedad/CIEI/CRIES/INVESP, 2000, pp. 59–82.

Caribbean and Central American Report—CCAR (London), 15 July, 1997.

Caribbean Policy Development Centre (CPDC). "Intervention of the CPDC to the 18th Meeting of the CARICOM Heads of Government, Jamaica, 1 July 1997." In *Pensamiento Propio* (Managua), no. 4 (May–August 1997): 140–148.

Ceara Hatton, Miguel. "El Caribe insular en la dinámica de la integración hemisférica" (The insular Caribbean in hemispheric integration dynamic). Paper presented at the Fifth Conference of the Association of Caribbean Economists, Havana, November 30–December 2, 1997.

———. "El Caribe: cumbres, creación de identidad e integración" (The Caribbean: summits, creation of identity, and integration). Unpublished manuscript, March 2000.

CPDC Bulletin (Bridgetown), December 1996.

CRIES (Regional Coordination of Economic and Social Research). Informational brochure, 1997.

de la Ossa, Alvaro. "Mecanismos políticos y económicos para la participación de los actores sociales en el proceso de regionalización" (Political and economic methods for the participation of social actors in the regionalization process). Paper, SELA/INVESP, Caracas, February 1996.

———. "Unificación centroamericana: la política primero, el desarrollo quién sabe" (Central American unification: first politics, development, who knows?). In *Anuario de la Integración del Gran Caribe 2000* (Greater Caribbean Integration annual report 2000). Caracas: Nueva Sociedad/CIEI/CRIES/INVESP, 2000, pp. 83–100.

———, comp. *La integración social: nuevas rutas hacia la discordia* (Social integration: new routes to disagreement). San José de Costa Rica: Fundación Fridrich Ebert/Fundación Centroamericana para la Integración, 1997.

Duncan, Neville. "Anglophone Caribbean Non-State Sectors in National Integration: A Vital Step in Caricom and Greater Caribbean Integration." Unpublished manuscript, 1997.

Girvan, Norman. "The ACS as a Caribbean Cooperative Zone." Paper presented to the Conference on Caribbean Survival in the 21st Century, Port-of-Spain, Trinidad, March 2000.

Gonzalez, Anthony "Globalización, regionalización y las relaciones entre el Caribe de habla inglesa y América del Sur en el contexto hemisférico" (Globalization, regionalization, and relations between the Anglophone Caribbean and South America in the hemispheric context). In *América Latina y el Caribe anglófono: ¿Hacia una nueva relación?* (Latin America and the Anglophone Caribbean: toward a new relationship?), edited by Andrés Serbin. Buenos Aires: Instituto de Servicio Exterior de la Nación/Grupo Editor Latinoamericano, 1997, pp. 193–239.

Hillman, Richard S., and Thomas J. D'Agostino. *Distant Neighbors in the Caribbean: The Dominican Republic and Jamaica in Comparative Perspective*. New York: Praeger Publishers, 1992.

Iniciativa Civil para la Integración Centroamericana (ICIC). "Posición y propuesta de las organizaciones aglutinadas en ICIC y CACI con respecto a la evaluación del sistema de integración centroamericana" (Position and proposal of the ICIC and CACI associated organizations with respect to the evaluation of the Central American integration system). In *Pensamiento Propio* (Managua), no. 4 (May–August 1997): 159–167.

———. "Plan de trabajo encuentro de los pueblos" (Plan of job placement in towns). Unpublished manuscript, Guatemala, August 30 and 31, 1997.

INVESP (Venezuelan Institute of Social and Political Studies). *La agenda sociopolítica de la integración en el Gran Caribe, Programa Regionalismo y Sociedad Civil* (The sociopolitical agenda for greater Caribbean integration). Folleto explicativo, 1996.

INVESP/CRIES. *The Second Greater Caribbean Civil Society Forum: Documents and Proceedings*. Caracas: INVESP, 1999.

Jácome, Francine. "Las sociedades civiles frente al proceso de integración." In *La otra integración: procesos intersocietales y parlementos regionales en el Caribe* (The other integration: intersocietal and regional parliamentarian processes in the Caribbean), edited by F. Jácome. Caracas: Cuadernos del INVESP, no. 4, 1999, pp. 73–105.

———. "El Foro Permanente de la Sociedad Civil del Gran Caribe: evaluación preliminar" (The Permanent Forum of Greater Caribbean Civil Society: preliminary evaluation). In *Anuario de la Integración del Gran Caribe 2000* (Greater Caribbean integration annual report 2000). Caracas: Nueva Sociedad/CIEI/CRIES/INVESP, 2000, pp. 179–197.

Kaul, Inge, Isabelle Grunberg, and Marc Stern. *Bienes públicos mundiales: Cooperación internacional en el siglo XXI* (Global public welfare: international cooperation in the twentieth century). New York: Oxford University Press, 1999.

Lewis, David. "Esquemas de integración regional y subregional en la Cuenca del Caribe" (Regional and subregional integration schemes in the Caribbean Basin). In *América Latina y el Caribe anglófono: ¿Hacia una nueva relación?* (Latin America and the Anglophone Caribbean: toward a new relationship?), edited by Andrés Serbin. Buenos Aires: Instituto de Servicio Exterior de la Nación/Grupo Editor Latinoamericano, 1997, pp. 95–142.

Nogueira, Uziel. "The Integration Movement in the Caribbean at Crossroads: Towards a New Approach of Integration." Working Paper, INTAL Series. Washington, DC: Inter-American Development Bank, April 1997.

Ramsaran, Ramesh. "Economías pequeñas, preferencias comerciales y relaciones con América del Sur: desafíos que enfrenta el Caribe de habla inglesa en una economía mundial cambiante" (Small economies, commercial preferences, and relations with South America: challenges that confront the Anglophone Caribbean in a changing global economy). In *América Latina y el Caribe anglófono: ¿Hacia una nueva relación?* (Latin America and the Anglophone Caribbean: toward a new relationship?), edited by Andrés Serbin. Buenos Aires: Instituto de Servicio Exterior de la Nación/Grupo Editor Latinoamericano, 1997.

Reinicke, Wolfgang, and Francis Deng. *Critical Choices: The United Nations, Networks, and the Future of Global Governance*. Executive Summary. Washington, DC: Global Public Policy Project, January 2000.

Rojas, Zaida. "Organizaciones civiles buscan espacio en la integración" (Civil organizations seek a place in integration). In *Boletín PIECA* (Guatemala), no. 3 (October 1997): 2–6.

Serbin, Andrés. *El Caribe: ¿zona de paz?* (The Caribbean: a peace zone?). Caracas: Comisión Sudamericana de Paz/Nueva Sociedad, 1989. Also published in English as *Caribbean Geopolitics: Towards Security Through Peace?* Boulder: Lynne Rienner Publishers, 1991.

———. "Los desafíos del proceso de regionalización de la Cuenca del Caribe: integración, soberanía, democracia e identidad" (The challenges of the regionalization process in the Caribbean Basin: integration, sovereignty, democracy, and identity). In *Revista Venezolana de Economía y Ciencias Sociales* (Caracas), no. 4 (1995): 75–112.

———. "Globalización, déficit democrático y sociedad civil en los procesos de integración" (Globalization, the democratic deficit, and civil society in the integration process). In *Pensamiento Propio* (Managua), no. 3 (January–April 1997): 98–117.

———. *Sunset Over the Islands: The Caribbean in an Age of Global and Regional Challenges*. London: Macmillan, 1998.

———. "Integración de la sociedad civil en el Gran Caribe: Balance de un año (1997–1998)" (Integration of civil society in the greater Caribbean: a one-year inventory, 1997–1998). In *La "otra" integración: procesos intersocietales y parlamentos regionales en el Gran Caribe*, edited by F. Jácome. Caracas: Cuadernos del INVESP No. 4, 1999, pp. 5–24.

———. "Globalización, regionalismo e integración regional: tendencias actuales en el Gran Caribe" (Globalization, regionalism, and regional integration: current trends in the greater Caribbean). In *Anuario de la Integración del Gran Caribe 2000* (Greater Caribbean integration annual report 2000). Caracas: Nueva Sociedad/CIEI/CRIES/INVESP, 2000, pp. 11–35.

Sutton, Paul. "El régimen bananero de la Unión Europea el Caribe y América Latina" (The banana regime in the European Union, the Caribbean, and Latin America). In *Pensamiento Propio* (Managua), no. 4 (May–August 1997): 25–53.

Yanes, Hernán. "Redes de ONGs e integración en el Gran Caribe" (NGO networks and integration in the greater Caribbean). In *Anuario de la Integración del Gran Caribe 2000* (Greater Caribbean integration annual report 2000). Caracas: Nueva Sociedad/CIEI/CRIES/INVESP, 2000, pp. 161–177.

Acronyms

ACP	African, Caribbean, and Pacific group of states
ACS	Association of Caribbean States
CACM	Central American Common Market
CARICOM	Caribbean Common Market and Community (a Caribbean economic community)
CARIFORUM	Forum of the Caribbean Common Market and Community
CBI	Caribbean Basin Initiative
CIA	Central Intelligence Agency
CIM	Inter-American Commission of Women
CRIES	Regional Coordination of Economic and Social Research
ECCB	Eastern Caribbean Central Bank
ECLAC	Economic Commission for Latin America and the Caribbean (United Nations)
EPZ	export-processing zone
EU	European Union
FL	Fanmi Lavalas
FSLN	Sandinista National Liberation Front
FTAA	Free Trade Area of the Americas
G-3	Group of Three countries (Colombia, Mexico, and Venezuela)
GDP	gross domestic product
GNP	gross national product
HDI	Human Development Index
IMF	International Monetary Fund
INVESP	Venezuelan Institute of Social and Political Studies
ISDHR	Institute for the Study of Democracy and Human Rights

ITCZ	Intertropical Convergence Zone
JLP	Jamaica Labour Party
JTA	Jamaica Teacher's Association
Mercosur	Common Market of the South
NAFTA	North American Free Trade Agreement
NGOs	nongovernmental organizations
NJM	New Jewel Movement
OECD	Organization for Economic Cooperation and Development
OECS	Organization of Eastern Caribbean States
PNC	People's National Congress
PNP	People's National Party
PPP	People's Progressive Party
PRD	Partido Revolucionario Dominicano; Dominican Revolutionary Party
PRG	People's Revolutionary Government
TWA	Trinidad Workingmen's Association
UFCO	United Fruit Company
UN	United Nations
UNDP	United Nations Development Programme
UNIA	United Negro Improvement Association
WIF	West Indies Federation
WTO	World Trade Organization

Basic Political Data

The United Nations Development Programme's Human Development Index (HDI) measures a country's achievements in terms of life expectancy, education (as reflected in adult literacy rates and combined primary, secondary, and tertiary school enrollments), and adjusted real income (through gross domestic product per capita in purchasing power parity in U.S. dollars). HDI scores range from 0.0 (low) to 1.0 (high), with higher numbers indicating a greater level of development in the specified areas.

The Netherlands Antilles, consisting of Bonaire, Curaçao, Saba, St. Eustatius, and St. Maarten, is a former Dutch dependency that is now autonomous in internal affairs under the charter of the kingdom of the Netherlands. Aruba, a former part of the Netherlands Antilles, assumed domestic autonomy as a member of the kingdom of the Netherlands on January 1, 1986.

Antigua and Barbuda
Capital City Saint John's
Date of Independence from Great Britain November 1, 1981
Population 66,487
HDI Score .795
Current Leader Prime Minister Lester Bryant Bird

Bahamas
Capital City Nassau
Date of Independence from Great Britain July 10, 1973
Population 307,153
HDI Score .820
Current Leader Prime Minister Perry Christie

Barbados
Capital City Bridgetown
Date of Independence from Great Britain November 30, 1966
Population 268,189
HDI Score .864
Current Leader Prime Minister Owen Seymour Arthur

Belize
Capital City Belmopan
Date of Independence from Great Britain September 21, 1981
Population 247,107
HDI Score .776
Current Leader Prime Minister Said Musa

Colombia
Capital City Bogotá
Date of Independence from Spain July 20, 1810
Population 43,035,480
HDI Score .765
Current Leader President Álvaro Uribe

Costa Rica
Capital City San José
Date of Independence from Spain September 15, 1821
Population 3,886,318
HDI Score .821
Current Leader President Abel Pacheco de la Espriella

Cuba
Capital City Havana
Date of Independence from the United States May 20, 1902 (occupation by the United States followed defeat of Spain in Spanish-American War of 1898)
Population 11,221,723
HDI Score .791
Current Leader President Fidel Castro

Dominica
Capital City Roseau
Date of Independence from Great Britain November 3, 1978
Population 73,199
HDI Score .800
Current Leader Prime Minister Pierre Charles

Dominican Republic
Capital City Santo Domingo
Date of Independence from Haiti February 27, 1844 (occupation by Haiti followed declaration of independence from Spain in 1821)
Population 8,505,204
HDI Score .722
Current Leader President Hipólito Mejía

Grenada
Capital City Saint George's
Date of Independence from Great Britain February 7, 1974
Population 99,000
HDI Score .795
Current Leader Prime Minister Keith Mitchell

Guatemala
Capital City Guatemala City
Date of Independence from Spain September 15, 1821
Population 12,974,361
HDI Score .626
Current Leader President Alfonso Portillo

Guyana
Capital City Georgetown
Date of Independence from Great Britain May 26, 1966
Population 766,256
HDI Score .704
Current Leader President Bharrat Jagdeo

Haiti
Capital City Port-au-Prince
Date of Independence from France January 1, 1804
Population 8,114,161
HDI Score .467
Current Leader President Jean-Bertrand Aristide

Honduras
Capital City Tegucigalpa
Date of Independence from Spain September 15, 1821
Population 6,575,264
HDI Score .634
Current Leader President Ricardo Maduro

Jamaica
Capital City Kingston
Date of Independence from Great Britain August 6, 1962
Population 2,668,230
HDI Score .738
Current Leader Prime Minister Percival J. Patterson

Nicaragua
Capital City Managua
Date of Independence from Spain September 15, 1821
Population 5,201,641
HDI Score .635
Current Leader President Enrique Bolaños Geyer

Panama
Capital City Panama City
Date of Independence from Spain November 3, 1903
Population 2,900,589
HDI Score .784
Current Leader President Mireya Moscoso

St. Kitts and Nevis
Capital City Basseterre
Date of Independence from Great Britain September 19, 1983
Population 41,082
HDI Score .800
Current Leader Prime Minister Denzil Douglas

St. Lucia
Capital City Castries
Date of Independence from Great Britain February 22, 1979
Population 158,134
HDI Score .749
Current Leader Prime Minister Kenny Anthony

St. Vincent and the Grenadines
Capital City Kingstown
Date of Independence from Great Britain October 27, 1979
Population 115,881
HDI Score .748
Current Leader Prime Minister Ralph Gonsalves

Suriname
Capital City Paramaribo
Date of Independence from the Netherlands November 25, 1975
Population 419,656
HDI Score .758
Current Leader President Ronald Venetiaan

Trinidad and Tobago
Capital City Port-of-Spain
Date of Independence from Great Britain August 31, 1962
Population 1,309,608
HDI Score .798
Current Leader Prime Minister Patrick Manning

Venezuela
Capital City Caracas
Date of Independence from Spain July 5, 1811
Population 24,632,376
HDI Score .765
Current Leader President Hugo Chávez

■ Nonindependent Territories in the Caribbean

Anguilla Associated state within the British Commonwealth (1982)

Aruba Member of the Kingdom of the Netherlands (1986)

Bonaire Member of the Netherlands Antilles (1954)

British Virgin Islands British crown colony (1967)

Cayman Islands British crown colony (1972)

Curaçao Member of the Netherlands Antilles (1954)

French Guiana Overseas Department of France (1946)

Guadeloupe Overseas Department of France (1946)

Martinique Overseas Department of France (1946)

Montserrat British crown colony (1966)

Puerto Rico Commonwealth ("free associated state") associated with the United States (1952)

Saba Member of the Netherlands Antilles (1954)

St. Barthélemy Administrative District of Guadeloupe (1946)

St. Eustatius Member of the Netherlands Antilles (1954)

St. Maarten Member of the Netherlands Antilles (1954)

St. Martin Administrative District of Guadeloupe (1946)

Turks and Caicos British crown colony (1976)

U.S. Virgin Islands U.S. territory with local self-government (1968)

Sources: The United Nations Development Programme Human Development Report, available online at http://hdr.undp.org; The World Bank, available online at http://worldbank.org; and *The CIA World Factbook*, available online at http:// www.odci.gov/cia/publications/factbook/index.html.

The Contributors

David Baronov is assistant professor of sociology at St. John Fisher College, Rochester, New York.

A. Lynn Bolles is professor of women's studies at the University of Maryland.

Thomas D. Boswell is professor of geography at the University of Miami, Florida.

Dennis Conway is professor of geography at Indiana University, Bloomington.

Thomas J. D'Agostino is executive director, Hobart and William Smith Colleges and Union College Partnership for Global Education, director, Center for Global Education, and visiting professor of political science, Hobart and William Smith Colleges, Geneva, New York.

Leslie G. Desmangles is professor of religion and international studies at Trinity College, Hartford, Connecticut.

H. Michael Erisman is professor and chair of political science at Indiana State University, Terre Haute, Indiana.

Stephen D. Glazier is professor of sociology at the University of Nebraska–Lincoln.

Richard S. Hillman is professor of political science and director of the Institute for the Study of Democracy and Human Rights at St. John Fisher College,

Rochester, New York, and the Central University of Venezuela, Caracas.

Duncan McGregor is professor of geography at the University of London, England.

Kevin Meehan is assistant professor of English at the University of Central Florida, Orlando.

Paul B. Miller is senior lecturer in the Department of Spanish and Portuguese, Vanderbilt University, Nashville, Tennessee.

Joseph M. Murphy is associate professor of theology at Georgetown University, Washington, DC.

Dennis A. Pantin is senior lecturer and coordinator of the Sustainable Economic Development Unit for Small and Island Developing States at the University of the West Indies, St. Augustine, Trinidad.

Stephen J. Randall is professor of history and dean of social sciences at the University of Calgary, Canada.

Andrés Serbin is director of the graduate program of international relations at the University of Belgrano, Buenos Aires, Argentina; professor of anthropology at the Central University of Venezuela, Caracas; director of the Venezuelan Institute of Social and Political Studies; and president of Regional Coordination of Economic and Social Research.

Kevin A. Yelvington is associate professor of anthropology at the University of South Florida, Tampa.

Index

About the Book

Designed to enhance readers' comprehension and appreciation of the traditions, influences, and common themes underlying the many differences within this complex region, *Understanding the Contemporary Caribbean* ranges in coverage from history to economics and politics, from the environment to ethnicity, from religion to the Caribbean diaspora.

The authors' thorough yet accessible analyses will serve equally well as a core text for Introduction to the Caribbean and Caribbean Politics courses and as essential background reading for visitors.

Richard S. Hillman is professor of political science and director of the Institute for the Study of Democracy and Human Rights at St. John Fisher College. He is author of *Democracy for the Privileged: Crisis and Transition in Venezuela,* editor of *Understanding Contemporary Latin America,* and coauthor, with Thomas J. D'Agostino, of *Distant Neighbors in the Caribbean: The Dominican Republic and Jamaica in Comparative Perspective.* **Thomas J. D'Agostino** is executive director of the Hobart and William Smith Colleges and Union College Partnership for Global Education.